BEYOND THE CLASSICS?

BEYOND

ESSAYS IN THE SCIENTIFIC

Edited by

with contributions by

 HARPER TORCHBOOKS

THE CLASSICS?

STUDY OF RELIGION

*Charles Y. Glock and
Phillip E. Hammond*

Norman Birnbaum
James E. Dittes
S. N. Eisenstadt
Alan W. Eister

Leonard Glick
Benjamin Nelson
Paul W. Pruyser
Talcott Parsons

Harper & Row, Publishers
New York, Evanston, San Francisco, London

First HARPER TORCHBOOK edition published 1973.

LIBRARY OF CONGRESS CATALOG CARD NUMBER: 72–13909

STANDARD BOOK NUMBER: 06–138755–x

STANDARD BOOK NUMBER: 06–136105–4 (HARDCOVER)

Designed by Ann Scrimgeour

To
The Society for the Scientific Study of Religion
in recognition of over twenty years of service
to its scholarly community.

CONTENTS

INTRODUCTION

Golden ages are not apparent in all fields of inquiry. There are some fields, however, which can look back to periods in their history where scholarly work achieved a zenith, not to be repeated or transcended. One of these fields is the social scientific study of religion.

The precise boundaries of its golden era may be subject to mild disagreement. Roughly, however, from the middle of the nineteenth century through the first decades of the twentieth a large number of highly gifted social scientists made contributions, now considered classic, to our understanding of the phenomena of religion. It is enough to mention Marx, Freud, Durkheim, Weber, James, Niebuhr, and Malinowski to indicate how remarkably productive the period was.

To identify a field as having had a golden age may seem offhand a negative attribution. It implies that the field has since become moribund and no longer creative. In the history of inquiry there are certainly examples where a period of greatness has been followed by a seemingly infinite time of shallowness. Golden ages can create the image that there are no new horizons to conquer or cause a field to become exegetical, devoted primarily to endless bickering about the meaning and correctness of what the classics had to say.

But moribundity need not be the fate of fields which have proceeded beyond a period of special creativity. Subsequent achievements may not be so spectacular, but by strengthening and building upon the foundations laid by the masters, a field can grow and gain in stature in ways not possible had there been no golden period.

Surprisingly, it is seldom self-evident which course a field has followed. Scholars are rarely given to this kind of introspection about their disciplines. Moreover, in most fields the standards by which progress is decided have never been worked out or agreed upon. By and large, it is left to history to decide what the abiding achievements have been.

In the end, of course, history *will* do the deciding. There is something to be said, nevertheless, for helping history along. Taking stock from time to time of where a field has been and where it appears to be going can heighten self-consciousness about the meaning and purpose of inquiry. It can also help to identify blind alleys which are being diligently but fruitlessly pursued. And it can help to clarify goals and provide new direction for their achievement.

Such stock taking of the scientific study of religion is the purpose of this book. It does not aspire to dissect and evaluate all that the field encompasses but to discover what has happened over the course of fifty to a hundred years to the ideas, theories, and insights contributed by the classical writers in the field. What has been their fate? How much do they continue to be the last word and in what ways have they been altered, extended, and elaborated upon by subsequent work? In effect, are we beyond the classics in the scientific study of religion or still mostly in the middle of them?

To answer these questions, we have commissioned a distinguished group of scholars, each an expert on some part of the classical literature in the scientific study of religion. Each contributor was asked to include in his essay a summary of the central ideas advanced in the classical writings, a report of subsequent work inspired by those ideas, an evaluation of the present status of the ideas, and a judgment about what direction future work might most fruitfully take.

Choosing the classical writings and writers to be covered was a collaborative enterprise. As editors, we made the initial selection. We then checked our choices informally with colleagues. As contributions were solicited, the choices were checked again. There was virtual agreement among those whom we contacted. Compromises were necessary in several instances, but the final selections were mostly unanimous.

Everyone agreed that Karl Marx ought to be included. While Marx never produced a work devoted only to religion, the insights and observations about the role of religion in social control scattered throughout his writings add up, it is felt, to a contribution of ground-breaking character which has contributed to shaping the course of the scientific study of religion and of religion itself.

Freud was also everyone's choice. As with Marx, there was no disposition to single out any one contribution for special attention. The review essay, it was felt, should encompass all of substance about religion that Freud had to say.

Emile Durkheim's *The Elementary Forms of the Religious Life* was singled out as especially worthy of classical status, as were Max Weber's *The Protestant Ethic and the Spirit of Capitalism* and his comparative studies of ancient Judaism and the religions of China and India. A choice from among the many contributions by anthropologists proved a difficult one; Bronislaw Malinowski was finally settled upon because it was felt that he had contributed most to opening up the modern era of the anthropological study of religion.

William James's *The Varieties of Religious Experience* was a nominee of the editors with which all consultants agreed, but the nomination of H. Richard Niebuhr's *The Social Sources of Denominationalism* produced disagreement. Objections were raised that its publication in 1928 put it outside of the classical period as we had defined it. Ernst Troeltsch, some thought, would be a better choice to represent the long tradition of work on church and sect. We finally prevailed with the argument that Niebuhr had done more than Troeltsch to put the concept of church-sect into theoretical perspective.

We ended up then with seven classicists. No others, in the view of our judges, were serious contenders.

The lives of these seven scholars span a 150-year period from 1818 when Marx was born to 1962 when Niebuhr died. Marx began to publish in 1840 and Niebuhr's last work was published (posthumously) in 1963, so that the productive period covers about 120 years. There was considerable overlapping in the life spans of these seven scholars. Indeed, the contiguity is virtually complete, except that Malinowski was born one year after Marx's death and Niebuhr, eleven years after.

The active periods in these men's lives also coincided to a considerable degree, thus offering opportunities for each to know about the others and to work collaboratively. By and large, however, these opportunities were not seized upon. There was no collaboration, and surprisingly little attention was paid by any one scholar to what the others were writing.

Marx completed his active career before any of the others began theirs and, consequently, his work could influence but not be influenced by theirs. Only Weber and Niebuhr build on and attempt to extend Marx's work. He is ignored virtually by everyone else. James was known to Freud and vice versa, but no mention of Freud is made in *The Varieties of Religious Experience* nor of James in any of Freud's writings. James was ignored by Weber and Malinowski. Niebuhr, who knew of James's work, makes no reference to it in *The Social Sources of Denominationalism*.

There is a record of Durkheim's having written a review of Weber's *The Protestant Ethic and the Spirit of Capitalism* but of no other recognition by Durkheim of Weber's work. In turn, Weber ignores Durkheim in all of his writings including those in the sociology of religion. Freud disregards Durkheim (except a minor reference in *Totem and Taboo*) and Weber, but this is reciprocated; neither Weber nor Durkheim makes any references to Freud.

Malinowski knew *The Elementary Forms of the Religious Life* intimately and has much to say in his work about it. But while acquainted with other of the classical writings, Malinowski finds no occasion to refer to them.

The scholarly interest of these classic writers far from coincided. Consequently, it would not necessarily follow, even in the best of all scientific worlds where communication is maximized, that they would be knowledgeable about, much less influenced by each other's work. Still, in such a world considerably more interaction than occurred would be expected to take place. Freud and Durkheim, for example, could scarcely ignore each other's observations on the origins of religion, nor could Weber and Durkheim overlook what each had to say about the relation between religion and the organization of social life. While it is impossible, of course, to say what the result would have been had there been such collaboration, a significant question for the scientific study of religion (and one the contributors address) is whether bridges begin to get built in subsequent work.

By today's standards none of the seven scholars qualifies as a specialist in the social scientific study of religion. Marx, Weber, and Durkheim are not considered especially to have been sociologists of religion, and Freud is not thought of as a psychologist of religion nor Malinowski an anthropologist of religion. Only James and Niebuhr specialized in religion but as philosopher and theologian, respectively, not as social scientists.

It was not, then, as a result of their having an inherent interest in religion per se that questions about it came to be absorbing for most of these scholars. In the context of their times the larger questions they addressed simply demanded that attention be paid to religion. It was not possible then, as it may be thought to be today, to ignore religion in any consideration of fundamental questions about the human condition or about the organization of social life.

What marks the work of these scholars, of course, is not that they attended to religion in their studies, but how they did so. Religion, after all, had been a subject of scholarly attention for centuries before them. The larger contribution of Marx, Freud, and the rest lies in their applying their genius to pioneering a new perspective of such study. Indeed, it is fair to say that this perspective, in combination with undisputed genius, truly distinguishes theirs from earlier work; the genius alone would not have yielded the same products.

In its essentials the new perspective involved borrowing the deterministic mode of explanation of the natural sciences and applying it to structure and change in the human personality and social arrangements. Religion was treated as both a dependent and an independent variable. Variations in the form and content of religion came to be understood as a result of observable natural, rather than unseen and unseeable supernatural forces, but religion also came to be recognized as an independent variable helping to shape personality and helping to create, reinforce, or challenge forms of social organization.

The seven scholars varied in how much their work was informed by this scientific perspective and also in the extent to which they gave the religion variable dependent (as opposed to independent) status. A scientific rather than a humanistic perspective predominates in Marx's and Freud's treatments of religion. It is also markedly in evidence in *The Elementary Forms of the Religious Life, The Protestant Ethic and the Spirit of Capitalism,* and the comparative studies. Marx and Durkheim give more emphasis to the dependent status of religion. Weber was the great tracer of the ways religious ideas influence the course of events. Freud's work examines religion both as a product of and an influence on the functioning of the human psyche.

Religion is a dependent variable in *The Social Sources of Denominationalism,* and this work, too, must be counted in the new mode. Niebuhr himself, however, was not permanently converted to the new perspective and abandoned it in subsequent work to return, especially in *The Kingdom of God in America,* to the more humanistic posture characteristic of his earlier writings.

Malinowski is the most difficult to classify. He was a thoroughgoing social scientist, but his research on religion is characterized as much by description as by explanation. Its borrowing from the natural science model, therefore, is more implicit than explicit.

The scientific perspective is least in evidence in *The Varieties of Religious Experience.* James, always more the humanist than the social scientist, was concerned essentially with cataloguing rather than accounting for variations in religious consciousness. *The Varieties of Religious Experience* has come to be accepted as a contribution to social science because it represents a breakthrough in conceptualization more than in explanation.

It has been said, and also denied, that an effect of subjecting religion to scientific study was to extend the existing conflict between religion and natural science. The work of the seven classicists supports such a view. On balance, the study was considerably more undermining than reinforcing of religion, especially in the traditional forms of religious expression. Marx and Freud were openly and personally hostile to religion, a stance both rooted and reflected in their scholarship. While Durkheim had no personal animus against religion and, indeed, proclaimed religion's positive social functions, his theory of the origin of religion was at odds with the prevailing religious conceptions of his time.

The validity of religion is not questioned directly in the work of Weber and Malinowski, yet their revelations about how social forces shape and are shaped by religion are scarcely consistent with a view of divinity as entering into and exercising control over human events. None of these five men was personally religious. Marx, Freud, and Durkheim were Jewish, but none was a practicing Jew as an adult, although Durkheim had trained for the rabbinate as a youth. Weber's parents were Protestant, his mother pietistically so, and he was trained in religion as a child and went so far as to be confirmed. He did so, however, out of respect for his mother rather than out of any religious conviction. Weber is best described as indifferent to religion as is Malinowski, who, though raised a Roman Catholic, never practiced Catholicism as an adult.

James and Niebuhr were both personally religious, James quite unconventionally so, Niebuhr in a more traditional way. Their works, or more correctly, those parts of them considered here, neither espoused religion nor attempted to subvert it. Yet, Niebuhr himself expressed reservations some time after *The Social Sources of Denominationalism* was published that subversion might be its effect, and he took pains subsequently to correct for this possibility. James, too, recognized that *The Varieties of Religious Experience* might have such a consequence, though only with respect to orthodox religion about which he was not personally concerned.

Only Niebuhr among these scholars gave explicit attention to the relationship of religious and social scientific perspectives, and he sensed them to be incompatible. Judging from the assumptions underlying their work, the works themselves, and the absence of a personal religious commitment, the others (except possibly James) would have agreed. Whether an incompatibility is acknowledged and demonstrated by subsequent scholarship in the scientific study of religion is a question left for the contributors to address.

Another reason for the classical status of the work of these seven persons can be advanced. It is this: Despite the obvious differences among them and despite the time span over which they wrote, these classical figures all deal in some global manner with the transition from premodern to modern society. Whether from magic to science, rural to urban life, self-destruction to eternal Eros, or pre-Reformation to rational capitalism, the focus of their study was on change. And not just change but upheaval, in the process of which humanity's religious consciousness—its symbols, motives, actions, and institutions—underwent revision. From different starting points certainly, and with different interests, methods, and conclusions of course, the authors of classics in the social scientific study of religion earn their title, it is suggested, by serving as *interpreters* of significant social change and religion's role in it.

It would be easy to explain their stature as a result merely of their having lived in *times* of significant change; by implication, then, less classical efforts result from living in less hectic eras. Such a claim not only smacks of self-illusion, however, but would have to be argued on extraempirical grounds. Who is to say when actual change is now greater, now less? Is not our sense of change brought about by those who help us see it? The classical status of these social scientists, we can suggest, stems in part from their having helped others to see and understand a changing social world. Indeed, it might even be suggested—especially in the cases of Marx and Freud—that they had a hand in bringing about that change.

It is appropriate here to introduce the contributors to this volume and at the same time to outline the organization of the book. The work of Karl Marx, who opened up the study of religion and social structure in contemporary settings, is the subject of Chapter 1. The author of that chapter is Norman Birnbaum.

Analysis of Max Weber's scholarship and heritage follows naturally on Marx with two chapters devoted to it. Chapter 2 by Benjamin Nelson focuses on *The Protestant Ethic and the Spirit of Capitalism;* Chapter 3 by S. N. Eisenstadt deals with Weber's comparative studies.

The work of Emile Durkheim is considered in Chapter 4. A contemporary of Weber's, Durkheim published *The Elementary Forms of the Religious Life* in 1912. The author of Chapter 4 is Talcott Parsons. Because Malinowski's work builds on Durkheim's, in part taking serious issue with it, analysis of it by Leonard Glick constitutes Chapter 5.

Two classical contributions to the psychology of religion are considered next. The work of Freud is examined in Chapter 6 by

Paul W. Pruyser, and James E. Dittes contributes Chapter 7 on William James's *The Varieties of Religious Experience.*

The final chapter by Allan W. Eister deals with H. Richard Niebuhr's *The Social Sources of Denominationalism.* Beginning with the earliest of the authors considered, then, we conclude with the most recent of the classical writers. A brief Epilogue concludes the volume.

BEYOND THE CLASSICS?

*the text of this book is printed
on 100% recycled paper*

1 BEYOND MARX IN THE SOCIOLOGY OF RELIGION?*

Norman Birnbaum

I INTRODUCTION

I have attached a question mark to the title—and for a number of reasons. In what sense may we, intellectual descendants of Marxism whether or not we claim to be attached to the Marxist tradition, go beyond Marxism with respect to the sociological analysis of religion? In the original Marxist *corpus,* a view of historical progress implied that religion and irreligion would both disappear with the self-creation of a new humanity. Clearly, as disabused descendants not alone of Marxism but of the entire nineteenth century, we at the moment entertain few hopes for that self-creation. The revolutionary means expected to realize a new humanity have usually, when applied, recreated old servitudes in new forms: for a transcendant God has been substituted

* I am grateful to the John Simon Guggenheim Memorial Foundation for a Fellowship which has given me the leisure to complete this paper and to the Fondazione Giovanni Agnelli, Torino, for its hospitality during the writing of it. An earlier version of the paper was delivered at the 1969 Annual Meeting of the Society for the Scientific Study of Religion, and a summary of this version was presented to the Eleventh Conference of the Conference Internationale de Sociologie Religieuse at Opatija, Yugoslavia in September 1971.

I should also wish to record my indebtedness to two colleagues and friends who work on similar problems. Three years of association with Professor Lewis Mudge of the Department of Religion at Amherst College, including a seminar we undertook together, have taught me much. My readers will have no difficulty, further, in recognizing the influence on my thought exerted by Henri Desroche. The English-speaking public may count itself fortunate that it now has two works by Desroche available in translation (1971, 1972).

for what Hobbes termed the mortal God, the state—or its antagonist, the movement or party. In societies which have experienced revolution, and in those which have not, new types of alienation have superseded or supplemented alienation arising from the labor process. It would be absurd to speak of a super- session of religion, even if we can verify the attenuation and transformation of some of its inherited structures and senti- ments.[1] Briefly, we confront no renewed or liberated humanity. The old gods may not be entirely with us, but neither have the new Adam and the new Eve appeared. In this sense we cannot go beyond Marx in the sociology of religion, but we have to go around the master in the search for other modes of analysis, new types of vision.

A second meaning of going beyond Marx, then, may attach to the familiar notion of secular progress in science—in this case, in social science.[2] In this account of things the privileged mode of interaction between historical experience and the human mind is codification. That codification proceeds by a formalized process of trial and error, seeks to explicate the essential elements and internal relationships of enduring or recurrent structures, and so brings to social phenomena the sharpness of vision developed in the natural sciences. Going beyond Marx in this sense would entail the substitution for the Marxist theory of religion of a superior one, superior not alone or even primarily because it deals with new phenomena, but because it deals differently with old phe- nomena. The last point is important because it marks a distinc- tion between a Marxist-inspired revision of Marxism (on account of new historical experience) and a rejection or severe emenda- tion of Marxism on a basis which claims to be scientific. Going beyond Marx in this last sense would entail a rupture with the Marxist epistemology, which holds that human purpose and value are inextricably bound to our notions of social process. In

[1] See Caporale and Grumelli (1971). This book contains the contributions to the Vatican Conference on the sociology of religion, valuable in their own right, and indicative of the current discussion of secularisation. See, also, the Introduction to the anthology edited by Lenzer and me (1969).

[2] The current discussion of method in the social sciences may be described as intense. See MacIntyre (1970), Friedrichs (1970), Gouldner (1970), Birnbaum (1971).

this view only the fusion of human purpose with historical experience can provide an adequate basis for knowledge.

The choice of a beginning point for this essay, then, implies a philosophical option. We may take the standpoint of conventional social science (which, to be sure, appears less conventional and monolithic the closer one examines it) and adumbrate a criticism of Marxism which rests on the progress of sociology. Alternatively, we may attempt to incorporate the legacy of this progress in a new historical vision which, like Marxism, fuses purpose and analysis. A splendid project, the latter, but rather vast for the briefer compass of this paper; the more so as, the Marxist anthropology fragmented, it is difficult to elaborate another one for our immediate requirements. Let us say frankly that this paper is a minor part of a search for a new vision like the Marxist one in scope. It will accordingly manifest the jaggedness and the contradictoriness of all such efforts, but perhaps this may be compensated for by a certain metaphysical openness. At any rate, we shall move from within the Marxist system to its boundaries and then outside these in the effort to find a new historical-philosophical location from which to examine the sociology of religion.

II THE MARXIST SOCIOLOGY OF RELIGION

The Original Theory

The exegesis of the original Marxist texts and of their historical sources seems to know no end. We are in possession of a very considerable critical and historical literature (most of it the work of scholars not living under Marxist regimes, whatever their own philosophical or political opinions).[3] Interestingly, some of this work has been accomplished by theologians: we may cite the work both of the German Protestants associated with the

[3] A recent international conspectus is provided by the International Social Science Council (1969). This was the UNESCO Conference of May, 1968, on the same theme—convened as the French student-worker revolt was breaking out. See also the valuable symposium cited by Lobkowicz (1967).

Marxismusstudien[4] of the German Protestant church and of the
learned monks of several orders in Paris (Calvez 1956, de Lubac
1969). These scholarly efforts have not been without political
meaning: the German Protestant effort to recapture the critical
part of the German philosophical inheritance has been a component in the loosening of the cultural and political rigidity (and,
let it be said, the crushing boredom) of the "restoration" of
German social structure after 1945. The French Catholic encounter with Marxism has been part of that movement of renewal and innovation in French Catholicism which took
dramatic form in episodes like *les pretres contestataires* and
their forerunners, the *Pretres ouvriers* (Petrie 1956), but it also
influenced the former Papal Nuncio in Paris, Cardinal Roncalli,
who became Pope John. The secular participants in this scholarly
effort have had other organizational and doctrinal concerns:
many were disappointed or dissident socialists engaged in a
search for a new humanistic fundament for a Marxist politics
which had become bureaucratized or tyrannical. Still others have
been concerned with the problem of the end of philosophy, with
the Marxist effort to effect a philosophical transcendence of a
reflective view of the world by developing a new type of human
praxis.

If the literature of exegesis and criticism is considerable, so is
the intensity of scholarly dispute contained in it. The relationship of the earlier to the later writings of Marx, the role and
continuity of Hegelian components in his thought, and the
weight to be assigned to human reflection in the Marxist conception of *praxis* are among the questions at issue. This is not the
place to review these controversies, but we may say that the
relationship of "material" to "ideal" factors in the Marxist
analysis now appears to be much more subtle and complex than
in schematic representations of an unequivocal and unilinear
determination of "superstructure" by a material "base." We
are entitled to conclude that the Marxist theory of religion has to
be conceived of in the light of these newer inquiries into the
original texts. Indeed, the matter is made simple by the fact that

---

4 Studienkommission der Evangelische-Kirche Deutschlands, *Marxismusstudien*, Vols. I–V (Tübingen: Möhr, 1954–59).

much of the interpretation has turned about the writings of Marx and Engels on religion.

For our purposes two major themes emerge from these writings. The first concerns the Marxist critique of the critical philosophers of the early nineteenth century. The second is the Marxist analysis of human alienation. Let us consider each in turn. I have termed Marx's immediate predecessors in philosophy critical and for good reason. Marx did not singlehandedly overturn an idealist metaphysics, much less develop his own system in a single leap of the metaphysical imagination. What he and Engels did was to utilize the intentions and contradictions of their predecessors to develop a new system (Löwith 1964a). Hegel voiced considerable respect for the historical function of religion in general and Christianity in particular, but he contributed no little to its relativization in describing it as one form among many of the manifestations of spirit. The Hegelian theologians Bruno Bauer and Friedrich David Strauss took Hegel at his word and examined Christianity in its context. The one concluded that the Gospels were the inventions of their apostolic authors, seeking self-understanding, the other, that Christian belief entailed a mythicization of human experience. All three were accused of inconsistency by Ludwig Feuerbach. The spirit, he held, was upon examination a manifestation not of itself but of human self-consciousness. The mythic object of deification in religion, and especially in Christianity, was humanity itself. The destruction of the Hegelian notion of the spirit, the reinterpretation of the work of the biblical scholars to uncover the human aspirations at the root of the Christian Gospels, were the preconditions for a new humanistic philosophy. German philosophy, Marx and Engels declared, had to go through a brook of fire (a play on the name of their colleague, Feuerbach) in order to be purified. Their conception of purification, however, rapidly took a more stringent emphasis.

Originally enthused by the young Hegelians' attack on the obscurity and abstractedness of Hegel's conception of spirit, delighted by their effort to make concrete the religious tradition of the West in universal human characteristics, Marx and Engels at first embraced the new philosophical anthropology (Easton and Guddat 1967). Their own dissatisfaction with it was a consequence of their realization, in their own terms, that it was a doctrine of humanity not much less abstract, no less remote from the concrete, than Hegel's notion of spirit. In the place of an abstract spirit the young Hegelians had set an abstract humanity. They had replaced the worship of God by a religion of humanity. And, to solve the concrete problems of a society stricken by exploitation and poverty, convulsed by industrialization, dominated by political tyranny, they could offer only the work of "critical critics"—philosophical discourse without reference to tangible historical realities.

Feuerbach, Marx and Engels declared, had depicted a humanity alienated from itself because it was subject to the creations of its own mind—to religious images of itself. Feuerbach's solution for this subjugation was to correct the images, to restore to or endow humanity with its own highest attributes. These, however, remained ideal, mental or spiritual creations with a humanistic content but still remote from the suffering of humanity in its concrete setting. Humankind needed religious imagery because it could not confront its own reality, but that reality was obscured by abstract humanistic conceptions in a manner not distinct from the workings of religion. The question was a different one: Why did humanity need religious or philosophical idealization? The initial answer could be found only in the misery and degradation of humanity's concrete conditions of existence, and we do well to remind ourselves that Marx and Engels (professing intellectuals) regarded a certain form of religious adherence as a higher but no less definite form of degradation than material exploitation or political subjugation. The Marxist search for the sources of religion and the Marxist effort to end religion were henceforth to be concentrated on the question of humanity's self-inflicted imprisonment in its own world—on the problem of alienation. Before considering the notion of alienation in greater detail, however, we must turn to another of the sources for the Marxist theory of religion: the notion of a secular community as a successor to the kingdom of heaven.

Marx and Engels took their view of society from three sources —German philosophy, what has been termed French socialism but what is better described as early French social thought, and

British political economy. Marx himself has noted ironically on the ways in which the laws of the market—as described in British political economy—curiously parodied the inscrutable workings of the Calvinist God. His conceptions of religion, however, may well owe much to Robert Owen's (1963) utopian view of a cooperative, nay, harmonious, human community. Owen's "New Moral World" was to be the result of a Christian critique of capitalism's destruction of human dignity and community. It paralleled themes found in some of the early French utopians and in the German social-religious thinker, Weiteling. The common element in these writing was the notion of a humanity come into possession of its religious heritage by realizing in new social forms the religious vision of community. Marx, of course, denied that humanity required a religious legitimation for its search for a true community: he dismissed the utopians as empty moralizers, again guilty of applying an abstract criterion to historical concreteness. Yet his own view of religion was immensely clarified by his encounter with these utopian Christians and post-Christian utopians. In one respect they demonstrated the close connection between religious ideals and a defective social reality: in a response to earthly misery which sought to heal the split in the actual human community by creating on earth a community hitherto reserved for heaven. In another respect they did provide Marx with elements he could transmute into his own version of eschatology: they insisted, in terms rather different from those of Aristotle, on Aristotle's definition of man as a political or communal being. Marx envisaged the self-realization of humanity as the creation of a new or true community. This was to develop from human need and through extreme conflict; it was to be produced, briefly, by the intolerability of its absence, by the self-destruction of its negation, the class society. Marx held that his morality was immanent in the historical process itself and, therefore, free of theological content. It was freed of theological content, however, by his transcribing theological terms into profane or secular ones.

A similar process, if with a somewhat different content, occurred with Saint-Simon's (1964) idea of a new community. Saint-Simon did not hesitate to use the term "the New Christianity," to describe his social ethic and political program. There were near-comical elements in it, as in the suggestion that the Papal Curia be replaced by a "Council of Newton." As did his disciple Comte, however, Saint-Simon admired the hierarchical order and spiritual discipline of medieval society (or what they thought was such). The notion of a secularized equivalent of Christianity serving to unite society—an equivalent to be constituted of positivistic doctrine—was drawn from the social theology of the Restoration. The thinkers of the Restoration hoped for a return to a society dominated by church and throne; Saint-Simon and Comte thought this impossible but were anxious to find new institutional supports for order. Marx's own revulsion for this sort of thought was very great, attached as he was to the tradition of the Enlightenment. Yet it was precisely Saint-Simon's program, which proposed to reconcile order and technological progress, which illuminated both the conservative functions of historical Christianity in Europe and the authoritarian bias of some of Christianity's critics. Saint-Simon's sociology of religion, which proposed to use a scientific equivalent for it to domesticate society, was in itself a caricature of the Enlightenment doctrine that institutional religion was a device for subjugating humanity. It would be absurd to deny the possibility that early Marxist texts can be found to substantiate the view that for Marx and Engels, communism was a "religion of mankind." As their critique of religion, and ideology, developed, however, they arrived at the position that a true religion of humanity was humanity itself, in its practice. That, however, required a liberated humanity, not one held together by a new or proto-religion, even if it spoke the language of science.

The Marxist sociology of religion, then, is inseparable from the radical humanism of Marx and Engels. That humanism opposed a true humanity to an inauthentic, or injured and subjugated one and propounded a general doctrine of the human condition in the analysis of alienation. The analysis was and remains a remarkable philosophical achievement. The Enlightenment, from which Marx and Engels drew so much, had opposed an authentic human nature to inauthentic or tyrannical institutions. The tyranny destroyed, human nature could flower. The achievement of Marx and Engels was, not least, the historicization of the antithesis. The real problem of history, they found, lay in the

interiorization of tyranny by the species, in its systematic deformation by and in its own historical structures. They opposed a
potentially fulfilled humanity to an actually degraded one. Recent scholarship has shown how the notion of alienation drew
upon the Hegelian legacy, upon romantic esthetics (the young
Marx wrote poetry and even in his most polemical and abstract
moments remained a great German prose stylist), and upon the
pedagogic and psychological theory of the French Enlightenment.

Two principal components constitute the elements of the theory of alienation. The first refers to human practice (or, as put
in the original texts, *praxis*). Hegel had developed at length the
notion of the exteriorization of the spirit. He had also, a point
seized upon by Marx and Engels, described the human form of
that exteriorization: the historical development of labor, particularly in bourgeois society. The key to human nature, Marx and
Engels held, was to be found in human *praxis*, and there was no
more important *praxis* than labor. Labor was, further, not
merely a means of self-reproduction for the individual: it was a
mode of self-reproduction for the species, and the relations of
work were the fundamental relations of all sociability. The
second component of the theory of alienation, then, was the
notion of sociability, perhaps best characterized as the notion of
community. Human beings were constricted, denied their full
development, because certain historical forms of the labor process
inevitably resulted in false or distorted communities. In these
the relationships of labor or production were relationships of
subjugation and not of fraternity. Moreover, the products of
human labor—under the advanced historical circumstances of
Marx's time—in effect assumed a life of their own, and ruled
over their producers. Humans related to one another through
these products, or through buying and selling them, and not
directly. True community, a direct relationship of humans to one
another, had no chance to develop.

The elements of the theory of alienation are, then, human self-
exteriorization in labor and the denial of the human community
in the relations of labor. The mechanism by which these elements
produced alienation was the division of labor. At bottom of the
idea of self-exteriorization lay, certainly, a notion of human

substance, of human wholeness. In the division of labor that wholeness was denied or, more specifically, fragmented. Humans produced to meet their needs but did so indirectly. The market mediated their relationships and placed the many, who had nothing to exchange but their labor power, at the disposal of the few, who controlled the means of production. It is important to note that for Marx and Engels, it was not private property (in the sense of ownership of the productive apparatus) which produced alienation, but alienation, in the form of the division of labor, which eventuated in private property. In a labor-divided society market forms of relationships inevitably developed once the forces of production had attained a certain degree of complexity. Bourgeois society was the market society par excellence, and it had driven the division of labor to its extreme point. Previous societies, like feudal Europe, had known the division of labor and, of course, exploitation. In these, however, production and exchange relationships were invariably combined with other, human relationships. Where, as in bourgeois society, production and exchange existed for and by themselves, the alienation of men from one another, and from their own possibilities of wholeness, was maximal.

The notions of wholeness and community which underlay the theory of alienation were used, then, to develop a negative account of human history. History was the record of humanity's failure to achieve fully human status. The Marxist account of history has, indeed, been described by Marx himself as, in effect, a prehistory: humanity can begin when alienation is overcome. It is in this context that we can insert the Marxist theory of religion: religion is a spiritual response to a condition of alienation. The Marxist theory of religion, however, was much more specific. It ascribed the religious forms of alienation to the specific forms of production, labor relationship, and relationship to nature found in the successive stages of human history. Perhaps we may put the matter in another way: in making concrete a general theory of religion as produced by human insufficiency, Marxism recorded the specific alienation of the several stages of history.

The precise mode by which religion was produced was a replica of the prevailing mode of production in human society.[5] In particular, Marx and Engels held, the division of labor had immensely significant consequences for spiritual and intellectual labor. Under very primitive conditions individuals and the societies to which they belonged themselves produced their own spiritual worlds—systems of codification and interpretation of experience. Where the society was closely and immediately dependent upon nature, natural religions developed. With the growth of the forces of production and the introduction of the division of labor, religious specialists appeared who concentrated on the production of systems of belief. These were important, nay, indispensable social functions; and if history records a progression toward a market system in commodities, it does not do so in the sphere of the spirit. What was produced, by whom, and for whom were matters of jealous interest to those in power in labor-divided societies. The general Marxist proposition that those who owned the means of production also owned the means of intellectual (or ideological) production was particularly true with respect to religion. Natural religions were transformed into state religions, and these, in turn, with the increasing density of the cultural tradition, into religions legitimated by (as well as legitimating) the state. With the consolidation of larger societies, polytheisms based on fusions of regional subsocieties (each with its gods) gave way to monotheism, proclaiming a strong and uniform moral discipline.

It may be objected that this does not sound particularly "critical" at all, but rather like conventional nineteenth-century accounts of the evolution of religion, of the sort we might find in the works of Taylor or Spencer. Just so. Marx and Engels were part of one of the first generations to profit from the new archaeological and philological inquiries into the history of religion. Their account of the facts and sequence of religious history, then, is different in no significant respect from that of their learned contemporaries. What did distinguish their work was the interpretative context in which it was placed, their

---

[5] To avoid burdening the text with citation after citation, it will be understood that I give a general sketch of the theory. See Niebuhr's introduction to Marx and Engels (1964), for a useful introduction to the texts.

account of the inner structure of religion and its relationship to society. Perhaps we may look at the matter in another way. For Marx and Engels the production of religious systems was part of the general process of the production of ideology: indeed, through most of human history religion was not alone the privileged but the exclusive mode of intellectual and spiritual discourse. As a mode of ideology religion shared its most general characteristic. Ideology was not, as is sometimes believed, a false account of the human condition or social situation. Rather, it is a partial one, determined by the imperfect development of humanity. We may say that ideology was the truth of a false condition, and this, by extension, included religion. Marx and Engels had an acute sense of the spiritual dimensions of human existence, as well as considerable knowledge of the Western religious tradition. Religious interpretations of the human condition were necessary, in their view, precisely because of the misery and degradation of that condition. Religion, as a derivative of alienation, could not be attacked frontally: when alienation was overcome, religion itself would dissolve. There was, however, a precondition to the political organization of the attack on alienation—or, rather, its causes—and this was a condition of (relative) enlightenment. Some parts of humanity, at least, had to be free of the sort of ideological domination contained in religion. This is the meaning of the famous remark at the beginning of Marx's "Contribution to the Critique of Hegel's Philosophy of Right": "For Germany, the criticism of religion is in the main complete, and criticism of religion is the premise of all criticism" (Marx and Engels 1964 : 41).

Let us ignore, for the moment, the ambiguities of the position (how may some attain insight into a world still alienated?) and consider yet other dimensions of the Marxist theory.

The impulses which produced religion were, for Marx and Engels, profoundly human: a demand at once for dignity and consolation, for explanation and moral coherence. Religion was a response to peoples' homelessness in the world, an effort to construct an imaginary home—a moral universe in which humanity could find repose—and an ideal image of itself. It is clear that this account of religion is far from a moral denigration of it; moral revulsion attached to the conditions which produced religion. Indeed, in his work *The German Peasants' War* (which remains a masterpiece of historical interpretation of the entire German Reformation), Engels declared that in religious epochs even critical and revolutionary thought had to find religious expression (Marx and Engels 1964: 97 ff.). Further, in his writings on early Christianity Engels likened its beginnings to the (then contemporary) beginnings of socialism among the European workers—as a spiritual movement for social dignity. With Marx, he was conscious of the progression of religious thought from tribalism to universalism, no doubt, a legacy of the Hegelian historical interpretation of the history of religion as a mode of the history of human self-consciousness and human development. Precisely that progression accounted for the original Marxist rejection of German classical philosophy: like the religious tradition from which it derived, it created a world of images and concepts remote from the actual structures of human reality. If philosophy in its abstract form was the legitimate successor of theology, all the more reason to concentrate the emancipatory activities of reason on the similarities between religion and philosophy (similarities contained in the general Marxist analysis of ideology, which encompassed both).

Moreover, concrete political consequences followed from the analysis of religion. The demand for religious emancipation, for freedom of religion from state control, was according to Marx simply a demand that people be free to enslave themselves. The freedom of religion guaranteed in the Declaration of the Rights of Man, and in the several American state constitutions, did not emancipate people: it made some of them citizens, perhaps, but not yet free people. Indeed, the bourgeois revolution, as it proceeded from seventeenth-century England to eighteenth-century France and the United States, ostensibly opened new possibilities for humanity while actually consolidating a new servitude. That revolution made the market the central institution of society and introduced, in effect, new types of religion. Christianity with what Marx termed "its cultus of abstract man" (Marx and Engels 1964: 135), particularly in its bourgeois and Protestant forms, was a precondition for the development of the abstract and universal market relations (with money as a common denominator) of capitalism. These relations having been introduced, a

curious regression occurred: a new type of fetishism appeared—
the fetishism of commodities—quite unlike the fetishism of
the primitives who were bound to nature. Bound to the market,
people conceived of themselves as dominated by the products of
their labor, commodities. They did not see that they had created
this world and that (granted the proper historical conditions)
they could undo it and create a humane universe. By a curious
paradox the apogee of the development of new human powers, in
the new productive apparatus of industrial capitalism, substituted for the religious conceptions of the past new phantasma-
goria—the reified world of commodity production. Humans, at
the point in their history when they were most remote from that
total dependence upon nature which characterized the primitive
stages of human development, were the opposite of sovereign.
They were also remote, however, from an element of primitive
existence which Marx and Engels valued rather strongly—integration in a community. They confronted a world they had
made, unaware that they had done so, isolated from one another,
fragmented and crippled in their common humanity. The replacement of theology by bourgeois political economy by no
means signified that the sources of alienation were gone. The
human needs to which religion was a response were as poignant,
their satisfaction apparently as impossible, as ever.

It was at this point that the radical humanism of Marx and
Engels proposed a transcendence of religion. The reconquest of
humanity by itself demanded, first of all, a process of self-
recognition. Humanity had to recognize the fact and the inner
structure of its bondage. It had to eschew religious and metaphysical solutions to its difficulties and learn to see itself as it
was. Therein, however, lay hope: a humanity thrown back upon
its own resources could realize its own potential. This reduction
of historical experience to a human essence, found in the process
of labor, had a rigorous metaphysical derivative of an antimeta-
physical kind. People had to see themselves as practical beings,
had to develop their capacities for autonomous activity free of
the fears rigidified in religion and free of the terrible limits set
by the bourgeois social order. No narrow (or even larger) utilitarianism was implied by this doctrine. It was not so much that
people were to be freed to follow their interests, but that they

were to free themselves—qualitatively—to follow new interests. As they did so, Feuerbach's project of a religion of humanity would dissolve: in possession of themselves, people would not feel compelled to worship an idealized image of themselves.

The philosophical and historical assumptions of the Marxist theory of religion, then, are inseparable from the theory of alienation. In the original Marxist texts the assumptions were stated more often than not. Nevertheless, we may phrase the Marxist sociology of religion in a somewhat different, possibly more concrete way. The components of this version of the doctrine are three: the development of the division of spiritual labor, the structure of the religious situation in the first half of the nineteenth century, and the problem of concrete transcendence.

The division of spiritual labor has proceeded, according to Marxism, *pari passu* with the division of material labor. In the original human community, the community had a direct relationship to nature: this was part of humanity's early and unfragmented apprehension of its own existence. As the productive forces grew, internal relationships of domination and exploitation developed in the once unitary human community. A particular and specialized spiritual production became necessary to legitimate the new division of labor, to explain it, and to assuage the fears and inchoate desires it evoked. That spiritual production took the most diverse forms—priests attending a polytheistic pantheon, caesaro-papist monarchs, charismatic churches, and heretical sects. In general, to the stages of the division of labor there corresponded phases in the division of spiritual labor and its product. The entire scheme is saved from excessive schematism by two elements frequently unappreciated by Marxism's critics.

The first is the Marxist appreciation of religious diversity and conflict attributed, of course, to differentiation and conflict in the society. Did not Engels attribute the rise of Christianity to the spiritual needs of the Roman Empire's proletariat to the death of the pagan gods (Marx and Engels 1964: 316 ff.)? The phrase "spiritual needs" gives us the second element in the theory. Human history, for Marx and Engels, is not alone the history of production and of the class struggles inextricably bound to production relationships. It is also the history of the spirit—if of the human spirit struggling against blindness, despair, and its own limitations. Marx, it should be recalled, was acutely aware of changes in the history of the spirit of the sort contained in the Reformation. Of the latter, he said that Luther had turned priests into laymen by converting laymen into priests, by internalizing what had been ecclesiastical discipline (Marx and Engels 1964: 51). His own anticipation of the modern analysis of the Protestant ethic was connected with a larger theme in his sociology of religion. The emergence and (temporary) consolidation of bourgeois society introduced a new form of (distorted) spirituality. What had been Protestantism became an egoism the more ruthless for the absence of any other historical possibilities of human relationship. Marx likened the workings of the market to the inscrutable decisions of the Calvinist God, but the doctrine of the fetishism of commodities implied a regression from monotheism to a more primitive spirituality. The ambiguity, the incompletion of historical development was indeed another theme in the Marxist sociology of religion. Monotheism was, for instance, depicted as the product of a higher, more developed civilization with a more dense and universal set of cultural contacts and, of course, production relations. Yet out of monotheism the thinkers of new epoch derived their metaphysical notions: to these, people were subjugated as surely as if they worshipped old gods.

It is at this point that we may turn to the Marxist analysis of the religious situation in its own period. The subordination of people to the market created not alone intolerable material deprivation, but severe spiritual suffering. In the resultant crisis some of the relationships of spiritual domination were becoming visible—not least, the uses of the churches as ancillary political organs. The Constantinization of Christianity, Marx and Engels implied, was a continuing process. They denied, however, that there was absolute utility to the demand for religious emancipation. This demand, which insisted on the separation of church and state, in reality called for the spiritual reproduction of market relationships. Just as people on the market were forced to sell their labor power in systems of exchange which they did not create, so people on the spiritual market would be cast into psychological dependence upon a supernatural order for want of the ability to perceive the natural and social order. Marx adduced the example of the United States, where the church was entirely separted from the state and where the separate churches flourished in a way unmatched in Europe. Germany (and other societies in Europe, like Italy and Russia) were no doubt historically backward: there, the struggle against religion and the churches was a preliminary to the real struggle against the conditions which made religion necessary. Where, however, capitalist production relations were developed in their full form, political atheism had to give way to unalloyed communism. Here again, Marx and Engels made use of the ambiguity of historical forms: they likened the beginnings of the socialist movement among the working class to the beginnings of Christianity (Marx and Engels 1964: 316). There are, indisputably, passages in the writings which give credence to the view that Marx and Engels thought of communism as a religion of humanity or as a successor to the historical religions. The proletariat, after all, was assigned the role of a surrogate for all of humanity. Humanity could regain itself only when the proletariat, as its most injured part, assumed the task of revolution—a mode of universal historical redemption. Yet the end of religion, in the Marxist theory, is perhaps best understood as part of the problem of concrete transcendence, to which we now turn.

The revolution anticipated by Marx was to bring about not alone a change in social relationships, but a spiritual change as well. Humanity would abandon the gods, because it would no longer need these: instead, it would learn to live with itself. In the place of the multiple spiritual alienations of its previous existence, humanity would live wholly—in a new *praxis*. This may be termed a concrete transcendence, because it would come (or was supposed to come) from an organic continuation of revolutionary activity. By revolting against the conditions of alienation, people would begin the process of ending alienation. The progression from one world to another, then, from the realm of necessity to the realm of freedom, was to be concrete. People required not theological images of the universe, nor yet their metaphysical derivatives: they had to meet the concrete tasks of

their history. Did this imply, for internal structure of Marxist
theory, a recourse to scientific modes of thought as the exclusive
model for the apprehension of reality? Is there not an undertone,
or a component, of pragmatic utilitarianism in these aspects of
Marxism? Perhaps, but we do well to recall that Marx himself
mocked the narrow utilitarianism of Bentham as philistine.
Equally, despite the relative infrequency and lack of development of Marx's ideas on science, he did not regard science as an
exclusively utilitarian pursuit. Rather, it was a development of
humanity's highest powers, an expression of the struggle against
inert nature, but also a realization of the human unity with a
higher nature, which encompassed the human potential. The
connection between science and *praxis* meant that science for
Marx was not strictly cognitive: it was, rather, a mode of social
existence. What we think of as social science, then, was part of a
general development of human power which also found expression in the rise of the natural sciences (what Marx [1953: 479]
once called the scientific power). The opposition between religion
and science, then, was for Marx not alone the familiar one of the
antithesis of falsehood and truth. It was, rather, the opposition
of an inauthentic—however necessary—stage in human development to an authentic one. Within what Marx designated as
human prehistory, religions and the beliefs attached to them
were more or less true. Bourgeois ideology, to draw an analogy
from the more general aspects of Marxist theory, was in fact a
truer statement about society than its predecessor—the organi-
cist theory of the early modern period—because it came closer to
the essential relationships which constituted society. The progression from metaphysics to metacriticism, as theology decom-
posed, was equally an approach to truth: out of the theoretical
humanism of the metacritics, the radical humanism of *praxis*
could develop.

It would be absurd to deny the secularized religious content of
the Marxist system as a whole: an extensive literature has drawn
the analogy, at times with profundity (Blumenberg 1966, Löwith 1964b). A secularized religious content, however, remains
secularized: the Marxist categories require, for our purpose, not
transformation back into their supposed religious sources, but
examination in their own terms. Before proceeding to that ex-

amination, we might well consider the treatment of religion in Marxist theory after Marx.

The Marxists after Marx

We may begin with Engels, despite his own role as Marx's early collaborator. His own pietistic background made Engels espcially sensitive to the religious dimensions of human existence, and his knowledge of the history of religions was not small. Engels's modification of the Marxist theory of religion had two aspects not unrelated to the general utilization of the theory found in his writings on a number of subjects. He did have a tendency, despite the religious sensitivity (what Max Weber might have termed religious musicality) he manifested, to describe religion at times as a direct expression of class interests. How the interests of a class may be identified, whether and under what conditions classes become aware of their interests, questions of the division of spiritual labor within given classes—these are matters which have long troubled students of the Marxists texts. The key to this emendation of Marxism is to be found in the word "direct" as applied to the expression of these interests: the burden of Marx's argument was that the situation of a class necessarily produced a situation of alienation, which in turn generated religion. That the specific forms and content of a historical religion were deeply influenced by the historical situation and social location of a class is, of course, a proposition Marxism shares with any number of other views of religion. The notion of religion as directly derived from class interests, in its reductionist form, is not compatible with the central tenets of the original Marxist analysis. Marx and Engels both were aware, of course, that at times religion was used or interpreted by classes high and low in terms consonant with their interests: this assertion is, however, not one about the origins of religion. The second tendency in Engels's thought stems from his assimilation of Darwinism. At times, he seemed to favor a doctrine of the natural selection of religions in situations of historical competition. The factors affecting natural selection, on this account, would be those at work in the general Marxist depiction of social process. We may note that this general depiction was, for all of its evolutionary and even naturalistic content, pre-Darwinian. People interacted with nature, but human labor, human society, and the human spirit were qualitatively distinct from nature. In the circumstances no mechanical causation of historical process was possible. History was a succession of structures, each with its own internal laws. A specific historical structure, given the general human propensity to develop religions, set limits to the religious systems that could live within it. This doctrine, whatever else it may be, is far from social Darwinism.

Perhaps I have made too much of these emendations of Engels. Let it be said at this point that he was at one with Marx in supposing that, within any historical structure, ideology (including, of course, religion) was not a mechanical derivative of production relations. In any given historical process, particularly in the short run, ideologies (including religions) had some autonomy. This is another way of saying that religion was an important historical force, not despite, but because of, its role as an expression of human alienation. The ambiguities in Engels's treatment of religion, however, were to lead to a certain crudification in the work of his successors, Kautsky (1910) and Bernstein (1895). There, religion was depicted as a reflection of class interests, as a direct means of class domination. The distinction (found in practice if not in theory in the original Marxist writings) between religion and ideology was erased: nothing of the substance of human spirituality was left in these analyses. Two curiously disparate reasons may be given for this development. These German Socialist thinkers (and politicians) took up positivism as a method. They proclaimed an almost total identification between the methods of the natural sciences and those of the social sciences. This is not the place to elaborate on the view that this frequently (as in some contemporary sociological studies of religion) leads to a position external to religion. By "external to religion," I mean a certain tendency to reduce religious structures to their observable contexts, to refuse a direct apprehension of religious consciousness, to treat it as solely epiphenomenal. This position is quite comprehensible when we connect it with the late nineteenth-century view that Marxism was a positive science, not a philosophical anthropology. On this view alternative interpretations of social existence were not just that: they were codification of error, radically different from and discontinuous with Marxism. The second reason for the positivistic insensitivity to religion in this version of Marxism is paradoxical. If Marxism were a science, if all other notions were in error, then Marxism's predictions as to the human future (a revolutionary utopia) had, somehow, to be verified mechanically and inevitably. No political movement can long maintain itself with a doctrine of inevitable triumph, however useful this may be for the purposes of converting those outside it and for maintaining the morale of those within it. Bernstein, in particular, met this problem by recourse to a Kantian morality. Socialism would come about because it ought to come about, not as a development of humanity's highest potential, but as an expression of humanity's actual moral characteristics. The element of qualitative and historical transformation was excluded; a static notion of humanity was introduced. In this setting, too, religion seemed at best arbitrary, at worst irrelevant or obscurantist—an element in history embarrassing to explain and most conveniently dispatched by treating it as a factor in prehistory. Kant's own interpretation of religion was rather different, but it was disregarded.

From Bernstein and Kautsky a line may be traced downward to Lenin (1947). Lenin's genius clearly resided in spheres other than the interpretation of culture or epistemology. The religion he knew best was the caesero-papism of Czarist Russia. The theory of knowledge he advanced was one in which human thought was a reflection of the real world. In the circumstances he dealt with religion as a pure and simple mystification. Lenin's views on religion marked, to some degree, a low point in the history of modern Marxist thought. We may say that it has taken decades for the official Marxist movement associated with Soviet communism to recover from the canonization of Lenin (which was followed, to be sure, by the domination of the movement by a former student of orthodox theology, Stalin). Current work in the Soviet Union and in the other state socialist regimes is increasingly vital and sophisticated: as it has yet to take definitive theoretical form, it will be dealt with in the section on the current sociology of religion.

Much of the most striking work on religion in the Marxist

tradition has been historical with a deepening or an emendation
of the Marxist theory as a by-product. We may therefore reserve,
equally, for subsequent treatment the writings of thinkers like
Borkenau, Goldmann, and Kolakowski. Two twentieth-century
Marxist theorists, however, merit our attention now. Lukacs
(1971) did almost no work on religion as such. However, his
insistence on the philosophical components of Marxism—and, in
particular, on the utility of concepts like *reification*—has contributed to the renaissance, more recently, of a serious Marxist
philosophical anthropology. In his work the concept of reification
is central; with it, the way has been opened to a critical consideration of religious ideas (and institutions) as reified sets of
symbols. The way has also been opened to those inside the
religious tradition for a purifying critique of the accretions
attaching to their own tradition. With the use of the concept of
reification, some religious thinkers have gone so far as to distinguish between authentic and inauthentic religion. Lukacs has
also contributed a notion of revolutionary *praxis* as a dialectical
leap into a human future as yet to be made. This had, clearly,
reinforced the secularized eschatological elements inside Marxism. At the same time, it has provided a somewhat more rigorous
theoretical framework for the Marxist notion of human development and contributed in this way to a possible specification of
the distinction between Marxism and religion. It must be said
that Lukacs's work on these themes, in his *History and Class
Consciousness,* was repudiated by Communist orthodoxy (and,
alas, by Lukacs himself). In no account did Lukacs move on to
consider religious phenomena explicitly. In his subsequent work
on esthetics, in which he attempts to ground esthetic experience in an idea of a humanity at once ideal and possible, his
use of religion is exceedingly fragmentary and unsystematic,
even shallow.

The personal religious inheritance of a thinker is important.
Lukacs was Jewish and, not surprisingly, developed an esthetics
with a heavy emphasis on the moral responsibility of the artist.
Antonio Gramsci (1966), the second original Marxist we have to
consider and the founder of the Italian Communist party came,
of course, from a culture steeped in Catholicism. The assimilation
of Gramsci's thought to modern Marxism, to modern thought as

a whole, is only now beginning. Gramsci insisted on the necessity of a Marxist analysis of culture and on the peculiarities of the Italian national culture. He conceived of the Roman Catholic church, historically, as rooted in the populace, as promulgating a doctrine complex, even subtle, for the intellectuals, but simple and comprehensive for the rest of the nation. What he admired in this process was its organic quality, its genuine synthesis of elements directly related to the activities and aspirations of a people. He derided the manipulative and political Catholicism which opposed Italian anticlericalism and socialism, but, in doing so, he in effect appealed to a more organic, more historically effective, version of religion. He did so in reflecting on the spiritual tasks before those who would organize a revolutionary, laicist party in Italy. Gramsci's Marxism is remarkable for its awareness of the educative tasks of a revolutionary party and in this respect is a concrete advance over what was programmatic in Marx himself—the modes by which humanity was to liberate itself from religion. Gramsci's most interesting work on religion is also fragmentary, and much of it was written in a fascist prison: its full development remains a task for his successors. We may note that his insistence on the educative tasks of a revolutionary movement has had considerable influence on Italy: the Italian Communist party has, in fact, doubled its vote (from circa 14 to circa 28 percent) since the end of the Second World War. The late Palmiro Togliatti, Gramsci's successor as leader of the party, in his celebrated "Political Testament," reminded the party that it had to take a differentiated and sympathetic view of religion (cited in Garaudy 1968: 118). This was more than a gesture at political coexistence with Italian Catholicism: it was an attempt to win again for political Marxism the theoretic legacy of the struggle against alienation. In the Togliatti "Testament," indeed, religion emerges as a potential force against alienation, as the possible bearer of humanity's aspirations along with socialism.

We are already anticipating the section on the Marxist-Christian dialogue. One of the striking results of the theoretical advances in Marxism achieved by Lukacs and Gramsci is the way in which these have been absorbed not by the socialist movement alone but by the oppositional party within Christendom. The critique of the ossification of its remoteness from human aspiration owes something to the doctrine of reification. The demand that the churches break their alliance with ruling elites and contribute to the practical education of subject populations draws, to some degree, upon Gramsci's reflection on Catholicism. For the moment, we may conclude that these advances in Marxism go some way beyond the original texts without radically transcending them or profoundly altering the original Marxist perspective. They constitute, then (a phenomenon observed more than once in the history of religions), a recovery of the past as well as an uncertain move into the future.

III   THE THEORETICAL CRITIQUE OF THE MARXIST SOCIOLOGY OF RELIGION

Introduction

The theoretical critique of the Marxist sociology of religion has two components. The first is straightforward enough—the development of other analytical assumptions, of different ideas about the relationship of religion and society. The second seems equally straightforward—direct criticism of Marxism, its emendation and refutation. The two are, of course, inseparably related: a critique of Marxism must always rest on its own theoretic foundations. More difficult still, the systems opposing Marxism usually share some assumptions with it. Indeed, they often have been influenced by Marxism and have incorporated some of its notions. We have to deal as well with inversions and reversals: the party of order, in early nineteenth-century sociology, insisted that only religion could hold society together and sought to buttress tottering thrones with refurbished altars. The critical party, to use Saint-Simon's terms, reversed the argument, and held that the elimination of religion was a precondition of social and political change. Moreover, the development of sociology at times seemed to verify the Marxist theses on ideology (and their underlying notions about alienation). Those thinkers who adduced permanent characteristcs of society were, often enough, eternalizing transitory historical phenomena—objectifying, in Marxist terms, structures actually created by people. Finally, sociologies of religion inevitably bear traces of the religious traditions within which, if only by opposition, they develop. We cannot briefly oppose to Marxism a uniform sociological critique: we have to turn, instead, to a multiplicity of sociologies of religion.

The Sociology of Religion in German Sociology

The encounter of German sociology with Marxism has always been direct. Not alone did Marx and Engels write (and think) in German: the German Social Democratic party represented a Marxist political and spiritual presence in German society. Moreover, the close relationship of German academic philosophy to German Protestant theology, the political role of the established Lutheran church, the *Kulturakampf* which set Catholics and Protestants against each other in the late nineteenth century, the very great impact on German culture of Darwinism all contributed to making religion a continuing problem for German social theory. It would be an absurdity to begin by stating that the non-Marxist Germans assigned primacy or even autonomy to spiritual factors in history. They did see religion (and ideas, generally) as constitutive of social reality, a proposition which is not entirely incompatible with Marxism, depending upon the larger framework in which the constitutive process is set. They were fully aware of the deep-rootedness of religious ideas in social process, not least Weber, whose sociology of religion at times loaned precision and verification to Marxist hypotheses. One major and enduring difference between German sociology and Marxism, however, will be found in philosophical anthropology. The Germans were historicists, but the ways in which people made their history were for them rather different than that described in the Marxist canon.

Toennies may be termed the founder of modern German sociology: his influence on Weber, for instance, has been underestimated. In one sense his *Gemeinschaft und Gesellschaft* (1964) may be thought of as an effort to find as many academic circumlocutions as possible for the phrase, "capitalist commodity production," which was not much in favor in the German universities at the end of the nineteenth century. Toennies was, indeed, a Social Democrat. His interpretation of human spiritual history, however, had a nostalgic, indeed romantic, cast. Industrialism in its capitalist form had torn apart the integument of human society, had replaced organic relationships with artificial ones, had generated a new and not necessarily more profound sensibility. The entire analysis of his work, in a descriptive sense, resembles nothing so much as an amplification of the characterization of bourgeois society found in the *Communist Manifesto,* where that society is taxed with having made profane everything held sacred by previous generations. Toennies clearly believed that only an organically united—and therefore authentic—community could develop conceptions of sacredness. Associative societies manifested rationalized modes of thought, discrete and individualized modes of feeling, a severance of the ties of people to nature and the human past embodied in religious tradition. Toennies provided no very systematic explanation of the transformation, even if he ascribed it to the emergence of market capitalism and its products—industrialization and urbanization. Indeed, even Toennies's description of a modern social mentality is just that—a description—and not a total explanation.

Toennies, then, interpreted religion (and the religious changes which, by the time he published his work in 1887, had already led to a large degree of secularization) as part of a total historical process. His critique of Marx was implicit in the implication that alienation was not a universal human condition but that it was a specifically modern disorder. Further, his analysis of modern society suggested very strongly that existence in it was possible without either God or human liberation. Put in another way, we may say that he interpreted history as having direction but not purpose. Toennies's work was part of a general German response to national social transformation. A philosophical response to this experience, with important consequences for sociology, was Dilthey's (1962) work.

Dilthey, as a philosopher of culture, proposed to answer the question, "How was historical knowledge possible?" by constructing a theory of history entire. Knowledge was possible because as knowers we intuited the human essence underlying historical flux. Yet flux was the form of history, in which, Dilthey here in effect paraphased Ranke, all epochs were equal in the sight of God. History was a succession of human value structures, modes of sensibility, knowledge, and judgment. The history of religion, in this view, was a partial aspect of a broader history. Insertion in a broader context, however, did not mean the analytical reduction of religion to other social factors. Indeed, religion as a privileged mode of crystallization of the human value structure merited our attention precisely as a way of seizing the peculiarity of a society or an epoch. Here was, in effect, a bourgeois humanistic response to the areligious humanism of the radicals and the conservative religiosity of the antihumanists. Religion could not be interpreted as a form of alienation, because there was no appeal for Dilthey from an actual to a potential humanity. Neither, however, could it be interpreted on its own terms, as a supreme and unique value universe. It was, on the contrary, the specific form taken by humanity in a given epoch. Something of the tension, nay ambiguity, of this position was transmitted by Dilthey to Weber.

The view that Weber's work on religion constituted a final and "scientific" falsification of Marxism is exceedingly difficult to sustain.[6] The Marxism Weber knew best was apparently—particularly with respect to the analysis of ideology and religion—the somewhat mechanical and positivistic doctrine of the German Social Democrats. Weber's fundamental differences with Marxism resided as much in the sphere of philosophical assumption and method as in the historical analysis of social structures. At first glance, it would seem that with respect to assumption and method the difference is enormous. The method of *Verstehen* involved the intuitive apprehension of the meanings imparted to social life by a divided humanity. Its division lay precisely in the plurality of value universes it constructed, the apparent axes about which Weber himself constructed his image of society. In fact, in his concrete historical analyses, the assumption of the construction of a human value universe was subordinated to the immediate exigencies of causal discourse, an element of ambi-

[6] See the debate on Max Weber at the German Sociological Association's celebration of his centenary (Stammer 1965).

guity in Weber which makes the interpretation of his legacy so difficult.

There is a demonic anthropology in Weber, in which the choice of values by humanity is utterly arbitrary (and so leads to a Darwinian or, rather, Hobbesian struggle among bearers of different values). This Weber combined with a pervasive belief in what he termed the metaphysical needs of the human spirit, which constituted the perennial psychological basis of religious experience. His theory of religion, however, did something other than combine universal human religious need with particular historical content arbitrary with respect to humanity, if lawful with respect to the specific conditions of existence of a historical group. Weber had an uncanny, almost perverse, grasp of the religious consequences of religious beliefs in this respect, not entirely unlike Marx. The historical process of rationalization, in which the transcendent elements were driven out of Western society, was for Weber a direct consequence of the Western religious tradition going back, before Latin Christianity, to the Old Testament. The similarities between Weber's description of rationalization and the Marxist concept of alienation have been noted, and for the moment we need only suggest three. The omnipresence of a means-end calculus meant that a certain kind of technical rationality pervaded all human relationships, a parallel to the conversion in Marxism of all human relations to market relations. The bureaucratic structures necessary to a rationalized society had an objective existence of their own, rather like the system of production relations in Marxism. Finally, the destruction of transcendence in rationalization also entailed the extirpation of previously glimpsed possibilities of human wholeness. This last seemed reasonably close to the notion of the denial of human wholeness contained in the idea of market-derived alienation. However, Weber envisaged no transcendence of rationalization, or, at any rate, none that could have intrinsically more moral and human value. He saw no authentic human possibility that could arise after the destruction of religious transcendence: the disenchantment of the world was final, and efforts to deny it were illusory and futile. Marx supposed that humanity's spiritual longings would be fulfilled by its own spiritual maturation. Weber's historical pessimism allowed him to believe only that the precious metal of the spirit would be converted to dross by history.

It is quite true that for Weber ideas, and above all religious ideas, were historic forces; but it is equally true that in this account of history, these ideas spend themselves. Protestantism, that fusion of inwardness and of rigorous ascetic discipline, ended in the banality of acquisitiveness, the philistinism of bureaucratic subjugation, the deep reflectiveness of caste ritual. The metaphysical splendors of Taoism allowed a profane system of family and emperor worship to regulate Chinese life. The prophecies of Israel have indeed been fulfilled—as Weber thought they might —in a small state with an army and (several) universities. Weber's unique contribution to the sociology of religion may consist of his depiction of the resistances encountered by the spirit, which eventually shaped and even subdued it. The analogy with Marxism is clear, but so is the difference. Weber supposed, in effect, that the products of the religious imagination of humanity would themselves fail in their original intention and so, in turn, generate new explosions of faith. Weber's colleague, Troeltsch (1956), contributed to this depiction of history in his account of the changing relations of church, sect, and mysticism in the history of Christianity. We may put the matter in extremely schematic form and say that for Marx, the spirituality distorted in production took religious form but that, for Weber, the spirituality authentically invested in religion was distorted by the relations of production.

These are clearly questions of metahistory. They should not obscure the very considerable contribution made by Weber to the analysis of the social context of religion. We may analyse his contribution in terms of the rubrics class, culture, and politic. In his essay on *The Protestant Ethic and the Spirit of Capitalism,* Weber (1930) was unequivocal: Calvinism, for all of its effects on Western social structure, had a class basis in the interests, culture, and aspirations of the petty and middle bourgeoisie. He largely ignored, as Borkenau was to point out later, the problem of the Calvinism of the nobility. The analysis of the class basis of Protestantism—and its forerunners among the late medieval sectarian movements—was deepened in the subsequent essay "Classes, Estates, Religion" in *The Sociology of Religion*

(Weber 1963). There, the urban and mercantile-productive style of life of the bourgeoisie was depicted as an indispensable element in what was to become the Protestant rationalization of Christianity. In his treatment of the world religions, without exception Weber gave precise accounts of the location of religiosity in the stratification system. The psychological mechanism by which religion was produced in these circumstances was, clearly, intuited by Weber without his specifying these. The notion of "elective affinity" had its role here, and the affinity was between the type of spirituality and religious duty emphasized by a religion and the concrete imperatives of existence of particular social groups. To the intellectuals (at first, in priestly form) fell the task of elaborating these affinities into coherent systems of belief. Not the least important aspect of Weber's sociology of religion is its emphasis on the role of religious specialists. Their emergence was the occasion for the introduction of a new possibility of stratification in not alone religious organizations, but in entire societies: the capture or appropriation of exclusive rights of access to divine wisdom or charisma by intellectuals clearly was an element in the struggle for power. In general, Weber saw the political uses of religion as dependent upon alliances between political and spiritual elites for the purpose of sacrilizing domination. (There is a direct connection to his analysis of bureaucratization, where secular versions of esoteric doctrine and practice are in the possession of a new type of intellectual.) Let us recall Weber's celebrated dictum that the negatively privileged fashion religions which legitimate what they will become, whereas the privileged elaborate doctrines which emphasize their being. Weber, at any rate, posited no absolute distinctions between religion and the rest of humanity's works. Assertions of his insistence on the autonomy of religion in society, therefore, do not seem to be unequivocally well-founded. There are, however, two senses in which he may be said to have gone beyond Marx. The first is in his profoundly pessimistic renunciation of hope for a transcendence of alienation, and that precisely at those points in his work at which Weber insisted on the human content of religion, on its dealienating function. The second is in his extremely detailed and careful specification of the social sources, institutionalization, and historical consequences of the world religions. Here, a good deal of Weber's work can be appreciated as an unintended tribute to Marx.

I have already said that Weber's analysis of the bureaucratic intellectuals evinces striking similarities to his view of the general role of the custodians of arcane doctrine. His predilection for treating aspects of secular existence as continuations or equivalents of religious phenomena is even more evident in his writings on the modern cultural situation. The interest of the intellectuals in esthetics (divorced from any moral or social purpose) and sexuality, he thought, were searches for substitute realms of the spirit. His analysis of the Socialist movement itself was not free of religious or ecclesiastical analogies, although he was careful not to deal with socialism *in extenso* as a secularized religious movement. Indeed, despite, or because of, his despair he did approach Marx on one point. The search for substitute realms of the spirit, the superficial similarities between modern bureaucrats and ancient priests did not lead him to posit a unilinear descent or equivalence between religion and nonreligion. He was sardonic about those who supposed that a religion fit for a rationalized society could be conjured out of the historical air: the time for belief, he held, had gone.

With Weber, the theoretical epoch in German sociology did not close. The twin caesurae of the Nazi triumph in 1933 and the postwar restoration of pre-1933 German social structure have impeded, however, the continuation of an original German contribution to social thought. For whatever reasons, the most original and internationally influential of recent German schools of sociology, the Frankfurt school, has given remarkably little attention to religion. From the dense mass of German sociological treatments of religion which have succeeded Weber, I select two for summary treatment. Mannheim (1952) is thought of, sometimes, as a successor to the Marxists. His theoretical debt to their work (and in particular to Lukacs) is obvious. What is less obvious is that his own depiction of religious movements, in *Ideology and Utopia*, used typological procedures and was, therefore, a retreat from the historicism of both Marx and Weber. The religious modes of apprehending reality, including chiliasm, seem to erupt from the substratum of history or succeed one another when abstractly conceived and classified conditions obtain. Briefly, Mannheim removed historical direction from his analysis and worked with a supposedly universal sociology. Was his interest in phenomenology responsible? I am at a loss to answer, but the phenomenological influences on sociology may point in another direction. The phenomenologists insist on the human construction of reality (Schutz 1967, Berger and Luckmann 1966, Luckmann 1967). Transposed to the analysis of religion, this would oblige us to interpret religious systems as the imposition of meaning upon the world. The empirical elements of this position were developed by Weber: their theoretical utilization in the sociology of religion might promise an extension of Marxism in quite unanticipated ways. In this account of the sociology of religion, the struggle against alienation is universal and perennial. There is, as yet, nothing in the method which enables us to distinguish between systems of meaning which contribute to maintaining alienation and those which constitute authentic efforts to humanize the universe. The use of the term "authentic" suggests, once again, that we have moved into realms not usually associated with sociology. Whether we have moved beyond Marx is, however, a different question.

Durkheim and a French Critique of Marxism

If Durkheim (1964) and his school, with their very great influence on the sociological analysis of religion, had simply propounded the thesis that religion was a mode of social integration, there would be little difficulty in dealing with them. We could remark that for Marx, at definite epochs (in fact, for most of the history of humanity), religion was equally that. If Durkheim had simply opposed to a society unaware, unconscious of its processes a model of sociological knowledge functioning as a technique for the mastery of history, again, we could note a considerable consonance with Marxism. The concrete religious studies of Durkheim's students—Mauss (1968) on the primitives Granet (1957) on the Chinese—and their wider influence (on, for instance, Febvre's [1932] studies of religious belief in the Renaissance and Marc Bloch's [1961a, b] medieval historiography) pose, in their concreteness, no overwhelming problem.

These establish close connections between religious forms and the rest of social organization, uncover identical meanings in each. This is different from the Marxist tradition (which insists on the transformation of concrete social existence in religion), but we could simply note the difference.

The difference of meaning, however, between the Marxist sociology of religion and the Durkheimians is far greater. In his recent Inaugural Lecture at the Collège de France, Raymond Aron (1971) (whom it is difficult to tax with excessive sympathy for Marxism) observed that he always found it difficult to accept the Durkheimians' curious disinclination to deal with social conflict. Durkheim's sociology, and in particular his sociology of religion, is a consensualist doctrine in a very specific sense. Today we employ the term "consensus" to designate an ultimate (or at least important) element of agreement about values in society. Durkheim certainly thought that this was present in society or, at least, described its absence as pathological. However, he made use, fundamentally, of Saint-Simon's concept of consensus: a description of the self-constitutive process of society, of the structural consonance of its parts. The intention of Durkheim's sociology was consensual in the sense that sociology was meant to identify and adumbrate that consonance. Further, it was supposed to offer pedagogically the society an occasion for self-reflection, or more precisely, self-recognition. The functions of sociology as an instrument of education (we might today term it a policy science or the supreme policy science) derived from its capacity to instruct people about two things: the constraints which bound them and the moral character of these constraints.

From this point of view, the striking thing about Durkheim's sociology of religion is that he portrays religion as having essentially the same tasks. It is true that religion operates with conceptions of the sacred, with realms of the spirit remote from scientific analysis. The source of religious beliefs and sentiments, the object of worship, however, is society itself. Religious symbolism transforms human dependence upon society into a different set of meanings. The sociology of religion is, in effect, a venture in interpretation employing symbolic rationality to establish the underlying rationality of social control. Marx proposed that religion be transcended as part of a process of tran-

scending a given and oppressive state of society. Durkheim
proposed that religion be understood so that the true source of
morality (and personal integration) could be known.

In this reading, Durkheim must be thought of (*horribile
dictu*) as a "conservative." We face a contradiction. Durkheim's own views of socialism were extremely critical, as he did
not see class conflict as the supreme mode of access to a just
society. Yet he was unequivocally reformist in his politics and,
indeed, saw one of sociology's chief tasks precisely in its potential as an agency of social intelligence. There is no reason to
suppose that a thinker must be consistent to be valuable, but we
cannot dismiss the contradiction as simply that. Two aspects of
Durkheim's sociology of religion may make it less of one than it
initially appears.

The first aspect, paradoxically, is its attention to the supra-
rational, spontaneous, even Dionysiac elements in religion. In
those moments when societies become aware of the sacred, in
which routine is transformed, societies attain the truth about
themselves. Moreover, they create (more accurately, re-create)
themselves. Religion, then, may be a force for the transformation
of a social order, for the propagation of a new set of ideas and
sentiments. Durkheim (1960: 609–11) described the French
Revolution as abortive but voiced his hopes for other transformations. Where, however, would these ideas and sentiments come
from? The second component of interest in Durkheim's sociology
of religion at this point is its evolutionary character. Durkheim
is sometimes read as a sociologist who propagated, or sought to
do so, invariant laws of social process. He did not, however,
always follow his own *Rules of Sociological Method* (1938).
There remained in his work an image of social development
derived from the evolutionary rationalism of Saint-Simon and
Comte. Religion, as the crucible in which social categories were
formed, was the predecessor of science. If science, however, was a
set of social categories, and if society was able at times to remake
its categories, then religion was not exclusively an expression of
humanity's passive dependence upon a (static) society. It was,
rather, an anticipation of freedom.

Perhaps so, but this libertarian interpretation of Durkheim
encounters a major difficulty. Nowhere does Durkheim define or

envisage a humanity apart from its concrete social forms. At no place does he oppose a vision of humanity transformed to his image of a humanity identical with its own transient structures. Like Marx, he may have anticipated a postreligious future; unlike Marx, he hardly grounded this philosophically. The creation and re-creation of society in religion was not, according to Durkheim, a mere reflection of its previous existence. The specificity of religion resided precisely in its creative capacity, in its making of society out of dispersed and atomized activities. We may say that Marx anticipated the development of this supreme human capacity precisely with the disappearance of the obscurantist, dehumanizing, functions of religion. Durkheim held that the capacity was perennial, and that if religion was to be replaced as a repository of the sacredness of society's awareness of itself, its functions would have to be assumed by science. Not only, then, the absence of a doctrine of alienation distinguished the two thinkers; their conception of transcendence differed radically as well. For Durkheim, society was alway intentionally created; for Marx, intention had as yet to come. The two thinkers spoke strikingly different languages; upon inspection, the profound differences between them are more impressive than the ones immediately obvious. Did Durkheim go beyond Marx? We can assert that only from within the premises of Durkheim's system.

Structuralism, Religion, Marxism

No recent method has been more discussed than structuralism and none with so little uniformity of terms. Structuralism may be thought of as the unexceptionable doctrine that behind the empirical flux of history, there are relatively enduring forms. It may be conceived of as a method which points to these forms and which cuts across some of the conventional boundaries of our traditions of social thought. We have had at least one version of Marxist structuralism (Althusser 1970) and yet another of Freudian structuralism (Lacan 1966)—both indubitably Parisian in accent. The spread of the discussion owes much to the fact that almost any discussion of structure will touch on perennial problems of method and substance in the social sciences: the relations of reality to appearance, of the one to the many, of process to form, of history to event, and of the mind to its object. For our purposes, we would do well to concentrate on structuralism as developed by Lévi-Strauss (1966) and his collaborators (Sebag 1964), a structuralism which in effect deals with the relationship of mind to society. The intellectual itinerary of Lévi-Strauss, from philosophy to social anthropology and back again, has been remarked upon often enough. Lévi-Strauss has indeed promulgated a theory of the universal characteristics of mind, or at the very least has engaged in an intensive search for one. Unlike his predecessors in the history of philosophy, Lévi-Strauss has not taken the view that professors of philosophy, by introspection and ratiocination, may discover in their own heads principles of mind visible only obscurely in the rest of humanity. Rather, his emphasis on arcane and esoteric data drawn from the interstices of modern societies and from its primitive predecessor and contemporary societies exemplifies one of his basic contentions: the unity of humanity is a spiritual unity. One initial point is clear: for all of his human sympathy, for all of his respect for the integrity of cultures often dismissed in the pejorative use of the term "savage," Lévi-Strauss sees them as the repositories of a cognitive reason. Spiritual yearning, terror, notion of transformation and transcendence are certainly far from absent in his work. Yet for him, religious phenomena are interesting precisely insofar as they constitute hidden cognitive systems. When we ask, therefore, what distinguishes structuralism from Marxism, it is the latter with which we must credit a more systematic appreciation of the emotive (rather than the denotative) component of religion.

Myths, religions, utopias, and social philosophies—all are systems of messages, languages by which a historically fragmented humanity explains nature and history to itself. The task of a sociology of religion, in the first instance, resembles that of cryptography: behind the specific imagery, content, and emphasis of the single language, sociology can and must discover a conceptual system. The particular conceptual system, further, operates with universal modes: antitheses, equivalences, rules for transformation. The whole constitutes a prescription for a universal grammar or decoding system. Once the operation of decoding is achieved—at least for one language—how may it be related to its setting?

It is at this point that the antithesis of Marxism and structuralism becomes clearer. In one way, no systematic relationship to a setting is possible for a religion (or any other human language) : it is the language, the symbolic system, which is the central constitutive element of the setting. Structuralism, here, has important links to the French tradition elaborated by Durkheim and the Durkheimians (Mauss was, indeed, Lévi-Strauss's teacher). An arbitrary or conceptual separation of social structure from its spiritual processes is possible in structuralism, but the conceptual separation rests on a premise, precisely, of separation. The systems of meaning contained in the coded vehicles of the spirit may be used by social forces external to these, but the meaning remains independent.

Structuralism, then, confronts the Marxist theory of ideology with two rather different arguments. The first insists that the human world is given order by the languages of the spirit: the distinction between ideology and *praxis* disappears. The second argument maintains the distinction but insists that it is total: the spheres interact blindly, but there can be no transfer of meaning. Indeed, there is no universal human meaning; myth, religion, philosophy are composed of universal elements but select and combine these in ways which are arbitrary from the viewpoint of a universal meaning. The notion of total human self-realization or the transcendence of alienation is incompatible with this argument. Indeed, for Lévi-Strauss and his colleagues, we may say that alienation (or something very like it) occurs precisely when a group is deprived of its particular system of meaning. (They partake of a general contemporary tendency, which we find equally in the works of so unsystematic a thinker as Fanon.)

Curiously, Lévi-Strauss himself has insisted on his affinity with Marxism. He locates this in his emphasis on processes of exchange. Groups exchange (products and messages) internally with other groups and with nature. Their systems of meaning are codifications of that process, indeed, they give it structure and direction. In the sense that Marxism supposes that people create their own environment, this is compatible with Marxism; but what else could Marxism or any other sociology in fact suppose? Structuralism denies direction to history, insists on history as a plurality of competing value universes, and treats the notion of transcending alienation as itself another myth. In any terms it has gone beyond Marxism; the real question is whether it has gone beyond many of our traditional conceptions of humanity itself.

Psychoanalysis, Marxism, and Religion

The similar intentions of Marxism and psychoanalysis have often been discussed. Each was a derivative of the Enlightenment. Each sought to replace irrationality and domination with reason and liberation. If we take into account their obvious differences of conceptual structure and object, may we see the two systems as complementary? The project is not unequivocal. First, we have to deal with profound differences of philosophic assumption. Marx remained a Hegelian and the later synthesis in his work of conceptions of the dialectic with data processed in an empirical-positivistic way (above all, in his political economy) is incomplete. Freud was a student of the German university generation marked by the Darwinian controversy: he employed the strict and naturalistic conceptions of causality of a laboratory physiologist. It is quite true that his transposition of these to the spheres of psychology and history posed great difficulties; we may say that he followed a trajectory which reversed that of Marx from empiricism to metahistory. The briefest examination of the theory of religion in Freud will pose some of these difficulties.[7]

In fortunate cases, Freud held, psychoanalysis could cure (in the sense of replacing one unconscious structure by another) neurosis. Yet, when he designated religion as "universal obsessional neurosis of mankind," he seemed to imply that the cure, if any, lay in the future. We may understand his theory of religion in three steps. The first concerns the beginnings of the psychohistory of humanity entire. Religion originated in a complex of

---

[7] See, of course, Paul Pruyser's extended essay on Freud, which is Chapter 6 in this volume.

rituals and beliefs which transposed onto a symbolic plane the original Oedipical act, the slaying of the primal father. Symbolic transposition enabled humanity to internalize the guilt resulting from this act, and, no less important, to develop internal psychic structures which made possible an irreducible minimum of social cohesion. The second plane entails the psychohistory of individuals, who, in effect, recapitulated in their psychic development the history of the human race. The noted (or notorious) equivalence of primitivism and infancy has its place here: primitive peoples lived all their lives in psychocultural structures which were (at least for a good deal of the time) transcended with the development of civilization. The third step is the latter: the progress of civilization entailed the repression of infantile belief, but it also entailed its continuation in the sublimated or socialized form of institutionalized religious tradition. Moreover, civilization was not unambiguous: it continued and even heightened repression, but the development of the human ego in science gave humanity a chance to understand itself and so to escape or at least minimize repression. Like so many nineteenth-century thinkers, Freud seemed to work with the evolutionary antithesis, religion-science, and, of course, he understood psychoanalysis as science.

Two conspicuous differences with Marxism emerge. Freud worked to a time scale which was much slower than the Marxist one, as well as with a humanity much more resistant to change, immensely recalcitrant to recognize its own highest interests and powers. Equally important, Freud denied (at times, quite explicitly) that institutional change could in and of itself create the preconditions for a triumph of reason. The repetition compulsion alone would re-create, in the individual psyche, the infantile conditions which generated religion. The task of reeducating humanity was just that, but it was a task which had to be entrusted (for the foreseeable future) to a small elite of the enlightened or the thoroughly analyzed. Further, the battle would have to be repeated in each generation. If new educational methods, new familial relationships, could minimize the incidence of neurosis, they could by no means eliminate the danger. A liberated humanity was a chimerical notion, a humanity slowly made aware of the necessity for a perennial struggle against the unconscious was not; but even this seemed infinitely difficult to attain.

There is another, starker way of posing the question. Freud ascribed a very different content and structure to human desolation than did Marx: their notions of alienation, superficially similar, are structurally diverse. Freud held that the transposition of the struggle against alienation (in his terms, neurosis) had to move from a generalized critique of religion to a specific attack on the psychic structures which generated religion. Again, the resemblance to Marx's critique of Feuerbach is superficial. The psychic structures which generated religion could not be changed; but they could be understood, and humanity could be taught to live without religious consolation or discipline. Freud hoped—with no very great conviction—that this could be true of humanity entire: for the foreseeable future, the only revolution he could envisage was one carried by a small elite. The concrete transcendence envisaged by psychoanalysis, then, had a dimension of sobriety, even resignation, as well as one of liberation. The radical elements of cultural criticism in Freud, as well as the specific analysis of religious systems, were carried further by some Freudians: these are best dealt with under the next general rubric of the paper.

IV HISTORICAL CRITIQUES OF THE MARXIST SOCIOLOGY OF RELIGION

Should I have termed this section an empirical-historical critique of the Marxist sociology of religion? It is common enough to classify studies of religion in three ways: comparative, empirical, and historical. The briefest of reflections will suggest that the generic rubric is historical: all of these studies are focused on phenomena apprehended in their historicity at a given time. If "empirical" is taken to mean quantitative studies, there is no reason why quantitative methods—rudimentary or complex— cannot be applied to historical or comparative data. (I at one point [Birnbaum 1959] enumerated the socioeconomic characteristics of the Zurich elite in Zwingli's time, the better to deal with the relationship of capitalism and nascent Protestantism in that society.) The term "historical" seems appropriate, both on general epistemological grounds and for reasons specific to Marxist theory, which above all claims to be one grounded in history.

If one thing needs saying, let it be said now. The literature on the relationship of religion to society is immense, and most of it has implications for the Marxist theory. Troeltsch once remarked that he had been criticized for not using primary sources to write his great book on the social doctrines of Christianity, but that had he done so, he would hardly have progressed beyond Saint Paul. This is not a Troeltsch-like effort, in either quantity or, alas, quality: it is, rather, a work of reflection. What I propose to do is not to survey the literature (which, now, would require the efforts of a well-endowed consortium of gifted scholars), but to set down a set of personal conclusions about it.

The Industrial Societies of the West

Three very general propositions may be derived from the Marxist texts with respect to the development of religion in the industrial societies of the West. I restrict these propositions to the West because (a) we confront, here, capitalist production relations and (b) we confront, equally, a specific version of the Judaeo-Christian tradition. These three are the following. With the development of capitalism and the profanation of all relationships religion must undergo an internal transformation: the notion of the fetishism of commodities refracts a more complex reality, in which total visions of transcendence give way to fragmented irrationalities. We may (even if Marx did not) describe these as substitute or inauthentic religions. Second, as important social groups—and above all, the working class—become aware of their real historical position and interests, they will free themselves of religious belief: in its early (authentic) or late (inauthentic) forms. Third, as power and property are threatened by organized socialism, the functions of the official churches as spiritual police agencies will become more compulsive and more evident.

What has, in fact, happened? Of a generalized decline in religious belief and sentiment with respect to the transcendent doctrines of the Judaeo-Christian tradition there can be little doubt. This decline has been most marked in areas of society most affected by the industrialization process. The evidence as to its causes, however, points in rather contrasting directions. One cause of the decline in belief seems to lie in the rise of technical-instrumental modes of mastering nature and society: disbelief among the more highly educated, the more technicized, groups of society is quite high. Another source seems to be the fragmentation, verging on destruction, of certain communal institutions—region, local community, extended family. We are more certain of the fact of decline in belief, even of its proximate sources, than we are about the phenomena which have replaced or succeeded belief.

A conceptual difficulty intrudes at this point. I have said that Marx employed, in a manner only half-explicit, a conception of inauthentic religion. It is surely possible that a superficial continuity in religious belief and practice for modern population groups conceals profound inner discontinuities. For obvious reasons, generalized studies of the inner structure and spiritual organization (if that is the term) of modern religious beliefs are sparse. It is easier to ascertain rates of decline in ecclesiastical participation, to compute answers to questionnaire inquiries about particular beliefs, than to make judgments about the whole. Pin's (1956) study in Lyon and Lenski's (1961) work in Detroit attempt to conceptualize the quality of piety in each case; Luckmann's interpretation of an "invisible religion" is another, more global effort of this kind. The German historian of ideas Blumenberg (1966) has suggested, in a book which must shake most sociologists of religion, that our operating assumptions about a unilinear process of secularization bear profound traces of theological thought. There is no easy way out of this difficulty, but just as the Marxist theory fuses evaluative and cognitive categories, responses to it (on one level, at least) tend to do the same. We can say with some conviction that the structure of industrial society, its fragmentation of roles in particular, makes a religious interpretation of it as a totality exceedingly difficult for those who live in it: the areas in which transcendence seems possible are ever more tightly constricted, if available at all.

Substitutes for transcendence (in its previous forms) are not difficult to hypothesize: nationalisms, regionalisms, and other compulsive forms of communalism constitute one genre, although it must be said that the self-defense or self-consciousness of a community, however attenuated or even distorted, is not necessarily a substitute religion. The end of the fusion between these communalisms and religion may, indeed, have invested them with energies once attached to religion. The same may be said of the modern cults of acquisitiveness and sexuality, both conspicuous in Weber's sociology of *ersatz* religiosity. Another path of inquiry would bring us to the jagged, inorganic, and intrinsically senseless universe of mass culture: a world of antisymbols. Upon reflection, we could say (with Adorno 1947) that this universe is marked by dreadful immanence. Repeating the surface of daily existence in industrial society, it embodies and legitimates its pervasive irrationality.

It is clear that efforts to verify or falsify the Marxist hypotheses on religion in industrial society entail interpretations of the data which go beyond a purely empirical plane to interpretations which may or may not be consistent with Marxism but which are equally global. A secular decline in the pervasiveness of religious belief (as well as of ecclesiastical control) is easy enough to establish. A causal analysis involves us in a historical time series which is not empirically verifiable by any one inquiry, however plausible it may appear. We can say that the decline of a belief in transcendence has left a vacuum, into which any number of contenders for the succession have rushed. We can say, equally, that the fragmentation of existence in industrial society makes any interpretation of the social totality difficult and that interpretations of a religious kind are especially difficult for those immersed in the technical-instrumental sectors of the society. The ascriptions of the multiple irrationalities in the culture of industrial society to capitalist forms of exchange is possible, but, rather than a verification of the Marxist thesis, it would constitute yet another application of it.

Perhaps more light may be shed on the theory when we con-

sider the religion of the industrial working class (Isambert
1961). Where that class has been organized in Socialist parties,
these are frequently antireligious or areligious. This, however,
may be due to an external association between the *ecclesiae* and
those with power and property. It may be due, equally, to the
inheritance by the Socialist movement of a bourgeois tradition of
anticlericalism and militant rationality (in Italy, the regions
with the highest Communist votes are those with a long-term
tradition of struggle against the papacy). That there has been a
pronounced decline in the religious adherence of the industrial
working class in general since the beginnings of industrialization
is obvious. Some other tendencies, however, complicate the
analysis.

There is evidence to suggest that Socialist movements may
have directly religious components. The role of the Methodist
churches and of Methodist leaders in British socialism has been
conspicuous. Left Catholicism is not merely the work of intellectuals: it has had, and has, solid working-class support. I do not
refer here to the varieties of corporativist anticapitalist doctrine
found in Catholicism, but to unmistakably Socialist Catholic
groupings aiming not at the modification of capitalism but at its
supersession. In Christian Socialist movements (which have to be
distinguished from Christian social movements, which have very
different political aims), the transition from religious notions of
community to profane utopias is exceedingly visible. It may be
said that in the recent transformation of the Catholic trade
union in France and similar developments in Italy (in both
countries, these unions are often more militant, less compromising, than the Communist-led ones) suggests that the transition
for some is now complete on an ideological level. Further, we
have to account for the fact that whatever the attitudes of adult
male members of the working class, the women until recently
have manifested more attachment to religion and to the churches.

Perhaps, however, the primary difficulty with the Marxist
thesis on the supersession of religion in the proletariat is this
(Birnbaum 1969: 106–166). A self-conscious proletarian attempt
to overthrow capitalism with the aid of a coherent revolutionary
doctrine has not been a consistent feature of the history of
industrial society. Instead, the Socialist movements (and their

trade union components) have often subsided into a politics which we may term reformist. Further, an ideological division of labor in the movement has assigned doctrine to the intellectuals, the laborious tasks of organization (and combat) to the workers. In some societies (Wilhelmian Germany and to some degree modern France and Italy) the working-class movement has itself constituted a counterchurch. Additionally, the working-class struggle to acquire bourgeois culture (with all that this implies) has meant that a genuinely working-class culture with a postreligious component has not developed. The cultural and social integration of industrial societies, as haphazard as it is, has worked against the emergence of such a culture. Interestingly, the foremost of the Latin Marxists, Antonio Gramsci, saw the development of such a culture—and, in particular, a critical view of religion—as an essential task for a revolutionary party in Italy. In short, the historical conditions for a test of this aspect of the Marxist theory have as yet to be realized. The theory has a self-confirming mechanism built into it: if the proletariat should accept its role, its Prometheanism would indeed supersede religion. For the moment, no part of Western humanity is Promethean. Whether or not the new Prometheus speaks Chinese, I cannot say.

The Marxist hypotheses on the churches as spiritual police agencies are somewhat easier to deal with. In part of industrial society the churches have identified with values (and with elites) we may term preindustrial. Here, the struggle against the churches, against integralism, has united an enlightened bourgeoisie and the Socialist movement. What was true of the Lutheran state church in Germany, or of Latin Catholicism, has not been true in societies with more ecclesiastical pluralism. There, a virtual stratification of the churches has occurred, such that churches of the dispossessed have been as prominent as the churches of the propertied. It is true that in the United States the main-line Protestant churches, in particular, have reinforced aspects of the national ethic which facilitated public attachment to a capitalist economy. These same churches, however, have repeatedly been the focuses of ideological conflict overflowing from other sectors of the society. Meanwhile, clerical integralism in the Latin societies has been challenged from within the Catholic churches themselves. In an epoch of global contestation, these have not been immune. We can say, in conclusion, that the churches have ceased to act unequivocally as spiritual policy agencies at the same time as they have ceased to serve as spiritual centers for society as a whole. The desperate efforts of ecclesiastical elites and of theologians (not the same parties, by any means) to adapt or modernize the churches suggest that long-term historical processes are working against them. It is difficult, however, to see either the opposition of a spiritually liberated working class or the churches' attachment to exploiting classes as the sole, or even primary, cause of the decline in the power and influence of the churches.

Studies of Religion in Preindustrial Europe

The number of such studies is, of course, enormous and may have been undertaken by historians (and a very few sociologists) aware of the implications of Marxist theory for their work. It may be suggestive, however, to see what resources are at our disposal in this vast field. We may begin with studies of heretical and Christian revolutionary movements (Werner 1956, Williams 1962). These have been explored in considerable variety and depth, from the early Middle Ages to the Reformation. Do any general conclusions emerge from data often esoteric in nature? (The study of medieval sects, obviously, calls for detailed knowledge of church history, theology, and social history and is made more difficult by the fact that, the sects having frequently been historical losers, their history has been recorded by the victors, their enemies). One negative result seems clear: we cannot assert that the heretical movements of the medieval period and the Reformation era were invariably and exclusively religions of the oppressed. The element of leadership, of ideological interpretation, is important. Just as, in our time, socialism has been an alliance of the working class and intellectuals who interpreted its historical position to it, so in the past theologians were indispensable to the Christian interpretation of popular discontent. Another conclusion suggests itself: where these movements were unequivocally movements of the oppressed, they often were urban in character involving the artisanate or the early urban proletariat. The peculiar quality of urban social relationships was a certain distance from the immersion in nature of rural society: this, apparently, encouraged critical reflection in the cities.

Max Weber attributed the origins of Protestantism to the concrete experience of urban production, the rational and visible connection between work and its results. He saw this as, in effect, demystifying. Weber's hypothesis is not contradicted by the historical literature; it is also perfectly compatible with Marxist notions on the emergence of profane thought. Are we entitled, however, to introduce a notion of historical progression (from religious belief to critical-causal social explanation) into the more obscure reaches of Western social history? Perhaps, but we would do better for the moment to say that urban heretical movements introjected different kinds of theological—both material and ethical—reasoning into the medieval cosmos. Legoff's (1957) studies suggest that the intellectually innovative scholastics were aware of their own artisanal status in the medieval division of labor without their invariably promulgating explicit heresies.

Heresy and revolution, then, were sometimes fused, sometimes distinct in the medieval period. The analysis of the social composition of the groups which espoused heresies without a prominent revolutionary component is, however, instructive. We find, to transpose a term from Marxism, multiple alienations. Oppressed or exploited regions, elites in situations of dislocation, women: these were some of the bearers of heresies. Moreover, in their theological content and ethical consequences, heresies almost always provided for alternative paths of life, new forms of social relationship. No doubt, analysis can trace the situations of spiritual alienation at the root of heresies to deeper changes in the medieval structure of production. These movements within a sacred society, however, raise a very general question. If we confront alienations within a total religious alienation, are we asserting something permanent—relatively irreducible—about the conflicts induced in humanity by its social nature? If we interpret heresies—revolutionary or not—as efforts to master alienation, do we not open a perspective in which the Marxist notion may be generalized? I shall return to this question later, but perhaps the distance between ourselves and the medieval period allows us to see this problem more clearly.

Let us turn to an area of inquiry which is a *locus classicus* of the discussion of the Marxist theory: the relationships of Protestantism to capitalism. Weber qualified his own researches, it will be recalled, by insisting on the necessity of complementary studies of the influence of social process on religion. Further, in his later works, he came much closer to ascribing some of the characteristics of Protestantism to a preformed style of life dependent upon a particular set of early bourgeois production relations. The literature, again, is enormous. I shall select two inquiries undertaken from a Marxist point of view. The first is the late Franz Borkenau's (1934; also Birnbaum and Lenzer 1969: 282–91) general study of the emergence of a modern mentality. Methodologically, Borkenau rejects a crude theory of religion and thought, generally, as a reflection of the relationships of production. What is at issue, Borkenau holds, is the total position of a group within a changing historical structure. He depicts Calvinism not alone in its urban setting but as a religion of the gentry, of displaced and threatened nobles; as in France and Scotland. His mode of analysis begins with the concrete social tasks presented by an environment to a group and proceeds to consider its spiritual resources for mastering these. Borkenau insists that Calvinism was not as central to Western spiritual development as Weber thought and establishes a rather different genealogy for both theoretical and bourgeois political economy and the practical morality of the nascent European capitalist class. For our purposes, what is important is the promulgation of a method of analysis sufficiently supple to account for the internal structure of a long-term historical process. Borkenau shows, in effect, that the antithesis of material or spiritual causation needs to be recast in terms allowing for the specification of the components of a long-term process.

A more recent Marxist effort to combine theory with historical analysis focuses on the French seventeenth-century Jansenists, Catholic equivalents, in effect, of the bearers of a Calvinist morality. Goldmann's (1955) study of *The Hidden God* makes use of a central device, the notion of a vision of the world. The vision of a world peculiar to a group expresses its aspirations, sufferings, and existential grammar. By concentrating in great detail on the inner differences among the Jansenists, their relationships to society and the state, Goldmann also arrives at the conclusion that their religion was a response to a threat. He identifies its bearers as a declining state nobility. We may note that in both cases the social alienation described by these Marxist scholars was experienced by elites—if elites in a situation of decline. We may also note that the recourse to specific historical studies has an important methodological consequence for the testing of the Marxist hypotheses: these, insofar as they are instruments of inquiry, are built into the data. What is remarkable about the contributions of Borkenau and Goldmann is the degree of precise specification they are able to supply as to the objects and limits of their examination of history. That they have cast considerable illumination on Western religious history, there can be no doubt. The synthesis of studies of this kind into a convincing critique or replacement for the Marxist historical hypotheses remains for the future. We may note, once again, a tendency for generalization of the notion of alienation, this time accomplished by the analysis of groups not always directly involved in production.

Religion in the State Socialist Regimes

A very obvious interest attaches to the study of religion in the state Socialist countries (see Klohr 1967, Birnbaum 1971: 162–80). Two questions in particular concern us. How far have these societies gone toward overcoming what they officially and formally conceive of as alienation in its religious form? Second, how do sociologists in these societies conceive of the survival of religion in their societies? It is easy enough to say that the first question exceeds the limits of this paper, but upon an answer to it turns our estimate of the disalienating potential of at least one version of Marxism. An answer is, in any case, rendered difficult by the fact that open inquiry into religious phenomena in these societies was difficult, almost impossible, in the Stalinist period. It has now resumed, with rhythms and results which vary from country to country.

In general, in examining religion in these societies, we have to distinguish between a role that can be termed oppositional and a role which can be designated as normal. (I hesitate to use the term, but hesitate even more to use the term "perennial.") Religion and, in particular, the churches have assumed oppositional roles in these societies as the locuses of beliefs and values (and communities) not integrated in the new political consensus. The relationship between the Orthodox church and the Soviet regime is now one of coexistence, but we may recollect that matters were far more antagonistic in the early years of the Russian Revolution. In countries like Poland and the German Democratic Republic, the Catholic and Protestant churches, respectively, have at times seemed to serve as countercommunities, even counternations. These phenomena are important enough, but on a Marxist basis they may be disposed of in a manner which is more or less straightforward. The Revolution in Russia did break the cultural fabric, it was intended to do so, and it was inevitable that a portion of the population—frequently, those who were most remote from urban society and culture in any case—should group itself about cultural values of a more traditional kind. To the objection that the peasantry, in particular, was one of the beneficiaries of the Revolution, it could be said that economic benefits and cultural traumas frequently coincide. The Revolutions in Poland and the German Democratic Republic were, as the Communists in these countries will freely admit, largely brought in by a foreign army. In the circumstances social resistance to the new regime coalesced with national resistance. Nothing, or almost nothing, follows for our long-term evaluation of the disalienating potential of the state socialist regimes except for the banal observation that if Rome was not built in a day, neither has Communism been constructed so quickly.

Suppose, however, that we take a rather different approach. Marx once discounted the separation of church and state, declaring that it would not lead to a diminution of the social role of religion as long as the production relations which gave rise to capitalist forms of alienation persisted. The state socialist regimes have entered a period of relative official neutrality with respect to religion. Production relations in the state socialist regimes are clearly not capitalist ones: what have been the consequences of allowing the citizens of these countries something very like freedom of religious (or irreligious) choice?

It is here that we have to use the work of our colleagues from the state socialist societies. Perhaps it would be useful to distinguish between data from the Soviet Union, which has had a Marxist regime for fifty-four years, and the other countries, which have had Marxist regimes for only about half of that time. In the Soviet Union our colleagues' data suggests that a decline in religious affiliation is closely correlated with urbanization. Not dissimilar findings come from the other societies, although the inquiries I have seen do not use urbanization as a global indicator of social change but refer, instead, to integration in new sectors of the labor force, new residential communities—in short, marked discontinuities with previous forms of existence. These findings seem to parallel our data from other societies. Let us recollect that the Communist vote in Italy has doubled since the end of the last war, not alone on account of vigorous political efforts but because of the industrialization and laicization of Italian society. On the face of it, the data from the state socialist regimes, recorded by sociological inquiry, do not show that a revolution was the necessary precondition for the decline in religious belief and in the influence of the churches.

It should not be thought that our colleagues from these societies are simple-minded, or single-minded, adherents of the thesis that a complete disalienation has occurred in principle in their nations. They are well aware of contradictions between reality and its propagandistic representation and of the fact that profound social changes are historical phenomena: they take time. For obvious reasons, our colleagues have hardly attacked another set of hypotheses. The nationalization of capital in the state socialist societies has not altered the facts (whether ineradicable or not) of domination and exploitation in these societies. Its modes have changed, the processes remain. Above all, the division of labor and relationships of domination within it are intact: whatever theoretical discussions are in progress in these societies on the fusion of manual and intellectual labor, practical progress in this respect does not seem very rapid. (The Chinese case comes to mind: the Cultural Revolution has claimed that it has made progress towards the fusion. I am unable in these pages to judge the claim or to consider its obvious implications for the spiritual history of humanity. The remark of a nineteenth-century sceptic about Christianity comes to mind: "Interesting," he said, "if true.") In the circumstances Marxist theory requires us to look for a considerable remnant of alienation in these societies. If alienation there is, religion or something like it must (on Marxist hypotheses) follow. We are forced to consider the hypothesis that Marxism itself, in its official or Constantine form, serves as a successor to religion in ways not anticipated nor wished for by Marx himself. There are indications that at some point in the near future, our colleagues may be able to explore this hypothesis. For the moment it remains a hypothesis.

The World beyond Western Europe and North America

Most of the population of the world lives in the nonindustrial or incompletely industrialized societies located beyond Western Europe and America. These societies manifest an astonishing variety of religious tradition. Some (as in Latin America) have transplanted European religions, others, syncretic fusions of European traditions with their own, yet others are embedded in different, often older (and no less profound) religious systems. Their entire religious history is, of course, a field for the exploration of Marxist hypotheses; it covers a good deal of the spiritual history of humanity entire. We do well to remember, however, that the Marxist theory of religion concerns primarily its supersession in the industrial West. Marx supposed that culture contact, imperialism, and industrialization would destroy other traditions and had, in any event, attitudes of a distinctly nineteenth-century kind toward these traditions, which he thought of as obscure and even barbarian.

It can be argued that one of the most successful applications to these societies of an aspect of the Marxist theory has been accomplished by Weber. His studies of China, India, and Ancient Judaism do not simply reverse the usual Marxist modes of analysis. Rather, they concentrate on property and production relations and their political correlates, and they treat religious organizations and symbolic structures as developments within the limits set by these material factors. True enough, Weber evokes the cases in which, having developed in what we may think of as a material basis, these religious factors themselves set limits to future material development. The interpretation, at this point, is so large that it leaves the territory of social history for that of the philosophy of history. To the notion of a progressive alienation in history, Weber opposes his own conception of a plurality of value universes existing, as it were, solipsistically. And to the notion of humanity as creating itself through labor (and labor's conceretization in production relations), he opposes the idea of humanity creating its universe by interpreting the problems of work and society. Marx and Engels did write of the interaction of production relations and other factors in history, but clearly Weber goes beyond this point to assert the occasional primacy of religion in the total historical process.

More recent inquiries touch upon the Marxist legacy at many points (Balandier 1955, Wertheim 1965). An entire series of studies on the millennial movements of primitive peoples supplies us with data of an astonishingly similarity to work on the Middle Ages. In these movements religious conceptions (revitalized and sometimes syncretically fused with new elements from without) legitimate protest and revolution at conditions of exploitation and domination by alien peoples. It is interesting that a distinguished French student of Islam, and of the third world generally (Bercque 1964), has written of the ''Dépossession du Monde.'' In his view colonialism and imperialism inflict alienation upon the cultures and peoples who are victims of Western society and who must, in turn, struggle to repossess their world. That struggle, however, often takes religious forms. One Marxist analysis would note the positive consequence of colonialism and imperialism: the forcible incorporation of backward peoples in the world market and, potentially at least, a new world culture. Another component of Marxism, however, would have to deal with the utilization of religion, an earlier form of alienation, against a later form.

The breadth and depth of the materials at hand, the richness of scholarship on the religions of the world and their social contexts, would require a separate analysis. While the beginnings of Marxist studies on these problems may be noted, the comparison of religions in different historical settings entails a conceptual grammar and raises philosophic problems, which may not be soluble in Marxist terms : is the self-contained world system of Confucianism a transcendent religion or a social ethic ? Further comparison may turn that upon Marxism itself. Is the notion of progressive direction in history itself a component of the Western religious tradition, even in its Marxist form ? The historical transcendency of Marxism itself was envisaged by Lukacs as an inevitable result of revolution, which would bring about a new society functioning according to different structural principles. Suppose that a comparative view results not in a transcendence of Marxism but in exposing its historical relativity ? We have already heard that history is a Western myth. If so, Marxism itself is part of it.

Psychoanalytic Studies of Religion

A good many practicing psychoanalysts have observed that the symptomatology of their patients has changed over the past decades. The disorders treated by the earlier generation of analysts seem to have become less prominent, and a generalized malaise—character disorder, as it is sometimes called—has become evident. Part of this observation may be due to changes in psychoanalytic technique and theory. Part, however, is no doubt due to real historical changes in the milieu from which both analysts and patients are drawn. This constitutes justification enough for treating psychoanalytic studies of religion as historical studies. We are unable to observe the process by which humanity becomes disalienated, since none of the historical conditions for that have occurred. Psychoanalysis, however, may, with all regard for the conceptual distinctions between psychoanalysis and Marxism, allow us to see the internal mechanisms of alienation at work in real people.

Case studies of individuals with religious beliefs or members of religious organizations are available, but these, for our purposes, have two drawbacks. The cases are drawn, inevitably, from a society in which secularization has occurred. The choice of religious belief, therefore, as an expression of the personality rather than, let us say, an exclusively scientific career may or may not tell us anything about the movement of the social whole. Second, these clinical studies inevitably (and properly, from the viewpoint of their own logic and aim) do not treat systematically of the relationship of individual to context.

We too have a literature of what may be termed clinical extrapolation, in which psychoanalytic concepts are used to explore the social role of religion. Erich Fromm's (1951, 1963, 1966) work in this area is interesting, not least for its own inner evolution. Fromm began by dealing with changes in family structure as precipitates of larger social changes (in production relations and authority systems). These changes in turn induced new patterns of psychological conflict in new generations, and these, again, found expression or stabilization in the symbolic sphere of religion. This, in turn, served as a system of reinforcement for social controls by defining reality in ways which precluded its concrete or political transcendence. Fromm's subsequent work on the Reformation implied a somewhat different approach in that it depicted a society (the nascent bourgeois society) unable to control the inner conflicts of humanity. Indeed, the terrible God of Calvinism generated more anxiety than the religion could assuage. Put in the language of a mode of sociological analysis, a functional response to a market society became disfunctional. Fromm also developed, to be sure, a conception of modal or typical character in a society—social character, which was constructed to perform the tasks imposed upon it. What Fromm had done to this point was to show the mechanisms (family structure and character formation) by which social conflicts were transformed into individual ones. Further, and most importantly, he held that these conflicts were systematic deformations of human potential, caused by society's need for social character of a compliant kind. It is not too much to assert that he sought and found conceptual equations for transforming the Marxist doctrine of alienation in religion into psychoanalytic vocabulary. Strikingly, after having established a progressive characterological deformation—accomplished in part by a religion—Fromm returned to a search for a universal human essence expressed in religion. He renounced, in other words, the notion that religion was an unequivocal sphere of

alienation. Instead, he now saw it as the historical repository of a
humanity denied expression in ordinary social routine, above all,
in the social routine of a society without God. The utilization of
psychoanalysis by anthropologists—Roheim (1969) among the
orthodox Freudians, Kluckhohn (1962) Kardiner and Linton
(1949), and Mead (1967, 1969) among these with less rigorously
classical Freudian views—has added new dimensions to our
understanding of primitive systems of production and exchange.
The addition of a new dimension of understanding, however,
does not necessarily constitute a modification of Marxist analysis. In particular, most of these studies are set in short-term
historical contexts. Where, as in the case of Mead's return to the
South Pacific or the retrospective analysis conducted by Linton
and the psychoanalyst Kardiner of change in a primitive society,
a historical direction is considered, we can, in effect, see the
transformation of the old gods. Mead's work on the assimilation
of a simulacrum of modern culture by primitives is particularly
instructive. The most we can say, however, is that new alienations seem to replace older ones. Alternatively, we have to
recognize that these inquiries were not directed to verification or
falsification of Marxist hypotheses: they may be combined with
these, or they may be used to assert a pluralization of historical
experience.

It is curious that Erikson's (1958, 1963, 1969) studies take us
deeper. Curious, not because of their obvious quality, but because
Erikson began on the terrain of psychoanalysis and worked both
outward and inward to history. His turn outward required
studies of the social organization and social history of the groups
and individuals he analyzed: these gave the demands of reality
on the psyche, the materials it had to master to keep a tenuous
equilibrium. His turn inward enabled him to put the psyche in
historical perspective. Not alone did humans confront an external
or fixed reality in the form of an enveloping social history. They
converted the elements of that history into modes of activity, into
the remaking of history. Erikson uses the Freudian notion of
conflict between culture and nature, history and the psyche, to
demonstrate the humanization of history. In his work neurosis
ceases to figure as historical accident or wound: it becomes the
mode in which individuals integrate themselves, poorly or well,

with tradition. Moreover, it becomes an area in which tradition is transformed. The term "dialectical" is much abused these days and I do not think it has appeared more than once or twice before in this essay. Let it be said that Erikson apprehends the relationship between historical movement and character as dialectical, as interpenetrating. With respect to religion, it is significant that his interest is in religious innovation, religious movements, such as in Luther's recasting of medieval Christianity, or Gandhi's interpretation of Hinduism. The social role of religion entails the opening of new possibilities of human development and experiences, as well as the fixation or stabilization of inherited relationships. Erikson once reported on a conversation he had had with a primitive psychotherapist, whom he obviously treated as a respected colleague: the struggle against alienation, for Erikson, involves psychoanalysis as one of its historical forms but is not new. Erikson avoids the notion of progressive direction in history, partly, to be sure, to avoid flattering his twentieth-century contemporaries, of whom his opinion is not excessively high. The elements of sociocultural criticism in his work, then, are frequently implicit. His depiction of the universality of neurosis or, more exactly in his terms, of characterological conflict, is in fact not a promulgation of a universal fatality. Just because those conflicts occur in historically specific forms, the possibility for their ultimate supersession is given. In that sense, Erikson's detailed historical and clinical work, his almost ascetic eschewal of larger political or social commentary, gives a radical cutting edge to his version of psychoanalysis. The history of humanity as a history of multiple alienations is not, in the end, entirely incompatible with the Marxist vision. Recall the title of the book, *Gandhi's Truth*: the truth in religion can be found in the universal aspirations it presents in culturally concretized form. Without intending to do so, Erikson may have taken us back to Feuerbach but this time, with the inner psychic structure of religion identified with the universal structure of the psyche.

Erikson's interpretation of the Freudian tradition, then, assigns to the ego a function analogous to the role of work in the Marxist account of human history. The work of the psyche transforms nature and history into a new, if impermanent, synthesis. To be sure, an analysis of this kind is not only present in the writings of Freud, but it pervades them: it remained for Erikson to draw conclusions and approach character as a historical phenomenon. Freud supposed that the struggle aganst religion had to become universal, if men were to understand their conflicts. Erikson views the struggle against religion (which includes, in his view, the search in some epochs for truer religions) as but one of the several forms of enlightenment. I have already said that Fromm, who began from Marxist positions, in the end found rather positive functions in religion. Are we experiencing—and not alone in psychoanalysis—a ''resacralization'' of Western thought?

V CONCLUSIONS

The Dialogue

I have before me a bibliography of the Marxist-Christian dialogue (Van der Bent 1969), which has hundreds of titles and is, according to those who compiled it, incomplete. The dialogue, as it now stands, has three elements. The first is an effort at understanding among intellectuals—Marxists on one hand, theologians on the other. A Marxist reconsideration of religion or, at least, of simple interpretations of religion and its social role, has been accompanied by a theological revaluation of radical humanism. The Marxists have found humanist elements in religion, and the theologians have returned the compliment: they have found transcendent elements in Marxism. Where, in fact, no such mutual recognition has taken place, the very discussion of fundamentally different positions has enabled each to be seen in somewhat new perspective by its protagonists.

The second aspect of the dialogue is an official one. The Marxist regimes and Marxist parties have sought some *modus vivendi* with Christian interlocutors. In countries like Poland and the German Democratic Republic, the churches have been powerful and autonomous forces not always well-disposed to the regime: the process of *rapprochement* has had obvious theoretical consequences. In the Latin Catholic countries (France, Italy, and Spain), the Marxist parties have recently spared no effort to find common ground with some, at least, of their Christian countrymen. In Chile, it may be recalled, Christian Democratic parliamentary votes helped to select President Allende, and a small Catholic Socialist party forms part of his government. The establishment by the Vatican of a secretariat for relations with nonbelievers and multiple contacts between the Vatican and the Marxist regimes are part of this tendency. It may be objected that some, at least, of the official relations between Marxism and Christianity are anything but spiritual: they have to do with the relations between two worldly powers.

That is precisely what bothers the third set of participants in the dialogue. These are the proponents of *contestation* in the churches, the trade unions, the universities, and near (but usually no longer in) the main-line Marxist parties. The youth revolt has manifested striking similarities of spiritual structure wherever it has broken out. A considerable anti-nomianism, an insistence on a return to the sources of the movements or institutions in question, a demand for and the practice of experiments in institutions, and, above all, the conviction that ideas have to be lived to be valid: these are its components. Young priests using Marxist political ideas, Marxist students seeking a life of apostolic spiritual purity in new communal forms, attest, each in their fashion, the new sort of dialogue.

I write here of a movement of thought and action so contemporary that it may be described as a mood or temper. Its ultimate consequences for the Marxist sociology of religion are still unclear. For the present, we may state the following. The philosophical-theological dialogue has led to a profound reconsideration of the possibilities of transcendence. The Christians have been induced to reexamine their own tradition, and some have given transcendence a far more concrete and earthly definition as a result. It is of note that one of the most influential Protestant theological works of recent years, Jurgen Moltmann's *Theology of Hope* (1969) bears the influence of the work of Ernst Bloch. Bloch, an independent Marxist, is himself Jewish and has a new interpretation of the Old Testament. In his view, its revolutionary elements were falsified by priestly and royal scribes. Bloch (1968) has recently declared that only a believer can be an atheist, and only an atheist can be a believer. In his version of the dialogue, religion is a record of humanity's perennial struggle for self-transcendence.

The official dialogue takes up themes contained in the discussion between theologians and Marxists but with pronouncedly different accents. A period of coexistence—indeed, of collaboration—between Marxism and Christianity, for an indefinite period means a renunciation of some of the more stringent Marxist positions. If the path to a more human future leads not through religion but can be taken only with those of a religious spirituality, clearly radical humanism has been severely attenuated. The precondition of revolution (or even of structural reform, which is all the Western Communists now seek, that proving difficult enough) is no longer the transcendence of religion. It is, rather, a more modest mutual recognition of our common humanity; more modest, perhaps, but no less unusual in its historical implications. This, again, is too conservative for those in the forefront of the youth revolt (a generic term for the entire movement of *contestation* in the West). The recognition of a common humanity strikes them as too much like a resignation to an old humanity. A humanity remade is what they seek. Their indifference to the struggle against religion as such, their utilization of religious tradition, has a very different basis than the official dialogue. In the youth revolt transcendence cannot take the form of a Marxist radical humanism, since this was too theoretical. A new form of practice is needed to supersede ideology and anti-ideology, religion and atheism. We seem back at Marx's own beginning point.

Reflections

I do not propose to give a theoretical summary of a theoretical essay. The word "essay" originally meant just that, a tentative effort to state a problem. For tentativeness and statement, I make no apologies. The Marxist sociology of religion is a finished and self-contained metatheory. A metatheory is a critique of historical existence, whereas a theory is a set of propositions about a movement within history. On the basis of the metatheoretical doctrine of religion as alienation, Marx and Engels

uttered a set of propositions about religion in history, chiefly
Western history. I have said that the examination of the truth or
falsity of single propositions cannot falsify the metatheory. It
infuses the theory, and were we to abandon the metatheory, our
theoretical grammar would be different, our theoretical propositions constructed of different elements. That much said, we may
still ask if the weight of the evidence about the Marxist doctrine
suggests points at which a reevaluation of it may begin. The
philosopher Hans Blumenberg, in a remarkable recent book, has
suggested that the very notion of secularism is a legacy of religious thought. The book is required reading for sociologists of
religion, since if we take it seriously, our present conceptual
apparatus dissolves. We are, Blumenberg suggests, still the pris-
oners of theological concepts, still looking for the reenactment of
a divine drama on earth. He has taken up anew a theme
prominent in Marxism with its demand for a radical humanism
which would transcend both religion and atheism. The historical
evidence, however, is that radical humanism of this sort comes
hard. Not alone is Western society still pervaded by institutions
and beliefs from its religious past, but secularization (I use the
term for want of a better one) requires newer, if less sublime and
less authentic gods. The fetishism of commodities, the reification
of power, the poor consolations of a desperate hedonism are as
prominent in the state socialist regimes as elsewhere. The attenuation of religion does not mean its transcendence. The absence of
God by no means entails the presence of a humanity more
mature, much less fulfilled.

The precise status of scientific-instrumental thought in Marxist theory still requires adumbration. There was a sense in which
Marx opposed science to religion. Religion was the science of a
false human condition, science was the practical expression of a
mature humanity true to itself. Modern science and technology,
whatever their potential, can hardly be seen as a true human
practice in Promethean terms. The scientists and technicians
hardly control the products of their own labor, which are expro-
priated by other social elites for purposes having to do with the
mastery of people, not in the interest of a mastery of nature for
all humanity. Should the scientists and technicians combine with
the more educated and skilled sectors of the contemporary labor

force to constitute a new revolutionary vanguard, they would rewrite the role of surrogate for humanity entire ascribed by Marx to the industrial proletariat. Indeed, for most of humanity (consider the peoples of the third world and a goodly section of the population in the industrial West) science and technology are modern forms of magic. An instrument of liberation, as Marx conceived of it, has become a new form of alienation.

Withal, we have to conclude that the Marxist hope of a total transcendence of alienation seems out of reach. Humanity without religion is no more human than humanity with it. Religion has been succeeded by multiple alienations, different in structure, not all that different (in the Marxist sense) in their consequences. The idea of a progressive direction in history, the Enlightenment's legacy to Marx, is difficult to sustain. No wonder, then, that Marxists and Christians have become reconciled: each seeks a kingdom not of this world (that the reconciliation is in part the work of Jewish intellectuals, working the derivatives of their traditions of commentary on eschatology, is a reminder of a component in Marx's own work). The humanizing function of religion, from our historical viewpoint, now seems a theme in the Marxist sociology of religion which has more than nostalgic functions. Humanity, for the time being, has not gone beyond the Marxist sociology of religion. Indeed, it has hardly arrived at Marx's own beginning point (Blumenberg 1966).

BIBLIOGRAPHY

Adorno, T. W., and Horkheimer, Max
   1947   *Dialektik der Aufklärung*. Amsterdam: Querido.

Althusser, L.
   1970   *For Marx*. New York: Pantheon.

Aron, Raymond
   1971   De la condition historique de la sociologie. *Informations sur les Sciences Sociales*, Vol. 10, no. 1.

Balandier, G.
   1955   *La Sociologie Actuelle de l'Afrique Noire*. Paris: Presses Universitaires de France.

Berque, J.
   1964   *Le Dépossession du Monde*. Paris: Seuill.

Bernstein, Edward
   1895   *Die Vorläufer des Neueren Sozialismus*. Stuttgart: Dietz.

Berger, Peter L.
   1967   *The Scared Canopy*. Garden City, N.Y.: Doubleday.
——, and Luckmann, Thomas
   1966   *The Social Construction of Reality*. Garden City, N.Y.: Doubleday.

Birnbaum, Norman
   1959   The Zwinglian Reformation in Zurich. *Archives de Sociologie des Religions*, No. 2 (1957).
   1969   *The Crisis of Industrial Society*. New York: Oxford.
   1971   *Toward a Critical Sociology*. New York: Oxford.
——, and Lenzer, Gertrud
   1969   *Sociology and Religion*. Englewood Cliffs, N.J.: Prentice-Hall.

Bloch, E.
   1968   *Atheismus im Christentum*. Frankfurt: Suhrkamp.

Bloch, Marc
   1961a   *Feudal Society*. Chicago: University of Chicago Press.
   1961b   *Les Rois Thaumaturges*. Paris: A. Colin.

Blumenberg, Hans
   1966   *Die Legitimät de Neuzeit*. Frankfurt: Suhrkamp.

Borkenau, Franz
    1934   *Die Übergang vom Feudalen zum Bürgerlichen Weltbild.*
            Paris: Alcan.

Calvez, Jean Yves
    1956   *La Pensée de Karl Marx.* Paris: Editions du Seuil.

Caporale, Rocco and Antonio Grumelli, eds.
    1971   *The Culture of Unbelief.* Berkeley and Los Angeles, Calif.:
            University of California Press.

Desroche, Henri
    1949   *Signification du Marxisme.* Paris: Editions Ouvrieres.
    1962   *Marxisme et Religions.* Paris: Presses Universitaries Fran-
            caises.
    1965   *Socialismes et Sociologie Religieuse.* Paris: Editions Cujas.
    1968   *Dieux des Hommes, Dictionnaire des messies, messianismes et
            millenarismes de l'ére chretienne.* Paris: Editions Mouton.
    1971   *The Shakers.* Amherst, Mass.: University of Massachusetts
            Press.
    1972   *Sociology of Religions.* Amherst, Mass.: University of Mas-
            sachusetts Press.

Dilthey, W.
    1962   *Pattern and Meaning in History: Thoughts on History and
            Society.* New York: Harper & Row.

Durkheim, E.
    1938   *The Rules of Sociological Method.* Trans. S. A. Soloway and
            J. H. Mueller, ed. G. E. G. Callin. Chicago: University of
            Chicago Press.
    1960   *Les formes elementaires de la vie religieuse.* Paris: Presses
            Universitaires Francaises: 609–11.
    1964   *The Elementary Forms of the Religious Life.* London:
            George Allen and Unwin.

Easton, Lloyd D., and Guddat, Kurt
    1967   *Writings of the Young Marx on Philosophy and Society.*
            Garden City, N.Y.: Doubleday.

Engels, Friedrich
    1966   *The Peasant War in Germany.* New York: New World.

Erikson, E.
    1958   *Young Man Luther.* New York: Norton.
    1963   *Childhood and Society.* New York: Norton.
    1969   *Gandhi's Truth.* New York: Norton.

Febvre, Lucien
   1942   *Le probleme de l'incroyance au xvi siecle, La religion de Ra-
          belais.* Paris: Michel.

Friedrichs, Robert
   1970   *A Sociology of Sociology.* New York: The Free Press.

Fromm, Erich
   1951   *The Forgotten Language: An Introduction to the Under-
          standing of Dreams, Fairy Tales and Myths.* New York:
          Holt, Rinehart and Winston.
   1963   *The Dogma of Christ and Other Essays on Religion, Psy-
          chology and Culture.* New York: Holt, Rinehart and Win-
          ston.
   1966   *Escape from Freedom.* New York: Holt, Rinehart and Win-
          ston.

Garaudy, R.
   1968   *From Anathema to Dialogue.* New York: Vintage.

Goldmann, Lucien
   1955   *Le Dieu Caché.* Paris: Gallimard.

Gouldner, Alvin W.
   1970   *The Coming Crisis of Western Sociology.* New York: Basic
          Books, Inc.

Gramsci, A.
   1966   *Il Materialismo Storico.* Torino: Einaudi.
   1966   *Il Risorgimento.* Torino: Einauldi.

Granet, Marcel
   1957   *Chinese Civilisation.* London: Routledge and Kegan Paul.

International Social Science Council
   1969   *Marx and Contemporary Scientific Thought.* Paris and The
          Hague: Mouton.

Isambert, F. A.
   1961   *Christianisme et classe ouvrière.* Paris: Casterman.

Kardiner, A. et al.
   1959   *The Psychological Frontiers of Society.* New York: Columbia
          University Press.

Kardiner, A., and Linton R.
   1949   *The Individual and His Society.* New York: Columbia Uni-
          versity Press.

Kautsky, Karl
    1910   *The Class Struggle.* Chicago: C. H. Kerr.

Klohr, O.
    1967   *Religionssoziologie, Internationales Forschungsbericht,* Jena.

Kluckhohn, Clyde
    1962   *Navaho Witchcraft.* Boston: Beacon Press.

Lacan, Jacques
    1966   *Ecrits.* Paris: Editions du Seuil.

LeGoff, Jacques
    1957   *Les intellectuells aux Moyen Age.* Paris: Seuil.

Lenin, V. I.
    1947   *Materialism and Empiro-Criticism, Critical Comments on a Reactionary Philosophy.* Moscow: Foreign Languages Publishing House.

Lenski, G.
    1961   *The Religious Factor.* Garden City, N.Y.: Doubleday.

Lévi-Strauss, C.
    1966   *The Savage Mind.* Chicago: The University of Chicago Press.

Lichtheim, G.
    1964   *Marxism, an Historical and Critical Study.* London: Routledge and Kegan Paul.

Lobkowicz, Nikolaus
    1967   *Marx and the Western World.* Notre Dame, Ind.: University of Notre Dame Press.

Lowith, K.
    1964a   *From Hegel to Nietzsche; the Revolution in 19th Century Thought.* New York: Holt, Rinehart and Winston.
    1964b   *Meaning in History.* Chicago: University of Chicago Press.

de Lubac, Henri
    1965   *La drame de l'humanisme athée.* Paris: Union Générale d'Editions

Luckmann, Thomas
    1966   *The Invisible Religion.* New York: Macmillan.

Lukacs, G.
    ·1971   *History and Class Consciousness.* Cambridge, Mass.: Massachusetts Institute of Technology Press.

MacIntyre, Alasdair, and Emmet, Dorothy, eds.
  1970 *Sociological Theory and Philosophical Analysis.* New York:
         Macmillan.

Mannheim, K.
  1952 *Ideology and Utopia: An Introduction to the Sociology of
         Knowledge.* New York: Harcourt Brace Jovanovich.

Marx, Karl
  1953 *Grundrisse der Kritik der Politischen Oekonomie.* Berlin:
         Dietz.
  ————, and Engels, Friedrich
  1964 *On Religion.* With an Introduction by Reinhold Niebuhr.
         New York: Schocken.

Mauss, M.
  1968 *Sociologie et anthropologie.* Paris: Presses Universitaires
         Francaises.

Mead, Margaret
  1967 *Male and Female.* New York: Morrow.
  1969 *Inquiry into the Question of Cultural Stability in Polynesia.*
         New York: A.M.S. Press.

Moltmann, Jürgen
  1967 *Theology of Hope.* New York: Harper & Row.
  1969 *Religion, Revolution and the Future.* New York: Scribners.

Owen, Robert
  1963 *A New View of Society.* London: Dent.

Petrie, John
  1956 *The Worker Priests.* London: Routledge and Kegan Paul.

Pin, Emile
  1956 *Pratique religieuse et classes sociales dans une paroisse
         urbaine,* Paris: Saint-Pothin à Lyon.

Roheim, G.
  1969 *Psychoanalysis and Anthropology.* New York: International
         Universities Press.

Saint-Simon, M. C.
  1964 *Social Organizaion, the Science of Man and Other Writings.*
         New York: Harper & Row.

Schutz, Alfred
  1967 *The Phenomenology of the Social World.* Evanston, Ill.:
         Northwestern University Press.

Sebag, L.
     1964   *Marxisme et Structuralisme.* Paris: Payot.

Stammer, O., ed.
     1965   *Max Weber und die Soziologie Heute.* Tübingen: Möhr (Sie-
             beck).

Toennies, F.
     1964   *Community and Society.* East Lansing, Mich.: Michigan
             State Universiy Press.

Troeltsch, Ernst
     1956   *The Social Teachings of the Christian Churches.* New York:
             Macmillan.

Van der Bent, A.
     1969   *The Christian Marxist Dialogue.* Geneva: World Council of
             Churches.

Weber, Max
     1930   *The Protestant Ethic and the Spirit of Capitalism.* Trans.
             Talcott Parsons. London: George Allen and Unwin.
     1963   *The Sociology of Religion.* Trans. Ephraim Fischoff. Boston:
             Beacon Press.

Werner, Ernst
     1956   *Pauperes Christi. Studien zu sozial-religiösen Bewegungen
             im Zeitalter des Reformpopsttums.* Leipzig.

Wertheim, W. F.
     1965   *East-West Parallels: Sociological Approaches to Modern
             Asia.* Chicago: Quadrangle Books.

Williams, George H.
     1962   *The Radical Reformation.* Philadelphia: Westminster Press.

2 WEBER'S PROTESTANT ETHIC: ITS ORIGINS, WANDERINGS, AND FORESEEABLE FUTURES

Benjamin Nelson

I WEBER'S HORIZONS IN HIS FIRST EDITION

A fresh balance sheet of the work done in review and criticism of Max Weber's *Protestant Ethic and the Spirit of Capitalism*[1] must begin by stressing the fact that our familiar current editions and translations have to be viewed as geological sites whose

---

[1] The most carefully conceived review of the recent controversial literature on the Protestant ethic will now be found in Little (1969: 226–37).

I am delighted to note the extent of convergence in our views of many of the most widely discussed critics of Weber—notably H. Trevor-Roper, H. Luethy, C. H. and K. George, W. Hudson, M. Walzer. S. N. Eisenstadt's (1968) review of the literature offers several interesting new perspectives on the transformative effects of Protestantism but does not sufficiently stress the marked discrepancies between approaches to critical issues by historians and sociologists (cf. *idem*, 1968a). The recently issued and enlarged edition of my *Idea of Usury* (1969) lists and summarizes the essays I have written in the effort to extend Weber's argument beyond the terms of his 1905 essay, in the spirit of the suggestions expressed in his ''Author's Introduction'' to the posthumously published *Collected Essays in the Sociology of Religion* (cf. Weber 1920, tr. Parsons 1930, reprinted 1958; also cf. Nelson 1969: 274–75).

At points in the above text I draw liberally upon my *Idea of Usury* and other published and unpublished essays of mine. Readers are referred to these works for the wider contexts and the detailed evidence. Also, in the references which are listed at the end of this chapter, entries are included which are not directly cited in the text or notes. This is done to suggest some of the relevant ranges of reference which could not be dealt with in detail within the limits of the present essay.

different strata are yet to be precisely mapped. A close look at the original text of the two parts of his famed study in the *Archiv für Sozialwissenschaft und Sozialpolitik* for 1904–05 reveals that Weber's original purposes were much more complex than those we have regularly attributed to him. Once we have bracketed all the allusions which were entered into the footnotes in the editions after 1905, it becomes clear that he was addressing himself less to experts in economic history than to the wider public of scholars and cultivated laymen interested in the relations of religion and history who were anxiously casting about in many directions for ways of explaining the historical grounds of the allegedly disenchanted secularism of the nineteenth and twentieth centuries.

Weber was intent on countering the following theses of theological and other partisans:

> 1. The thesis of Protestant polemicists that the secularization of the modern world was due to the "rationalism" and secularism of the French Enlightenment *philosophes* who had been bred in Catholic "culture areas."
>
> 2. The thesis of the Catholic polemicists that the secularism of the modern world had begun with Protestantism itself with the "rationalism" growing out of Luther, Calvin, and the Protestant scholastics.

Weber devoted his first essay to proving that "rationalism" in the narrower senses used by theological—and for that matter professional historical—controversialists was, in fact, not either the decisive spur to nor the distinctive hallmark of the very largely rationalized economic cosmos of the nineteenth and twentieth centuries. The critical clue to this, Weber was convinced, might be found in the persistence, in however attenuated and spectral a form, of the sense that people had a *religious duty* to labor selflessly, methodically, conscientiously in their callings *in this world* without undue preoccupations with personal pleasures, sensuous indulgences, and sportive play. So unnatural a notion, Weber reasoned, was not traceable to human biological nature, nor could it be explained in terms of calculated prudence. Only the force of religion, sustained by the promise of theological rewards and sanctions, could effect this end. The *vocational asceticism* of the modern world must have had spiritual roots (Weber 1905, tr. 1930: 90,153–54).

It was Luther, Weber became convinced, who ignited the spark here. It was the new teachings of Luther and Calvin in respect to the notion of "calling" which had the effect of overcoming the *dualism* of otherworldly and innerworldly asceticism and creating a uniform obligation of all to struggle unremittingly in the calling to which they had been assigned or had chosen. As Weber put it, adapting a phrase from Sebastian Franck, the world itself had now become a monastery and all laymen had become brothers living under regulated discipline in the service of the Lord.

Being thoroughly versed in medieval history and, indeed, having already turned his eyes to the wider horizons later to command his undivided attention, Weber recognized that the passage to the new ethos involved the overcoming of dualisms of various sorts: the dualism between otherworldly asceticism expected in the early period only of the "religious," who dwelt under the triple vow of poverty, chastity, and obedience, and the incessant round of striving and sin which masked the everyday world of all who were its inhabitants.

Already before his first essay had ended, Weber had distinguished himself not only from the Catholic and Protestant disputants referred to above, but from the already renowned economic historian, Werner Sombart, who as early as 1902 in the first edition of his *Der moderne Kapitalismus* had laid stress on the derivation of the *"spirit of capitalism"* from the calculative *"rationalism,"* strongly manifested in profit-oriented activities in trade, commercial farming, and accounting in the pre-Reformation period.

We cannot exaggerate the strength of Weber's conviction that prior writers and controversialists had been mistaken in treating rationalism—"speculative" and "practical" alike—as the moving force and mainspring of the distinctive culture and organization of modern society. How close this issue was to the crux of Weber's argument can be seen from the sharpness of his warning (1905, tr. 1930: 77–78) against the forgetting of a "simple proposition" about rationalism:

> one may . . . *rationalize life from fundamentally different basic points of view and in very different directions.* Rationalism is an historical concept which covers a whole world of different things. It

will be our task to find out whose intellectual child the particular concrete form of rational thought was, from which the idea of a calling and the devotion to labor in the calling has grown, which is, as we have seen, so irrational from the standpoint of purely eudaemonistic self-interest, but which has been and still is one of the most characteristic elements of our capitalistic culture. We are here particularly interested in the origin of precisely the irrational element which lies in this, as in every conception of a calling.[2]

As we shall soon see, Weber was to devote a very large part of his later years to herculean attempts to separate the different strands, aspects, appearances, and manifestations of the workings of "reason" and "rationality." How comprehensive and consistent these efforts were to be, the reader will better be able to judge at the end of the present chapter.[3]

The close of the first part finds Weber intent on clarifying his position in respect to the multiple conflicting interests, influences, and factors—"ideal" and "real" alike—in the emergence and workings of the modern world order. The very last lines of the first part (Weber 1905, tr. 1930: 91–92) finds him insisting that he had no intention

> of maintaining such a foolish and doctrinaire thesis as that the spirit of capitalism (in the provisional sense of the term explained above) could only have arisen as the result of certain effects of the Reformation, or even that capitalism as an economic system is a creation of the Reformation. In itself, the fact that certain important forms of capitalistic business organization are known to be considerably older than the Reformation is a sufficient refutation of such a claim. On the contrary, we only wish to ascertain whether and to what extent religious forces have taken part in the qualitative formation and the quantitative expansion of that spirit over the world. Furthermore, what concrete aspects of our capitalistic culture can be traced to them. In view of the tremendous confusion of interdependent influences between the material basis, the forms of social and political organization, and the ideas current in the time

[2] The italics in the above text are mine.
[3] In a series of papers listed in the references, I have emphasized the difficulties resulting from Weber's discussions of the expressions of rationality and rationalization in sociocultural process; cf., for example, Nelson (1968b, 1969). In these and other writings I have used the term "structures of *rationales*" to describe operative structures of principles, evidentiary canons, logical and metalogical rules connected with confirmation procedures and proofs which are found to serve as regulative decision matrices in all spheres of action and opinion, behavior and belief. Extensive discussions of Weber's view on rationalization will be found in Parsons (1937, ed. 1968: esp. 567–78, 751–53; cf. Abramowski, 1966).

of the Reformation, we can only proceed by investigating whether and at what points certain correlations between forms of religious belief and practical ethics can be worked out.

Part II, precisely entitled "The Practical Ethics of the Ascetic Branches of Protestantism," undertook to illustrate the "religious foundations of the four principal forms of *ascetic* Protestantism: (1) Calvinism, (2) pietism, (3) Methodism, (4) the sects growing out of the Baptist movement."

Here Weber sought to specify the theological quandaries and psychological states associated with the Calvinist sense of the stages and signs of the regenerated life. He tried to lay bare the religious foundations of the new sense of strenuous methodical action oriented to the collective as well as individual achievement of God's design in this world. Here, too, he inquired into the complex changing correlations of predestinarian theology with the probings for signs of God's election in life and good fortune here on earth. Here, Weber touched upon "the unprecedented inner loneliness of the single individual," the "complete elimination of salvation through the church and the sacraments," the carrying forward to its logical conclusion of the "elimination of magic from the world," the "antagonism to sensuous culture," the "roots of that disillusioned and pessimistically inclined individualism which can even today be identified in the national characters and the institutions of the peoples with a Puritan past, the disappearance of private confession, the spread of the sense that "God helps those who help themselves," the idea of the "necessity of proving one's faith" in worldly activity.

The work came to a close with a summary chapter, "Asceticism and the Spirit of Capitalism." To clear away possible confusion, Weber detailed the outcomes of the new asceticism for the rationalization of conduct in respect to the regulation of time and dedication to calling; he distinguished between the "pariah-capitalism" associated with the Jews and the "rational" organization of capital and labor which was the hallmark of Puritanism.

To the very end, Weber struggled to escape stereotype and dogmatism in the framing of his general historical and sociological statements. His (1905, tr. 1930: 183) closing lines bear exceptionally poignant witness to his scholar's faith:

Here we have only attempted to trace the fact and the direction of its influence to their motives in one, though a very important point. But it would also further be necessary to investigate how Protestant Asceticism was in turn influenced in its development and its character by the totality of social conditions, especially economic. The modern man is in general, even with the best will, unable to give religious ideas a significance for culture and national character which they deserve. But it is, of course, not my aim to substitute for a one-sided materialistic an equally one-sided spiritualistic causal interpretation of culture and of history. Each is equally possible, but each, if it does not serve as the preparation, but as the conclusion of an investigation, accomplishes equally little in the interest of historical truth.

One of our main tasks in the following pages will be to chronicle and to illustrate major episodes in the disappointment of Weber's hopes.

We bring our reading of the book to a close by citing the never-to-be-forgotten characterization of our own era which constitutes its climax (Weber 1905, tr. 1930: 181–82).

The Puritan wanted to work in a calling; we are forced to do so. For when asceticism was carried out of monastic cells into everyday life, and began to dominate worldly morality, it did its part in building the tremendous cosmos of the modern economic order. This order is now bound to the technical and economic conditions of machine production which to-day determine the lives of all the individuals who are born into this mechanism, not only those directly concerned with economic acquisition, with irresistible force. Perhaps it will so determine them until the last ton of fossilized coal is burnt. In Baxter's view the case for external goods should only lie on the shoulders of the "saint like a light cloak, which can be thrown aside at any moment." But fate decreed that the cloak should become an iron cage.

Since asceticism undertook to remodel the world and to work out its ideals in the world, material goods have gained an increasing and finally an inexorable power over the lives of men as at no previous period in history. Today the spirit of religious asceticism—whether finally, who knows?—has escaped from the cage. But victorious capitalism, since it rests on mechanical foundations, needs its support no longer. The rosy blush of its laughing heir, the Enlightenment, seems also to be irretrievably fading, and the idea of duty in one's calling prowls about in our lives like the ghost of dead religious beliefs. Where the fulfillment of the calling cannot directly be related to the highest spiritual and cultural values, or when, on the other hand, it need not be felt simply as economic compulsion, the individual generally abandons the attempt to justify it at all. In the field of its highest development, in the United States, the pursuit of wealth, stripped of its religious and ethical meaning, tends to become associated with purely mundane passions, which often actually give it the character of sport.

No one knows who will live in this cage in the future, or whether at the end of this tremendous development entirely new prophets will arise, or there will be a great rebirth of old ideas and ideals, or, if neither, mechanized petrification, embellished with a sort of convulsive self-importance. For of the last stage of this cultural development, it might well be truly said: "Specialists without spirit, sensualists without heart; this nullity imagines that it has attained a level of civilization never before achieved."

II CAPITALISM AND RATIONALIZATION

The poet's lament should serve to remind us that whatever their authors may intend, *books will have their fates.* Our fresh reading of Weber's original pages establishes that his main aim was neither to write an essay in economic history nor, for that matter, to controvert historical materialism. All his notices to the reader, all his *caveats* notwithstanding, these very issues have been at the hub of the polemical exchanges from the first appearance of the work to the present hour. Despite Weber's earnest efforts to bring the exchanges to a temporary halt in 1910 (Winckelmann 1968: 283–345; Baumgarten 1964: 192–214) the controversy has so far shown little sign of abatement.

The sections of the present essay are written in hope that the time may now be opportune to attempt advances beyond the polarized frames of reference which so often in the past blocked productive research and discussion. In any case, we must strive to expand our powers to settle disputes in this troubled area by enlarging our understanding of many tangled levels of theory and fact.

Weber's book began to undergo its puzzling fate early. Despite his anxious efforts to guard against misconstruals of his aims by professional political and economic historians, it was they who led the attack on him for making provocative claims which went far beyond the evidence. Hardly one of the central elements in the Weber account escaped rebuttal at their hands.

Some of his opponents insisted that a matured "Protestant ethic" and the "spirit of capitalism" existed well *before the Reformation,* namely in classical antiquity, the Middle Ages, or the Renaissance; some reviewers suggested that the Reformation did not involve a notable alternative of the churchly or moral regulative patterns of previous eras; yet other, less friendly, critics set out to disprove the entire structure of Weber's arguments on the role of religious influences in the career of capitalism in different lands of Europe.

From the perspectives adopted in the following pages, little of the spirit or substance of these approaches seems acceptable. In my view, Weber seems to have been largely correct in his interpretations of the historical developments. What his original critics missed—what many continue to miss today—is the critical fact that "capitalism" in a narrow sense was not the central interest of Weber's essays on the Protestant ethic. He was, indeed, not to give explicit attention and treatments to the "economic history" or "economic" institutions of "capitalism" until his last series of lectures on *General Economic History* which appeared posthumously (Weber 1922).

The central object of Weber's interest was the uncovering of cultural, so-called spiritual, foundation of the distinctive bureaucratic enterprise, organization, and outlooks of the modern Western world. Prudent "rationalism," he insisted, was not the view which spurred the spread of the vocational, innerworldly asceticism, as the dominant *ethos* of the modern industrial era. Far from being smooth and straight, the roads to modernity were paved with "charismatic" breakthroughs of traditional structures. These breakthroughs, forged in an atmosphere of religious and social effervescence, had their issue in the overcoming of the invidious dualisms which had hitherto inhibited new rationalizations (and new rationales) affecting all patterns of action and conviction relating to work, wealth, welfare, regulation of self and society, political order, the sense, ultimate worth, the experience of justification, and so on (Nelson 1949, 1969: 229–47). As the years passed, Weber was to strengthen his desire to discover whether and why the rationalization process had been more intensive and extensive in the West than anywhere else. Already, indeed in his first edition, however, the *civilizational* differences in the central orientations to "religion" and "world" proved to be of critical importance for his way of thinking.

What Weber saw was that the distinctive hallmark of the Protestant ethic was a radical change in the orientations of people to self, destiny, work, world; orientations which proved traceable to the work of the reformers and the Reformation. In the absence of a new ethos, he was convinced, the *industrial* division of labor would never come out of the cocoon. Nor, for that matter, would business and commerce have so readily attained the assured respectability required for the maintenance over many generations of a continuing commitment to the advancement of corporations, firms, and families. The *consecration* of regulated work *within the world* could only come when a set of new theological and religious "premia" were developed for the work done in the world, when all people were equally considered to be called to religious vocations in the service of God. In earlier days, certainly in the medieval period, as Weber well knew, no such supposition could ever evolve to a position of dominance.

Weber never intended to say that notable economic developments of varied sorts had occurred prior to the elaboration of the Protestant ethic. A student of Levin Goldschmidt (1891), the author of *The Universal History of Commercial Law* (Koenig and Winckelmann 1963: 12, cf. Nelson 1965: 12), and himself at home in the economic and legal developments of the high and late Middle Ages, Weber (1905, tr. 1930: 194–201, cf. 1956: 516–90) needed no one to tell him that commerce, banking, money changing, money lending, had all attained high levels in the Middle Ages. He could not, however, overlook the fact that the pre-Reformation era continued to give great stress to *otherworldly* asceticism, and as long as this was so the dualism of "religion" and "world" prevailed. The outcome of this dualism was to consecrate only that work which was directed to the service of God in religious offices. *Other* work done in the world might be useful, expedient, legitimate, illegitimate, honorable, *but not consecrated* (for the price of the neglect of this distinction, see Nelson 1969: 236–39, 1971a).

Such were the accents in Weber's depiction of the crystallization and workings of an *ethos* related to the mastery of self and world. It cannot be too often repeated that this issue was the core of Weber's emphases. Until people in any society become committed to a *universalist* ethic of disciplined conduct, a regulation of character and a readiness to move forward toward widened expression of divine-human imperatives, we have not yet found the "Protestant ethic," nor have we found the basis for the transformation of older, traditional societies rooted in particularities of place, of tribe, of kindred, of class, of caste, and so forth. In this respect there was a great kinship in the views of Weber with Durkheim and Maine (Nelson 1971c).

III WEBER'S EXPANSION OF HIS SCOPE

Weber himself seems not to have been immediately aware of the full scope of his claims and the evidence needed to establish them; this understanding came slowly with his comparative studies between 1911 and his death in 1920 of other civilizational complexes; the new insights did not attain their best expression until his Author's Introduction to the posthumously published *Collected Essays in the Sociology of Religion* (1922, 1954).

Here Weber makes it utterly clear that he was committed to exploring *all of the elements*—extraeconomic as well as economic ones—which had cooperated to bring about the, until then, unique transformation of parts of Western Europe in the direction of rationalization, rationalism, industrialization, rationality, modernity, in respect to the organization of conduct, the division of labor, the management of affairs, the orientations to "world" and "religion," the achievement of perfection. His perspective was, despite his reluctance to think so, civilizational and crosscultural (Nelson 1971c).

The widened contexts needed for the fuller understanding of Weber's theses were, indeed, not available to the general public until the early 1920s and 1930s with the posthumous publications of working editions of the various volumes of his *Gesammelte Aufsätze zur Religionssoziologie* and his monumental *Wirtschaft und Gesellschaft*. Unhappily these studies entirely escaped the attention of his historian critics. From this perspective, *The*

Protestant Ethic was only an intimation of a program, a provocative sketch.[4]

It is no wonder, then, that Weber's notions have been imperfectly comprehended by his historian-critics from Felix Rachfahl in 1909 to R. H. Tawney, who initiated new phases in the discussion in 1926 and 1933, respectively,[5] and to the most recent critics—Kurt Samuelsson, H. Trevor-Roper, and Herbert Luethy in the 1950s and 1960s.[6]

For many of the misconstructions of his theses Weber has himself to blame. Had he truly found ways of presenting his own materials in a more straightforward and systematic way, his work might have escaped many criticisms. There would have been a clearer understanding everywhere that he was not contending that Protestant theology was the source and spur to capitalistic economic activity in the narrow sense or that Protestant theology and capitalistic economic activity were inextricably connected with the spirit of acquisitiveness or that capitalism was the one main interest of his argument.

Weber wrote in an excessively condensed style, covering vast masses of details with a few sentences and making critical distinctions in a phrase. His subtle reflections were soon lost in the thicket of his footnotes, which, for the most part, remain unknown territory to this day. There is also the case that too few of his critics could follow him into the religious spheres he understood so well. The exceptional illustration of Max Scheler (1964) highlights this fact.

Only a small number of Weber's contemporaries were prepared to understand what he was doing in *his own contexts.* Scholars in related careers knew of the strife raging on the methods proper to all the social sciences and the humanities, above all, the point of departure for sociology, economics, and

[4] Parsons stated this view clearly from the outset (1930, 1937), and he has continued to stress this down to the present day (1962, 1968). Reinhard Bendix has also emphasized this perspective (1956, 1960, 1964, 1968, 1970, chaps. 6, 7, 9), also, in Bendix and Roth (1971: chap. 10).
[5] For an analysis of the earlier history of this discussion, see Fischoff (1944); on H. M. Robertson, see Parsons (1935), Nelson (1949, 1969: 104n.)
[6] On Samuelsson see Parsons (1962, Nelson 1962, Morgan 1963). For Luethy and Trevor-Roper, see their writings listed in the references; also Nelson (1969: 241–45).

even history. Yet few could come abreast of his breakthrough in point of method, style, scope; few could follow the leaps he had made beyond the frontier methodologists such as Windelband, Dilthey, and Rickert and frontier historians such as Werner Sombart, Georg Jellinek, and Eberhard Gothein.[7]

Weber's sophistication in method was too great for all but a few of his philosopher contemporaries. Not without justification, historians continued—and continue—to take him to task for the omissions dictated by his selective ideal-typical historical analysis. In this process, however, they forgot—or missed the fact—that Weber had a superb documentary knowledge of ancient and medieval history, historical theology, law, and the development of law and legal institutions. Not one of his critics early or late could match him here—not Sombart, Lujo Brentano, not Tawney, not Pirenne, nor Henri Sée; this is surely true of many less widely trained Americans.

Now there is no longer any excuse for skipping what Weber tells about the "Protestant ethic" in the subsequent comparative studies he included under the title, *Economic Ethic of the World Religions,* which were translated into English: "The Social Psychology of the World Religions," *The Religion of China,* "Religious Rejections of the World," *Hinduism, Ancient Judaism.* Nor may we forget the essays and lectures of the last years of his life: "Science as a Vocation," "Politics as a Vocation," and the *General Economic History.*

It is only as the exact terms of the thesis are more fully grasped in these wider horizons that Weber's generic intentions in his early essays can be set forth. Weber is not talking about the "Protestant ethic" in the idiographic sense as much as the role it played as the paradigmatic illustration, crucial for the West, of innerworldly vocational asceticism—a structure of sentiments and disciplines, incentives and religious rewards spurring people to systematic conscientious, methodical conduct in this world.

It behooves us at this point to recall that the decisive contribu-

[7] For some of Weber's remarks on Jellinek's influence on his work, see Bendix and Roth (1971: 308–10, cf. Koenig and Winckelmann 1963: 15). Oddly, valuable clues to Gothein's influence on Weber will be found in the strange book by Steding (1938: xxvi, 345, 547–48, 610, 740–41).

tion to the wider and more informed understanding of Weber's work was made by Talcott Parsons in his magisterial *Structure of Social Action*. First published in 1937, that work remains the indispensable point of departure for all wishing to trace the backgrounds and scope of Weber's famed sections in *Collected Essays in the Sociology of Religion*.[8]

The widened scope within which Weber's work must be viewed is not, however, a common foundation of work even today.

> 1. The prime site for the test of Weber's theory preferred by a majority of American sociologists is *present evidence* of the *present force* of the "Protestant ethic" in the narrower sense of legitimating the "acquisitive motive" in *American life*. If we do this, our answer as to the continuing relevance of Weber's theory is chiefly of one sort; our research tends to become mainly social-psychological and overly confined to surveys of current attitudes and opinions.
>
> 2. Alternatively, Weber's argument is treated chiefly as an historical problem to be settled by close search of the settings in which the "Protestant ethic" is claimed to have had its greatest crystallization. If we conceive the issues exclusively in this spirit, we will miss the main message of Weber.

From this point forward, this essay will proceed on the assumption that stresses of the two above sorts are not nearly so important or central as other sorts of emphases. My own commitments (1969 : 247–48) on this head may be put as follows :

> 1. Weber set out to do a great deal more than to prove the affinities of Protestantism, capitalism, and mammonism. Consequently, it will not suffice, as many historical and sociological specialists have done, to treat the "Protestant ethic" purely in terms of a local historical proposition on the relations of economy and religion in the sixteenth or seventeenth centuries.
>
> 2. Weber always intended the notion of the "Protestant ethic" to refer to the existential and cultural foundations of any society committed to the mastery of this world through intensive discipline and consensual organization of the personal and social orders.

---

[8] The full scope of Parsons's contributions to the understanding of Weber and the issues growing out of his *Protestant Ethic* will doubtless have to wait for memorial volumes now being gathered in his honor to receive the documentation it deserves. Only a handful of the papers and statements he has done on Weber over a period of close to forty years can be listed herein. (See Parsons 1937, 1967 : 500–677, 1962, 1964, 1968). In addition to these contributions Parsons had a leading part in the training of a number of younger men who have made decisive contributions to the documentation of Weber's influence. Among these we would need to mention Robert Merton, Robert Bellah, Clifford Geertz, Jan Loubser, and David Little. A few of the younger men were also influenced by James Luther Adams.

3. In the end, therefore, the proving grounds for Weber's views are not Prussia or even England, but the Soviet Union, the Far East, the Near East, Africa—in short, the world.

IV   LIMITED PERSPECTIVES

In my view the approaches that have been least productive in recent years have been those which have construed Weber's purposes narrowly in one or the other of the following ways:

1. Those who reject the possibility that religious and cultural forces of any sort can be effective factors in change (orthodox Marxist and other sorts of "materialists").[9]
2. Those who deny that religious outlooks and communities have ever been found to foster the spirit of capitalism (K. Samuelsson).
3. Those who have sought to establish definitive proof that the spirit of capitalism and the analogues of the Protestant ethic were fully elaborated before the Protestant Reformation (L. Brentano, C. H. George, C. Bec).[10]
4. Those which seek to show that the existence of Protestantism in one or another area in no way guarantees the development of capitalism in that area (S. Burrell).

Views of this sort represent simplifications of the tenor and bearing of Weber's argument. Actually all research which in any way documents the relevance of cultural and religious variables in the development of economic institutions, ethics, organizations is consonant with Weber's mature views. Recent research, even when it attacks him, is likely to be congruent with the positions he adopted from 1910 on, especially in the essays and monographs gathered in his *Collected Essays in the Sociology of Religion* and his *Economy and Society*.

From the very first there has been continuing dispute as to the presence long before Calvin of a distinctively "Protestant ethic" in the medieval and Renaissance eras. The source of almost all the literature here was Sombart's book, *Der Bourgeois*, which was translated into English under the title, *The Quintessence of*

[9] The most interesting recent variant of this view will be found in such writers as Lichtheim and Hobsbawm, who think of Weber as a Marxist epigone (cf. Nelson 1969: 167–273).
[10] For Weber's replies to arguments along these lines see (1930: 194, 202, 262, Nelson 1969: 235, 1971a).

Capitalism. According to Sombart, Leon Battista Alberti antici-
pates Benjamin Franklin throughout his work, *On the Family*.[11]

Weber's efforts to clear up these issues never convinced those
disposed against his views. In my opinion, Weber was right in the
main to distinguish between prudential ethics that derived out of
older family and lineage patterns and rooted in estate moralities
or simple family acquisitiveness and what he called "the Protestant ethic." (1904, tr. 1930: 194–98). A great number of notable
historians have gone astray on this issue. The roster includes the
great Henri Pirenne (1914).

In very recent years the issue has been put on a new footing by
Christian Bec, who for the first time has systematically attempted a sorely needed close analysis of all the books of conduct
of the period. Without here entering into the details of his evidence, I would have to say that in the end Bec's results prove
inconclusive and that he is of divided mind. The books themselves do not at all prove his proposition that the spirit of capitalism was rampant in fourteenth-century Florence. Indeed, the
special studies he himself has carried forward established beyond
doubt that in that very same area and territory ruling attitudes
were decidely noncapitalist or precapitalist or even anticapitalist
(cf. Bec 1967, 1969).

In the same spirit, historians who have not followed the argument closely enough have made too much of the development of
double-entry bookkeeping during the fourteenth century and
exaggerated the theological rewards offered for the conscientious
and methodical practice of so-called economic virtues. One does
not convert Weber by proving that St. Thomas and other scholastics had rational structures of ethical analysis. Weber (1904,
tr. 1930: 73–78) is emphasizing the special character of the
Protestant ethic and its special grounding in ontological propositions and orientations, the very irrationality out of which there
came as an unanticipated by-product the rationale methodizing
of all life.

The two most widely discussed current critiques of Weber

---

[11] This work is now newly translated (Watkins 1969). Joan Gadol has
argued that notions analogous to Weber's Protestant ethic may be clearly
found in Alberti's *De icearchia* (Gadol 1970). For indications of my approach to views of this sort see Nelson (1971a).

which have issued in recent years are those by Hugh Trevor-Roper (1968) and Herbert Luethy (1964, 1965). Both writers seem to be concerned to do for our times what R. H. Tawney did for his time; both writers ask to see a widening of the historical horizons of the analysis. Neither of the authors, however, has as great a command of the relevant historical materials as Tawney had and both begin by initial simplifications of Weber's thesis. Having dealt with their views elsewhere (Nelson 1969: 236, 238, 241–45, 256, 265), I would here simply repeat that our understanding of the issues developed by Weber is, at least, as often weakened as it is advanced by their contributions. Whether Trevor-Roper and Luethy know so or not, they, in effect, deny that Protestantism was one of the central roads to the modern world: both seem guilty of great simplifications in their analyses of the relations of Protestantism and Catholicism in the sixteenth and seventeenth centuries. It is not the case that Erasmus was a powerful factor in the spread of more liberal views on economic activity, nor is it helpful to assume that it was more the retarding influences of Catholicism after Trent than the propulsive forces within Protestantism itself which are to be treated as the explanation of the breakthroughs to the modern society and outlook (see Little 1969). Neither author captures Weber's understanding of the critical importance of the development of rationalizations (cf. Gothein 1908, Borkenau 1934, Groethuysen 1927–29, 1968, Weber 1956, 1958).

Trevor-Roper and Luethy do deserve our thanks for calling attention to the need to study developments in Catholic culture areas in the sixteenth to eighteenth centuries. Oddly, neither of these authors mentions truly notable efforts of the past (Honigsheim 1914, Magendie 1925, Speier 1935). The most important omission is the very learned and thorough study by Bernard Groethuysen (1927–29; 1968) which might very well have been entitled "The *Catholic Ethic* and the Spirit of Capitalism." Groethuysen's work offers great help in appreciating the locales and atmospheres of the passages to the bourgeois blends of religion and world which came to be characteristic of Catholic France in the seventeenth and eighteenth centuries.

In this entire sphere of the comparative attitudes of Catholics and Protestants to work, religion, and world Weber might have spared us if he had placed more explicit stress on the changes in the structures of experience, conscience, and consciousness. Having argued this point at length elsewhere (Nelson 1969: 239–47), I must be content to say here that had Weber adopted this emphasis, it would have been ever so much easier for him to make clear the contrast between the systematic and sanctified pursuit of one's calling encouraged by Protestantism and the calculative taking advantage of expedient concessions which characterized Catholic orientations. We need again and again to stress the contrast between the accommodations allowable through traditional casuistry and the positive religious rewards reinforced by the ringing affirmations of a new conscience.

In recent years attempts to employ and test Weber's notions in the study of the problems of development and modernization have been made by many sorts of social scientists—economists, social psychologists, econometricians, economic historians, political scientists, and others. Three of the outstanding men in this connection are David McClelland (1961), Everett Hagan (1962), and W. W. Rostow (1960). Of the three Rostow seems to have come closest to grasping the import of Weber's stresses on the new structural incentives to take-off as well as Weber's implied emphases on the importance of rationalization. Limitations in Rostow's understanding of Weber have, however, been stressed by Niles Hansen (1963).

McClelland has placed prime stress on critical importance of the so-called need-achievement syndrome for the social spread of innovative entrepreneurial activity. A vast literature has already accumulated on the exact claims made by his theory and research from the vantage point he has stressed. His work seems to give undue prominence to the social-psychological springs of innovative activity and inclines to overidentify innovation with risk-taking antitraditionalism in an entrepreneurial sense.

Particular exception has been taken to his efforts to prove his theory statistically. An especially strong critique of the applications of the theory to the need-*achievement* scores of African groups today will be found in a study by Szymon Chodak (in progress).

One must applaud Everett Hagan for making so thorough an attempt to arrive at new ways of talking about psychological

sources of dispositions to innovation. In the end, however, his
theory seems to rest too heavily upon inferences schematically
drawn from Robert Merton's paradigms (see esp. Merton 1938,
1968b) and not heavily enough on depth-historical analysis of
sociocultural processes. Hagan's stress on the status-withdrawal
factor has not lived up to its initial promise in recent analysis.

V "REFORMATION" AND THE ROADS TO MODERNITY

The "Protestant Reformation" needs to be considered as one
among the decisive developments on the roads to modernity in
the West (Weber 1956). These roads do not begin at one point
nor do they go along a single path nor do they converge on a
single end point. They include such processes as:

> 1. The development of the medieval cities and other related
> breakthroughs in the social and cultural Renaissance of the twelfth
> century (Weber 1956a: 1212–1372, Martindale 1966, Pirenne 1956,
> Clagett et al. 1961).[12]
> 2. The Reformation and the break from the structures of con-
> straints and grammars of assent of the medieval church to the
> pluralization of churches and sects of the pluralization of new maps
> of life and knowledge (Nelson 1969).
> 3. The various phases of the revolutions in science, philosophy,
> technoculture, and sensibility in the sixteenth and seventeenth cen-
> turies (Nelson 1968c).
> 4. The fusions at white heat of the wider—often unintended—
> by-products of the Protestant Reformation and the scientific revolu-
> tions, especially in Napoleon's France and Bismarck's Germany,
> issuing in the accelerated thrust toward total "rationalization" of
> the spheres and institutions of belief, instruction, and action.

It was Weber and not Troeltsch, Stephen Berger (1971) recalls,
who is the point of departure of the insight into the importance
of sects in the carrying through of notable changes in the
passages from received structures. Berger's pages summarize
limitations of prevailing images of the church-sect distinction.

For my part, I must here admit that one difficulty I find in

---

[12] A provocative suggestion in this sphere has recently been made by Mc-
Intosh (1970). My views on the issues posed by McIntosh are on their way
to the press now.

current discussion of sects, as well as in many other problems in the sociological study of religion and in theoretical sociology generally, is that so much research proceeds upon a mistaken supposition that the linguistic repetition of concepts establishes their material identity to their contents or their logical constancy in use. Again and again sociologists continue to fall into a trap of treating the same word as though it necessarily included or comprised the same contents. Under given sets of historical circumstances it may, indeed, be the case that movements to new phases do require the activity of new sects. We are not, however, to suppose that sect-like structures which emerged during the early Reformation were by any means necessarily dedicated to the rationalization of the world along the lines conceived by Weber. Many sect-like structures were closer in spirit to Catholicism than they were to the Reformation (Nelson 1949, 1969). This was indeed perceived by Luther himself and by other reformers. So far as the perspectives of comparative historical sociology of sociocultural process are concerned, we need to note that the turns and fortunes of the Reformation as a movement were marked by the elaborations of precarious balances between spiritualism and legalism, mysticism and political realism, enthusiasm and organization, civil war and treaties of concord, rejections as well as acceptances of "the world." (This was noticed by Troeltsch [1912:II] as well as by Weber [1910].)

Reserving some further details of Weber's analysis of sects for later pages, we must take note of what may be considered the most ambitious recent effort to offer a social-structural, genetic-causal analysis of the Reformation, that by G. E. Swanson (1967), *Religion and Regime.*

Swanson (1967: 2) plainly announces that his aim is to go beyond Weber in developing a causal analysis of the origins of Protestantism. As he puts it:

> My purpose in this book is to offer an explanation for the Reformation and to examine the consistency between that account and the historical record. More generally, my purpose is to offer an explanation for the acceptance or rejection of belief in the imminence of whatever men consider of ultimate value and to provide one test of that explanation.

Moving forward along the lines of an explanatory model he had previously applied in his *The Birth of the Gods* (1960),

Swanson seeks to establish the view that Catholicism persisted in areas characterized by specific sorts of regimes, which he calls "commensal and centralist," that provided "legitimate role in Government (gubernaculum) for special interest, that is for constituent bodies, as such." By contrast, he continues, three other sorts of regime—"heterarchic, limited centralist and balanced regimes—came to be associated with the adoption of Protestantism." In the areas that were to become Protestant the constituent bodies played large parts in the formulation of central policies by which the state was guided and administered. In a limited centralist regime constituent bodies participated only in the application of such policies to subdivisions of the body politic.

The wider setting which Swanson stresses is the rejection by the reformers of "the idea that God was immanent in creation" which, in his view, did mean that the central governments of European societies had once been experienced as immanent in history and that in some of these societies it was no longer so.

To sum up his own statement (Swanson 1967: 60) of results:

> As I evaluate the evidence, 21 of the 41 societies under study had commensal or centralist regimes. All but two of these societies remained Catholic. Of the 20 societies I judge to have had heterarchic, limited centralist, or balanced regimes, all adopted Protestantism. All societies with limited centralist regimes adopted the Anglican or Lutheran reforms. All societies with balanced or heterarchic regimes adopted Calvin's doctrines.

The bulk of Swanson's work is dedicated to elaborating and illustrating the central hypothesis, which, he suggests, allows us to understand even the critical differences in the recent and current patterns of political structures in Europe.

Space will not allow a full discussion of Swanson's theories and proofs in these pages. His work has already received careful review and criticism by informed scholars and historians of the stamp of Roland Bainton (1968), William Bouwsma (1968), and Robert Kingdon (1969). From the point of view of the present paper the following would need to be said: Notwithstanding Swanson's apparent use of comparative and statistical techniques, his method falls short of being sociological *in the contemporary sense*. As I retrace the threads of his argument, his main suppositions have their ultimate source in segments of

Feuerbach and Durkheim. This base is then reinforced from point to point by derivations from Talcott Parsons and others.

I am not now protesting the constituent elements of the compound or the compound itself. Indeed, I would grant that with certain safeguards Swanson's postulates might prove exciting starting points for interesting programs of research, but it hardly seems compatible with present-day sociological analysis to apply these perspectives in so exclusive a fashion as Swanson has done.

Actually, the author's work has greater likelihood of proof in the anthropological study of primitive societies than in the depth-historical sociologies of complex civilizations. We must beware lest the proof we derive from primitive societies often proves to be self-fulfilling hypotheses. His "proofs" of the exact fit of the primitive and early modern cases weaken, rather than strengthen, the argument. The only structures whose force Swanson acknowledges in the development of the religious identifications of the sovereign territories are the *supervening* political structures allegedly operating in the early modern era.

Swanson begins his book by explaining that he is not truly asking or answering Weber's questions. I doubt that Swanson has successfully asked or answered his own questions (cf. Nelson forthcoming).

A strong contrast to Swanson's work will be found in the very stimulating study by David Little (1966). His work takes its point of departure from the effort to explain what he explains is a real dilemma in Puritanism both in England and America, a simultaneous inclination toward regimentation and toward voluntary self-determination. As he observes (1966 : 425) :

> The entire theological and ethical conception of a new order in Puritan literature is rooted in the Calvinistic doctrine of a voluntary order which demands above all voluntary human obedience. Under God's sovereign authority, the new order requires a distinctive style of life that is set apart from the world of natural necessity and coercive political determination: "We must be a law to ourselves; we must be voluntaries, without constraint, yielding subjection to the will of God."

We must be grateful to Little for an especially clear criticism of Michael Walzer's work (cf. Walzer 1965). In Little's view

(1966: 429), Walzer fails to grasp main themes of Calvin and
Calvinism.

> To argue, as Walzer does, that Calvinist and Puritan thought may
> be reduced to an obsessive search for political security is to convey
> two erroneous notions: (a) *that only Calvin and the Puritans were
> frantically concerned about order;* b) *that the order they sought
> was exclusively political.*

The development of Puritanism both in America and England
illustrates a "genuine dilemma involving simultaneously *both* an
*inclination towards regimentation and towards voluntary self-
determination."*
Little directly disputes the suggestion of Walzer that there is
nothing in Puritanism that could constitute a positive or *constructive foundation for legitimating the voluntaristic* and universalistic norms of modern society.
Little (1966: 428) concludes by insisting that:

> Max Weber remains one of the few interpreters of Calvinism who
> enables us to make good sense of an experience that leaves most
> people bewildered. . . . As Weber understood, the mystery can be
> solved, in large part, only by examining the theological sources and
> content of Calvinistic Puritanism. When that is done, the Puritan
> experience emerges as a twofold commitment: as a commitment to
> "an order founded on a voluntary choice," in Miller's words, and as
> a commitment to the use of involuntary means to extend this or-
> der. . . . They are perplexities born of a special perception of
> order, and they are perplexities that continue to disturb the souls
> of men in today's world.

VI   PERSONAL LINES OF WORK

I allow myself some lines on the development of certain of the
emphases and outcomes of my own researches into themes critical
to Weber's Protestant ethic.
As I have elsewhere written (1969: 239–40):

> Given Weber's overriding interest in uncovering the "spiritual
> roots of the vocational asceticism of Occidental rationalism," and
> given his commitment to the conduct of "thought experiments" by
> the "ideal-type" method, Weber was correct, *from his point of view,*
> to stress the decisive importance of the notion of *innerweltliche
> Askese.*

In this spirit he again and again minimized the relevance to his concern of the changes in the doctrines of usury which had been a point of departure of my own researches. As the years passed, my emphasis was bound to become different from Weber's. My growing concerns with the structures of consciousness, including the principal legitimations and casuistries of action, spurred me to press forward to explore the *rationales* proposed by the contending groups locked in struggles over a whole series of theological, social, economic, and other issues. I sought to understand how the norms governing the settlement of disputed questions in all spheres came to be decided; how the bases for political obligation were reared; how conflicts at the level of self, community, civilization were moderated. The more intensively I searched the documentary remains for answers to questions of this nature, the more I appreciated the central position traditionally given to *conscience* by older historians of the last century. The issue of usury implicated the entire fabric of *opinions and actions* rooted in *conscience* and all the forms of the imbeddedness of *conscience,* including casuistry and the cure of souls.

Suddenly, indeed, the historical emphases ascribed to the notion of *conscience* gained fresh meaning. It was not that Luther or Calvin invented this fateful idea—a systematic exploration of that concept had already been started by others in the Middle Ages—but that these leaders of the Reformation gave everything a new axis and a new center by the scope of their attacks on every aspect of the culture of conscience—its structures, its *decision-matrices,* and its very *rationales.*

My own point of departure came to rest on the following perspectives: To understand the *makings* of early modern cultures we need to understand the *makings* of early modern minds and, therefore, need to have a proper sense of the change in the central paradigms as well as the restructuring of axial institutions in the society. If I may use the language of my current research, the makings of early modern cultures are most clearly in evidence when we study them from the special point of view of the revolutions in the rationale-systems in the sphere of conscience in its dual bearings in the spheres of moral action and intellectual opinion.

It will be recalled that during the entire period under discussion the logics were interdependent: in fact, they were woven together in a single fabric of propositions centering around the notion of conscience. As continuing Continental usage should serve to recall, the Latin *con-scientia* referred both to the *moral conscience,* or "the proximate rule of right reason in the moral sphere," and opinions and beliefs in the philosophic and scientific spheres. It is, therefore, no wonder that all important cultural and social innovations in our period had to involve an attack upon or a reconstruction of the *logics of decision* in the spheres of action and thought, in the scientific and moral domains alike.

For the present purpose, we need say only that the revolution called the Reformation was a breakdown and reconstruction of the court Christian and the received logics of moral decision. All fundamental images and ideals of self, spiritual direction, and group life were reshaped in the ensuing correlations of newer elements and reconstituted older elements released by the dissolution of the older complex.

I continue to be convinced that the notion of the new sort of "brotherhood" which I have called "universal otherhood," where all become *equally* rather than *differentially* others, was born in the era of the Reformation. Time and ongoing research continue to add evidence that advances in the direction of universal otherhood will remain one of the hallmarks of "ecumenical Protestantism." At the present time, indeed, as I have written elsewhere (1965c : 596), "the 'Protestant ethic' is now being exported to every corner of the earth along with energy packages, the computer, the bank, the department store, the central office and the Board Room."

In my own recent writings I have been striving to open new approaches to areas Weber neglected to cultivate sufficiently, partly because of his very strong commitments to predominant social-psychological images of action (purpose rationalization models). I find myself now disposed to reopen many questions in the light of the wider images he offers in his retrospective Author's Introduction to the *Collected Essays in the Sociology of Religion.*

In a series of special essays I have investigated the theoretical and empirical issues involved in the conflicts and fusions among the elements and outcomes of "the scholastic rationales of conscience, the early modern crises of credibility, and the scientific-technocultural revolutions of the seventeenth and twentieth centuries."

In several papers now in progress I seek to explain why Weber was so hesitant to develop structures of analysis necessary for the full exploration of his own materials. It is interesting to note that his diffidence was especially great in the following spheres: the depth-historical analysis of processual flows in the cultural and civilizational spheres, the systematic analysis of changes in the structures of conscience and consciousness, the structures and processes of intercivilizational content (Nelson 1969: 240–41, 1971c).

Again and again one is driven to the sense that, had Weber lived beyond 1920, he might very well have reworked many of the structures given some prominence in his earlier essays. We are led to this conclusion by a number of proofs:

1. There are, indeed, inconsistencies and differences of emphasis between sections of his *Economy and Society* and his *Collected Essays in the Sociology of Religion*. These are not mere matters of changes in the choice of perspective. One of the most troublesome points at issue is the degree to which Weber was prepared to emphasize the importance of urbanization and the development of city constitutions and social conflict in cities as factors working toward the rationalization of conduct and elimination of magic.

2. Another, and from my point of view, more impressive evidence is the growing awareness on Weber's part of the need to see the particular rationalization of conduct effected with the help of the Protestant ethic placed in the wider setting of the development of rationalization in the West. Again, it is the retrospective Author's Introduction which forces upon us an awareness of his belated stress upon what I have elsewhere called "structures of rationales, cultural logics, symbolic technologies." It proves that Pythagoras, Plato, Aristotle, Euclid, and Archimedes, Gaius, and Ulpian were at least as important in the development of the distinctively Western structures as were Luther and Calvin (Weber 1930: 13–17).

The unhappy pressure Weber placed upon himself to subordinate the development of science to the study of rationalization process encouraged a view from which we are only now recovering. Weber knew very well himself that the revolution in early modern science and philosophy did not need to wait upon the emergence and spread of the Protestant ethic. However, his

continuous assimilation of science to the rationalization of conduct made it easy to miss his point. Weber rarely wrote on
science or, for that matter, technology as such, but it is possible
to recognize that few men had so deep an understanding of the
problems involved in discriminating the dimensions of sociocultural process. His long essay, ''The Rational and Social
Foundations of Music,'' is a striking testimony in support of the
position taken in his retrospective Author's Introduction.

A further testimony to the probable ways in which the work of
Weber may need to be reconceived may be found in the growing
awareness revealed in the current discussions of the need to
fortify, collate, and correlate Weber's analyses of both the
''rational'' and ''social'' foundations of music. In respect to the
social foundations, we are coming to increasing awareness that a
fuller understanding of the transformations associated with the
influence of the Protestant ethic involves our perceiving that it
took the energies and structures of consciousness of new groups
to break the morale of traditionalism and open the roads to
modernization. Under certain circumstances it is possible for
traditional values themselves to be given a new momentum and
to be made the source of new attacks on the temporary dominant
structures.

Very helpful insights into the latter phenomena are to be
inferred from a number of essays by Bellah (1957, 1965a, 1965d,
1970), Bendix (1968a), Eisenstadt (1965, 1968b) and others
(see esp. Vallier 1967, 1969, 1970, and essays by E. Willems,
M. Ames, and G. Germani in Eisenstadt 1968b).

VII CALVIN, PLYMOUTH ROCK, AND BEYOND

It would not be realistic to expect that historians of American
social development, religion, and churches would agree as to the
soundness and relevance of Weber's views for developments on
this side of the Atlantic. In the main, indeed, relatively few
American historians have found it necessary to see Weber in his
own terms and develop a wide view of the implications of his work

or to construe his more familiar theses against the background of his mature reflections.

It is not surprising, therefore, that very few American historians have brought into single focus Weber's various statements of life and religion in America. Thus, scant attention has been given to Weber's remarkable letters (Brann 1944), which he sent home during his trip to this country; and, again, very few writers have thought to comment on the bearing of his views on sects (see now Berger 1971) and voluntary associations for the understanding of American life (see Weber 1910, Adams 1971).

American Protestant historians of great renown have continued to insist that Weber's discussion of the Protestant ethic is a gross caricature of the Reformation. This is especially clear, it is claimed, in Weber's discussion of Calvin and the Calvinist sects (e.g., Hudson 1949, 1961).

I find myself unable to agree with the extreme criticisms of Weber. As I have remarked, Weber does in places allow the impression that the spirit of Calvinism found its ultimate expression in the spirit of acquisitiveness, but this was not his underlying view nor, for that matter, was it even necessary in his main argument. The many criticisms of Weber by unsympathetic American church historians can readily be shown to go far beyond the evidence.

Luckily, a select company of our most eminent American historians of Puritanism and colonial religion have been able to maintain a judicious reserve in respect to these defensive polemics. Here one would especially mention the sympathetic understanding of Weber to be found in the writings of Perry Miller, Kemper Fullerton, A. Whitney Griswold, Edmund Morgan, Frederick B. Tolles, Gillian Gollin, E. Gaustad, and others. Professor Morgan is reported to be at work on a major history of the Protestant ethic in the United States. The promise of this contribution is immense. Also to be mentioned in this connection are the lives and recent studies of such men as Andrew Carnegie, Henry Ford, and Frederick Winslow Taylor.

There is no reason to deny that Weber committed errors and excesses in some of his views and pages. Thus, we are obliged to reject Weber's supposition that whenever and wherever we encounter religiously related voluntary associations and sect-like groups we are looking at phenomena which have their primary meaning as credit-certifying agencies. Weber has overstated something here, treating an aspect of the surface at the expense of other features. The development of sects and fellowships of various sorts in the United States has had as much to do with the breaking out of restrictive molds inhibiting response to new experience as it has had to do with the assurance of a satisfactory rating at the bank. Weber seems not to have understood that each of the formalized sects created extreme restraints against mingling across denominational boundaries. The phenomena he saw during his trip to the United States often involved the successful overcoming of the severe inhibitions (see Weber 1908, Adams 1971, cf. Berger 1971).

We are in need of extensions of Weber's views of sects so as to include the wider voluntary associations which are interdenominational, intercultural, crossing political and ethnic boundaries. Again and again in the course of American history fixed structures which are Continental in origin are forced to be loosened in favor of more flowing structures which are more inclusive. A critical key to the American society has been the openings of freedoms of exit from structures on the point of becoming ossified and fossilized and freedoms of entry into new associations (Arieli 1966).

Weber did not quite catch the full thrust of these dynamical flows. His American followers have tended to be even less aware of process than he was. Our contemporary understanding of the variety of group structures and processes needs to be enlarged. The familiar polarities which have come down do not now suffice. The most interesting forms are those which illustrate mixes and meshes of different points of view, different balances of structural-counterstructural modalities (see suggestions in Turner 1966).

The influence of the Protestant ethic in America is sometimes very easy, sometimes very hard to uncover. When it is hard, it is like correlating particle traces in a cloud chamber served by a billion-volt linear accelerator. The reason for this may be put simply: in our land Protestantism seems to take form less in sharply differentiated institutions than to express itself at every point in the social and cultural life process in a volatilized form. Rather, as a way of life, Protestantism secretes itself into the activities of the business organization, the board room, the exchange, the town council, the legislative session—in short, in all the conventionalized structures which are then taken-for-granted ways of proceeding in the worlds of education, business, and law. The Protestant ethic is at work wherever Protestants act as whole people or in accordance with the norms of the institutions they have established.

Until recently, Catholicism and Protestantism have tended to manifest themselves in different ways. Traditionally incorporating a strong support for otherworldly *dualism,* Catholicism continues to give strong emphases to acosmic *caritas*-related life or to the activities of conventicles associated with charismatic persons or offices. Ascetic Protestantism has usually functioned to restructure the orders of the world. Catholicism has tended to support the development of orders parallel to but outside of the conventional orders.

VIII   THE "PROTESTANT ETHIC" IN CONTEMPORARY AMERICA: GREELEY, LENSKI, AND OTHERS

The evidence on the present relevance in American belief and behavior of the Protestant ethic is exceedingly elusive. An ambitious statistical study by Mack, Yellin, and others (1956) sees no evidence against the null hypothesis that identification, whether with Catholicism or Protestantism, is indifferent so far as motivation to achievement on the job is concerned. On the other hand, other studies (Goldstein and Eichorn 1961) on other corners of the American scene produce the result that the Protestant ethic of high work drive and low propensity to spend can be found strongly in certain rural communities.

Clearly, the evidence adduced by American researchers of American situations neither decisively establishes nor decisively disestablishes the Weberian thesis in any simple sense. With very

few exceptions, however, the jurors have voted in the negative
(e.g., Greeley 1964, Demerath and Hammond 1969).

Andrew Greeley (1964) has proposed that the Weber thesis
might well be set on the shelf for all its use in helping us understand the rated motivations and performances of American
Catholics, Protestants, and Jews. I find myself ready to acknowledge the ingenuity of Greeley's review of current research. I find
myself unready to come to his conclusions. His own closing pages
also make clear that research on Weber's theses needs to include
careful stipulations as to the parameters and dimensions of the
analysis. If many American Catholics seem to reveal behavioral
traits and orientations comparable to those of Protestants, this
evidently must be so because of the fact that America is prevail-
ingly a Protestant culture area. Any consideration of the phenomena here which did not place due stress on civilizational
ascendencies within given areas would miss the point.

So far as survey method is concerned, many of the most critical questions in this area occur in the recently published exchange
between Howard Schuman and Gerhard Lenski over the findings
of Lenski's Detroit area study. Schuman (1971: 33–40) specifically questions Lenski's conclusions that, so far as Protestant-
Catholic differences in economic ethic go, "that as a general rule
commitment to the Spirit of Capitalism is especially frequent
among white Protestants and Jews (and is much less frequent
among Catholics)." Schuman examines the data under the heading of work values, attitudes toward work, other attitudes and
values regarding work and consumption, especially: (1) belief in
the possibility of success, (2) divine concern with economic
striving, (3) use of leisure time, (4) concern with thrift, (5)
follow-up to installment buying. He then proceeds to review the
materials on "positional and performance measures."

One must be grateful to Schuman for realizing that the terms
"Protestants" and "Catholics" are vague and have an omnibus
nature. He writes: "For one thing 'Protestant' covers very many
different denominations and sects in America, and Weber was at
pains to detail differences as well as similarities among these."

Lenski's reply (1971: 49) is a model of judicious analysis. He
begins:

I would not want to claim that differences in rates of occupational mobility of the type reported in *The Religious Factor* and these other studies have yet been confirmed, but neither would I concede that they have been refuted. If anything, the net balance of subsequent research on this intriguing subject seems to suggest that as recently as the 1950s, differences between the two major religious groups still survived in American society, and Schuman's findings suggest a reason for this.

Lenski's closing remarks (1971: 50) offer an especially telling contribution to the area.

Times are changing, and some of the most important changes in the religious realm have been of a kind that few would have predicted as recently as the early 1960s. Even now, Vatican Council II seems to have been more a sport than a natural outgrowth of a dominant earlier trend. Vatican Council II was a major religious revolution: it legitimatized dissent within the Church, thereby re-ordering the whole structure of authority both organizationally and intellectually and thus sweeping the Catholic Church swiftly into the mainstream of contemporary life. In effect, it was a kind of belated consummation of the Protestant Reformation. Because of this, I am inclined to think that such differences as existed between Catholics and Protestants a decade ago have been seriously eroded and are likely to diminish even more in the decade ahead. Thus, *The Religious Factor* is, at best, a picture of an era that has ended.

If I have any real criticism of Howard Schuman's otherwise excellent piece of research and analysis, it is that he seems to lack an interest in change. Nowhere in his article did I find a reference to Vatican Council II, yet that historic series of meetings took place between the time of my study and the time of his replication. Like many of the rest of us, he has probably been overly influenced on the theoretical level by structural-functionalism with its curiously synchronic, ahistorical orientation, and on the methodological level by the technique of the sample survey with its built-in timeless bias. Personally, I believe that these limitations can be overcome and must be overcome. Structural-functional theory should be replaced by theories which take the time-dimension explicitly into account and which make social change a prime concern, and sample surveys should be designed, not merely for replication (important as that is), but even more for time-series analyses. But I say this less as a criticism of Schuman than as a suggestion for all of us.

Lenski's observations drive home the argument of the current essay. The terms "Protestant" and "Catholic" are not to be conceived of as logical constants. The precise meaning to be attached to these terms will clearly vary with wider associational, societal, and even civilizational contexts. Complications

presented with the evidence in one or another locality can never
be taken as final confirmation or disconfirmation of the theses;
no single experiment may be deemed crucial. We have yet to
introduce into our thinking the strictness of design which applies
in descriptive astronomy or in the tracking of particles in cloud
chambers. The mixes "Protestant"-"Catholic" with other societal and associational imperatives vary greatly from place to
place and from time to time. Whoever wishes to test Weber's
views must first come to understand the exact nature of his
theses and then to establish the methods of tracking the phenomena in the social and historical universes which are relevant.

IX   SCIENCE AND TECHNOLOGY

Weber found it impossible to close his work without specifying a
series of new tasks which would need to be carried forward in
support of the wider project. Thus he writes (1930: 182–83):

> The next task would be rather to show the significance of ascetic
> rationalism, which has only been touched in the foregoing sketch, for
> the content of practical social ethics, thus for types of organization
> and the functions of social groups from the conventicle to the State.
> Then its relations to humanistic rationalism, its ideals of life and
> cultural influence; further to the development of philosophical
> and scientific empiricism, to technical development and to spiritual
> ideals would have to be analysed. Then its historical development
> from the mediaeval beginnings of worldly asceticism would have to
> be traced out through all the areas of ascetic religion. Only then
> could the quantitative cultural significance of ascetic Protestantism
> in its relation to the other plastic elements of modern culture be
> estimated.

In retrospect it is hard to grasp why sociologists and scholars
were so slow to relate to the challenges posed by Weber's view on
the possible relations of the Protestant ethic and sciences. The
reasons must have been many.

At no time in his basic monograph did Weber squarely face
the issue of the relations of the Reformation and science. Indeed,
in the years between 1915 and 1920 Weber wrote very little
directly on science or technology and did not devote any special
paper to the problem. Among the footnotes in *The Protestant
Ethic*, Weber (1930: 182–83) proposed the relation between

scientific positivism and the pietist sense of God's nature and will. His most important statement on the issue of the cultural backgrounds of science appears in his "Anti-Critical Last Word" in 1910 (see Winckelmann 1968). Here he declares that it was never his intention to contend that early modern science had to wait for the emergence of the Protestant ethic. From that time forward Weber did not devote a single paper to the "rational *and* social foundations of science," as, for example, he did in the case of music.

American scholars have largely been unaware of the disputes associated with the names of Franz Borkenau and Henryk Grossmann. In a carefully conceived study on the transition from the world view of the feudal era to that of the age of manufacture, Borkenau (1934) contended that the central structures in the images of science and philosophy were derived from the rationalization of labor in the era of manufacture in the sixteenth and seventeenth centuries. The philosophy of mechanism seems to him to be the fruit of the actual rationalization of mechanical activity. Henryk Grossman (1935), a collaborator in the Institute for Social Research, took very strong exception to this view. In a detailed critique he insisted that the sources of the mechanical world view were to be found in the evidences of the workings of actual machines and mechanisms rather than from the rationalization of labor. It is to be hoped that the arguments will become more widely known and reviewed.

The outstanding American response to the challenge expressed in Weber's statement of *agenda* was Robert K. Merton's doctoral dissertation, which was first published in *Osiris* in 1938. In this truly astonishing work, now newly published with a new introduction (1970), Merton undertakes to show that seventeenth-century England, especially the circles of Puritans, provided an especially favorable climate for the development of science, technology, and society.

In a series of recent papers I have sought to show that very many writings on the subject of the relation between the "Protestant ethic" and the origin and development of the scientific revolution are defective, at least in the popular forms circulated in textbooks. Weber himself never claimed that the formation and success of the Protestant ethic was an indispensable precondition of the origin and development of modern science. Indeed, as he tells us clearly in 1910 (''Anti-Critical Last Word''), he did not wish to be identified with a proposition so transparently false.

Weber recognized that many of the foremost pioneers of the early modern revolution in science and philosophy were reared in Catholic settings and were cordial to Catholic outlooks and world views; moreover, those who were Protestants were by no means opposed to religion or religious expression (see Winckelmann 1968 : 324–25).

If Robert Merton (1970: intro.) sounds different from Weber on this issue, it needs to be remembered that the focus of Merton's study is on the scientific movement in seventeenth-century England; it does not set out to explain the distinctly *scientific* revolution connected with the names of Copernicus, Galileo, Descartes, Newton, and so on (see Hall 1963).

There is no need to dispute the view that the spread and success of the scientific movement as a social movement in England was affected by the instrumental activism and the respect for scientific universalism in the seventeenth and eighteenth centuries and powerfully influenced the Protestant ethic.

Acting under the goad of these and other difficulties, I found myself having to review the scientific-technocultural revolutions of the seventeenth and twentieth centuries. I had also come to be convinced that the two movements—the Protestant Reformation and the scientific revolution—needed to be seen in their similarities and differences alike.

In words I have used elsewhere (1968b : 164) :

> Our story falls under two rubrics as follows :
> 1. *The Protestant Reformations* saw the successful challenge to the Court of Conscience, and other directive agencies of the medieval church, in respect to regulation of action and decision in the moral-religious spheres. In the wake of these developments, all the fundamental images and ideas of self and group religious responsibility and political responsibility, religious destiny and spiritual direction were reshaped in idiomatic ways in the distinctive *new orders* which came to be constituted in the different Protestant culture-areas. . . .
> New cultural structures fusing newer elements and reconstituted older elements occurred everywhere and, indeed, efforts were occasionally made everywhere to restore integrated medieval patterns. But again and again the embattled core of Protestantism has resisted

attempts to reunite "conscience-casuistry and the cure of souls" in a single tribunal or institution. Protestantism has persisted in moving in the direction of new structures of personal and social order.

2. *The Scientific and Philosophical Revolution.* The medieval union of "conscience-casuistry-and cure of souls" also forms a critical part of the background of Copernicus, Galileo, Descartes, Pascal and many others who pioneered in the "Early Modern Revolution in Science and Philosophy"—a fact yet to be duly appreciated by many sociologists and historians of the movements of science and philosophy. The appearance of the newer developments in Catholic backgrounds and in Catholic culture-areas made it inevitable that the aforementioned pioneers of the early modern Revolution in Science and Philosophy would come into head-on conflict with the principles and procedures of the estimated directive systems.

The Protestant ethic is everywhere making headway now in this twentieth century, along with the spread across the world of technologies and outlooks which have been powered by Protestant lifeways. As I have elsewhere written (1968b: 165–66, cf. 1970b):

> For the revolutions of the *rationales* of conscience to come to their fruition, the *Protestant Ethic* had to pass beyond Weber. The legacies of Luther and Calvin, Galileo and Descartes, had truly to be linked together and become united.
>
> The new ethics, energies, and life-ways which had arisen in the successful Protestant Revolution had to be placed at the service of what contemporary scientists call "new world-models"—the natural philosophy, the mathematical physics, and the revolutionary new logic and algorithm, which oddly enough flowered first in Catholic centers, but were slowed in their progress there by official resistance, political no less than ecclesiastical.
>
> Western civilization had to wait longer than many have supposed to arrive at the contemporary take-off and "exponential growth-points." First a series of great fusions had to occur. These fusions were not effected, as so many have freely assumed, in 18th Century England, the time in which the first industrial revolution gained momentum. *Pure Science* was less a source than a beneficiary of 18th Century technology—an insight we owe to A. N. Whitehead, Lawrence J. Henderson, and too few others after them. The Revolution through which we are now passing is Science's Revolution, actually a *Perspectival-Technological-Organizational* Revolution. Our Revolution altogether dwarfs the earlier development.
>
> In short, I am proposing that the reshapings of the rationales of conscience compose fundamental phases in the *makings* of early *modern* cultures and that from the late 19th Century forward, first mainly in Germany after an abortive episode in Napoleonic France, then in the United States and elsewhere, the by-products and the off-shoots of these *makings* were fused at great heats. If we find the pathos of Weber's judgments overwhelming, it is because Weber

was a supreme witness of what in the spirit of German philosophy and sociology—Hegel, Marx, Simmel—he construed as a succession of fatal *mechanizations* of the spirit.

Regrettably, I must reserve for the future any extended show of evidence that the dynamic political and administrative environments of Continental Europe, notably Germany and France, proved to be the setting for the decisive fusions of the regenerated Logics of science, technology, industry, and education. It is the thrust which occurred in Germany after 1870 to which Weber bears witness. A startling expression of the way things seemed to stand at the outbreak of World War I will be found in an unforgettable, but rarely cited essay by Paul Valéry.

In present-day America is the highest point reached so far by the runaway processes here described. Not far behind in the race are current allies and former enemies—the Soviet Union, the European Powers, Japan, China. Hourly reports from the world's capitals, laboratories and battlefields all spell out the story: A new format is spreading as new societies, new nations, a new world, and indeed, a new universe are in the throes of coming into being. The greatest intensity yet known of high-speed and fully-automated mechanical technologies and high-speed and fully-automated nonmaterial and information-systems and electronic microcircuitries is now upon us. 1917 and 1945 have been left far behind.

X AGENDA

One persistent stress of the present paper is that it is a mistake to treat any locus as being the place for the ultimate test of the Weber hypothesis. We have rejected the identification of Weber's theory with the fixation in the notion of motive; thus, the "Protestant ethic" is not to be equated with achievement need. Again we have sought to draw attention to the multiple ways in which the Protestant ethic lead precipitates and undergoes distillations in the most unexpected places in the culture. Thus, for example, it is an error to identify the increase in the interest in spectator sports as a sign of the waning of the Protestant ethic. The fact is that there is no understanding the extraordinary rationalization of skills and division of responsibility in these sports without referring to the processes described by Weber.[13]

It is only a depth-historical comparative sociology which can

---

[13] This is attested by many recent biographies and autobiographies of sports stars.

protest against regularly falling into the mistake of treating a current element as the sum and substance of a complex, highly rationalized culture. The least we can do in our efforts to develop the potentials of Weber is to apply as strictly as possible the cautions which Durkheim and his followers sought to exercise in the carrying on of sociological comparative research.

It is the claim of this writer that there is much fruit to be harvested from the adroit and precise application of Weber's clues. Masses of patterns remain to be disclosed as the "civilizational" structures he identified go their way from West to East, and areas hitherto remote from the so-called Protestant ethic start on their way toward a fuller rationalization.

In this horizon, we dare not forget that if the so-called West is going East, the so-called East is coming West (Nelson 1971c). The study of Weber's *Protestant Ethic* is thus a main point of entry into the study of civilizational complexes and the patterns of intercivilizational contacts and conflicts.

Selected themes deserving of close regard of future researchers may be mentioned by way of bringing this essay to a temporary close.

Rationalization

It is odd to report that there have been so few studies of American social development from the point of view of the processes of rationalization, and yet there have been few countries in the world in which the thrust toward rationalization has had such profound impacts in recent decades as in our own land. Our own twentieth century has witnessed massive efforts to advance the rationalization of all the spheres of thought and action. The systematic rationalization of means and ends in the spheres of conduct and belief—e.g., war, business, sports, automation and collectivation of knowledge, and so forth—has gone at least as far in our country as in any other.

He who would write the history of the "Protestant ethic" in the United States would be obliged to devote many sections to such notable figures as John D. Rockefeller, Sr., Henry Ford, Frederick Winslow Taylor, Frank Galbraith, Thomas J. Watson, and many others too numerous to mention. (See now Jardim

1970, Kakar 1970, Kovel 1971, Rischin 1965). The underlying motif in the life and work of all these men was to drive toward the fullest rationalization of conduct and organization so as to generate the greatest possible outputs of incomes over losses and costs. The men above named are paradigms of the Protestant ethic in action. This fact has been perceived by their biographers, and it is startling to realize that as yet so few authors have thought to include their lives in the assessment of Weber's hypothesis.

Impersonal Service and Impersonal Goal vs. Imitatio Dei

Too few writers have recognized the crucial importance for Weber of the Protestant emphasis on impersonal service on behalf of a superpersonal goal. Many clues to contemporary structures can be found in a review of earlier historical forms.

In the medieval and early modern eras this contrast takes the form of a difference between the pursuit of a selfless ministry in the interest of God's mastery of the world and a personal, or as we say today, an existential imitation of Christ's love, friendship, and suffering for humanity in every act oriented to any other person or object.

Throughout antiquity and the Middle Ages friendship was conceived as the union that transcended all calculation and egotism, whether of family or of person. From at least the time of Plato forward, the moralists and novelists insisted upon the preeminence of friendship, going so far as to deny that members of one's own family or one's spouse could truly be one's friends in the highest sense. The stress on Christ as the perfect and true friend continued into Renaissance Italy and the Elizabethan period in England.

Interestingly, the first powerful assault on the idea of friendship came with the opponents of Elizabeth and the courtly style. The Puritans correctly grasped that, so long as friendship and friendship circles were held in the highest esteem, there was no possibility of achieving sanctification for the special love within the family. Too few studies have been done in this area. We can say, however, that it was the Puritans above all who mounted the attack on the ethos of friendship which prevailed in England until their day. The very idea that charity begins at home involves the sanctification of the home. Too few have noticed that such a sanctification goes far beyond the idea that we are to love ourselves as we love our neighbors. The notion "that charity begins at home" is the sacralization of the collective egoism of the family and its property. This represents the indispensable base of the newer system which came into being with the Protestant ethic (Weber 1930: 224; see also Nelson 1949, ed. 1969: a54, a56, a62, 163). There is another side to this story.

Placation vs. Performance

Too few writers have given enough stress to the shift in orientation involved in the passage from person-oriented placation-compliance to the performance of a task in an objective spirit. It is only with Protestantism that this emphasis of impersonal service on behalf of a superpersonal goal can develop the morale necessary for concerted group function in an advanced division of labor. To speak of bureaucracy excessively in terms of domination and imperative coordination is to miss the fact that under one light bureaucracy represents the activity of a collective animated by a commitment to the realization of objective ends and organizational purpose. For many different sorts of reasons, this emphasis is today at bay in many parts of the Western world.[14]

The World of Missions

Another exceedingly important field for future research would be the study of the character of missions inspired by variant structures of religious ethos. As Weber realized, Protestantism was committed from the first to the notion of explicit knowledge and explicit proclamation of faith, whereas the Catholic view accepted the congruity of autochthonous faiths so long as the habits of the indigenous people were not in direct conflict with the law of Christ. If we are to reconceive the program of research necessary for the confirmation or disconfirmation of Weber's thesis, we would need to look into the ways in which

---

[14] For earlier signs of awareness of changes in the person-organization relation, see Riesman (1950, Whyte 1956, cf. Nelson 1969).

Catholicism and Protestantism spread from Europe to other lands. We would need to discover what the effects of the two structures were for the development of character and conduct in these countries. Preliminary evidence indicates that wherever, with rare exceptions, Protestantism has taken hold, institutions having the character of the Protestant emphasis on transformation have taken hold (e.g., Capéran 1934, Bellah 1970: 123–24). Catholicism has always managed to give less direct strain to previous cultural and civilizational tendencies.

There is a sense in which the United States can itself be conceived of as an illustration of a new nation in which Protestant strains had unique opportunity to receive continent-wide elaboration (e.g., Lipset 1967, Mead 1963, Brauer 1950, 1961, Arieli 1961). The spread of the "Protestant ethic" into the Far East is too complex and ambiguous a story to follow any further in these pages.

The Roads to Modernity

In a properly defined *comparative depth-historical sociology of sociocultural process* (Nelson 1961c), structures of orientations and actions having the character of the "Protestant ethic" can be expected to be found regularly on the roads to modernity.

It is no wonder that contemporary writers have seen the desirability of extending the "Protestant ethic" concept to lands which were far from the center of Protestantism—Japan, Russia, India. Robert Bellah's first move (1963) to establish the evidence for the relevance of the "Protestant Ethic Analogy in Asia" was an inspired move in the right direction. Philip Siegelman's too-little noticed study of the Chettyars of Madras (1964) deserves to be better known; I deem it a strong confirmation of a tack I have taken in my *Idea of Usury*. In my view, therefore, Niles Hanson (1963) is correct when he speaks of the "Protestant ethic" in this broader sense as the prerequisite of modernization anywhere and everywhere.

The newer research has definitely established that one of our most urgent needs is to study the roads to modernity in the light of the changes in the orientations to action and belief influenced by the changes in the structures of consciousness and conscience.

Integral to this process is the understanding of the struggles now to advance, now to oppose, rationalized schemes of control, rule, and order: now to hold fast to tradition; now to shake up existing structures so that great awakenings that move toward widened participations might occur (Nelson 1971c). Wherever we have movements comparable to the Reformation in any lands, we may expect to see regulative cultural transformation of political and juridical orientations and orders involving novel balances and rules of individual options (Nelson 1969).

XI IN RETROSPECT

If debate continues to rage in this field, part of the reason must be and is the fact that authors start with very different assumptions as to what Weber is saying. Many wrongly supposed that he is contending that the Protestant ethic was a sufficient condition of the emergence of the spirit of capitalism and of the full institutionalization of the structures of enterprise and outlook which have come to be the hallmark of the contemporary Western world.

This was never his argument. From the first essay to the last Weber very clearly understood that all sorts of conditions which were antecedent to the full elaboration of distinctively modern capitalism had existed long before the development of Protestantism, long before, indeed, the emergence of Christianity. What he undertook to ascertain was what set of circumstances or what set of changes proved to be a critical catalyst in the constellation of elements which came to be uniquely influenced by one or another factor at a particular time.

He tells us plainly that he is applying Mills's "Method of Difference" and, therefore, looking for the factor or chain of circumstances which helped to explain some unique outcome of a given experiment. The unique outcome, as he saw it, in the Protestant ethic was the spread of a rationalized sociocultural order based on the assumption of vocational asceticism. In his later work, his comparative work, he sought to show that all other components which were involved in the Western fusion could be found separately and in combination in other places,

but these had not undergone the spur which was supplied by
Luther, Calvin, the Protestant ethic, and the spirit of capitalism
in the West. His successive writings on the social psychology of
the world religions—the Confucianism—and Taoism—religious
objects of the world—Hinduism and Buddhism—and the religion of Ancient Judaism—were all devoted to further testing of
this hypothesis. And lastly, throughout his *Economy and Society*
and in his *General Economic History* he makes it as clear as possible that he is not arguing; that the one and only cause which
produced the modern capitalistic cosmos is the Protestant ethic.
It was never his intention, to paraphrase him, to substitute a
foolish and doctrinaire spiritualistic causal interpretation of
culture and history for one-sided Marxist materialism or economic interpretation of history (Weber 1930: 92, 183).

Those American writers who have neglected to look into
Weber's other works beyond the *Protestant Ethic* have done
themselves a *disservice*. Moreover, there are two places in particular where Weber is as clear as can be on these issues. One is
the last chapter of the posthumously published lectures, entitled
General Economic History. The chapter itself is called "The
Evolution of the Capitalistic Spirit." The other place is the
Author's Introduction to the *Collected Essays in the Sociology
of Religion*. Indeed, it is here that Weber makes it evident that
so far as he was concerned the Protestant ethic was a tiny part in
a very much larger process—the progress of the spirit of rationalization, which has had until now a unique thrust, spread,
and persistence in the West.[15]

If we wish to go beyond Weber, we must strive to go to the
roots of his theoretical structures; we must earnestly review his
achievements and his miscues. Above all, we must prepare ourselves to look freshly at the tumultuous cultural processes of our
own day and indeed of the half-century which has elapsed since
his death in 1920 (see Nelson 1971). We will surely find ourselves needing his help—and the help of others commemorated
elsewhere in this book—if we are to make sense of our fates and
our hopes.

[15] The account in Parsons (1937, II: 500–78) remains indispensable here.
See also Loewith (1960, 1923, cf. Mommsen 1965, Abramowski 1966, Nelson
1968b, 1970a).

BIBLIOGRAPHY

Abramowski, Günter
  1966 *Das Geschichtsbild Max Webers Universalgeschichte am Lietfaden des okzidentalen Rationalisierungsprozesses.* Stuttgart: Klebt.

Adams, James L.
  1971 The Voluntary Principle in the Forming of American Religion in Elwyn Smith, ed. *The Religion of the Republic.* Philadelphia: Fortress Press.

Arieli, Yehoshua
  1966 *Individualism and Nationalism in American Ideology.* Baltimore, Md.: Penguin Books.

Bainton, Roland
  1968 Review of G. E. Swanson, *Religion and Regime: A Sociological Account of the Reformation. Journal of Church and State* Vol. 10, no. 3 (Autumn), pp. 445–47.

Baumgarten, Eduard
  1964 *Max Weber: Werk und Person.* Teubingen: Mohr (Siebeck).

Bec, Christian
  1967 *Les marchands écrivains á Florence.* The Hague: Martinus Nijhoff.
  1969 *Il libro degli affari proprii di casá di Lapo di Giovanni Niccolini de Sirigatti.* Paris: S.E.V.P.E.N.

Bellah, Robert N.
  1957 *Tokugawa Religion.* New York: The Free Press.
  1963 Reflections on the Protestant Ethic Analogy in Asia. In S. N. Eisenstadt, ed. 1968b: 243–51. Also in Bellah 1970. Originally published in 1965.
  1965 *Religion and Progress in Modern Asia,* ed. New York: The Free Press.
  1965a Ienaga Saburo and "The Search for Meaning in Modern Japan." In Marius E. Jansen, ed. *Changing Japanese Attitudes toward Modernization.* Princeton, N.J.: Princeton University Press.
  1965b Japan's Cultural Identity. *Journal of Asian Studies,* 24 (August): 573–93. Also in Bellah 1970.
  1965c Meaning and Modernization. See now Bellah 1970, 64–75. Originally published in 1965.

1965d   The Religious Situation in the Far East. *Harvard Divinity Bulletin:* 27ff. Also in Bellah 1970 : 100–113.

1970   *Beyond Belief.* New York : Harper & Row.

Bendix, Reinhard
1956   *Work and Authority in Industry: Ideologies of Management*
(1962)   *in the Course of Industrialization.* New York : Wiley. Also available as a Harper Torchbook.

1960   *Max Weber: An Intellectual Portrait.* Garden City, N.Y.: Doubleday. Also available in Doubleday-Anchor paperback edition.

1964   *Nation-Building and Citizenship.* New York : Wiley.

1968a   The Cultural and Political Setting of Economic Rationality in Western and Eastern Europe. In Bendix, ed. *State and Society: A Reader in Comparative Political Sociology.* Boston : Little, Brown and Company.

1968b   Max Weber. In D. Sills, ed. *International Encyclopedia of the Social Sciences,* Vol. 16. New York : Crowell-Collier and Macmillan.

1970   *Embattled Reason.* New York : Oxford University Press.

———, and Roth, Guenther
1971   *Scholarship and Partisanship: Essays on Max Weber.* Berkeley and Los Angeles, Calif.: University of California Press.

Berger, Stephen D.
1971   The Sects and the Breakthrough into the Modern World : On the Centrality of the Sects in Weber's Protestant Ethic Thesis. *Sociological Quarterly* 12 (Autumn) : 486–89.

Biéler, André
1959   *La pensée économique et sociale de Calvin.* Geneva : Librairie de l'Université.

Borkenau, Franz
1934   *Der Übergang von feudalen zum bürgerlichen Weltbild.* Paris : Librairie Felix Alcan.

Bouwsma, William J.
1968   Swanson's Reformation. *Comparative Studies in Society and History* 10 (July) : 486–91.

Brann, H. W.
1944   Max Weber and the United States. *Southwestern Social Science Quarterly* (June) : 18–30.

Brauer, Jerald C.
  1950 Puritan Mysticism and the Development of Liberalism.
        Church History 19 (September) : 151–70.
  1961 Images of Religion in America. *Church History* 30 (March) :
        2–16.

Burrell, Sidney A.
  1960 Calvinism, Capitalism, and the Middle Class: Some After-
        thoughts on an Old Problem. In S. N. Eisenstadt, ed. 1968b:
        135–54.
  1964 *The Role of Religion in Modern European History,* ed. New
        York: Macmillan.

Capéran, Louis
  1912 *Le problème du salut des infidèles.* Toulouse: Grande Sémin-
 (1934) aire. Original edition in 2 volumes.

Cardwell, Jerry D.
  1971 Multidimensional Measurements of Interfaith Commitment.
        Pacific Sociological Review 14 (January) : 79–88.

Carnegie, Andrew
  1962 *The Gospel of Wealth and Other Timely Essays.* Cambridge,
        Mass.: Harvard University Press.

Chodak, S.
        *Man, Political Systems and Development: Conclusions from
        Comparative Analysis.* Forthcoming.

Clagett, Marshall, Post, Gaines, and Reynolds, Robert, eds.
  1961 *Twelfth-Century Europe and the Foundations of Modern
        Society.* Madison, Wis.: University of Wisconsin Press.

Clark, S. D.
  1948 *Church and Sect in Canada.* Toronto: University of Toronto
 (1965) Press.

Demerath, N. J., III, and Hammond, Phillip E.
  1969 Protestantism and Capitalism—Two Developments in Search
        of a Relationship. Chapter 3 of Demerath and Hammond
        1969a: 80–114.
  1969a *Religion in Social Context: Tradition and Transition.* New
        York: Random House.

Dilthey, Wilhelm
    1966   *Einleitung in die Geisteswissenschaften: Versuch einer
            Grundlegung für das Studium der Gesellschaft und der
            Geschichte* 6th ed. Stuttgart: Teubner. Gesammelte Schrif-
            ten, Band I.

Eisenstadt, S. N.
    1965   Transformation of Social, Political, and Cultural Orders in
            Modernization. *American Sociological Review* 30: 659–73.
    1968a   The Protestant Ethic Thesis in an Analytical and Compara-
            tive Framework. In S. N. Eisenstadt, ed. 1968b: 3–45.
    1968b   *The Protestant Ethic and Modernization. A Comparative
            View.* New York: Basic Books, Inc. Authors excerpted in-
            clude H. Luethy, M. Walzer, S. A. Burrell, C. H. and K.
            George, R. N. Bellah, M. Ames, C. Geertz.

Fischoff, Ephraim
    1944   The Protestant Ethic and the Spirit of Capitalism: The His-
            tory of a Controversy. *Social Research* 2: 61–77.

Freund, Julien
    1966   *The Sociology of Max Weber.* Trans. Mary Ilford. New
            York: Random House-Pantheon. Original French ed. 1966.
            Cf. review by Nelson in *American Sociological Review* Vol.
            35, no. 3 (June 1970), pp. 549–50.

Fullerton, Kemper
    1928   Calvinism and Capitalism. *Harvard Theological Review* 21:
            163–95.

Gadol, Joan
    1969   *Leon Battista Alberti: Universal Man of the Early Renais-
            sance.* Chicago: University of Chicago Press.

Gaustad, Edwin S.
    1968   *The Great Awakening in New England.* Chicago: Quad-
            rangle.

Geertz, Clifford
    1968   *Islam Observed: Religious Development in Morocco and
            Indonesia.* New Haven, Conn.: Yale University Press.

George, Charles H., and George, Katharine
    1961   *The Protestant Mind of the English Reformation, 1570–1640.*
            Princeton, N.J.: Princeton University Press.

Gerschenkron, Alexander
   1968   *Continuity in History and Other Essays.* Cambridge, Mass.:
          Harvard University Press (Belknap).

Gerth, Hans, and Mills, C. Wright
   1953   *Character and Social Structure.* New York: Harcourt Brace
          Jovanovich.

Glock, Charles Y., and Stark, Rodney
   1965   *Religion and Society in Tension.* Chicago: Rand McNally.

Goldschmidt, Levin
   1891   *Universalgeschichte des Handelsrechts,* Vol. I. Stuttgart:
          Enke.

Goldstein, Bernice, and Eichhorn, Robert L.
   1961   The Changing Protestant Ethic: Rural Patterns in Health,
          Work and Leisure. *American Sociological Review* 26 (Au-
          gust): 557–65.

Gollin, Gillian L.
   1967   *Moravians in Two Worlds.* New York: Columbia University
          Press.

Gothein, Eberhard
   1889   *Die Aufgaben der Kulturgeschichte.* Leipzig: Duncker und
          Humblot.
   1892   *Wirtschaftsgeschichte des Schwarzwaldes.* 2 vols. Stras-
          bourg: K. J. Trübner.
   1895   *Ignatius von Loyola und die Gegenreformation.* Halle: Max
          Neimeyer.
   1908   "Staat und Gesellschaft des Zeitalters der Gegenreforma-
          tion." In Staat und Gesellschaft in der Neuernzeit. Teil II,
          Abteilung V, I, Der Kultur der Gegenwart.

Greeley, Andrew
   1964   The Protestant Ethic: Time for a Moratorium. *Sociological
          Analysis* 25 (Spring): 20–33.

Griswold, A. Whitney
   1934   Three Puritans on Prosperity. *New England Quarterly* 7
          (September): 475–93.

Groethuysen, Bernard
   1927– *Die Enstehung der bürgerlichen Welt-und Lebensan-*
   1930   *schauung in Frankreich.* 2 vols. Halle.
   1968   *The Bourgeois: Catholicism vs. Capitalism.* Introduction by
          B. Nelson. New York: Holt, Rinehart and Winston.

Grossmann, Henryk
    1935   Die gesellschaftlichen Grundlagen der mechanistischen Phi-
            losophie und die Manufaktur. *Zeitschrift für Sozialforschung*
            4 : 161–231.

Hagan, E.
    1962   *On the Theory of Social Change.* Homewood, Ill.: Dorsey
            Press.

Hall, A. R.
    1963   Merton Revisited or Science and Society in the Seventeenth
            Century. *History of Science* 2 : 1–15.

Hammond, P. E., and Johnson, B., eds.
    1970   *American Mosaic: Social Patterns of Religion in the United
            States.* New York: Random House.

Hansen, Niles M.
    1963   The Protestant Ethic as a General Precondition for Eco-
            nomic Development. *Canadian Journal of Economics and
            Political Science* 29 (November) : 462–74.

Hertz, Karl H.
    1962   Max Weber and American Puritanism. *Journal of the Scien-
            tific Study of Religion* 1 : 189–97.

Hill, Christopher
    1961   Protestantism and the Rise of Capitalism. In F. J. Fisher,
            ed. *Essays in the Economic and Social History of Tudor and
            Stuart England.* New York: Cambridge University Press.

Honigsheim, Paul
    1914   *Die Staats und Soziallenhnen der französischen Jansenisten
            im 17ten Jahrhundert.* Heidelberg: Historical Dissertation.
    1968   *On Max Weber.* Trans. Joan Rytina. New York: The Free
            Press.

Hudson, Winthrop
    1949   Puritanism and the Rise of Capitalism. *Church History* 18 :
            3–17.
    1961   The Weber Thesis Reexamined. *Church History* 30 : 88–99.

Hughes, E. C.
    1910   See Max Weber 1910a.

Jardim, Anne
    1970   *The First Henry Ford.* Cambridge, Mass.: Massachusetts
            Institute of Technology Press.

Jellinek, G.
    1895   *Die Erklärung der Menschen-und Burgerrechts.* Munich:
            Duncker and Humbolt.
    1901   *The Declaration of the Rights of Man and of Citizens: A
            Contribution of Modern Constitutional History.* Trans. of
            1895. New York: Holt, Rinehart and Winston.

Johnson, B.
    1964   Ascetic Protestantism and Political Preference in the Deep
            South. *American Journal of Sociology* 69 (January): 359–
            66.
    1966   Theology and Party Preference among Protestant Clergy-
            men. *American Sociological Review* 31 (April): 200–8. Re-
            printed in Hammond and Johnson 1970: 242–54.

Kakar, Sudhir
    1970   *Frederick Taylor: A Study in Personality and Innovation.*
            Cambridge, Mass.: Massachusetts Institute of Technology
            Press.

Kingdon, Robert M.
    1969   Review of G. E. Swanson, *Religion and Regime. American
            Sociological Review* 34 (January): 843.

Koenig, René, and Winckelmann, J., eds.
    1963   *Max Weber zum Gedächtnis.* Köln und Opladen: Westdeut-
            scher Verlag. Constitutes Kölner Zeitschrift für Soziologie
            und Sozialpsychologie hgb. von René Koenig. Sonderheft 7.

Kovel, Joel
    1971   The Right Neuroses at the Right Time. Review of books on
            H. Ford and F. W. Taylor by A. Jardim and S. Kakar,
            respectively. *New York Times Book Review,* February 14,
            p. 5.

Lenski, Gerhard
    1961   *The Religious Factor: A Sociological Study of Religion's
            Impact on Politics, Economics, and Family Life.* New York:
            Doubleday. Rev. ed. 1963. Garden City, N.Y.: Doubleday-
            Anchor.
    1971   The Religious Factor in Detroit, Revisited. *American So-
            ciological Review* 36 (February): 48–50.

Letwin, William
    1963   *The Origins of Scientific Economics: English Economic
            Thought 1660–1776.* London: Methuen.

Lipset, S. M.
　　1967　*The First New Nation.* Garden City, N.Y.: Doubleday-
　　　　　　Anchor. 1st ed. 1963. New York: Basic Books, Inc.
　　———, and Bendix, R., eds.
　　1960　*Social Mobility in Industrial Society.* Berkeley and Los
　　　　　　Angeles Calif.: University of California Press.
　　———, and Solari, Aldo
　　1967　*Elites in Latin America.* New York: Oxford University
　　　　　　Press.

Little, David
　　1966　Max Weber Revisited: The "Protestant Ethic" and the
　　　　　　Puritan Experience of Order. *Harvard Theological Review*
　　　　　　59: 415–28.
　　1969　*Religion, Order and Law: A Study in Pre-Revolutionary
　　　　　　England.* Introduction by R. Bellah. New York: Harper &
　　　　　　Row.

Loewith, Karl
　　1923　Max Weber und Karl Marx. In K. Loewith. *Gesammelte*
　　(1960)　*Abhandlungen.* Stuttgart: Kohlhammer.

Loubser, Jan
　　1963　Puritanism and Liberty: A Study in Normative Change in
　　　　　　Massachusetts, 1630–1850. Dissertation on deposit in Har-
　　　　　　vard University Library, Cambridge, Massachusetts.
　　1968　Calvinism, Equality and Inclusion: The Case of Afrikaaner
　　　　　　Calvinism. In S. N. Eisenstadt ed. 1968: 367–83.

Luethy, Herbert
　　1959　*Le Banque Protestante en France de la Révocation de l'Édit
　　　　　　de Nantes à la Revolution.* 2 vols. Affaires et Gens d'Affaires
　　　　　　19, 1–2. Paris: S.E.V.P.E.N.
　　1964　Once Again: Calvin and Capitalism. *Encounter Magazine* 124
　　　　　　(January): 26–38.
　　　　　　See B. Nelson 1964b.
　　1965　Max Weber—Luethy's Reply (to Benjamin Nelson). *En-
　　　　　　counter Magazine* 136 (January): 92–94.
　　1970　*From Calvin to Rousseau.* New York: Basic Books, Inc.

MacIntyre, Alasdair
　　1967　*Secularization and Moral Change.* London: Oxford Univer-
　　　　　　sity Press. The Riddell Memorial Lectures, 36th Series,
　　　　　　delivered at the University of Newcastle upon Tyne, Novem-
　　　　　　ber 11, 12, and 13, 1964.

Mack, R. W., Murphy, R. J., and Yellin, S.
  1956 The Protestant Ethic. Level of Aspiration, and Social Mobil-
         ity. *American Sociological Review* 21 (June) : 295–300.

Magendie, M.
  1925 *La politesse mondaine et les théories de l'honnêteté en
         France, au 17me siècle, de 1600–1660.* 2 vols. Paris: Librairie
         Felix Alcan.

Martindale, D.
  1966 Prefatory Remarks. In Weber. *The City*. New York: The
         Free Press: 9–62.

Masur, Gerhard
  1961 *Prophets of Yesterday.* New York: Macmillan. Also avail-
         able in paper as a Harper Colophon Book, 1966.

Mayer, Albert J., and Sharp, Harry
  1962 Religious Preference and Worldly Success. *American So-
         ciological Review* 27 (April) : 218–27.

McClelland, David C.
  1961 *The Achieving Society.* Princeton, N.J.: Van Nostrand.

McIntosh, Donald
  1970 Weber and Freud: On the Nature and Sources of Authority.
         American Sociological Review 35 (October) : 901–11.

Mead, Sidney
  1963 *The Lively Experiment.* New York: Harper & Row.

Means, Richard L.
  1970 Methodology for the Sociology of Religion: An Historical
         and Theoretical Overview. *Sociological Analysis* 31 (Win-
         ter) : 180–96.

Merton, R. K.
  1938 Social Structure and Anomie. Now available with continu-
         ities in R. K. Merton 1968a: 185–248.
  1968a *Social Theory and Social Structure.* Enlarged ed. New
         York: The Free Press. Originally published in 1949.
  1970 *Science, Technology and Society in Seventeenth-Century
         England.* New Introduction by the author. New York:
         Harper Torchbooks. Original publication 1938.

Miller, Perry
  1956 *Errand to the Wilderness.* Cambridge, Mass.: Harvard Uni-
         versity Press.

1967   *Nature's Nation.* Cambridge, Mass.: Harvard University Press (Belknap).

Mitzman, Arthur
1969   *The Iron Cage: An Historical Interpretation of Max Weber.* New York: Knopf.

Mommsen, W.
1965a   Universalgeschtliches und politisches Denken bei Max Weber. *Historische Zeitschrift* 201 (December): 557–612.
1965b   Max Weber's Political Sociology and His Philosophy of World History. *International Social Science Journal* 27: 23–45.

Morgan, Edmund
1963   Review of K. Samuelsson, *Religion and Economic Action. William and Mary Quarterly,* Series 3, no. 18 (January) pp. 135–40.

Nelson, Benjamin
1949   *The Idea of Usury: From Tribal Brotherhood to Universal Otherhood.* Princeton, N.J.: Princeton University Press. 2d enlarged ed. Chicago: University of Chicago Press and Phoenix Books, 1969. 2d ed. includes following additions: "After Two Decades: Notice to Readers," New Postscript, New Annotated References, New Acknowledgments.
1962   Review of K. Samuelsson, *Religion and Economic Action. American Sociological Review* 27 (December): 856.
1964   Max Weber's The Protestant Ethic: 1904–64. Abstracts of Papers, 59th Annual Meeting, American Sociological Association. Montreal, Canada 1964.
1964a   Religion and Development. In T. Geiger and L. Solomon, eds. *Proceedings of the Sixth World Conference, Society for International Development.*
1964b   In Defense of Max Weber. Rely to Herbert Luethy. *Encounter Magazine* 131 (August): 94–95.
1965a   Self-Images and Systems of Spiritual Direction in the History of European Civilization. In S. Z. Klausner, ed. *The Quest for Self-Control.* New York: The Free Press.
1965b   Probabilists, Anti-Probabilists, and the Quest for Certitude in the 16th and 17th Centuries. In *Actes du Xme Congrès internationale d'histoire des sciences (Proceedings of the 10th International Congress for the History of Science),* Vol. 1. Paris: Hermann.

1965c   Max Weber's The Sociology of Religion: A Review Article. *American Sociological Review* 30 (August) : 595–99.

1967   Casuistry. In Encyclopaedia Britannica, Vol. VI. Reprinted from 1963 ed.

1968a   The Early Modern Revolution in Science and Philosophy: Fictionalism, Probabilism, Fideism, and Catholic "Prophetism." In R. S. Cohen and M. Wartofsky, eds. *Boston Studies in the Philosophy of Science,* 3. Dordrecht, Holland: D. Reidel.

1968b   Scholastic *Rationales* of "Conscience," Early Modern Crises of Credibility and the Scientific Technocultural Revolutions of the 17th and 20th Centuries. *Journal for the Scientific Study of Religion* 7 (Fall) : 155–77.

1968c   Introduction. In Bernard Groethuysen. *The Bourgeois: Catholicism vs. Capitalism in Eighteenth Century France.* New York: Holt, Rinehart and Winston.

1969   *Conscience* and the Making of Early Modern Cultures: The *Protestant Ethic* beyond Weber. *Social Research* 36 (Spring) : 4–21.

1970   See J. Freund 1968.

1970a   Theologies, Sciences, Machines, Faiths: Historic Encounters since the Middle Ages. Paper delivered at United Presbyterian-American Jewish Committee Colloquium on Judaism and Christianity View the Technological Future, February, Princeton, N.J.

1970b   On the Roads to Modernity: "Conscience," Casuistry, and the Quest for Certitude. Paper presented to the American Historical Association, December, Boston. Manuscript forthcoming.

1971a   The Medieval Canon Law of Contracts, Renaissance "Spirit of Capitalism," and the Reformation "Conscience": A Vote *for* Max Weber. In R. B. Palmer and R. Hamerton-Kelly, eds. *Philomathes: Studies and Essays in the Humanities in Honor of Philip Merlan.* The Hague: Nijhoff.

1971b   Conscience, Casuistry, Crises of Credibility, and Quests for Certitude: From Abelard to Galileo. Paper presented to Sixth Conference of Medieval Studies, May, Kalamazoo, Mich. Manuscript forthcoming.

1971c   Communities, Societies, Civilizations: Post-Millennial Views on the Masks and Faces of Change. In M. Stanley, ed. *Social Development: Critical Perspectives.* New York: Basic Books, Inc. In press. Originally presented to the Symposium on Frontier Issues on Social Development Theories, April 1969, Syracuse, N.Y.

1971d   McIntosh on Weber and Freud. Manuscript forthcoming.

1971e   Max Weber on Race and Society, I. Trans. J. Gittleman. Ed. and intro. B. Nelson. *Social Research* Vol. 38, no. 1 (Spring), pp. 30–41.

1971–72 E. Durkheim and M. Mauss, Note on the Notion of Civilization (1912). Trans. and intro. B. Nelson. *Social Research* Vol. 38, no. 4 (Winter 1971), pp. 808–13.

1972   On R. K. Merton, *Science, Technology, Society* . . . A Review-Article. *American Journal of Sociology* July 1972, in press. Cf. Merton, 1970.

O'Dea, Thomas F.

1970   The Sociology of Religion Reconsidered. *Sociological Analysis* 31 (Fall) : 145–52.

Parsons, Talcott

1928–29 "Capitalism" in Recent German Literature. Sombart and Weber. *Journal of Political Economy* 36 (December) : 641–61; 37 (February) : 31–51.

1935   H. M. Robertson on Max Weber and His School. *Journal of Political Economy* 43 : 688–96.

1949   *Essays in Sociological Theory.* New York : The Free Press.

1958   Introduction. See Weber 1958.

1962   Address. Proceedings of the Hazen International Conference on the Sociology of Religion, Washington, D.C.

1963   Introduction. In translation of Max Weber. *The Sociology of Religion.* Boston : Beacon Press.

1967a   Christianity and Modern Industrial Society. In E. A. Tiryakian, ed. 1967. Originally published in 1963.

1968   *The Structure of Social Action.* 2 vols. New York : The Free Press. 1st ed., 1937. New York : McGraw-Hill.

1968a   Christianity. In D. Sills, ed. *International Encyclopedia of the Social Sciences,* Vol. 2. New York : Macmillan.

———, Shils, E., Naegele, K., and Pitts, J., eds.

1961   *Theories of Society.* 2 vols. New York : The Free Press.

Pirenne, Henri

1903   *Histoire économique de l'occident médiéval.* Bruges : Desclée de Brouwer.

1914   The Stages in the Social History of Capitalism. *American Historical Review* 19 : 494–515.

1956   *Economic and Social History of Medieval Europe.* Trans. I. E. Clegg. New York: Harcourt Brace Jovanovich. Originally published 1936, London.

Pope, Liston
1948   Religion and the Class Structure. *Annals of the American Academy of Political and Social Science* 156 (March) : 84–91.

Renouard, Yves
1949   *Les hommes d'affaires italiens au moyen âge.* Paris: Colin. 2d rev. ed., 1969. English trans. in progress by B. Nelson and collaborators.

Riesman, David, Denney, Reuel, and Glazer, Nathan
1952   *The Lonely Crowd: A Study of the Changing American Character.* New Haven, Conn.: Yale University Press. Also available in paper from Doubleday-Anchor.

Ringer, Fritz R.
1969   *The Decline of the German Mandarins: The German Academic Community, 1890–1933.* Cambridge, Mass.: Harvard University Press.

Rischin, Moses, ed. and intro.
1965   *The American Gospel of Success: Individualism and Beyond.* Chicago: Quadrangle Books.

Robertson, H. M.
1933   *Aspects of the Rise of Economic Individualism: A Criticism of Max Weber and His School.* New York: Cambridge Univiersity Press.

Robertson, Roland
1970   *The Sociological Interpretation of Religion.* New York: Schocken Books.

Rosen, Bernard C.
1959   Race, Ethnicity, and the Achievement Syndrome. *American Sociological Review* 24 (February) : 47–60.

Rostow, W. W.
1960   *The Stages of Economic Growth. A Non-Communist Manifesto.* New York: Cambridge University Press.
1963   *The Economics of Take-off into Sustained Growth,* ed. New York: St. Martin's Press.

Samuelsson, K.
    1961   *Religion and Economic Action: A Critique of Max Weber.*
           Trans. E. G. French. New York: Basic Books, Inc. Paper-
           bound edition, New York: Harper Torchbooks, 1964.

Scheler, Max
    1964   The Thomist Ethic and the Spirit of Capitalism. Trans.
           G. Neuwirth. *Sociological Analysis* 25 (Spring): 4–19.

Schneider, Louis
    1970   *Sociological Approach to Religion.* Toronto: Wiley.
    1970   The Sociology of Religion: Some Areas of Theoretical Po-
           tential. *Sociological Analysis* 31 (Fall): 131–44.

Schuman, Howard
    1971   The Religious Factor in Detroit: Review, Replication and
           Reanalysis. *American Sociological Review* 36 (February):
           30–48.

Sée, Henri E.
    1928   *Modern Capitalism. Its Origin and Evolution.* Trans. H. B.
           Vanderblue and G. Doriot. New York: Augustus M. Kelley.

Shiner, L.
    1967   The Concept of Secularization in Empirical Research. *Jour-*
           nal for the Scientific Study of Religion 6 (Fall): 207–20.

Siegelman, Philip
    1964   Religion and Economic Activity: The Chettiars of Madras.
           In T. Geiger and L. Solomon, eds. *Motivations and Methods*
           in Development and Foreign Aid: Proceedings of the Sixth
           World Conference, Society for International Development.
           March 16–18, Washington, D.C.

Speier, Hans
    1935   Honor and the Social Structure. *Social Research* 2 (Febru-
  (1952) ary): 74–97. Reprinted in H. Speier, *Social Order and the*
           Risks of War: Papers on Political Sociology. New York:
           Stewart.

Sombart, Werner
    1915   *The Quintessence of Capitalism. A Study of the History and*
           Psychology of the Modern Business Man. New York: E. P.
           Dutton.

1951   *The Jews and Modern Capitalism.* Trans. M. Epstein. Biblio-
        graphical Note prepared in association with B. Nelson. New
        York: The Free Press.
1967   *Luxury and Capitalism.* Introduction by Philip Siegelman.
(1913) Ann Arbor, Mich.: University of Michigan Press. Originally
        published as *Luxus und Kapitalismus.* Munich: Duncker and
        Humblot.

Stammer, Otto, ed.
1965   *Max Weber und die Soziologie heute. Verhandlungen des
        fünfzehnten deutschen Soziologentages.* Teubingen: Mohr
        (Siebeck). Includes relevant papers and statements by
        T. Parsons, H. Marcuse, R. Bendix, B. Nelson, D. Gold-
        schmidt, and others.

Steding, C.
1938   *Das Reich und die Krankheit der europäischen Kultur.* Ham-
        burg: Hanseatische Verlagsanstalt.

Swanson, Guy
1960   *The Birth of the Gods.* Ann Arbor, Mich.: University of
        Michigan Press.
1967   *Religion and Regime: A Sociological Account of the Ref-
        ormation.* Ann Arbor, Mich.: University of Michigan Press.

Tawney, R. H.
1958   *Religion and the Rise of Capitalism. A Historical Study.*
        New York: New American Library.

Taylor, Frederick Winslow
1947   *Scientific Management.* New York: Harper & Row.

Thorner, Isidor
1953   Ascetic Protestantism and the Development of Science and
        Technology. *The American Journal of Sociology* 58 (July
        1952–May 1953): 25–33.

Tillich, Paul
1932   *The Religious Situation.* New York: Holt, Rinehart and
        Winston.

Tiryakian, E. A., ed.
1967   *Sociological Theory, Values and Sociocultural Change. Es-
        says in Honor of Pitirim A. Sorokin.* New York: Harper
        Torchbooks.

Tolles, F. B.
    1945   Quietism vs. Enthusiasm, The Philadelphia Quaker, and the
           Great Awakening. *Pennsylvania Magazine of History and
           Biography* 69 (January) : 26–49.
    1947   Benjamin Franklin's Business Mentors: The Philadelphia
           Quaker. *William and Mary Quarterly* 4 (January) : 40–69.
    1948   *Meeting House and Counting House.* Chapel Hill, N.C. :
           University of North Carolina Press.

Trevor-Roper, Hugh
    1968   *The Crisis of the Seventeenth Century.* New York : Harper
           & Row.

Troeltsch, Ernst
    1912   *The Social Teaching of the Christian Churches.* 2 vols. Trans.
  (1960) Olive Wyon. New York : Macmillan. Paperbound edition
           available from Harper & Row.
    1912   *Protestantism and Progress.* Trans. W. Montgomery. New
  (1958) York : Putnam. New edition, Boston : Beacon Press.

Turner, Victor W.
    1968   *The Ritual Process: Structure and Anti-Structure.* Chicago :
           Aldine.

Vallier, I.
    1967   Religious Elites: Differentiations and Developments in
           Roman Catholicism. In S. M. Lipset and A. Solari (1967) :
           190–232.
    1969   Comparative Studies of Roman Catholicism: Dioceses as
           Strategic Units. *Social Compass* 16 : 147–84.
    1970   *Catholicism, Social Control, and Modernization in Latin
           America.* Englewood Cliffs, N.J. : Prentice-Hall.

Veroff, Joseph, Feld, Sheila, and Gurin, Gerald
    1962   Achievement, Motivation and Religious Background. *Ameri-
           can Sociological Review* 27 (April) : 205–17.

Walzer, Michael
    1965   *The Revolution of the Saints: A Study in the Origins of
           Radical Politics.* Cambridge, Massachusetts : Harvard Uni-
           versity Press.

Watt, Ian
    1965   *The Rise of the Novel.* Berkeley and Los Angeles, Calif. :
           University of California Press.

Weber, Max

1904–1905   *Die protestantische Ethik und der Geist des Kapitalis-*
(tr. 1930   *nus. Archiv für Sozialwissenschaft und Sozialpolitik*
and 1958)   XX–XXI. *The Protestant Ethic and the Spirit of Capitalism.* Trans. with an Introduction and New Preface
by Talcott Parsons. New York: Scribner's.

1908   The Protestant Sects and the Spirit of Capitalism. Chapter
12 in Weber 1946.

1910a   Diskussionsrede zu E. Troeltsch's "Vortrag uber 'Das
stoischchristliche Naturrecht.' " In Weber 1924 : 462–70.

1910b   Proposal for Sociological Study of Voluntary Associations.
Trans. of Weber, Geschäftsbericht. From *Verhandlungen
des ersten deutschen Soziologentages von 19–22 Oktober,
1910.* Frankfurt. Teubingen.

1920a   *Gesammelte Aufsätze zur Religionssoziologie.* 3 vols. Teu-
(1922–23)
bingen: Mohr (Siebeck).

1920b   Author's Introduction. *The Protestant Ethic and the Spirit
of Capitalism.* Trans. Talcott Parsons. New York: Scribner's. Originally appeared posthumously in *Gesammelte
Aufsätze zur Religionssoziologie.*

1922   *The Sociology of Religion.* Trans. Ephraim Fischoff. Intro-
(tr. 1964)
duction by Talcott Parsons. Boston: Beacon Press.

1922   *Max Weber on Law in Economy and Society.* Trans. Edward
(1954)   Shils and Max Rheinstein. Cambridge, Mass.: Harvard
University Press.

1924   *Gesammelte Aufsätze zur Soziologie und Sozialpolitik.* Teubingen: Mohr (Siebeck).

1946   *From Max Weber: Essays in Sociology.* Trans. H. Gerth and
C. W. Mills. New York: Oxford University Press.

1956   *Economy and Society.* 3 vols. Eds. G. Roth and C. Wittich.
(tr. 1968)
Trans. G. Roth and C. Wittich. Totowa, N.J.: Bedminster
Press.

1956   *Soziologie—Weltgeschichtliche   Analysen—Politik.*   Ed.
J. Winckelmann. Introduction by E. Baumgarten. Includes
a helpful chronology of Weber's career and a systematic
bibliography of his writings. Stuttgart: A. Kroener.

1958   *The Rational and Social Foundations of Music.* Carbondale,
(1969)   Ill.: Southern Illinois University Press. Paperback edition
available from Arcturus Books.

1922   *General Economic History*. Trans. F. H. Knight. Last chap-
(tr. 1966)
        ter, The Evolution of the Capitalist Spirit, is especially rele-
        vant here.
1968   *Methodologische Schriften*. Frankfurt am Main: S. Fischer
        Verlag.

Whitehead, A. N.
1968   *Science and the Modern World* (Lowell Lectures 1925). New
        York: New American Library.

Whyte, William H., Jr.
1956   *The Organization of Man*. New York: Simon and Schuster.

Wilson, Bryan
1961   *Sects and Society*. Berkeley and Los Angeles, Calif.: Uni-
        versity of California Press.

Winckelmann, Johannes, ed.
1956   See Weber 1956.
1963   See Koenig and Winckelmann 1963.
1968   *Max Weber: Die protestantische Ethik, II: Kritiken und
        Anti-kritiken*. Munich.
1969   *Max Weber: Die protestantische Ethik, I*. 2d enlarged ed.
        Munich.

Wrong, Dennis, ed.
1970   *Max Weber*. Englewood Cliffs, N.J.: Prentice-Hall.

3 THE IMPLICATIONS OF WEBER'S SOCIOLOGY OF RELIGION FOR UNDERSTANDING PROCESSES OF CHANGE IN CONTEMPORARY NON-EUROPEAN SOCIETIES AND CIVILIZATIONS

S. N. Eisenstadt

I

Weber's studies of non-European (or non-Christian) religions constitute the largest part of his *Sociology of Religion*, comprising most of the *Aufsätze zur Religionsoziologie* (1920–23), as well as large parts of his treatment in *Wirtschaft und Gesellschaft* (1956).[1] Included, as is well known, are relatively full-blown studies of Jewish, Chinese (Confucian), and Indian (Hindu and Buddhist) civilizations and more dispersed but very rich appraisals of diverse aspects of other religions. These studies are focused on the internal dynamics of religions and on their relations to crucial aspects of social structure, especially political organization, economic life, and social stratification.

Quantitatively, these studies of the non-Christian religions comprise a much larger part of Weber's work than his analysis

[1] The complete collection is now available in English translation. See Weber (1930, 1946, 1952, 1958, 1964).

of Christian religion in general and of Protestantism in particular. And yet, they seem to be mostly—if not only—a derivative of his concern with the Protestant ethic thesis. This is most clearly evident in the analysis contained in the *Aufsätze zur Religionsoziologie* (1920–23) which seeks to explain why these religions or civilizations—the Jewish, Chinese, and Indian— have not given rise to that type of orientation which generated the development of modern rationalism in general and modern capitalism (and also modern bureaucracy) in particular.

This question is especially pertinent for Weber because all these "great civilizations" or religions—and also, by inference, Catholic Europe and to some extent Japan and Islam, with which he deals only passingly—have developed many of the structural characteristics or preconditions of capitalism.

His well-known answer to this problem, as put forward in the essay on the Protestant ethic (1930), was that in Europe it was the specific type of this-worldly religious orientation which developed out of the Protestant (especially Calvinist) ethic that provided, *from a broad comparative point of view*, the potential push to such developments.

Accordingly, he attempted, then, to analyze the various non-European religions or civilizations to see what it was in the structure of their beliefs, orientations, and organization that prevented them, as it were, from generating the same type of push toward what nowadays would be called modernization. He found it, as is well known, in the respective *Wirtschaftethik* of these different religions.

II

The general lines of his argument in this respect are rather well known, and we can follow Parsons (1937), Bendix (1960), and, more recently, Warner (1970) in summarizing them. In general Weber judged that religions may influence the direction of such *Wirtschaftsethik* in three basic ways: (1) religious prescriptions of conduct, especially the more realistic ones, could have a direct impact on economic activities; (2) religious ideas could be a source for the legitimization of social and political institutions;

and (3) through religious sanctioning, human motivations and interests might be channelled in the direction of different types of goals.

Thus, with regard to China, he depicted Confucianism as containing a utilitarian and worldly ethic whose practical precepts are without a metaphysical foundation and are concerned with peoples' conduct in this life for its own sake. The hereafter is disregarded except for the imperative of leaving this world with a good and honored name.

The Confucian *Weltanschauung* depicts an ordered cosmos and world which is extended to a belief in the "sacred" structure of the state. Great value is placed on classical literary education. Socially there is the overriding injunction to honor and obey the head of the family: an injunction which extends from the emperor to the mandarins, to the artisans in cities away from the ancestral villages, and so forth. The acceptance of order, static learning, and filial piety is essentially conservative and preserving of a social structure at an early stage of development, that is, a society which is pervasively traditionalistic.

In the economic sphere these and other elements of Chinese society mediate against the development of a capitalist economy. The extended kinship groups function as protective associations by defending the "individual member against economic adversities in his relations with landlords, moneylenders and employers. . . ." The sale of land is made difficult by the central government or the family. The prevailing ethic of becoming a universal person by studying the classics precludes specialization and the acquisition of new knowledge. The particularistic tradition of Confucianism precludes a universalism needed to institute natural law. Finally, capitalism is prevented due to the Confucian tolerance of the masses' interpretation of Taoism's mystical contemplative doctrine: as magical superstition arises among the masses, technical inventions are opposed in the belief that they will disturb ancestral spirits. Indeed, the emotional satisfaction which magic gives to the people is used by Confucians to defend the social order against reforms as well as against dictatorship by the emperor.

In India the Hindu *Weltanschauung* is based on the beliefs in transmigration (each soul exists perpetually and passes through

an unending series of rebirths) and in ethical compensation
(each act has an immutable effect on the actor's soul). Tied to
these beliefs is the additional one of "dharma," the duty to
continue the prescribed tradition of one's caste so as to improve
chances of reincarnation into a higher caste. Thus, the real interest of the individual lies not in upsetting the system but in
improving one's caste in the next life.

Orthodox Hinduism excludes the possibility of a personal
transcendental god-creator. God is to be found within the order,
and thus the explanation of the universe justifies the existing
social system. Popular Hindu belief in a pantheon of gods develops as a concession to the need for a personal god. Different
gods become the inspiration for the emergence of sects which are
taught by gurus (teachers), some of whom later become so
revered by the people (despite their lack of knowledge of San-
skrit) that they overshadow the status of Brahmins. Neither
such gurus nor the Brahmins, however, seek an improved caste
status (although they could have become gods) but rather "salvation"—a permanent escape from the worldly existence by
mysticism or asceticism.

Buddhism, which at one time held dominance in India, carries
the contemplative life and other-worldly orientation to a further
extreme. Without sanctioning any social system, Buddhists are
ideologically anticaste; the egalitarian principle is used by con-
querors to popularize the religion. However, the religion's commitment to contemplation, to dispassionate intellectual discourse,
and to the belief that the layman could do his best toward
salvation only by supporting monks are scarcely supportive of
upturning existing social arrangements. As a result, the caste
system has been effectively retained during both Buddhism's
ascendency and decline as a major religious force in Indian life.

The caste system, according to Weber, originated and spread
for several reasons. The conquest of the Indian subcontinent by
the Aryans created a color line with typical disdain of the in-
vader for intermarrying with the natives, as well as differentiation of tasks and tax collection from the natives. The Hinduiza-
tion of tribes which possessed varied occupations and degrees of
wealth and territory also augmented the caste system. The

resulting subdivision of existing castes had the effect of further elaborating the system.

Weber sees the caste system as insulating the Indian people from the political realm; its tenets effectively freeze economic development as well. While craft and merchant guilds emerge and trading, war material, tax farming, and the like contribute to the initial stage of capitalism, these developments are hampered by the immobility imposed by caste on vocational choice and on place of residence. Again, the imperative of attaining salvation through the performance of traditional acts and the deprecation of this world effectively prohibits the emergence of the capitalist system.

But however much his analyses of the non-Christian religions were geared to issues bearing on the Protestant ethic, Weber also undertook in his comparative studies very detailed investigations of many other aspects of these civilizations and their religions. In so doing, he provided a much fuller analysis of their origin, structure, and development than he did of Protestantism (or Catholicism). Moreover, as shall be seen in greater detail later, his comparative work also went beyond some of the analytical concepts and emphases which he developed in the *Aufsätze* (1920–23) and even beyond some of the richer analytical concepts and problems which he has developed in the chapters devoted to the analysis of religion in *Wirtschaft und Gesellschaft* (1956).

III

Given Weber's own emphasis on the analysis of the non-European religions from the perspective of the Protestant ethic thesis, including his stress on the ''Wirtschaftsethik'' of these various religions, it is not surprising that most of the initial criticism or exegeses of Weber's analysis focused on these problems. It is only much later that the broader implications of Weber's work for the study of modernization are given wide-spread attention. To understand the development of the studies which take up from Weber's analysis of non-European religion, it is necessary first to survey briefly the development of the response to the Protestant ethic thesis itself.

In another place I have traced two stages in the controversy about this thesis (Eisenstadt 1968: 3–45). In the first stage Weber was understood to be claiming a direct causal relation between the rise of Protestantism (and especially Calvinism) and the development of capitalism (and in other places in Weber's version, of modern institutions in general). But as the comparative studies began to be published and the initial work on the Protestant ethic came to be more widely known, it was recognized—even if often only gradually and intermittently—that this is not the correct interpretation of Weber's thesis. In this second stage Weber was conceived of as dealing with the *transformative* potentialities of Calvinism, that is, its possibility to create from within itself new types of orientations and activities, after the failure of its initial totalistic socioreligious orientations and types of formal organization.

This shift to the analysis of the transformative capacities of religion pointed to the possibility that, under certain conditions, different religions may foster new types of activities which go beyond the original *Wirtschaftsethik,* that is, that there may take place a transformation of the original religious impulses which may, in turn, lead to far-reaching changes in social life and institutional organization.

This interpretation of Weber's work with its emphasis on the transformative potential of religion on individual behavior and social organization in particular has been of special importance when attempts are made to draw a comparative implication from Weber's analysis.

IV

The evaluation of Weber's analysis of non-Christian religions has to a degree paralleled the stages of controversy around the Protestant ethic thesis.

The first stage is characterized by a detailed exposition and criticism of Weber's analysis, first of his exposition of the respective *Wirtschaftsethik* of these religions or civilizations and second, of his more general analysis of the major institutional aspects of these religions and their repercussions on historical development.

Here mention may be made of the older work of Julius Guttman (1925), which provides a very detailed, and on the whole, only partially favorable criticism of Weber's analysis of Judaism. Guttman judges that Weber overemphasizes the importance of the distinction between prophetic and rabbinical Judaism. He also finds unacceptable Weber's contention that there developed a tendency in postexilic religious orientations toward a double standard of morality in economic activities for inside and outside groups. Weber's conception of a pariah religion also draws Guttman's criticism.

More recently J. Katz (1961: 72–75) in his work on traditional Jewish society briefly analyzes Weber's evaluation of the different types of religious sanctioning of economic activities. Largely following Weber, Katz notes that Jewish religion did not negate the pursuit of mundane affairs. Moreover, its tradition of learning greatly facilitated the development of a rational attitude toward such pursuit. At the same time, however, Katz points out, economic activities were never sanctioned in religious terms as the *central* dimension of human endeavor. (See also F. Raphaël [1970] for an even more recent overall evaluation of Weber's analysis of ancient Judaism.)

As to Weber's work on China and Confucianism, the most important evaluators are O. Van der Sprenkel (1964) and C. K. Yang (1964). Both acknowledge the overall validity of Weber's analysis of Chinese civilization in general and of Confucianism in particular, a feat made all the more remarkable, they note, given the relative paucity of data available to him. Yang, while recognizing some limitations, conceives Weber's analysis to be useful to understanding Chinese modernization in the more recent past as well.

Among the criticisms of Weber's work on India, Milton Singer's (1961) is among the most detailed. Singer expresses a high appreciation of Weber's work but is skeptical about its adequacy, especially that it does not afford a perspective from which to address the contemporary scene. Singer writes:

To evaluate Weber's conclusions is not easy. In view of the complexity of Hinduism, and of Asian religions generally, any characterization of them or any comparison of them with Western
religion is going to involve large simplifications. Certainly Weber
has brilliantly constructed a characterization based on an impressive
knowledge of both textual and contextual studies. But one may
wonder whether the construction does justice to elements of Asian
religions. Some of these are: a strand of this-worldly asceticism;
the economic rationality of merchants, craftsmen, and peasant;
theologically consistent system of impersonal determinism in Ve-
danta and Buddhism, with direct consequences for a secular ethic;
the development of "rational empirical" science; religious individualism; and personal monotheism. Weber is certainly aware of all
these elements and discusses them in his study. . . . But in the
construction of the "Spirit" he does not give very much weight to
these elements. With the evidence today before us of politically
independent Asian states actively planning their social, economic
and scientific and technical development, we would attach a great
deal more importance to these elements and see less conflict between
them and the religious "spirit."

Singer and the critics referred to earlier provide a detailed
appraisal of Weber's analysis of specific religions or traditions
and very often are contributions in their own right to their
study. By and large, however, these critics are not concerned with
examining and assessing the broader comparative implications of
Weber's hypotheses. Such commentary came from other sources
and, on the average, somewhat later in time.

V

The upsurge in the social sciences of interest in development or
modernization and the general broadening of the scope of comparative macrosocietal studies has generated widespread new
interest in explicating and in testing the broader implications of
Weber's analysis of the non-European religions. These studies
have developed in directions roughly parallel to those adopted in
the discussion of the Protestant ethic thesis proper. As in the
search for a causal link between Protestantism and capitalism
the religious beliefs and practices of different religions have been
reexamined to assess the degree to which they facilitate or sanction the undertaking of some continuous, systematic, this-worldly,
secular, and especially economic activities.

In these studies (for a discussion of these studies, see Bellah

1963), two aspects of various religions which Weber singled out in his analysis have been taken up as possible explanations of differences among religions to facilitate the development of "secular" institutions in general and economic ones in particular. One of these is the extent to which any religion or religious system is focused on a "multiple of very concretely defined and only loosely ordered sacred entities" which emphasize separate, discrete, ritual, magical activities and which encourage a continuous dissipation of energies and resources in such immediate situations.[2] Or, stated obversely, the extent to which religious concepts are "rationalized" and remain "apart," "above," or "aloof" from the concrete details of ordinary life. The other aspect is the degree to which such religions tend to emphasize "this-worldly" as against "other-worldly" orientations and concerns in their doctrine, ritual, and precepts. The general conclusion that can be derived from these studies is that of these two aspects it is the first—the extent of "rationality"—that has more potential influence on whether or not economic and other secular activities are encouraged. Religions which have, in principle, positive orientations to this-worldly activities may yet, insofar as they emphasize discrete, magical orientations and activities, give but little support to any more continuous systematic activities in any field of activity.

Thus in many of these studies (some of which are discussed in Pieris 1963; Eisenstadt 1968a: 3–45), it is often claimed that the more magical or discrete a religious system, the less does it facilitate the development of more continuous secular activities. This is the claimed effect of the multitude of dispersed religious rituals found in more primitive religions. It is also seen to be the result of the many nonrationalized religious emphases which can be found in many of the peripheral areas of the higher religions —Buddhism, Hinduism, Islam, or Eastern Christianity. Muslim Ramadan, for example, is one of many customs of such other-worldly higher religions which is inimical to sustained economic effort.

On the other hand, religions whose main stress is other-worldly may yet facilitate a positive attitude to certain types of

---

[2] The nomenclature here follows Clifford Geertz (1964).

secular activities in two different ways. They may first enjoin their adherents to perform their secular duties. Second, insofar as they have developed a certain level of rationality, they may also encourage some continuous systematic effort and activity in various secular spheres.

But although such rationalization constitutes, in some instances, a basic prerequisite for the encouragement or facilitation of more sustained activities in various secular fields, it does not in itself tell us the extent to which within these religions there may also develop more positive, transformative orientations to the secular world. That is to say, the existence of some broad, generalized support for economic or other secular activities does not in itself inform us as to the extent to which these religions give *full religious legitimation* and sanction for continuous secular activities, how much they endow various activities in the secular world with direct religious meaning, or to what degree such activities became the focus of religiosity (see Pieris 1963).

Such full religious legitimation of secular activities is a relatively rare phenomenon in the major world religions, whatever their concrete attitudes to this world, especially as long as their activities are set within a relatively "traditional" setting. This does not necessarily preclude the possibility, however, that in the more congenial environment of modernizing situations there may develop from within them some such transformative orientation, just as was, according to Weber, the case with Protestantism.

VI

This brings us naturally to the second—to some degree chronological, but mostly analytical—stage of the effort to draw out the implications of Weber's thesis about the non-European religions. The major characteristic of this stage is the search for more or less exact equivalents to the Protestant ethic within these religions, that is, a search for ascetic, religious groups with a strong emphasis on this-worldly—and especially economic, commercial, or industrial—activities. Included in this stage are studies of

Islam, especially in South Asia, of Hinduism, of Buddhism, and of the religions of Japan.

The expansion of Islam into Southeast Asia provides a fascinating study because its carriers, among others, were ascetic, especially Sufi groups. These groups strongly emphasized personal discipline in work and in daily behavior, and they appealed successfully to middle-class, urban (mostly merchant) elements. The result was the development of a new stratum in the society, most notably of the Santri groups in Indonesia.

In a series of articles and books Clifford Geertz (1956, 1960, 1963) has described the development of different parts of this stratum and examined their potentialities for and ultimate failure to evolve a modern or capitalistic type of entrepreneurship (as distinct from the more politically based economic activities developed by the more traditional aristocrats and from the more traditional market small entrepreneur). Geertz's rich and intricate analysis of Javanese religions treats of considerably more than the Weberian problem and belongs, in sense, to the next generation of studies concerned with religious changes in Southeast Asia. Yet in various parts of Geertz's work—especially in *Peddlers and Princes* (1963)—the older Weberian starting point is still very discernible. It is a point of departure for several later studies of Java as well. (See Castles 1967; and Peacock 1968, 1969).

Also characteristic of this stage is Singer's (1956; see also Srinivas, Karve, and Singer 1958) already-mentioned critique of Weber's analysis of Indian society. As has been seen previously, Singer, contrary to many current interpretations of Weber's analysis of Hinduism as necessarily leading to economic stagnation, emphasizes that there does exist within the whole of Hinduism strong emphases on this-worldly activities. These may be reinforced by many aspects of the family and caste structure and, under propitious circumstances, may indeed generate a more active, generalized orientation. In this same vein, Joseph Elder (1959) has presented evidence that the Indian caste ethic is being transformed into a universalistic ethic of occupational responsibility detached from its earlier anchorage in the hereditary caste structure. This theme has been taken up and further developed in other studies of contemporary India, as for instance

Khare (1970) and Rudolphs (1967). Similarly, Ames (1963, 1967) in his study of Ceylonese Buddhism attempts to connect certain internal transformations among some Buddhist groups in the direction of greater asceticism and a weakening of the emphasis on ritualism with a tendency to engage in organized, self-disciplinary, this-worldly activities in the economic, educational, or political sphere.

The systematically most far-reaching study of this stage is undoubtedly Robert Bellah's *Tokugawa Religion* (1957).[3] Bellah looks for appropriate equivalents of the Protestant ethic and finds them in the general ethos of the Samurai with its stress on achievement orientation, on responsibility to collectivity, and on relatively autonomous criteria for judging the exercise thereof. This ethos is backed up by a combination of Shintoism and Confucianism as developed by the Singaku sect. Its ascetic, this-

[3] Also to be mentioned is a most fascinating analysis of a non-Christian religion which, without directly referring to Weber, does yet constitute one of the closest parallels to Weber's analysis of the transformative potential of religious sects. This is G. Sholem's (1962) analysis of the Shabtai Zvi and Frankist movements of heresies which developed in the seventeenth and eighteenth centuries in Judaism.

In this analysis he shows how the overt failure, because of Shabtai Zvi's conversion to Islam, of the messianic hopes held up by him gave rise among many parts of the Jewish population to sects which developed the belief that this act of conversion was only an external one, and the Messiah really "went underground" and will still come. These groups have developed a series of rather unorthodox and even antinomian beliefs and practices, emphasizing the relative unimportance of external observances as against inner faith.

Gradually many members of these groups, and especially, but not only the ones formed in Eastern Europe in the eighteenth century after the rather continuous disappointment of their hopes, became a breeding ground for assimilations. Out of them came many people with high ideological semi-religious motivation who were absorbed in the emerging open European society of the late eighteenth and nineteenth centuries. Many of them tended to participate in some of the more radical intellectual groups of that time.

Thus, in a sense we have here a rather very close parallel to the transformative tendencies and activities of some of the radical Protestant groups, which can be, at least to some extent, accounted for by a rather similar basic religious orientation—a high degree of transcendental orientation and commitment, the gradual growing up of accepted traditional mediation between God and people—as well as by some structural similarities in the placement of these groups, that is, their being in a somewhat secondary elite position within their own society as well as in a marginal, potential secondary elite position in the opening up broader society.

worldly orientations are found by Bellah to be an important factor in promoting Japan's modernization.

VII

Most of these studies largely parallel those which analyzed the spread of Protestantism in Catholic countries such as Italy and various parts of Latin America. The latter have shown how minority Protestant groups tend indeed to develop vigorous entrepreneurial economic activities, even if they cannot transmit their ethos onto the broader society. Studies of various religious groups and movements outside the West, however, have produced quite different findings.

Four major themes emerge from such studies. First, unlike the Protestant groups in Catholic countries, potentially "modernizing" entrepreneurial Islamic and Buddhist groups in Southeast Asia, even when they are possessed of some equivalent of the Protestant ethic, rarely, if ever, succeed in developing a continuously viable "modern" institutional structure. Castles's (1967) study of the Kudus cigarette industry of Java affords an illustration of the derailing processes at work. He says (1967: 90–91):

> In the struggle of Indonesian leadership groups in the present century to step into the shoes of the departing colonial elite, the group rooted in the *santri* business class and its Outer Island allies was a strong contender. . . . Ignoring the part played by the wisdom and skill of individual leaders and other fortuitous events (important though these may have been), the chief proximate causes of the failure of this group seem to have been two. In the first place by the strictness of their Islamic emphasis they alienated vitally important sectors of Indonesian society, both of the masses and of the elite. And in the second place the leadership group closest to the *santri* businessmen was unable to retain the support of the *santris* is general.
>
> This political failure of the *santri* middle class (especially its inability to retain sufficient support among the *santri* masses of Java) can be attributed largely to its continued precarious and marginal economic position.
>
> What light does the Kudus case, and especially the failure of the Kudus group of entrepreneurs, throw on the question of the economic limitations and consequent political weakness of the *santri* business class? First the successes of the Kudus group should be

mentioned. They did create the industry. They also met successfully a series of shocks and challenges in changing economic and political conditions.

The other failures of the Kudus entrepreneurial group have been political or social rather than economic. On the one hand the distinctive middle class ethos which was developing before the war in contradistinction to the aristocratic *prijaji* ethos has been diluted. In a sense this is a social victory, as it indicates that the doors to higher education and intermarriage with the elite are now open to the children of Kudus businessmen. But the result is that the possibility of a self-conscious middle-class ideology overcoming the ideological legacy of Indonesia's two-class system is diminished.

Yet on the other hand the Kudus *santri* businessmen have failed to maintain their functional links with other social groups. They have little influence in the trade unions. They are out of sympathy with the most influential religious and political leaders in the Kudus region, the Nahdatul Ulama *kiajis*. And their relationships with the regional administration are generally characterized by dependence and avoidance.

A second theme stresses that even when the existence of some equivalent of the Protestant ethic has been a spur to modernization, especially economic development in non-Western societies, it has not been accompanied by a full-scale, "total value transformation" of the society. On the contrary, the effect is to distort such development.

This theme has been most effectively sounded by Bellah (1963) in his response to Japanese criticism of his *Tokugawa Religion:*

> Looking at economic growth as our criterion, we are inclined to consider Japan as a rather unambiguous success story. But to Japanese intellectuals who feel as acutely as Weber did the failure of modern Japan to carry through certain critical structural transformations which are associated with modern society, the evaluation of Japan's modern history is much more problematic. It would be convenient for social scientists and policy makers if economic growth were an automatic index to successful structural transformation. This does not, however, seem to be the case. Indeed, where economic growth is rapid and structural change is blocked or, as in the Communist cases, distorted, social instabilities result which, under present world conditions, are serious enough to have potentially fatal consequences for us all. A broader perspective than has often been taken, would seem then to be in order.

A third theme, best represented in the work of M. F. Wertheim (1961, 1964) and of S. H. Alatas (1963, 1970) is that, in contrast to Europe and Latin America, potentially modernizing religious and social movements in Southeast Asia are rooted much more frequently in the peasantry than in urban groups.

And, finally, a fourth theme, most recently sounded by Mendelson (1970) and especially Tambiah (1970, 1971), is that insofar as there has been innovative entrepreneurial activity in non-Western settings, its initiators and promoters have been politicians and bureaucrats rather than the structural equivalent to the Western middle class.

These themes have been sounded in works inspired directly by Weber. They are repeated and elaborated upon in other more general studies of contemporary religious development, especially in Asia. These studies (for example, Binder 1963, Smith 1966, 1970, 1971, Sarkisyan 1965, von der Mehden 1963, King 1964, Roff forthcoming) highlight the quite different this-worldly orientations of organized and popular religions in the setting of New States. They demonstrate the great variety of movements and activities, ranging from communal-populistic through more esoteric sects up to more fully developed organizations, which arise from within these religions. They also show such movements to be much more oriented to the political than to the economic field, and they point to the great importance of religious "messianic" symbolism for the development of nationalistic and communal symbols and aspirations.

As Weber himself did in his broad comparative studies of religion, contemporary research also indicates that not all religions or religious movements are necessarily change oriented and that what seems to be change or heterodoxy in the religious sense need not necessarily always have direct impact on broader institutional settings, that is, provide religious sanctioning of general institutional changes. On the contrary, religious organizations often develop far-reaching accommodative relations to existing political regimes. Such accommodations may, in situations of change, have far-reaching consequences but not necessarily in the institutional directions envisaged by the original Protestant ethic thesis or by the search for its equivalent.

VIII

The upshot of all these critical themes does not necessarily negate either the importance of religions as potential carriers of social and political innovation or of the general importance of rational economic and political innovation for the functioning of a modern polity. They make it clear, however, that the social carriers and institutional locus of such innovation need not be the same as those that were originally envisaged by Weber in his analysis of the Protestant ethic and by those who have searched for its direct equivalents in other, non-European settings.

In sum, a large body of contemporary scholarly opinion appears committed to two different yet complementary views about the possible implications of Weber's work for the analysis of Asian religions and societal development. One view calls for continuing analysis of religious organizations and movements as these are related to social and political order in general and to processes of change and modernization in particular. This view is largely in accord with Weber's *general* work in the sociology of religions, especially that contained in *Wirtschaft und Gesell-schaft*. There, it will be recalled, he develops a series of typologies of religious organizations and of their relationships to the social, political and economic order. The other view would place the emphasis on continuing examination of the possibility of a total value transformation of these societies.

IX

Most of the research on non-Western religion derived from Weber, as well as a further development of Weber's own insights, indicates the possibility of a much differentiated and yet analytically focused approach to the study of the transformative potentials of different religions.

A fruitful starting point for such a differentiated approach, in my judgment, is one of the central analytical concepts developed by Weber—namely that of *Wirtschaftsethik*. As is by now well known, *Wirtschaftsethik* neither connotes specific religious injunctions about proper behavior in the economic field, nor is it just a logical derivative of the intellectual contents of the theology or philosophy predominant in a given religion. Rather, as especially Weber's analysis of the non-European religions indicates, *Wirtschaftsethik* has to do with a general mode of religious or ethical orientation. Included in this orientation is an evaluation of a specific institutional sphere based on the premises of a given religion or tradition about the cosmic order and its relation to human and social existence and, consequently, the organization of social life.

Thus, *Wirtschaftsethik* is, in a sense, a code, a general formal orientation, a deeper structure which programs or regulates the actual concrete social organization. Unlike many modern structuralists, however, Weber did not conceive of the code as a purely formal means to organize only a set of abstract, symbolic contents. Rather, he conceived of it as the key to unlocking the basic symbolic structural and organizational elements of human and social existence.

Although most of Weber's work dealt explicitly with the relation of such codes to the economic sphere, his work in general, and on non-European civilizations in particular, contains extremely important analyses into what may be called status ethic and political ethic of the great religions, that is, the religious evaluation of the political sphere or of different dimensions of status (see Eisenstadt 1968a). Different codes of any given religion operate together in exerting their influence on the institutional setting of the society or civilization within which the given religion operates and on the direction of change within it. Weber made it clear that among the most important carriers of such codes are various religious movements of orthodoxy and heterodoxy.

Especially important in this respect is his exploration of the relation between organizational and structural aspects of religions in general, and of movements of heterodoxy within them in particular, on the one hand, and the respective *Ethik* or codes of these religions on the other. It is in this combination that the special strength of Weber's analysis can be found. The movements of orthodoxy and heterodoxy were identified by him both as carriers of continuity in the basic codes of these civilizations and as indicators of possible changes in their range. He shows how out of different constellations of such movements there develop the potentialities of change of the major religions, and he shows the different concrete ways in which such potentialities were actualized. His analysis of the non-European religions or civilizations provides a very detailed exposition of the interrelations between these codes and of different changes within them.

But in this analysis he does not go beyond the traditional settings of these civilizations. As we have seen, Weber's central question was why they did not develop in the direction of European modernity; and he did not ask himself whether they might develop beyond their traditional settings in a way different from capitalism or modernity in Europe.

Because of this he does not envisage—or at least does not discuss—the possibility of the development of parameters of modernity differing from the ones that developed in Europe. In a sense he took this type of modernity for granted. Implicitly, however, in his exploration of the specific characteristics of Western rationality and of the relations between *Zweckrationalitaet* and *Wertrationalitaet,* Weber touches on the possibility of the existence of different combinations of these various rationalities, hence, also—very indirectly and only implicitly—on the possibility that there may perhaps develop types of modernity differing from the European ones. But the type of analysis he attempted with respect to the historical development of non-European civilizations and religions can be transposed to the modern setting of these societies, to illuminate the process through which these societies have been developing their own response to the challenge of modernity and their own types of posttraditional social and political orders.

X

The transposition must begin with the recognition that a great variety of different patterns of modernity of a posttraditional order are likely to develop. Unlike what has been often assumed in the classical paradigms of modernization, development or modernization does not constitute a unilinear demographic, social, economic, or political process leading to some plateau, whose basic contours—whatever the differences in detail—will be everywhere the same. Rather, modernization has to be seen as a process or a series of processes with a common core generating similar problems, but to which different responses are possible.

Growing differentiation, social mobilization, the breakdown or weakening of central traditional premises confront the societies on which they impinge with the problems of regulating newly emerging groups, of resolving conflicts which develop among them, of integrating these groups within some common institutional framework, and of developing some new focuses of collective national identity.

The responses to these common problems in different societies vary greatly on almost all the crucial dimensions of social and cultural organization. First, they vary structurally in the bases adopted for strata formation, for occupational distribution, for example, the relative importance of agrarian vs. urban occupations, for organizational development, and for the formulation of allocative and regulative mechanisms.

Second, they vary symbolically in the emphases given to different dimensions of human existence. Third, they vary as to whether an active or passive attitude toward participation in the social and cultural orders and in their formation is taken. And, finally, they vary in the ways change itself is conceptualized, understood, and responded to.

The net result of such variation in response is to produce differences in types of new political and cultural centers, in the boundaries of different collectivities and orders, in the rights of various groups for access to the major sociocultural orders and their centers, in the conception of the centers' posttraditional legitimation and its relation to the periphery, in the basic policies of the center and in the demands of the periphery, and in the system of stratification. It is these differences which at least partially explain the dynamics of each of these posttraditional orientations and take them beyond the original scope of the Protestant ethic thesis.

XI

It is in the attempt to understand the variations in responses, both within single civilizations and between different ones, that we may come back to Weber's analysis of the possible place of religious orientations and movements in governing them.

In this situation of change the importance of heterodoxy and movements of reform and rebellion as carriers of changes tends here to become even more fully articulated than in Europe, mainly because of the fact that the very encounter with the West intensifies such movements of protest.

But at the same time here protest tends to become much more closely interwoven with processes of formation of new centers. Hence, these two aspects or referrents of various basic codes, that of protest and that of center formation, tend to become closely combined.

Moreover, in these situations it is indeed in the political sphere that the major impact of change and impulse to institution building usually develops, and the major orientation of the various movements of rebellion and change are focused above all on this sphere. Therefore, it is especially important to analyze here different movements of heterodoxy and protest in their impact on the political sphere, on the *Politische Ethik,* on the codes relating to the political sphere, and through them on other institutional spheres. Such analysis may help us to bring out the different cultural and institutional implications of some of the codes prevalent in these groups, the possibilities of changes and transformations within them, and their impact on the concrete constellations of different posttraditional social and cultural orders. It may also help us in the understanding of the development of new combinations of rationalities, especially of different types of *Wertrationalitaeten,* with the *Zweckrationalitaet* characteristic of modern, differentiated, structural and organizational settings. In this way it may indeed build on Weber's analysis of non-European civilizations to the study of the relations between the codes of the great non-European religions, their carriers, and the responses of their societies to the impact of modernity.

BIBLIOGRAPHY

Alatas, S. H.
  1963 The Weber Thesis and Southeast Asia. *Archives de Sociolo-gie des Religions* Vol. 8, no. 15, pp. 21–35.
  1970 Religion and Modernization in Southeast Asia. *European Journal of Sociology* Vol. 9, no. 2, pp. 265–96.

Ames, Michael
  1963 Ideological and Social Change in Ceylon. *Human Organization* 22 : 45–53.
  1967 Magical Animism and Buddhism. In E. D. B. Harper, ed. *Religion in South Asia.* Seattle, Wash.: University of Washington Press.

Bellah, Robert N.
  1957 *Tokugawa Religion.* New York: The Free Press.
  1963 Reflections on the Protestant Ethic Analogy in Asia. *Journal of Social Issues* Vol. 19, no. 1, p. 59.

Bendix, Reinhard
  1970 *Max Weber: An Intellectual Portrait.* Garden City, N.Y.: Doubleday.

Binder, L.
  1963 *Religion and Politics in Pakistan.* Berkeley and Los Angeles, University of California Press.

Castles, Lance
  1967 *Religion, Politics, and Economic Behavior in Java: The Kudus Cigarette Industry.* Cultural Report Series, No. 15. New Haven, Conn.: Southeast Asia Studies, Yale University.

Eisenstadt, S. N.
  1966 *Modernization, Protest and Change.* Englewood Cliffs, N.J.: Prentice-Hall.
  1968a The Protestant Ethic in Comparative and Analytical Perspective. In Eisenstadt, *The Protestant Ethic and Modernization.* New York: Basic Books, Inc.
  1968b Reflections on a Theory of Modernization. In A. Rivkin, ed. *Nations by Design.* Garden City, N.Y.: Doubleday-Anchor Books.
  1968c *Max Weber: On Charisma and Institution Building.* Chicago: University of Chicago Press.
  1971 *Political Sociology.* New York: Basic Books, Inc.

Elder, Joseph W.
    1959   Industrialism in Hindu Society: A Case Study in Social
            Change. Unpublished Ph.D. thesis, Harvard University.

Geertz, Clifford
    1956   Religious Belief and Economic Behavior in a Central Java-
            nese Town: Some Preliminary Considerations. *Economic De-
            velopment and Cultural Change* Vol. 5, no. 4, pp. 134–59.
    1960   *The Religion of Java.* New York: The Free Press.
    1963   *Peddlers and Princes.* Chicago: University of Chicago Press.
    1964   Internal Conversion in Contemporary Bali. In J. Bastin and
            R. Roolvink. *Malayan and Indonesian Studies.* New York:
            Oxford University Press.

Guttmann, Julius
    1925   Max Weber's "Soziologie des Antiken Judentum's." *Monat-
            schrift für Geshichte und Wissenschaft des Antiken Juden-
            tum* 69: 195–223.

Kapp, Karl William
    1963   *Hindu Culture, Economic Development and Economic Plan-
            ning in India.* New York: Asia Publishing House.

Katz, J.
    1961   *Tradition and Crisis.* New York: The Free Press.

Kessler, C. S.
    Forth-   Islam, Society and Political Behvior: Some Comparative
    coming   Implications of Malay Case. *British Journal of Sociology.*

Khare, R. S.
    1970   *The Changing Brahmins: Associations and Elites among the
            Kanya-Kybjas of North India.* Chicago: University of Chi-
            cago Press.

King, W. L.
    1964   *A Thousand Lives Away: Buddhism in Contemporary Burma.*
            Cambridge, Mass.: Harvard University Press.

Mendelson, E. Michael
    1970   The King of the Weaving Mountain. *Royal Central Asian
            Journal* 48: 229–37.

Moans, G. P.
    1969   The Role of Islam in the Political Development of Malaysia.
            Comparative Politics 1: 264–84.

Parsons, Talcott
1937   *The Structure of Social Action.* New York: McGraw-Hill.

Peacock, James L.
1968   *Rites of Modernization: Symbolic and Social Aspects of In-
donesian Proletarian Drama.* Chicago: University of Chicago
Press.
1969   Religion, Communications, and Modernization: A Weberian
Critique of Some Recent Views. *Human Organization* Vol.
28, no. 1 (Spring), pp. 35–41.

Pieris, Ralph
1963   Economic Development and Ultramundaneity. *Archives de
Sociologie des Religions* Vol. 13, no. 15, pp. 95–101.

Raphaël, Freddy
1970   Max Weber et le Judaisme Antique. *Archive European de
Sociologie* Vol. 11, no. 2, pp. 297–336.

Roff, William R., ed.
Forth-   *Religion, Society and Politics in a Malay State: Essays
coming   on Kelantan.* Ithaca, N.Y.: Cornell University Press.

Rudolph, Lloyd I., and Rudolph, Susanne Hoeber
1967   *The Modernity of Tradition: Political Development in India.*
Chicago: University of Chicago Press.

Sarachandra, Ediriweera R.
1965   Traditional Values and the Modernization of a Buddhist Society: The Case of Ceylon. In Robert N. Bellah, ed. *Religion
and Progress in Modern Asia.* New York: The Free Press.

Sholem, G.
1954, 1969   *Major Trends in Jewish Mysticism.* New York:
Schocken.

Singer, Milton
1956   Cultural Values in India's Economic Development. *Annals
of the American Academy of Political and Social Science*
305 (May): 81–90.
1961   Review: The Religion of India: The Sociology of Hinduism
and Buddhism. *American Anthropologist* Vol. 43, no. 1
(February), pp. 143–51.
1966   Religion and Social Change in India: The Max Weber Thesis, Phase Three. *Economic Development and Cultural
Change* Vol. 14, no. 4 (July), 497–505.

Sirkisyanz, E.
   1965   *Buddhist Background of the Burmese Revolution.* The
          Hague: M. Nijhoff.

Smith, D. E.
   1966   *South Asian Politics and Religion.* Princeton, N.J.: Prince-
          ton University Press.

Srinivas, M. M., Karve, D. F., and Singer, Milton
   1958   India's Cultural Values and Economic Development: A Dis-
          cussion. *Economic Development and Cultural Change* 7: 1–12.

Tambiah, S. J.
   1970   *Buddhism and Spirit Cults.* New York: Cambridge Univer-
          sity Press.
   1971   Buddhism and This Worldly Activity. Paper presented to
          the International Congress of Orientalists, Canberra.

Van der Sprenkel, O. B.
   1964   Max Weber on China. *History and Theory* 3: 348–370.

Von der Mehden, F. R.
   1965   *Religion and Nationalism in South East Asia.* Madison,
          Wis.: University of Wisconsin Press.

Warner, R. Stephen
   1970   The Role of Religious Ideas and the Use of Models in Max
          Weber's Comparative Studies of Non-Capitalist Societies.
          Journal of Economic History Vol. 30, no. 1 (May), pp. 74–
          87.

Weber, Max
   1920– Gesammelte Aufsätze zur Religionssoziologie. 3 vols. Tü-
   1930   bingen: Möhr (Siebeck).
   1930   *The Protestant Ethic and the Spirit of Capitalism.* Trans.
          Talcott Parsons. New York: Scribner's.
   1946   *From Max Weber: Essays in Sociology.* Trans. ed. and in-
          troduction, Hans H. Gerth and C. Wright Mills. New York:
          Oxford University Press.
   1952   *Ancient Judaism.* Trans. and preface Hans H. Gerth and
          Don Martindale. New York: The Free Press.
   1956   *Wirtschaft und Gesellschaft: Grundriss der Verstehenden
          Soziologie*
 (tr. 1968) Tübingen: Möhr. Available in English as *Economy and
          Society: An Outline of Interpretive Sociology.* 3 vols. Ed.
          Günther Roth and Claus Wittica, trans. E. Fischoff and
          others. New York: Bedminster Press.

1958   *The Religion of India: The Sociology of Hinduism and
        Buddhism.* Trans. Hans H. Gerth and Don Martindale. New
        York: The Free Press.

1964   *The Religion of China: Confucianism and Taoism.* Trans.
        Hans H. Gerth, introduction, C. K. Yang. New York: Mac-
        millan.

Wertheim, W. F.

1961   Religious Reform Movements in South and South-East Asia.
        Archives de Sociologie des Religions 12: 53–62.

1964   Religion, Bureaucracy and Economic Growth. *Transactions
        of the Fifth World Congress of Sociology* Vol. III. London:
        International Sociological Association.

Yang, C. K.

1964   Introduction to Max Weber on China. *History and Theory*
        3: 348–370.

4 DURKHEIM ON RELIGION REVISITED: ANOTHER LOOK AT THE ELEMENTARY FORMS OF THE RELIGIOUS LIFE

Talcott Parsons

I

Since more than thirty years ago I wrote a long chapter (1937: 640–96) on Durkheim's analysis of religion based mainly on the *Elementary Forms of the Religious Life* (Durkheim 1910), and I had only sporadically gone back to this focal book of Durkheim since then, it seemed that full rereading of the *Elementary Forms* was the best way to prepare myself to write a chapter in the frame of reference of the present book, namely: how do Durkheim's contributions in the field of religion look at the present time? It should be kept in mind that from the very beginning of his published work, Durkheim was deeply concerned with normative order as a fundamental constituent in the nature and structure of society. It was this emphasis on which I initially focused attention in my own first serious study of Durkheim's work. It seemed to me, and I think rightly at the time, that the *Elementary Forms* constituted the culmination for its author of a long and complex process of the deepening and clarification of his understanding of this very central problem area. Along the road, building on his analysis in the *Division of Labor in Society* (1893), Durkheim arrived at the full statement of the conception of internalization of moral norms in the personality of individuals and of the seminal conception of *anomie*, and I think very importantly of what I have called institutionalized individualism. Conspicuously, this last began with his analysis of the reasons why Protestants had higher suicide rates than Catholics.

Looking back, I think I was somewhat ambivalent about two features of the *Elementary Forms*. The first was Durkheim's concentration on studying the religion of a single primitive society, indeed the most primitive about which he could find what he considered to be adequate evidence. The second was the stress he laid in the book on problems in the difficult boundary areas of epistemology and of the sociology of knowledge, which I had a certain feeling were being somewhat gratuitously "dragged in" a study which I interpreted to be focused mainly in the sociology of religion.

As the background of a great deal that has happened to me intellectually in the long intervening period, I can say that I have come out of the rereading with a substantially altered perspective, an alteration which definitely enhances my appreciation of the greatness of the book. In the first place, stimulated along the way by Robert Bellah's (1959) significant paper, "Durkheim and History," I think I have come fully to understand the sense in which Durkheim had, by the time he wrote the *Elementary Forms*, come to be committed to a theory of evolution not merely of human societies in the analytical sense, but of the human condition generally. The choice of empirical material for the book and its main pattern of organization were clearly to a major degree determined by this commitment.

Second, I have come to see that the book is not primarily a study in the *sociology* of religion, but rather of the place of religion in human action generally. In the terms that I have used in recent years, it is couched primarily at the level of what I have called the general system of action, which includes the theory of the social system but also of cultural systems, personality systems, and of behavioral organisms. In a very important sense the last of these four references proved to be unexpectedly important in interpreting what Durkheim was doing. Above all, it makes much more intelligible the grounds for his concern with problems that I have called those of epistemology and the sociology of knowledge. Many of his formulations about the societal

origins of the categories of the understanding, of space and time
and the idea of force and, hence, causality that were unacceptable to me in earlier years are still unacceptable as adequate
general statements, in the sense that I think the basic insights
that he had can be reformulated in more acceptable terms. A
very central shift of his, however, from the inherited traditions
of the theory of knowledge was his placing of culture, including,
of course, empirical knowledge, in a perspective which was only
partly epistemological.

What I take to be his basic theorem is that human society and
the cultural framework of the human condition, including
knowledge, have evolved concomitantly from a common basis
and, in relatively advanced stages of sociocultural development,
have come to be differentiated from each other. This conception
of common origin is very different indeed from a one-way
conception of determinism, namely, that of society as an independently existing entity, determining the nature of the organization of knowledge. This, of course, has been the common sense
of what might be called the vulgar sociology of knowledge, of
which Durkheim most definitely was not a proponent.

Durkheim's position in epistomology was definitely Kantian,
emphasizing the strong duality of the problems of sense data and
their sources on the one hand, and the categorial structure of
knowledge on the other hand. Indeed, in his conclusion Durkheim
cites Kant's sound conviction that the grounding of cognitive
knowledge and that of moral judgment should be treated as
linked through the fact that they both concern universality of
reference, as distinguished on the one hand from the data of the
senses, and on the other from what he called the appetites. This
is indeed the fundamental conceptual scheme of Durkheim's
analysis: the duality on the one hand of the universal and the
particular, on the other hand, the crosscutting duality of the
cognitive and moral references.

II

It is here that the famous distinction between the sacred and the
profane enters in. I had earlier correctly understood, indeed it

was very difficult to miss, that this distinction was in the religious context the equivalent of the distinction between moral authority and the utilitarian or instrumental pursuit of interests in the secular sphere. I did not, however, fully appreciate the last-mentioned implications of it, namely, the extent to which he identified the distinction in the moral sphere with that in the cognitive. At present, however, it seems correct to say that he thought of the category of the sacred as the synthesis or matrix of the other two primary categories of universality, namely, the categories of the understanding and the related cognitive rubrics and the category of the moral. This identification and the corresponding identification of the profane with *both* instrumental interests and sense data is by no means incompatible with a difference of relation of these pairs to social systems on the one hand and to the individual on the other. I take it that the really fundamental meaning of Durkheim's thesis of social origin is the evolutionary one that at sufficiently early stages, society and culture were undifferentiated from each other.

This brings us to another very central point, namely, Durkheim's assertion that sacred things are symbols, the meanings of which should not be interpreted in terms of their intrinsic properties. This, it will be remembered, was one of the main points of his, to me, devastating critiques of the theories of animism and naturism concerning religion. When, however, the question arose: symbols of what, Durkheim's tendency, disturbing to so many including myself, was to say symbols of society. In the usual received senses of the concept ''society,'' this seemed very close to being nonsense. If, however, one looks at the problem in the evolutionary perspective and speaks of symbols of the grounding of human existence, which is always inherently, at least in major part, social, it seems a much more reasonable formula. I think that in both the cognitive and the moral contexts, Durkheim was essentially speaking of the basic framework of order, which must be assumed in order to make the phenomena of human life, with special emphasis on its social aspect, intelligible. Indeed, in the conclusion he speaks of a concentration in human society of the forces, I think it is fair to say, determining the functioning of living systems which is unique in the aspects of the universe we know. I should interpret this assertion in terms, which have become current since Durkheim's day, of the evolution in the direction of negative entropy of the organization of living systems, and the significance of the references lies in their revealing the fundamental conditions of this order of evolution. This interpretation gives a certain reasonableness to Robert Bellah's (1970) suggestion that we ought to speak of symbolic realism in the sense of abandoning the attempt so prominent in Durkheim's case, but also in that of Freud, to interpret sacred and some other symbols as always representing something outside themselves.

III

In all these discussions on Durkheim's part there is a persistently recurring note, namely, the emphasis on separateness of the moral from the appetitive, of the categorial from the empirical, of the sacred from the profane. But second, there is the theme of the relation of categorial, moral, and sacred components to long-run concerns, as distinguished from day-to-day concerns, of the systems in which they form a part. It was this emphasis on a quite different time span which alerted me on my rereading to the very striking formal similarity between Durkheim's series of distinctions and the historic distinction in biological theory between those aspects of biological systems which are embodied in the *genetic* constitution of organisms as members of species and those which characterize the individual organisms. One formulation is the distinction between germ plasm and somatoplasm; another, genotype and plenotype; another, phylogenetic and ontogenetic references. The problem of separateness was fought out in the famous post-Darwinian controversies over the question of the inheritance of acquired characteristics with the negative view finally clearly prevailing.

Since what we have been calling behavioral organisms is an essential constituent of what we call action systems, it seems reasonable to assume that this dichotomy, which is fundamental to the understanding of all organisms, should also apply to the human organism in its role in action. If this is true, then why should not a closely related distinction be extended from the organic aspect of human action systems to the others? It seemed to me that many of Durkheim's discussions and observations were consistent with the view that this was one of the principal messages that he was trying to convey in his analysis.

In interpreting this it should be kept in mind that Durkheim was writing at a time when the social sciences, and sociology in particular, were fighting a strenous battle against what has often been called biological reductionism. Durkheim's own, perhaps most important, single polemical opposition, namely, to Herbert Spencer, was part of that battle. Durkheim strenuously asserted that society was a "reality *sui generis.*" It is not an organism in the then current sense of the term "biological." Since that time, however, biological theory has undergone a profound process of change which in many respects, to much surprise, assimilates the understanding of the functioning of organisms far more closely to that of personality and social systems than had previously been thought reasonable. At least for the moment, the culmination of this change has been the development of the new genetics, with its conception of DNA as embodying, in its chemical structure as a very complex molecule, a code which can govern the reproduction of previous patterns of organization in living cells in the development of new cells. (Stern 1970, Stent 1970, Olby 1970). This extremely general feature of the operation of living systems is continued in many different respects but above all with respect to genetic constitution in the processes of bisexual reproduction.

Seen in this perspective, it has become increasingly clear that Durkheim's three separate categories could all be interpreted as pointing to, if not fully analyzing, the presence in the governing of human action processes of codes analogous in some respects to the genetic code. The parallel recent development of the science of linguistics has strongly reinforced this perspective in the intellectual atmosphere of our time. When one looks at Durkheim's discussions in this perspective, some very striking parallels in pattern of analysis emerge, of which I had been totally unaware in my readings in the 1930s.

Though in the realm of the sacred there are many particularized elements, I think we can correctly say that in Durkheim's conception beliefs about the sacred are organized in their core in terms of a cultural code, which is the primary focus of the stability of the complex action system. It is not, however, only a focus of stability, but also the locus of introducing variability, both in adaptation to changing conditions and of a sort which has evolutionary consequences. From this point of view, the culture may be conceived of as constituting a very major evolutionary emergent phenomenon which has enabled socially organized humans, who are culture bearers, to transcend many of the constraints of the more rigidly bounded life of organisms without culture. It is, of course, by now very well known that the mammalian brain, in its most highly developed form in the human organism, is the most fundamental organic bearer of the processes which make cultural communication and creativity possible.

Durkheim, of course, did not anticipate these developments in biology and linguistics, but he analyzed the phenomena of action systems in a frame of reference within which these phenomena fit in terms which are remarkably congruent with the theory which has developed in these other fields. It seems to me that this congruence places the significance of his views in a quite different light from that in which they appeared in terms of the initial impact of the *Elementary Forms* on the social science community, which we should remember was overwhelmingly unfavorable, especially in the English-speaking world.

IV

We may now turn to another set of themes that are closely related to those just reviewed. They are somewhat different but have another very interesting connection with biological thinking. It will be remembered that in Durkheim's whole discussion of religion and quite explicitly in his definition, the concept moral community appears very prominently. He defined religion, that is, as a set of beliefs and practices which unite those who adhere to and practice them in a *moral community,* which, he added, is called the church, a component of his definition which needs some comment. This emphasis on the moral community is, as I have already suggested, a major theme of Durkheim's work throughout his career, centering on his famous concept of the *conscience collective* in the connotation that *conscience* should be translated more nearly as conscience than as consciousness. His insights about the nature of this community, however, came to a certain kind of culmination in the *Elementary Forms,* building, of course, on his theory of internalization.

Closely related to the concept of moral community is that of the social environment of the individual, the *milieu social.* This figured in Durkheim's earliest attempts to define the problems of sociology, especially his early concept of social facts, to which he applied the Cartesian criteria of exteriority and constraint. This paradigm was formulated from the point of view of the acting individual in his relation to a social environment. The great break from the Cartesian tradition was not in the paradigm itself, but in the conception of *social* facts, within the conception that society is a "reality *sui generis.*" It is perfectly clear that Durkheim meant the term "reality" in this phrase as an object or set of them in the Cartesian sense.

There followed a great revolution in Durkheim's thinking which culminated in the insight about internalization and the meaning of constraint as constraint by moral authority. I had not, however, been fully aware of the extent to which the progression from the Cartesian conception of the facticity of the *milieu social* to the idea of constraint by moral authority was not simply progress from a more to a less elementary theoretical position but was the framework within which *both* conceptions came to be combined in a unique manner. The realization that this is the case has, I think, been basically dependent on the conception that much of Durkheim's thought was couched at the level of the general theory of action and not only of the social system.

The upshot is that I think it is quite clear Durkheim's conception of the *milieu social* should be interpreted as the internal environment of the system of action. The concept of the internal environment was of course introduced by the great French physiologist, Claude Bernard (1957), who was a contemporary of Durkheim's. W. B. Cannon's (1932) conception of *homeostasis,* is, of course, closely related. This, at a different level from that of the primary cultural codes, may be conceived as a focus of relative stability of human action systems. I stress here the level of action rather than, as Durkheim himself tended to do, society, if one interprets society or social systems to be a primary subsystem of action rather than action itself. The essential paradigm, complicated since Durkheim's early days, is that the *milieu social*, that is, the environment shared by the participants in the same society, is both a given, empirically present environment, which must be cognitively understood and instrumentally taken into account if, as one may put it in current terms, one is to act rationally. At the same time, however, those who act in relation to the same empirically given *milieu social* constitute a moral community, and this is the distinctive feature of what Durkheim calls society as a reality *sui generis* as distinguished from the predominantly physical environment which was the focus of the Cartesian tradition.

Indeed, this duality carried over from his earlier work provides the primary rationale of the inclusion of the two primary differentiated focuses of the normative components in human action as Durkheim saw them in the *Elementary Forms,* namely, the cognitive and the moral, which in his conclusion he so dramatically associated in his comment on Kant. To repeat, the essential thing is the inclusion of *both* references in the same formula, not the shift in interest from the cognitive to the moral.

Here, however, another very interesting problem arises. In his famous definition of religion, as I have noted, Durkheim said the moral community of which he was speaking could be called a church. Certainly, in the case of Australian Totemism there was no structural differentiation between the social community as a network of interlocking clans and whatever entity and subentities had religious significance, notably both the tribe and its constituent clans. In modern societies, however, with the differentiation and later the separation of church and state, it is by no means a simple and obvious question in what sense what is usually called secular society, if it is to be a society at all, should also be called a church. It seems to me that a major contribution to the solution to this problem has been made by Robert Bellah (1967) in his, I think, now famous paper, "American Civil Religion." In this paper Bellah showed that, precisely in the Durkheimian sense, the American societal community did indeed have a religion, with a relatively full panoply of beliefs and practices and that this could be considered both constitutive of and expressing the moral community which constituted the nation. It is not necessary for present purposes to spell out the details of Bellah's analysis, but it is quite clear that in some sense a belief in God and, therefore, the transcendental sanction of the nation as an entity is central to it, and he points out that after the tremendous national trauma of the Civil War and its culminating symbolic event, the assassination of Lincoln, a new note of martyrdom and sacrifice entered into the symbolization of the community, which brought the civil religion nearer to Christian patterns in that Lincoln was frequently conceived of as having died that the nation might live.

V

There is another striking resemblance to the conceptual structure of genetic theory in biology. In his chapter on the Australian idea of the soul, Durkheim sets forth the idea, which was well known to me and many others of his readers, that they believed in a theory of reincarnation. That is, an ancestral spirit which is conceived to remain for long periods in some sacred place (a water hole, a rock, or something of this sort), was conceived of as entering the body of a woman, and this event was interpreted as that of actual conception. Beliefs with respect to the male role in reproduction have been somewhat equivocal. All this is familiar, but what I had not remembered from previous reading was that it was not the *whole* of the ancestral spirit substance which became reincarnated in the newly conceived child, but a *part*, split off, as it were, from the main spirit substance. This splitting is not necessarily believed in by all of the Australian tribes, but Durkheim cites chapter and verse with respect to some.

This is highly suggestive of what you might call the logic of the germ plasm. The chromosomes themselves and, it is now clear at the molecular level, DNA are conceived of as dividing and reproducing themselves; in DNA the two helical components divide, in the chromosomes one unites with a matching chromosome from the other parent of the offspring. In either case, what goes into a daughter cell is not the *whole* of the genetic material but is, as it were, a fragment or a fraction which has been split off from a continuing stock of such material. In other words, the genetic heritage embodied in chromosomes and DNA molecules is not embodied in *any particular* mortal cell or organism but continues as the basis of continuity of the organic type, most familiarly, the species. That such a belief should turn up in a very primitive society and that Durkheim should see fit to emphasize it is to me a very striking development, which is strongly suggestive of the basic theoretical continuity between the biological sciences and the sciences of action.

Another very striking feature of the new theory of genetics has been, as was noted, the conception of a code which is biochemically embodied in the structure of the DNA molecule, which, of course, would vary according to species but with a basic continuity in the pattern of the code itself (Stent 1970). This code then is conceived of as being the template on which, by way of RNA, the enzymes which are, in turn, the agents of synthesis of other complex molecules are developed. We have noted that there is a striking logical resemblance of the conception of the genetic code in its function to the theory of linguistics, which again has developed enormously since the time when Durkheim wrote. Language, however, may be treated as, in certain respects, the prototype of what we have come to call culture, and, surely, the two primary cultural categories of Durkheim's concern in the *Elementary Forms,* namely, codes defining moral order and those defining cognitive structures, are, in certain fundamental respects, isomorphic with linguistic codes.

It was indeed suggested some twenty years ago by the biologist Alfred Emerson (1956), probably among others, that there is a fundamental functional equivalence between the gene, that is, the genetic constitution of species, and what Emerson called the symbol, which we might amplify as the codified culture of human action systems. In both cases they constitute the primary locus of the continuity of organizational type, transcending, in the case of the genes, the individual organism and its subunits down to cells and, in the case of action, individual organisms and personalities and, indeed, social systems. In these codes, both genetic and cultural, serving as templates, it is possible to synthesize, in the terminology of linguistics, messages or utterances, which can be individualized and particularized and yet carry the element of commonness, which in the language case is necessary for effective communication.

VI

We have seen that the religious component centering in category of the sacred, the moral and the categorial or, for Kant, the a priori components of the cognitive system, constitute the grand triad of the fundamentals of a human action system as Durkheim worked them out in the *Elementary Forms*. In the terms I have been accustomed to using, these should be regarded as three primary focuses of the cultural system, namely, what I had called constitutive symbolization, moral-evaluative symbolization, and cognitive symbolization. They are then both institutionalized in societies in the analytical sense and internalized in personalities and behavioral organisms.

According to the theory of action, there should be a fourth central category at both the cultural and the other levels. At the cultural level it is what we have referred to as expressive symbolization, which links, in what loosely may be called social-psychological terms, with the category of affect which I, contrary to much current usage, tend to identify as a generalized medium of interchange primarily anchored in the *social* system, but specifically mediating primary interchanges with both personality and cultural systems (Parsons 1970). Where does this stand in Durkheim's analysis?

It seems to me that there are several clues. It will be remembered that just as he contrasted sense data with the categorical component of knowledge, he contrasted what he called the appetites with the element of moral authority and order. "Appetite" is a term which was rather widely current in the psychology of Durkheim's time but has largely gone out of use.

There are, then, two other extremely important references. In his handling of the descriptive material about ritual in the Australian system, Durkheim continually emphasizes the phenomenon he calls effervescence, which is that participants in the rituals and significantly the collective rather than magical versions, that is, those which he would call religious, manifest states of high emotional excitement, of exultation, and, in certain connections such as funeral ceremonies, despair leading to self-mutilation of a rather serious character. We may suggest that for Durkheim this emotional excitement is both genuine in the psychological sense and socially ordered. In the latter context he emphasizes that the pattern of action and interaction is laid down in detail in the tradition of the tribe prescribing who should do what, in relation to whom, at what point in the time sequence. Thus, though the excitement is psychologically genuine, it is not a matter of spontaneous reaction to immediate stimuli. This meticulous ordering, of course, relates very much to the fact that the ritual actions are permeated with symbolic meanings, which refer in Durkheim's emphases in particular to the structure and situation of the social system.

We think that these three aspects of religious ritual may legitimately be identified with the structure of what we may call the affective complex at the general level of action. The symbolization, we would suggest, must be culturally ordered, and this, in turn, suggests that there must be a code aspect of expressive symbolism, which is parellel to that in the cognitive and the moral realms. This is perhaps most explicit in Durkheim's chapters (1912: book III, ch. 3, 4) on the mimetic and the representative rites. The articulation with the personality of the individual seems, above all, to be indicated in a phenomenon of effervescence, including a very important interpretation which Durkheim puts on the rites, and the psychological states of the participants. This is his interpretation that the rites do, in fact, not only reinforce, but generate what he explicitly calls "faith." He very specifically states that beliefs alone do not suffice but that the believer is only fully a believer if he translates the meaning of his beliefs into actions. It is in this connection that Durkheim states his famous aphorism about religion, *C'est de la vie sérieuse.*

The societal references are involved, it seems to me, at two levels. The first, which figures prominently in Durkheim's analysis, refers to the social content of at least a very large proportion of the symbolization. From a certain point of view, the totem animal or other species of object symbolically speaking *is* the clan, and frequently the participants in ceremonies, especially as later work has shown, feel themselves actually to be the mythical symbolic entities whose actions their ritual patterns represent (Bellah 1970: 20–50, Warner 1958). We may very broadly say that the closeness of this identification of ritual symbolism with societal content is, at least in part, an index of the primitiveness of the religious system Durkheim is analyzing.

The other principal societal reference is in the very conspicuous interpretation of Durkheim that a primary function of religious ritual is the reinforcement and, we might even indeed say the creation, of solidarity. Solidarity, of course, is a concept which figured very centrally in Durkheim's theoretical thinking from his first published writings until his death. There is, then, a certain linkage between faith and solidarity, because those who share a common faith constitute precisely in Durkheim's own formula a moral community, which, in the case of what we in the modern world would call a church, is primarily religious but is also a secular social system; whereas what we think of as secular society also has the kind of religious aspect which Bellah analyzed as the civil religion. It is a question of relative primacies, not of presence or absence.

With respect to the code aspect of the expressive-affective system, we think that there are some extremely significant emphases in Durkheim's treatment which he did not attempt to codify theoretically but which link with a good deal of comparative evidence. On the one hand, there are a good many references to the ritual significance of blood and the shedding of blood in ritual contexts. The most conspicuous in the Australian case concerns the initiation ceremony. There is, of course, a note of deliberately inflicted pain and hardship, but, at the same time, blood is clearly a sacred symbol. In a recent book David Schneider (1968) has analyzed the significance of the symbol of blood in the context of such expressions as "blood relations" in American kinship, and this would certainly apply much more widely. Anyone interested in comparative religion, then, to cite only one case which was surely in Durkheim's mind, cannot miss that significance in the Christian institution of the Eucharist, which is the central ritual of Christianity. The wine is explicitly declared to be the blood of Christ.

Schneider also strongly emphasizes the symbolic significance for kinship of sexual intercourse, which has a dual reference, namely, to the recreation and extension of the nexus of blood relationships, since it is through sexual intercourse that human procreation takes place and the children of a couple are related to each other and to both their parents in this symbolic sense by blood, though the incest taboo prevents the parents from being related in that way to each other.

It is striking here that first Durkheim calls attention to the general tendency of rituals of what he calls the positive cult to generate sexual excitement as part of the effervescence, and, second, he points out references to actual cases of ritual sexual intercourse which have the extremely interesting feature of being incestuous in terms of the Australian rules of exogamy. Presumably such incestuous relations, which generally do not involve members of nuclear families, are confined to the ritual context. The suggestion is that blood and sexual intercourse are both part of a symbolic complex in which the references which Durkheim calls those to faith on the one hand, to social solidarity on the other, are central. The intercourse of a married couple is the primary symbol of their very special solidarity. Their assumption of the burden of parenthood may be said to be a primary symbol of their faith, that is, in the societal future that extends beyond themselves and their personal interests.

There is a second very prominent theme of ritual symbolism, in this case involving the function of eating. On the one hand, Durkheim claims it is generally true that in all, in his sense, profane circumstances, the totem is taboo as a food source for the members of the clan of which it is a totem. This taboo, however, like that against clan incest, is ritually broken on certain specific occasions when there are ceremonial totemic meals. Again, this seems to be a very general theme in ritual systems. Thus, the standard Hebrew sacrifice to Jahweh was the burnt offerings of animals specifically in a context of edibility. In Christianity the second main component of the Eucharist is the mutual partaking of bread, and this is explicitly declared to be the body of Christ; but it also symbolizes membership in the church as an actual social collectivity. Finally, it can hardly escape notice that a very special symbol of family solidarity is the act of eating family meals together, very specifically heightened in significance on special occasions in our culture, such as Thanksgiving, Christmas, and birthdays of family members.

There are many things about this complex that are obscure, but it seems to me very likely that Durkheim, following particularly on the work of Robertson Smith and the study of sacrifice by his own associates Hubert and Mauss (1964), contributed notably to the beginning elucidation of a very general code of ritual symbolism, which is culturally expressive rather than primarily cognitive or moral, which is intimately concerned with the maintenance of levels of motivation in the individual, but which is also intimately connected with social solidarity. It is probably significant that these symbols relate very specifically to aspects of the organism, which is in a certain sense the common groundwork of all the other aspects of human action.

VII

With this, we think that Durkheim was at least well on the way to rounding out a highly generalized analysis of the principal system references and components of action. In so doing, he made great advances toward placing his conception of society and its solidarity in the kind of broader context which is necessary if many of the perspectives of misunderstanding through narrow interpretation, which have plagued the discussion over Durkheim's work for at least two generations now, should be overcome. It should be evident that we are convinced that this step to a higher theoretical level than the overwhelming proportion of the discussion over Durkheim, including my own earlier discussion, will lead to a much fuller integration of biological theory with the theory of human action than has existed for a very long time, indeed, since the break of the social sciences with the older, evolutionary biology.

I think it can correctly be said that Durkheim's initial focus was on society as such on the one hand and on the problem of normative order with respect to it on the other, which led him directly to the moral component, especially in his conception of moral authority. In the evolution of his thought which led to the

Elementary Forms he not only, as it were, went behind his conception of the moral component in society, but he followed it to the levels of what Tillich (1952) called ultimate concerns, which were more or less explicitly religious. If, however, this was all that he had done, it might have constituted only a reversal of his original positivistic position and a return to a relatively conventional religious point of view, either that of the Judaism in which he was brought up or of the Catholicism which was the dominant explicit religion of France.

This, however, was not all that he did. First, he remained faithful to the emphases of the great positivistic tradition in by no means abandoning powerful stress on the significance of the cognitive component. He remained in a certain sense a Cartesian to the end but built his Cartesian frame of reference into a much wider paradigm of analysis. This appears in his consistent emphasis on the importance of the belief systems of his Australian subjects, however primitive and weird they may seem to the modern mind. Indeed, one can say unequivocally that placing, as he did, his great series of chapters on totemic beliefs before the chapters on ritual was a thoroughly considered decision on his part. He was never tempted by the kind of sociology of knowledge which would tend to make belief systems an altogether secondary function of other variables in the action system.

At the same time, however, he insisted on the centrality on the still further aspect of the more ultimate organization of an action system, namely, that expressed especially in ritual. This following up certain other developments in his earlier work, notably the conception of internalization and its relation to *anomie,* led him in a direction which would have included very close relations to psychology, namely, in those aspects which dealt with the nonrational. He did not go far along this path. For example, there is little evidence that he was very much aware of the beginnings of psychoanalysis. One must remember, however, that the first decade of the twentieth century saw only a very minimal dissemination of psychoanalytic ideas (A. Parsons 1956, 1969).[1] Nevertheless, Durkheim certainly in his anal-

---

[1] The last chapter has been published in English translation as ''Diffusion of Psychoanalytic Concepts'' in A. Parsons (1969).

ysis of ritual in its twin relations to faith on the one hand and solidarity on the other and the beginnings of the working out of the actual structure of symbolic codes made a very great contribution which can surely be integrated with those stemming from more technically psychological origins.

One may indeed perhaps say that, in line with many of the great traditions of Western thought, the most fundamental set of problems with which Durkheim was struggling concerned the conception of rationality and its limits. The problem was the nature of the cognitive component in human action, how was it related to noncognitive components, those ultimately involved in religious faith on one side, those involved in the motivations of human nature and the parameters of the human condition, all of these involving the question of the relation between rational, nonrational, and irrational aspects.

Certainly rereading the *Elementary Forms* strongly reinforces my conviction that Durkheim was one of the great contributors to the clarification of this very fundamental aspect of the human adventure. In the first instance, as a social scientist he had to have a very deep commitment, not only to the desirability of rationality, but to the feasibility of conducting studies by rational methods and producing verifiable results. At the same time, like his great contemporaries, especially Weber and Freud, he showed very deep sensitivity to the importance of the respects in which, shall we say, people as actors, as distinguished from people as scientists, could not be rational beings in the traditional sense of the Enlightenment. He not only arrived at certain general conclusions in this sphere, but he made immense progress in clarifying the theoretical framework in which these problems will have to be approached in the coming phase of our cultural history.

VIII

This chapter as originally submitted failed to fulfill one major request of the editors of this volume, namely, to deal with the fate of the ideas about religion put forward by the author in question in the intellectual development subsequent to the time of his writing. It has not been possible in the time available for me to do the scholarly work necessary for a thorough review of this question comparable, for instance, to that done by Benjamin Nelson on the aftermath of Max Weber's study of the Protestant ethic. A somewhat impressionistic outline will, however, be presented.

In spite of a great deal of obtuseness figuring in the discussion of Weber's Protestant ethic thesis, it has clearly been a major focus of attention in a variety of fields of the study of religion and society. When this attention is combined with that given to the concept of charisma and, somewhat less, to the comparative studies in the sociology of religion, it can probably be said that Weber's influence has been the most important of any scholar of his generation in that branch of the study of religion which connected closely with sociological problems.

By comparison, the impact of Durkheim strictly in this field seems to have been rather meager. Very broadly, my own interpretation of this fact is essentially that intellectually Durkheim was too far ahead of his time and that, with very few exceptions, the social scientists, who are the only ones who have paid serious attention to Durkheim's work, have simply not been ready to appreciate the importance of the kinds of considerations which Durkheim put forward in the *Elementary Forms* and in some other writings as they have been reviewed in the body of this paper. It is perhaps not an entirely rash prediction to suggest the possibility of a rediscovery of Durkheim in the relatively near future which will give him a very different place in cultural and intellectual history than he has so far enjoyed.

There has been a very serious blocking over what Durkheim meant by the concept of society and its relation to the individual. In the field of religion this has been most obviously manifest in the interpretation that he spoke of religious entities, notably the concept of God, as simply symbolic representations of society, meaning by ''society'' a concrete, empirical entity. For a variety of reasons this interpretation has been substantively unacceptable to most modern social scientists. It has, however, been used positively, especially by anthropologists, through its relation to their use of Durkheim's conception of the social functions of religious ritual as serving to reinforce social solidarity. This point of view has, of course, above all been put forward by Radcliffe-Brown (1939) and carried on by a number of his students and followers. Notably, perhaps, E. E. Evans-Pritchard (1956), W. E. H. Stanner (1969), and W. Lloyd Warner, the latter not only in his book, *A Black Civilization* (1958), which dealt with an Australian tribe, but in his study of American quasireligious rituals as exemplified by the study of Newburyport, Massachusetts (1959). With the exception of Warner, this line of thought has been most conspicuous in British social anthropology. Theoretically, I think Stanner (1969) has gone beyond the others.

Somewhat different emphases have appeared in the French tradition which in certain respects have been mediated by Marcell Mauss (1954) and in the present generation especially by Claude Levi-Strauss (1962, 1968). Levy-Strauss's structuralism, I think, can be said to owe a great deal to Durkheim, and its implications extend into the religious field. I would think also that the very great generalization of this point of view by Jean Piaget, as summarized in his recent little book *Structuralism* (1970), clearly also owes a great deal to Durkheim. Again, this is a very general, theoretical point of view which only in part relates to the study of religion.

Preoccupation with the problem of the status of the concept of society has, however, seriously obscured a very central theme in Durkheim's thought which is very much concerned with religion. This is the idea he referred to as "the cult of the individual," as connected with organic solidarity in Western societies. His postulation of the nature of the collective system has so offended Western traditions of individualism, above all, those in the English-speaking world, that he has almost universally been interpreted to be the great denier of the essential reality and importance of the individual. This is, it seems to me, a profound misinterpretation. I have referred to Durkheim's basic conception in this area as one of institutionalized individualism in which a very special synthesis of individuality and social solidarity has been developed in the modern Western world. This theme was somewhat further developed by Mauss (1968) in a notable article that on the religious front has, to my knowledge, only been taken up by Robert Bellah. Few have realized to what an extent Bellah's (1967) very seminal conception of the civil religion is grounded in Durkheim's thinking. A much more extensive review of Bellah's relation to Durkheim in this and other respects is contained in his Introduction to the volume *Emile Durkheim on Morality and Society* (forthcoming). Indeed, this Introduction, which became available to me only just as I was drafting this supplementary statement, makes it clear that Bellah stands virtually alone in not only the profoundity of his understanding of Durkheim's theoretical thinking, especially as it bears on the study of religion, but also in his positive use of Durkheim's insights in his own work. There are many points at which this becomes clear in the volume of Bellah's (1970) essays. It is particularly notable that the idea of the cult of the individual, but within the context of institutionalized individualism, is very central to Bellah's thinking.

Two other writers may be singled out for mention in this connection, though others might be. One, Kenneth Burke, is not a sociologist. I think here particularly of Burke's volume *The Rhetoric of Religion* (1961), but it is difficult to say how far Burke has been directly influenced by Durkheim. I would imagine not very much. There is, however, particularly in Burke's analysis of the symbolic content of Judaism and early Christianity in the essays of that volume, what seems to be a very definite convergence with the fully mature Durkheimian point of view in the *Elementary Forms*. Burke is one of the very few who have taken seriously the attempt to formulate what might be called a symbolic code as constitutive of basic religious orientations in the first case for the first three chapters of Genesis and in the second, in his analysis of the thought of St. Augustine. These seem to me to be specific studies which are directly in the line of development which Durkheim sketched out some sixty years ago.

Another very stimulating writer is Peter L. Berger, notably in his volume *Sacred Canopy* (1967). On the level of his analysis of religious symbol systems in the first four chapters of the book, it seems to me that Berger has developed a remarkably lucid picture which is basically very Durkheimian, though the extent to which, again, it is actually derived from Durkheim's influence remains unclear. Unfortunately, however, in the latter part of the book where Berger turns to the analysis of the process of secularization, he departs radically and, in my opinion, unfortunately from a Durkheimian perspective in what seems to be a kind of Neo-Marxian direction. The basic problem seems to be that he conceives of the world of the sacred as set totally over against the secular world, which to him is primarily focused on economic interest and the structure of markets. The all-important intermediate area of the solidarity of societal groups and communities is simply squeezed out, and, therefore, anything like a Durkheimian interpretation of the relation of religion to the nature and problems of modern society is radically precluded. Nevertheless, I think it can be said that Burke, who originated as a literary critic, and Berger, who is a sociologist specializing in religion, have been among those who have approached most closely to developing the lines of thought which Durkheim initiated. These books and the work of Bellah, which is as yet somewhat fragmentary, and also of such persons as Clifford Geertz (1968) seem to give a certain basis for the optimistic hope that the Durkheimian influence with special reference to religion has a fair prospect of coming into its own fairly soon.[2]

---

[2] How far the sociological profession still has to go in order to generalize such a level of appreciation of Durkheim's contributions is vividly illustrated by a chapter in a recent volume of essays by Reinhard Bendix and Guenther Roth (1971). In chapter 25 (written by Bendix), which is entitled "Two Sociological Traditions," a contrast is drawn between Weber and Durkheim with special reference to their respective contributions to the sociology of religion. Bendix is clearly one of the most culturally sophisticated of contemporary sociologists and a major contributor to the discipline in a number of fields. Yet the view of Durkheim which he presents, especially with respect to the field of religion, must be considered to be a caricature, not an interpretation. He accepts Durkheim's early statements of what I once called his "sociologistic positivism" at their face value, including the literal and naïve version of the view that God symbolizes society. This is to say that Bendix, as he put it in an earlier volume of essays (1970), treated Durkheim as a sociological reductionist, treating religion and various other phenomena as simple functions of an allegedly unproblematical entity called society—in a parallel fashion he there treated Freud as a biological reductionist—both in highly unfavorable contrast with Weber. The contrast of this picture of Durkheim with that presented by Bellah (forthcoming) and, if I may say so, in the body of the present essay, could hardly be sharper.

BIBLIOGRAPHY

Bellah, Robert N.
  1959   Durkheim and History. *American Sociological Review* Vol.
          24, no. 4 (August), pp. 447–61.
  1967   Civil Religion in America. *Daedalus* Vol. 96, no. 1 (Winter),
          pp. 1–21.
  1970   *Beyond Belief: Essays on Religion in a Post-Traditional
          World.* New York: Harper & Row.
  Forth- Introduction to *Emile Durkheim on Morality and Society.*
  coming Heritage of Sociology Series. Chicago: University of Chi-
          cago Press.

Bendix, Reinhard
  1970   *Embattled Reason: Essays on Social Knowledge.* New York:
          Oxford University Press.
———, and Roth, Guenther.
  1971   *Scholarship and Partisanship: Essays on Max Weber.* Berke-
          ley and Los Angeles, Calif.: University of California Press.

Bernard, Claude
  1957   *An Introduction to the Study of Experimental Medicine.*
          Trans. H. C. Green. New York: Daler.

Burke, Kenneth
  1961   *The Rhetoric of Religion.* Boston: Beacon Press.

Cannon, W. B.
  1932   *The Wisdom of the Body.* New York: Norton.

Durkheim, Emile
  1893   *De la division du travail social.* Paris: Librarie Felix Alcan.
  tr. 1933 *On the Division of Labor in Society.* Trans. George Simp-
          son. New York: Macmillan.
  1912   *Les formes élémentaires de la vie religieuse: Le système to-*
  tr. 1915 *temique en Australie.* Paris: Librarie Felix Alcan. *The
          Elementary Forms of the Religious Life.* Trans. Joseph W.
          Swain. London: George Allen and Unwin.

Emerson, Alfred E.
  1956   Homeostasis and Comparison of Systems. In Roy R. Grinker,
          Sr., ed. *Toward a Unified Theory of Human Behavior: An
          Introduction to General Systems Theory.* New York: Basic
          Books, Inc.

Evans-Pritchard, E. E.
  1956   *Nuer Religion.* Oxford: Clarendon Press.

Geertz, Clifford
    1968   Religion as a Cultural System. In Donald R. Cutler, ed. *The Religious Situation*. Boston: Beacon Press.

Hubert, Henri, and Mauss, Marcel
    1964   *Sacrifice: Its Nature and Function*. Trans. W. D. Halls. Chicago: University of Chicago Press.

Lévi-Strauss, Claude
    1962   *Totemism*. Boston: Beacon Press.
    1963   *Structural Anthropology*. New York: Basic Books, Inc.

Mauss, Marcell
    1954   *The Gift*. London: Cohen and West.
    1968   A Category of the Human Spirit. In Benjamin Nelson, ed. *Histories, Symbolic Logics, and Cultural Maps*. A special issue of *The Psycho-Analytic Review* Vol. 55, no. 3 (September), pp. 457–81.

Nelson, Benjamin
    1949   *The Idea of Usury*. Princeton, N.J.: Princeton University Press.

Olby, Robert
    1970   Francis Crick, DNA, and the Central Dogma. *Daedalus* 99 (Fall): 938–87.

Parsons, A.
    1956   La pénétration de la psychoanalyse en France et aux Etats Unis. Doctoral dissertation. Sorbonne.
    1969   *Belief, Magic and Anomie*. New York: The Free Press.

Parsons, Talcott
    1937   *The Structure of Social Action*. New York: McGraw-Hill.
    1970   Some Problems of General Theory in Sociology. In John C. McKinney and Edward A. Tiryakian, eds. *Theoretical Sociology: Perspectives and Developments*. New York: Appleton-Century-Crofts.

Piaget, Jean
    1970   *Structuralism*. Trans. and ed. Chaninah Maschler. New York: Basic Books, Inc.

Radcliffe-Brown, A. R.
    1939   *Taboo*. New York: Cambridge University Press.
    1952   *Structure and Function in Primitive Society*. New York: The Free Press.

Schneider, David M.
    1968   *American Kinship: A Cultural Account.* Englewood Cliffs,
           N.J.: Prentice-Hall.

Stanner, W. E. H.
    1969   *On Aboriginal Religion.* Melbourne: Oceania Monographs
           #11.

Stent, Gunther S.
    1970   DNA. *Daedalus* 99 (Fall): 909–37.

Stern, Curt
    1970   The Continuity of Genetics. *Daedalus* 99 (Fall): 882–908.

Tillich, Paul
    1952   *The Courage to Be.* New Haven, Conn.: Yale University
           Press.

Warner, W. L.
    1958   *A Black Civilization: A Social Study of an Australian Tribe.*
           New York: Harper & Row, rev. ed.
    1959   *The Living and the Dead: A Study of the Symbolic Life of
           Americans,* Vol. 5 in The Yankee City Series. New Haven,
           Conn.: Yale University Press.

5 THE ANTHROPOLOGY OF RELIGION: MALINOWSKI AND BEYOND

Leonard Glick

As a true officiating magician in a savage tribe would have to do, I have to recite the whole list, so that the spirit of the works (their 'mana') may dwell among us.

(Malinowski 1926)

I

The contribution of modern anthropologists to the study of religion can be summed up by saying that they have taught us to take seriously all religions, no matter how exotic or bizarre on first acquaintance, and to make an effort to understand them as other ways of thinking about the world and responding to it.[1] Perhaps this lesson is now an accepted part of our intellectual perspective, but it is a relatively new lesson, nevertheless. Prior to this century and well into its early decades the religions of most people in the colonial world were looked upon as of interest primarily for the light they could shed on the early history of humanity, for it was assumed that the religions of civilized people were of a different, more advanced order from those of the heathens whom they missionized and dominated. To put this an-

[1] This paper was completed in December 1969 and does not take into consideration anything published after that date. A number of colleagues at the University of Wisconsin commented helpfully on this paper. For extensive suggestions, most of which were incorporated into the final draft, I am especially indebted to Catharine McClellan and Phillip E. Hammond.

other way, one studied primitive religions not so much for what they might have to teach about religion as for the insights they might afford into the mysterious workings of the primitive mind.[2]

This tradition is rooted in European intellectual history, and we can only take fleeting notice here of some of the major ideas and themes that lie in the background of anthropology as we know it today (cf. Hodgen 1964). Some anthropologists would have us trace our lineage back to Herodotus, but I am more in accord with those who would begin the story with the Age of Discovery and the awakened curiosity of Renaissance people about other peoples and places (Hallowell 1965). Next must be mentioned the writings of Enlightenment philosophers on progress in human thought and institutions, for from their ideas it was a short step to the nineteenth-century theory of cultural evolution. According to this theory, which found fullest expression in the work of E. B. Tylor (1871), by studying the cultures of primitive peoples one might reconstruct the cultural history of our species stage by stage from the customs and beliefs of the lowliest aboriginal to those of the most cultivated European. Given this profoundly ethnocentric intellectual milieu, it is not difficult to understand why in the conception of James Frazer and other turn-of-the-century scholars, folk beliefs and rituals were interpreted not as religious systems on a par with our own, but as evidences for stages in the evolution of human thought. In short, the anthropological study of religion was conducted as a kind of adventure into the past—an intellectual exploration into the primitive origins of the modern mind.

By around 1910 a few ethnologists had begun to reject evolutionism in favor of less ambitious studies of how specific cultural

---

[2] The final and most penetrating statements of this point of view were in the writings of the French philosopher-ethnologist Lucien Lévy-Bruhl (1923, 1926). In advancing his concept of the "prelogical" mentality, Lévy-Bruhl did not deny ordinary human mental capacities to other peoples; he simply maintained that their logic was based on nonscientific premises. A more defensible proposition would have been that all peoples exhibit logical and "prelogical" dimensions in their thinking. See Evans-Pritchard's chapter on Lévy-Bruhl in *Theories of Primitive Religion* (1965). See also Needham (1965).

For reasons that may be apparent the word "primitive" is out of fashion in anthropology. My use of it in historical context should not be taken for a personal statement on its appropriateness for anthropology today.

traits or clusters of related traits had developed and undergone reinterpretation as they diffused from one geographical-cultural area to another. But although their work was on the whole more rigorous and nearer to modern standards than that of their predecessors, they were still tracing the lives of customs and artifacts rather than describing and interpreting particular ways of life.

In the decade beginning in 1910, one of the leading ethnologists in England was C. G. Seligman of the London School of Economics. Having conducted substantial field research in Melanesia, Ceylon, and the Sudan, Seligman was sensitive to the value of thorough ethnographic studies (Firth 1965 : 2). In retrospect, however, his most enduring contribution to ethnography was not his own work but his sponsorship of the field studies of his most creative student, Bronislaw Malinowski.

Malinowski had arrived in London in 1910, "a pale, bespectacled student with a high forehead" (Firth 1957 : 5), already possessed of a doctorate in physics and mathematics from his native Cracow and an additional term of study under Wundt at Leipzig (Métraux 1968). Within two or three years he had become an established anthropological scholar (e.g., Malinowski 1913), and Seligman secured for him a modest grant for field research in Melanesia. In 1914 he departed for the South Pacific. In June 1915, following a brief and not particularly distinguished term of work among the Mailu of Papua, he arrived in the Trobriand Islands, near the eastern tip of the island of Papua-New Guinea. He remained there until May 1916 and returned for a second year from October 1917 to October 1918. His experiences there were the turning point in his career and underlay all that he wrote thereafter.

It would be a distortion to maintain that in the course of this work Malinowski was totally liberated from the biases of his predecessors. He consistently referred to the Trobrianders as savages (e.g., 1929), and we know now that while among them he endured more ennui, depression, and even repulsion than most anthropologists would ever admit to (cf. Malinowski 1967). But with that acknowledged, the fact remains that his field methods and their results were unique :

The most crucial innovation was that he actually pitched his tent in the middle of the village, learned the language in its colloquial form, and observed directly at first hand just how his Trobriand neighbors behaved throughout the 24 hours of an ordinary working day. No European had ever done this before and the kind of ethnography that resulted was completely new. Where his predecessors had spent their time describing the manners and customs and artifacts of a primitive tribe Malinowski found himself describing a way of life (Leach 1965).

Even before his field work was completed, Malinowski published a remarkable essay on Trobriand religion. This was "Baloma," a study of beliefs about the soul, death, and the afterlife (1916). Although seldom cited nowadays,[3] "Baloma" has reached a new audience in a paperback edition (1954, with "Magic, Science and Religion" and "Myth in Primitive Psychology")[4] and deserves attention as a prototype for Malinowski's better known ethnographic achievements. For here already displayed are those qualities which distinguished his work from that of his predecessors: his ability to convey ethnographic work as a deeply personal experience and to document that experience richly, while at the same time demonstrating that ethnography does not mean just amassing a "chaos of facts" but "grasping what is essential" and "subordinating it to general rules" (1954: 238).

Malinowski was not altogether consistent in his theoretical writings over the years, but it should be explained that the "general rules" to which he refers have to do with the realization that the various parts ("institutions") of a culture are interdependent and that each satisfies particular biological and psychological needs. Both can be remembered in connection with the term "function" (which Malinowski did much to popularize). The first principle—that parts of a culture are "functionally" interrelated—is perhaps best demonstrated in the celebrated *Argonauts of the Western Pacific* (1922), in which a description of a trading arrangement leads into extensive discourses on canoe making, magic, and other aspects of Trobriand life. The second principle—that the "function" of institutions is

---

[3] But see Gluckman's comment (1963: 263).

[4] All references to these three essays will be to this readily available edition.

to satisfy basic needs—is most memorably expressed in all his writings on magic and religion, including "Baloma."

In "Baloma" Malinowski stated for the first time the essence of his theory of religion: the heart of religious belief and practice lies in man's inability to accept the prospect of his own individual extinction. Beliefs in spirits are a logical expression of the human need to believe that the essential person lives on after bodily death and may continue to participate in human affairs. In a later essay on "The Foundations of Faith and Morals" (1936) he cited "belief in Providence" and "belief in Immortality" as universal religious affirmations, but of the two it was the latter—the conviction that "beyond the brief span of natural life there is a compensation in another existence" (1962 : 335)—that he perceived as the very core of religion.

The role of religion, then, is to deny death and to affirm life. But what is one to do when life, as it must, proves to be one long succession of difficulties, dangers, and disasters? How can one preserve health, prolong life, and avert death in a world that seems to care nothing for people and their purposes? Malinowski found the answer—or rather discovered other people finding the answer—in magic. More than any other aspect of Trobriand culture, magic seems to have decisively captured his attention; it is the key to much of his most important work, including *Argonauts of the Western Pacific* (1922) as well as *Coral Gardens and Their Magic* (1935). In these books and others one fundamental argument appears and reappears: The people of the Trobriands (and, by extension, primitive people everywhere) live with ordinary human needs—food, health, security—in the forefront of their minds. But ordinary human powers are never adequate to guarantee that these needs will be satisfied, that fears of starvation, disease, and disaster will not be realized; and so people turn to magical rites and "spells" in hopes of more firmly securing that which can never be wholly secured. No less rational or practical than we ourselves, they turn to these seemingly inadequate devices not because they are foolish or childish, but because hard empirical experience tells them that life seldom proceeds according to plan and that only by employing every available source of power and control can they anticipate success.

But it is in his classic "Magic, Science and Religion" (1925) that Malinowski most vividly develops this argument. The key to "Magic, Science and Religion" is that although religion occupies more of its pages, magic is its pivotal subject. In this connection it should be noted that Malinowski conceived of the essay as being an extension of the work of the man whom he looked upon as his most illustrious predecessor: Sir James Frazer, author of *The Golden Bough*. Despite his enduring reputation,[5] Frazer has long since fallen from his pedestal in professional ranks (Leach 1966); the annual Frazer lectures have become a ritual of rejection in which anthropologists select a Frazerian theme and demolish it (cf., e.g., Firth 1955, Fortes 1959). But in Malinowski's eyes Frazer was anthropology's finest flower and *The Golden Bough* the embodiment of its promise:

> If I had the power of evoking the past, I should like to lead you back some twenty years to an old Slavonic university town. . . . I could then show you a student leaving the medieval college buildings, obviously in some distress of mind, hugging, however, under his arm, as the only solace of his troubles, three green volumes with the well-known golden imprint, a beautiful conventionalized design of mistletoe—the symbol of *The Golden Bough*. . . . [M]y first attempt to read an English masterpiece in the original. . . . [N]o sooner had I begun to read this great work, than I became immersed in it and enslaved by it. I realized then that anthropology, as presented by Sir James Frazer, is a great science, worthy of as much devotion as any of her elder and exact sister studies, and I became bound to the service of Frazerian anthropology.
>
> (Malinowski 1954: 93–94)

Nor did Frazer, despite his years (*The Golden Bough* first appeared in 1890), represent only the past; in Malinowski's view he had paved the way for his successors. Malinowski tells us that while he was in the Trobriands letters from Frazer "helped me more by suggestion, query and comment than any other influence" (1944 : 182); and indeed, although he dedicated *Argonauts* to Seligman, he asked Frazer to write the preface. But most important for our immediate concerns, in "Magic, Science and Religion" he takes his lead explicitly from Frazer:

> The extended and deepened outlook of modern anthropology finds its most adequate expression in the learned and inspiring writings of Sir James Frazer. In these he has set forth the main problems of

[5] "It may be said without reasonable fear of contradiction that no other work in the field of anthropology has contributed so much to the mental and artistic climate of our times" (Gaster 1959: xix).

primitive religion with which present-day anthropology is busy: magic and its relation to religion and science; totemism and the sociological aspect of early faith; the cults of fertility and vegetation.

(1954: 18–19)

In short, Malinowski conceived of his mission in "Magic, Science and Religion" as being amplification of Frazer's leading themes, most especially the role of magic in primitive life. Indeed, the very title of the essay reveals the impact of Frazer's anthropology. *The Golden Bough* is about many things, but its central theme is magic. In the final abridged edition of the book (1922) the two key chapters are those entitled "Sympathetic Magic" and "Magic and Religion." Here Frazer sets out the thesis with which Malinowski was to take issue (but only in the role of loyal *epigone*): In primitive stages of human mental development, people believed (as some continue to believe) that objects and events can influence one another through a mystical relationship—"a secret sympathy" (1922: 14). This assumes two basic forms: the "law of similarity," expressed in "homeopathic magic," asserts that "like produces like, or that an effect resembles its cause"—in other words, that an effect can be produced by imitating it; the "law of contact," expressed in "contagious magic," assumes that "things which have once been in contact with each other continue to act on each other at a distance after the physical contact has been severed" (1922: 12).

Magic in Frazer's view is thus "a spurious system of natural law" (1922: 13) having the same goals as science but grounded in false principles. Both magic and science assume that the world is orderly and events are controllable by people, but the one is the "bastard sister" of the other (1922: 56–57). The magician may postulate the existence of spirits but he "constrains or coerces" them to achieve his ends. Religion stands apart from both magic and science in postulating the existence of superior powers which cannot be controlled by such means but only by "conciliating or propitiating" them (1922: 59). Frazer interprets this as a more complex system of thought and therefore concludes that an "Age of Magic" must have preceded an "Age of Religion" in human development.

This is not the place for an extended critique of Frazer's anthropology (cf. Leach 1966). But as we return to Malinowski, we should keep in mind not only the manner in which he reworks Frazer's theories but also the experience from which each man's approach derived: Frazer's, from library research into literally hundreds of sources of diverse vintage and quality; Malinowski's, from a single intensive field study which had no contemporary parallel.

Magic, then, is the pivotal subject of "Magic, Science and Religion," just as it was in *The Golden Bough,* but with this fundamental difference: Malinowski rejects the idea of ages of magic and religion; replying explicitly to Frazer and other evolutionists of similar persuasion, he asserts that no people have ever been without religion.[6] For that matter, he also rejects the assumption that any people lack a form of science, which he takes to include any empirically derived knowledge.

"Magic, Science and Religion" thus takes issue with the "learned and inspiring writings" of the honored predecessor at such a fundamental level that only the subject of inquiry reveals their kinship. Malinowski is responding to Frazer but not in the Frazerian idiom. He has now completely rephrased the problem as follows: All people have religion, and all have some form of science; but why do some people also depend so heavily on magic? His answer, once again, is that where human powers alone are insufficient for the realization of human needs and desires, magic helps fill the gap. Obvious though this may seem now, it represented a significant departure from Frazer and indeed from all anthropology that interpreted primitive thought as something generically distinct from our own; for as Malinowski presents the case, though Trobriand magic, examined alone, might appear to be irrational, in the context of Trobriand culture it is understandable as a powerful adjunct to wholly rational practices and purposes.

But, he insists, it is only an adjunct. For primitive people are by no means lacking in rudimentary science, if by that term we refer simply to empirical knowledge. Institutionalized science in the Western sense they obviously lack, but it does not follow that they are therefore incapable of rational, pragmatic thought and

---

[6] The opening sentence of the essay comes right to the point: "There are no peoples however primitive without religion and magic." The words "however" and "and" bear more weight than may be immediately apparent.

action. To the contrary, this is as much the stuff of their lives as of our own. The difference lies in their placing more trust than we ordinarily do in magical *reinforcements* to such activities.

As for religion, this too he explains as not only rational but indispensable to the fulfillment of human needs in a social context. The distinction between magic and religion, as Malinowski sees it, is that the former is addressed to the immediate needs of the individual (his or her reaching out for security in the face of imminent uncertainty and danger) and is thus largely a personal thing, while the latter comprehends the most important events of a lifetime—especially those associated with role transition—and endows them with meaning and value transcending individual concerns. In other words, although religious rituals, like magical practices, gratify the needs of individuals for support and reassurance, they also express fundamental social values that serve the needs of individuals only indirectly. Malinowski rejects equations of society and religion, insisting that they support one another but are not the same thing. But since he is so often described as sociologically naïve, we should note that he was not unaware of the social element in religion, only convinced that there is more to it than that. For while plainly recognizing the public character of ritual as one of its definitive features, he still maintains that "the social share in religious enactment is a condition necessary but not sufficient" (1954: 69), which is to say that religion must satisfy something within individuals or it would not play such a preeminent role in human affairs.

Taking up several other Frazerian themes—totemism, initiation, sacrifice, communion—Malinowski arrives in each case at the same conclusion: Religion is an essential institution in every human society because it meets certain basic needs that can be met by no other institution.

As in his other writings, Malinowski reiterates his conviction that "of all sources of religion, the supreme and final crisis of life—death—is of the greatest importance" (1954: 47). Here again he so extends and reinterprets Frazer's conclusions as to end up rejecting them. Frazer had asserted that "probably the most powerful force in the making of primitive religion" had been "fear of the human dead" (1922: vii). Malinowski discovers fear to be but one aspect of a complex response to death compounded of "passionate attachment to the personality still lingering about the body and a shattering fear of the gruesome thing that has been left over" (1954: 48), and he demonstrates that mortuary rites reflect this ambiguity. But ultimately hope triumphs over fear, and the promise of enduring life for the spirit assuages grief over death of the body: "into this play of emotional forces, into this supreme dilemma of life and final death, religion steps in, selecting the positive creed, the comforting view, the culturally valuable belief in immortality, in the spirit independent of the body, and in the continuation of life after death" (1954: 51). In short, the ultimate purpose of religion is to assure people that they are not mere mortals.

Nadel rightly observes (1957: 205–6) that Malinowski was less sure of his ground in discussing religion than in discussing magic. Perhaps the weakest section of "Magic, Science and Religion" is that in which he sums up the case for distinguishing magic from religion, for the distinction is largely academic. Both magical and religious practices mobilize extrahuman powers to serve human purposes, and the determination of whether an action is magical or religious is not as clear-cut as Malinowski made it out to be. If, as Nadel maintains, he ended up demonstrating that "religion was little more than a bigger and better kind of magic" (1957: 200), he was on the right track.

Summing up now, what can be said about Malinowski's legacy to anthropology and specifically to the anthropological study of religion? Perhaps his most vital contribution should be mentioned first of all: Having experienced another way of life with such compelling intimacy, Malinowski came to appreciate the role of religious belief and practice in the everyday affairs of living men and women, and to reject interpretations grounded in the idea that the religions of primitive peoples are exotic relics of the "childhood" of the human species. Thus he insisted that there could have been no "Age of Magic" or "Age of Religion" but rather that magic, religion, and even science were the common possessions of humanity in every era. In accord with his concept of "functional" relationships, he showed that not only do the people of the Trobriands exhibit magical, religious, and scientific elements in their behavior, but that each has its rational purposes and its place in a larger scheme. Finally he demonstrated, often dramatically, that magic and religion satisfy peoples' needs for certainty and security in a hostile and otherwise hopelessly arbitrary world.

Malinowski's writings have gradually assumed the status of classics among anthropologists of every persuasion. The Trobriand Islanders, their *kula* trading ring and their magic, have become such standard illustrations, not only among anthropologists but for everyone writing about primitive culture, as to hardly require citation. It will be well to remember, then, as we proceed and sometimes lose sight of Malinowski for a time, that his contributions to anthropological method and thought were so fundamental as to be taken for granted by many authors who were indebted to him for their most essential heritage.

II

The year in which *Argonauts of the Western Pacific* appeared also witnessed the publication of another anthropological classic, *The Andaman Islanders,* by A. R. Radcliffe-Brown (1948, orig. 1922).[7] Although quite different from *Argonauts* in style, this book also embodied a critical departure from traditional ethnography, having undergone such radical revision from its initial form that information collected for the author's original purposes had to be relegated to a lengthy appendix. For Radcliffe-Brown's field research had been conducted from 1906 to 1908, while Malinowski was still a physics student in Cracow, and his goal at the time had been a traditional reconstruction of culture history:

> It was largely from this point of view that I approached the study of the Andaman Islanders and attempted, by an investigation of physical characters, language and culture, to make a hypothetical reconstruction of the history of the Andamans and of the Negritos in general.
>
> (1948: vii)

But by 1914 he had rewritten the book in the form in which it eventually reached publication, and this was far removed from historical reconstruction. In fact, he had explicitly rejected

[7] He was A. R. Brown then, but the name soon expanded along with his reputation.

historical ethnology in favor of a synchronic and comparative approach resembling that of the natural sciences: "intensive investigation of each culture as an adaptive and integrative mechanism and a comparison one with another of as many variant types as possible" (1948: ix). (Later he insisted that he and his students were strictly "comparative sociologists" and abandoned the term "culture" to Malinowski and the Americans.)

Radcliffe-Brown was heir to the positivist tradition in the study of religion, exemplified in the preceding generation by the work of the Scottish theological historian Robertson-Smith (1889) and that of Emile Durkheim (1912). Simplifying somewhat, their legacy may be said to resolve into two key propositions. First, ritual, as opposed to belief ("myth"), is the essential and sole observable component of religion, hence the proper subject for scientific study. Second, ritual is social behavior and must therefore be interpreted sociologically. Though Radcliffe-Brown formally adhered to these dicta, he held more in common with Malinowski's psychologically slanted "functionalism" than is generally recognized.

Despite its noncommittal title (perhaps a carry-over from the author's original plan), five of the six chapters in *The Andaman Islanders* have to do with religion. Indeed, the book can be epitomized as an attempt to answer one question: Why do Andaman Islanders adhere to certain religious beliefs and perform certain rituals?

Radcliffe-Brown's answer combines sociological and psychological explanations (1948: 230). It hinges on the principle that each element in religion has a "function," meaning that each is an integral and supportive component of a social-cultural system (see esp. chap. 5). Although his interpretation is thus primarily sociological in emphasis, it is also psychological, because the intervening variable between ritual and society is what he calls "sentiments" (a term borrowed from the social psychologist Shand):

> I have tried to show that the ceremonial customs are the means by which the society acts upon its individual members and keeps alive in their minds a certain system of sentiments. Without the cere-

monial those sentiments would not exist, and without them the social organization in its actual form could not exist.

(1948: 324)

Some twenty-three years later, when he summed up his thoughts on religion and society, his views were essentially unchanged:

Rites can be seen to be the regulated symbolic expression of certain sentiments. Rites can therefore be shown to have a specific social function when, and to the extent that, they have for their effect to regulate, maintain and transmit from one generation to another sentiments on which the constitution of the society depends.

(1952: 157)

In their later years Malinowski and Radcliffe-Brown both maintained that their ethnographic theories held little in common. Neither went to great lengths to spell out their differences, although Radcliffe-Brown mentioned briefly one major point of disagreement in his essay entitled "Taboo" (the 1939 Frazer lecture). Here he argues against Malinowski's contention that because magic serves practical purposes, it is plainly distinguishable from religion, which is "simply expressive"; to the contrary, he maintains, many religious beliefs and rites are practically grounded, and in fact the distinction between magic and religion may turn out to be little more than a problem in definition (1952: 137–38).[8]

But more important than such disagreements are the striking correspondences in the work of these two pioneers. Comparing the key chapter of Radcliffe-Brown's ethnography (5: "The Interpretation of Andamanese Customs and Beliefs: Ceremonial") with the first and final chapters of *Argonauts of the Western Pacific,* we see how similar they are at the core. Both emphasize the importance of recording statements in a people's own vernacular. Both recognize that the various components of a culture are "functionally" related. Both demonstrate that reli-

[8] Whereas Malinowski saw the function of ritual to be relief from anxiety, Radcliffe-Brown maintained that anxiety was generated when rituals were not performed properly or on time. Homans (1941) resolved this tempest in a teacup with an economical interpretation embracing both arguments and drew the appropriate moral: "two distinguished persons talking past one another rather than trying to find a common ground for discussion."

gion promotes fundamental social values. Both cite the mixture
of fear and affection with which people regard dead kinspeople
and draw implications from this apparent paradox. Most important, both maintain that all religions, no matter how exotic, are
understandable as coherent systems of belief and practice serving universal human needs and purposes.

Although not nearly as prolific a writer as Malinowski, Radcliffe-Brown profoundly influenced a generation of students
throughout the world. Indeed both he and Malinowski thoroughly dominated British anthropology until the 1940s and
molded every member of the generation of social anthropologists
who achieved prominence around that time. But meanwhile in
the United States another anthropological tradition, closely related to the work of Malinowski in particular but sufficiently
distinct to require separate consideration, was developing under
the mentorship of another European, Franz Boas. Until around
mid-century his students, who identified themselves not as social
but as cultural anthropologists, pursued studies in cultural history and cultural psychology which set them more or less apart
from British anthropologists. As the name indicates, culture—
conceived of as the total constellation of beliefs, behavior, and
products of behavior characteristic of a particular way of life—
became the focal concept of the Americans and underlay nearly
everything they wrote. In contrast, their British counterparts
were working in the Durkheimian sociological tradition established in the main by Radcliffe-Brown.

But by the beginning of the next decade the two schools were
drawing much nearer together. Radcliffe-Brown and Malinowski
had both contributed to this process. The former taught at the
University of Chicago from 1931 to 1937 and left a permanent
imprint on anthropology at that institution especially. Malinowski visited the United States several times to teach and
study, and ended his career at Yale University, where he taught
intermittently from 1939 until his death in 1942. It would appear
that his experiences with students in this country were not
altogether gratifying (Métraux 1968: 546), but in the perspective
of another thirty years there can be no question about his impact
on American anthropology.

By the 1950s the interests of cultural and social anthropologists, particularly many of the younger scholars, had grown so close together that their work may be considered as variants of a single tradition. In the next two sections, therefore, I shall first examine developments in the United States from the time of Boas until mid-century or thereabout; after which we should be prepared to discuss work over the past two decades as an international endeavor embracing British and American anthropologists as well as those from other nations.

III

Although studies of American Indian life and associated theorizing about relations between primitive culture and civilization were well underway in the United States by the late nineteenth century, it was not until after the turn of the century that anthropology was established as a professional discipline with university affiliations. The credit for this transition is generally accorded to a single man, Franz Boas, a German physical geographer who came to America in the 1880s to study Eskimos and Northwest Coast Indians and remained to become professor of anthropology at Columbia University. Hardly a more striking contrast to Malinowski in personality and working style could be imagined. If empiricism was a working principle for Malinowski, for Boas it was almost a religion; for he was convinced that nothing short of rigorous fidelity to native texts was essential if anthropology was ever to achieve credibility as a scientific discipline, and he was determined that it should. In this respect his own ethnographic writings on religion can be instructively compared with those of Malinowski. Restricted in large measure to unedited texts and word-for-word translations, all but devoid of interpretive comment, they stand like mines of unworked ore in contrast to Malinowski's multifaceted and deliberately styled literary creations. To grasp the difference in full one need only compare, for example, Boas's writings on Kwakiutl religion (e.g. 1927, 1930) with "Magic, Science and Religion."

But whatever the ultimate judgment on Boas's ethnographic work (cf. Harris 1968: chaps. 9–11, Goldschmidt 1959), there can be little question that the flowering of outstanding research which characterized the period between about 1915 and 1950 in the United States must be credited largely to his teaching and writing. The goal he set before his students was cultural history —that is, the history of how particular cultures and their component parts had developed and influenced one another—based on careful, detailed investigations of individual cultures. Although world ethnology was their ostensible goal, the cultures with which these scholars were in fact to be primarily (almost exclusively) concerned were those of American Indians. More than may be immediately apparent, this shaped their work and distinguished it from that of their British counterparts.

For one thing, they were conducting research not in overseas colonial territories but among people who had been uniquely victimized by the very nation which now, paradoxically, looked upon them as part of its own vanishing natural heritage. Cultural anthropology was thus in a sense conceived of as being a kind of natural history. Moreover, because most American Indians were no longer living in intact *societies,* the emphasis necessarily fell on their *cultures*—cultures sometimes remembered only by the elderly and, in any event, no longer lived or experienced in aboriginal form. This meant, for instance, that one might learn about an aboriginal ritual and perhaps see objects associated with its performance but never be able to observe the ritual as part of an ongoing way of life. Finally, in contrast to the British, who were studying African and Pacific societies which were said to have no discoverable history, American anthropologists understandably looked upon history as the cornerstone of their ethnology.

With these points in mind we can understand why cultural anthropology, which clearly resembled Malinowski's work in a number of important respects (emphasis on field work, deep interest in cultural particulars, rejection of evolutionary schemes), nevertheless differed from it in one major respect. Whereas Malinowski relied almost entirely on his own observations of everyday behavior, American anthropologists characteristically employed their subjects to tell them about the traditional culture of times past. Phrasing this somewhat differently, we may say that whereas Malinowski set out to explain the *behavior* of individually observed human subjects, American anthropologists set out to explain *cultural phenomena* on the basis of what their subjects told them about traditional life.

Let me elaborate on this by describing a brief study by the man most often cited as the outstanding cultural anthropologist of his generation, A. L. Kroeber. This is a chapter entitled "The Growth of a Primitive Religion" which appeared in the first edition of his textbook, *Anthropology* (1923). The word "growth" epitomizes Kroeber's perspective on cultural anthropology. He looked upon it as a branch of natural history concerned with the life of cultures—how they grew, changed, developed variants, achieved climactic expression, disappeared; and how they might be classified into natural groupings based on demonstrable relationships, much as the biologist established taxonomic groupings (1923: 295; cf. Kroeber 1952: 3–11, 57–62). In this chapter his subject is ritual practices of the Indians of California. His purpose is to determine the order in which particular rituals appeared (and, if possible, to date these appearances), then to set them in context by correlating "religious development" with "cultural development" (1923: 314–15). Beginning with distributions—some rituals are found throughout the California area, others only in subareas—he applies the so-called age-area hypothesis (the more widespread a cultural trait, the older it probably is) to establish periods of religious development. We see then that he approaches religious traditions as cultural traits (or trait clusters) whose evolution and diffusion can be traced and compared.

Note that Kroeber is not describing the rituals of a particular community; he is concerned, rather, with the history of rituals, conceived of as cultural forms existing independent of the people who performed them. This is not to say, of course, that he was unaware that rituals require people for their performance, only that his subject was the history of the rituals themselves.

This concept of cultural anthropology as the history of customs and institutions also contrasted with Malinowski's approach in that it rather self-consciously avoided psychological considerations as constituting a different order (or phenomenological level) of explanation which had to be kept separate. This was Kroeber's view (1952) and that of one of his most outspoken contemporaries, Leslie White (1949b), and it generated controversies which continue to this day. But many anthropologists, especially those primarily interested in religion and modes of thought, found that various kinds of psychological explanation were an essential component of their work (Hallowell 1954).

For a number of Kroeber's contemporaries this simply meant taking account of the fact that ultimately it is individuals, not cultures in the abstract, that believe in religions; hence, that rituals and beliefs cannot spread to new societies if they do not appeal to the needs of individual men and women in those societies. For example, we find another student of American Indian culture history, Leslie Spier, applying basic psychology to an otherwise traditional ethnological study of how the Sun Dance ceremony of the Plains Indians developed and diffused from one group to another (1921). Spier treats the Sun Dance as a trait complex—that is, an assemblage of related traits which may diffuse separately or together, depending on the receptivity of new hosts. What distinguishes his work from Kroeber's is his more explicit concern with the conditions under which aspects of the ceremony have been accepted or rejected by particular peoples. In other words, he is posing another kind of question: he is asking how and why specific possibilities for behaving fit or fail to fit the culturally determined psychological characteristics of potential recipients. Although his work is clearly ethnological, then, in the sense that his primary concern is to explain cultural variation and to reconstruct cultural history, Spier is also concerned with individual motives and needs as determinants of cultural processes. I might add that although it would be a distortion to equate Spier's work with what Malinowski was doing at about the same time, these remarks should indicate that the distance between them was not as great as might be supposed on first acquaintance.

The same general conclusion applies to two books entitled *Primitive Religion* which appeared during this period, one by Robert Lowie (1924), the other by Paul Radin (1937). Lowie had already achieved prominence with an earlier volume on *Primitive Society*, and the book on religion, his second attempt to sum up a major segment of cultural anthropology in textbook fashion, may be taken as thoroughly representative work for this period. Although Lowie stood firmly in the tradition of historical ethnology and had in the past rejected psychological explanations for other kinds of ethnological problems, here he maintains that in the study of religion "it is the psychological view that requires emphasis" (1924: v). The book is, in fact, devoted in large measure to psychological considerations. His ventures into psychology and social psychology are perhaps superficial in many places, but the evidence is plain that he was making an effort to view religion comprehensively, from the psychologist's perspective as well as that of his own discipline. The book begins with ethnographic sketches of four religions: Crow Indian religion, known to him at firsthand, and three others based on various sources. Then follows a critique of the various theories of religion advanced since Tylor's day; but although A. R. Brown (Radcliffe-Brown) enters the discussion along with other prominent contemporaries and Frazer (among others) receives a thorough refutation, it is interesting to note that nowhere is Malinowski mentioned, not even in a chapter on magic.

The remainder of the book is devoted to a regional-historical outline, followed by chapters on what appear at first to be a diverse assortment of topics but all of which concern aspects of the psychological dimension in the anthropology of religion: history and psychology as complementary forms of explanation for religious phenomena (e.g., the reception of the Ghost Dance by the Dakota Indians and the response of the Winnebago to the peyote religion); the role of sexual differences and sexuality in religious belief and practice; the significance of individual variability in religious experience; and psychological relations between religion and art. Finally in this connection there is a long chapter on the subject of mental associations: how ideas and symbols are associated in various cultures, how associations are expressed in ritual and belief, and the question of whether some such associations are pan-human.

Lowie discovers the essence of religion in the "sense of mystery or weirdness" (1924: xvii) attaching to divine power. His conclusions in this regard were in line with the writings of the older British anthropologist R. R. Marett (1914), whom he knew and respected, and of the German philosopher Rudolf Otto, whose *The Idea of the Holy* had appeared shortly before and with which Lowie was almost certainly familiar. But we might also note that the people Lowie knew best were the Crow Indians, and his ultimate model for religious experience seems always to have been the Plains Indian vision which endowed an individual with supernatural power. He discovers the "central fact of Crow religion" to be an "extraordinary subjective emotional experience" (1924: 19–20), that is, the emotional excitement associated with visions and other religious events; and perhaps it was this more than any other consideration that led him to insist on the importance of psychology for the study of religion.

Radin was more concerned than any of his contemporaries with the role of the individual in cultural processes. A lifelong student of the culture of the Winnebago Indians but concerned with the thought worlds of people in all other cultures, Radin was drawn to the capacities for philosophical depth and poetic expression which he discovered in a few individuals in each society. Like ourselves, he maintained, other societies have their thinkers and doers, their people of affairs and their philosophers. It was on the accomplishments of the latter that he chose to focus attention (1927). But although he pays native theologians their due in his *Primitive Religion,* the central thesis of the book is not unlike that of Malinowski: the roots of religion, he declares, lie not in peoples' musings about spirits but in their everyday struggles to survive. Always in every society there are those few persons for whom religious meditation is a way of life, but for the great majority the business of living comes first and last, and religion is valued only insofar as it lends support in the struggle: ". . . religion comes from life and is directed towards life. In itself it is nothing" (1937: 58).

Anthropologists writing on "culture and personality" have nearly all contributed to the anthropology of religion. The prototype for this tradition was the work of Ruth Benedict. Like most other cultural anthropologists of her day, Benedict conceived of her primary mission as explaining how and why cultural traits were distributed in particular arrangements. One problem in this connection captured her attention. Among American Indians she discovered an affinity for ecstatic religious experience which was absent in only one major culture area, that of the Southwestern Pueblos. Her early library researches into the vision experience

(1922) and the concept of the guardian spirit (1923) had impressed on her the fervor with which most American Indians sought and received personal supernatural power. But later, working among the Pueblo Indians of Cochiti and Zuni, she encountered people dedicated to diametrically opposite values: placidity, self-control, immersion in collective ritual; "an *ethos* distinguished by sobriety, by its distrust of excess, that minimizes to the last possible vanishing point any challenging or dangerous experiences" (orig. 1930; Mead 1959: 249).[9] Following Nietzsche, she labeled this the "Apollonian" way of life, as contrasted with the "Dionysian" ways of other American Indians.

It will be apparent that what Benedict perceived here was not simply a contrast in religions in the narrow sense but a contrast in whole life styles and, underlying these, in what she identified as "fundamental psychological set":

> There is in their cultural attitudes and choices a difference in psychological type fundamentally to be distinguished from that of surrounding regions. It goes deeper than the presence or absence of ritualism; ritualism is itself of a fundamentally different character with this area, and without the understanding of this fundamental psychological set among the Pueblo peoples we must be baffled in our attempts to understand the cultural history of this region.
>
> (1959: 249)

For her next paper on the same general subject she chose the term "configurations" to express the idea that cultures are consistently shaped particular psychological modes, but eventually she settled on "patterns" for the title of the book in which these efforts culminated. *Patterns of Culture* (1934) begins and ends with chapters introducing cultural anthropology about as well as has ever been done, and on this alone its enduring reputation probably rests in part; but the core of the book comprises three chapters extending her comparative method farther than she had hitherto attempted. Turning to the Zuni Indians once again as the exemplification of the "Apollonian" way of life, she contrasts them with the "Dionysian" Kwakiutl of the Northwest

---

[9] In a paper on religion published in 1928, Benedict's friend, the distinguished anthropologist-linguist Edward Sapir, had called attention to this contrast. See Sapir (1949: 350–51).

Coast, studied by her mentor Franz Boas, and with the people of
Dobu, an obscure Melanesian island south of the Trobriands,
studied by Reo Fortune (1932). Fortune had found little to
admire in Dobuan life, and Benedict followed his lead: the
Dobuans are "lawless and treacherous," addicted to "suspicion
and cruelty"; their culture "fosters extreme forms of animosity
and malignancy which most societies have minimized by their
institutions" (1934: 131, 172).

As one might anticipate with generalizations of this sort,
Benedict's work has been subjected to relentless criticism by
those who doubted that all Zuni are as serene, all Kwakiutl as
vainglorious, or all Dobuans as perfidious as she imagined (see
Harris 1958: 404–7). Nevertheless, her work has so far retained
its place as possibly the most widely read book in anthropology.
Her durability, like that of Malinowski, is attributable at least in
part to the essential modernity of her work, which is evident
despite all its shortcomings. Sharing the conviction, "most
clearly voiced by Malinowski," that cultures must be understood
as "organic and functioning wholes" (Benedict 1932: 1), she
produced her own distinctive version of that fundamental insight. Her comprehensive approach to religious belief and its
ritual expression as key components of something at once larger
and more fundamental foreshadowed much of the recent work in
world view, symbolism, and "structuralism" to be considered
shortly.

The terms "pattern," "configuration," and "ethos" were
adopted by a number of other anthropologists, some of whose
work took a turn similar to that of Benedict. Clyde Kluckhohn
(1941, 1943) proposed that each term be applied to a different
aspect of "structural regularities" in culture: *pattern,* to regularities in "overt culture," that is, consistencies in observable
behavior; *configuration,* to regularities in "covert culture," or
the premises underlying behavior; and *ethos* to a people's
"single dominant master configuration" (1943: 218), the one
overriding concept of existence around which their lives were
oriented. He applied these definitions to some of his own work on
Navaho culture, but they did not take hold elsewhere. Kluckhohn
later followed through along related lines with research into

values and value-orientations among ethnic groups of the Southwest (e.g., 1951, 1956), demonstrating that people living in the
same general environment but belonging to diverse cultural
traditions (Navaho, Zuni, Mormon, and so forth) were behaving
according to different, sometimes diametrically opposite, existential premises.

A definition of *ethos* that has found more general acceptance
appeared in Gregory Bateson's *Naven* (1936, 2d ed. 1958), an
unorthodox ethnographic study of a single ritual performed by
the Iatmul people of New Guinea. In the course of his analysis
Bateson distinguished between *ethos* and *eidos:* the former has to
do with the "emotional emphases" of a culture, or the channels
it affords for affective expression; the latter, with its "cognitive
emphases," or the basic intellectual categories and premises of
its members. The two concepts, he noted, could be thought of as
subdivisions of Benedict's "more general concept, *Configuration*" (1958 : 32–33).

In distinguishing cognitive from affective emphases, Bateson
was calling attention to a distinction that was current in psychology but had received little recognition from anthropologists.
To appreciate the implications of this distinction for the study of
religion, let us return briefly to "Magic, Science and Religion."
It will be recalled that in Malinowski's scheme, religion and
magic, the domain of the sacred, satisfy basic human needs for
security and emotional reintegration in the face of adversity; in
Bateson's terms, this is the affective dimension of culture, and
religion may be said then to serve affective functions. In contrast, science, the domain of the profane, which Malinowski
explicitly equated with knowledge (1954 : 25), has to do with the
cognitive dimension of culture. In other words, religion and
magic serve the human need to *feel* satisfactorily about experience, science has to do with the need to *know* enough in order to
perform satisfactorily. (This is not to overlook Malinowski's
emphasis on the pragmatic value of magic, only to call attention
to its function, which he conceived of as feelings of comfort and
reassurance.) Benedict and others implicitly accepted the distinction insofar as they described the psychological dimensions
of religious experience primarily in affective terms. Bateson was

pointing toward a more comprehensive perspective, one in which the domain of knowledge blends imperceptibly into that of religion. Indeed from such a perspective the terms "know" and "believe" are revealed as distinctions made only by outsiders, whereas what is specifically of interest in this connection is a people's *own* conception of the world around them: their identities as individual selves, the identities of other persons, nonvisible beings and forces, natural and cultural objects in the environment, the nature of time and space, the origin and form of the cosmos—in short, their total cognitive experience.

The anthropologist who has gone furthest in exploring this dimension of culture and in developing its implications for the study of religion has been A. I. Hallowell. Trained at the University of Pennsylvania under Frank Speck, Hallowell inherited his teacher's interests in Algonkian Indians and has devoted himself primarily to studies of the Ojibwa (Chippewa) of Manitoba and Wisconsin. Speck also transmitted a point of view, one that emerges in much of his work but nowhere more clearly than in his exceptionally sensitive study of the religion of the Montagnais-Naskapi Indians of Labrador (1935). The emphasis in this book was on what has come to be called "world view" (Redfield 1962: 269–80), concept which Hallowell took up and developed along lines that were distinctively his own. Hallowell's work derived its particular quality from his ancillary interests in Gestalt psychology (1954: 201–2), ego psychology, and primate evolution, all of which he eventually combined into a challenging synthesis (1963).

But for a closer examination of his contribution it is best to begin with his doctoral dissertation (1926), where his potential for innovation beyond the traditional concerns of his generation is already in evidence. This was a study of ritual behavior centering on bears and bear hunting in the northern regions of North America and Eurasia. Why, he inquires, do people of the North ritually address bears and apologize to those they have killed as though these animals were capable of understanding human speech and human purposes? In a limited sense such questions were characteristic of the times; for like Spier writing on the Sun Dance and Benedict on the guardian spirit concept, Hallowell may be said to have been concerned with how and why a particular cluster of cultural traits (ceremonial responses to bears) came to be distributed over a particular cultural area. But in Hallowell's perspective these "traits" had to be understood as modes of *behavior* corresponding to modes of *perception* induced by immersion in a particular cultural environment:

> . . . man does not envisage natural phenomena afresh, but looks out upon the animal and plant life of his environment, the solar bodies, and all the rest of the world about him, through the cultural spectacles with which the accident of birth has provided him (1926: 18).

It is important to note that in answering the question of why bear ceremonial developed where and as it did, Hallowell rejected explanations depending on assumptions about universal psychological responses to bears or to their peculiarly human-like behavior. The ceremonial treatment accorded these animals, he insisted, is "primarily a cultural point of view" (1926: 153). In other words, this particular way of thinking about bears and behaving in response to bears was to be understood as a product of cultural conditioning.

Hallowell's writings on Ojibwa religion indicated even more plainly his interest in the cognitive world of his subjects (1934) and in the way in which their culture molded them to perceive and respond to their environment (1955: chaps. 9 and 11). Following the lead of the Gestalt psychologist Koffka, he adopted the term "behavioral environment" to describe his subject: "From a psychological standpoint the environment of man is always a culturally constituted behavioral environment" (1954: 201) ; that is to say, the world that a person perceives and acts in is one that his culture has created for him. Moreover, the environment of every human being is construed as a scene in which one's own self operates in relation to everything else identified as not oneself, including of course other persons: each individual becomes human through learning "to discriminate himself as an object in a world of objects other than himself" (1955: 75). The evolution of this capacity for self-objectification and self-discrimination was a key element in the humanization of our species (1963: 478–90).

What has this to do with religion? The anwer is that every religious system postulates interaction between persons, *human*

and nonhuman;[10] moreover, that the foundations of morals rest
in each individual's possessing a sense of self with rights and
responsibilities in respect to others—including, once again, not
just human beings but also nonhuman beings in the form of
animals, diverse natural and geographical phenomena, and invisible denizens of the spiritual world. In short, religion is our term
for concepts and precepts guiding interaction in a behavioral
environment peopled by other beings of every sort:

> The entire psychological field in which they live and act is not only
> unified through their conception of the nature and role of "persons"
> in their universe, but by the sanctioned moral values which guide the
> relations of "persons." It is within this web of "social relations"
> that the individual strives for [personal fulfillment in life] (1960:
> 48).

While traditional culture and personality studies have declined in recent years, there has been a proportionate awakening
of interest in cognitive studies, and a number of these have been
addressed to problems in religion. Hallowell's interests were
adopted in part by his student Anthony Wallace, whose recent
textbook on religion (1966), for example, while arguing for the
primacy of ritual in religious experience, goes on to explore its
cognitive foundations and psychological functions. Wallace's
noteworthy paper on religio-political responses to extreme sociocultural stress, which he labeled "revitalization movements"
(1956), is another case in point. The recently emergent field of
what has been somewhat faddishly called "ethnoscience" (and
with which Wallace, incidentally, has been closely associated)
has found Charles Frake describing beliefs about illness (1961)
and religious behavior (1964) in a tightly controlled framework
centering on cognition and modeled on the economy and repli-
cability of linguistic description.

Finally must be mentioned a number of studies, American and
European, of world view (e.g., Forde 1954; Horton 1962, 1967),
values (e.g., Lee 1949; Kluckhohn 1949, 1951), systems of
thought (Fortes and Dieterlen 1965), culture as "religious

---

[10] Melford Spiro (Hallowell's former student) defines religion as "an institution consisting of culturally patterned interaction with culturally postulated superhuman beings" (1966: 96). Lienhardt, a social anthropologist,
defines the religion of an African people (the Dinka) as "a relationship
between men and ultra-human Powers encountered by men" (1961: 32).

structure" (Miller 1964), and religion as "cultural system" (Geertz 1966), all of which are rooted in the proposition that religion is another term for, or at very least an essential dimension of, human designs for living.[11] Among the most appealing essays in this group is Dorothy Lee's widely cited study of "being and value" in Trobriand Island culture, in which Malinowski's writings are mined for fresh insights into the "philsophic basis" (1940: 401) of Trobriand life. Malinowski himself had insisted that the ultimate goal of ethnography should be "to grasp the native's point of view, his relation to life, to realise *his* vision of *his* world" (1922: 25, original italics). If he achieved his goal in large measure, Lee, reviewing his work from a new perspective, seems to have grasped even more firmly the Trobriand vision of the world. The point of her paper is that Trobrianders "are concerned with being, and being alone" (1949: 401) in contrast to ourselves, for whom change and becoming are fundamental premises. But without attempting to summarize her arguments here, let it suffice to say that the appearance of such a paper, some twenty-five years after "Magic, Science and Religion," tells how far anthropology had come in that time and reaffirms our debt to Malinowski and the kind of ethnography he urged on us.

IV

During the past quarter-century the number of anthropologists writing on religion has multiplied several times over; but despite the diversity that this naturally entails and despite claims for innovation on all sides, it is not far off the mark to say that there is still widespread agreement on three fundamental (and not necessarily contradictory) ways of explaining religious belief

---

[11] Forde uses the term "world-outlook" (1954: vii). The presence of several French contributors in this volume is not by chance. French ethnologists have been consistently attracted to the study of *systèmes de connaissance* (Dieterlen 1965). Two good examples of their work are Griaule and Dieterlen on the Dogon, in the Forde volume, and Lebeuf on the Fali, in the Fortes and Dieterlen volume (1965). See also (Richards 1967). Horton's outstanding papers compare African and Western world views.

and behavior. Briefly these can be characterized as theories about religion and society, about religion as a system of thought, and about religion as a cultural institution serving human needs.[12]

It might be asked at once why an anthropological approach to religion should not take account of all dimensions of the human condition, and it goes without saying that ideally this would be the case in every study. The third category above, because it is potentially the most comprehensive, impresses me as ultimately the most promising in this regard. I might add that it can hardly be called new, however, since it derives more or less directly from Malinowski's theoretical efforts, a point to which we shall return. In any event, by dividing our review of the modern period into three broad categories, we should be able to impose at least tentative order on what otherwise might appear to be an impossibly diverse assemblage. I shall introduce each topic as a statement about religion, then give some indication of what has been accomplished by briefly reviewing representative work. It should be added that more often than not bare mention will have to suffice for work deserving more attention.

1. Religion reflects, sustains, and legitimizes the social order.

This is the approach transmitted by Radcliffe-Brown to his students, the social anthropologists who began to achieve prominence in the 1940s. Despite a somewhat restricted perspective which makes for dry reading at times, there is no denying the quality of their accomplishments. For example, Raymond Firth's studies of the Polynesian island of Tikopia (1936, 1967a, 1967b) and his related theoretical writings (1961, 1964) might be summed up as studies in the relation of religion to social organization, but this would hardly do justice to the sensitivity and humanistic insight he brings to the subject. I can do no more than call attention to his work here; likewise for the ethnographic achievements of such social anthropologists as S. F. Nadel (1954), Monica Wilson (1957, 1959), John Middleton (1960), and Jack Goody (1962), all of whom have worked in

[12] For more historical perspective on the first two categories see Evans-Pritchard (1965).

Africa and have concentrated on the social foundations of religion and ritual as their primary (but not necessarily exclusive) theme. Despite differences in emphasis, the work of these ethnographers is grounded in the principles set forth in Radcliffe-Brown's 1945 lecture on "religion and society" (1952: 177): Understanding a religion means studying "religious actions" (rituals) in their social context and demonstrating their "social function," which is to foster in individuals the "sentiments" on which societies depend for their coherence and continuity.

Among the earliest to demonstrate the virtues of this approach was Meyer Fortes, whose writings on the social structure and religion of the Tallensi, a West African people, span the entire period under consideration (1945, 1949, 1959, 1965). The Tallensi are not a "tribe" but a loosely bounded grouping of two peoples of different ancestry, called Talis and Namoos, who are linked by networks of social relations, by shared cultural idioms, and by cooperative rituals into a cluster of affiliated communities. Ultimately their unity, such as it is, resolves into the fact that they all reside in Taleland. Although Talis and Namoos are linked by extensive bonds of kinship, they retain individuality as clusters of clans with distinct myths, food taboos, and ritual traditions. Persons belonging to Tali clans sacrifice at ancestral shrines representing exogamous lineages, several of which reside together in a particular locale as a "composite clan" (that is, not necessarily linked by bonds of kinship). In addition to their socioeconomic ties, lineages are linked to those of other clans by two forms of cooperative ritual: sacrifices with related lineages at collective ancestral shrines, and sacrifices with unrelated lineages at so-called earth shrines. Finally, at an annual cycle of "Great Festivals," all the clans of Taleland, Tali and Namoo alike, come together for a complex series of cooperative rituals "in which the greatest common interests and values of the whole society are dramatized and affirmed" (1949: 3).

In brief, we see here how a society, composed of peoples whose diverse ancestry corresponds only roughly to their present residential locations, is held together in what Fortes calls a "dynamic equilibrium" largely by a network of ritual obligations. His implicit argument, then, is that the essential function of religion is to unite social groups and ensure their integrity and continuity. For the ultimate basis of Tallensi social existence, he says, is

> a body of moral and jural norms and values accepted as binding by all Tallensi, and defended from the disruptive action of conflicting sectional interests by the most solemn ritual sanctions of Tale religion. The function of ritual collaboration between clans and lineages is to maintain the unchallengeable validity of these norms and values; for upon their observance the attainment of the common good ultimately depends. (1945: 115)

But social life is seldom as balanced and serene as this passage suggests, and much of the more recent work of social anthropologists has been addressed to the subject of conflict and change. In several studies which deal with conflict while retaining the notion of social equilibrium, Max Gluckman has called attention to African rituals involving symbolic rejection of accustomed roles by women and of a ruler by his people (1954, 1955, 1963). Gluckman argues that these "rituals of rebellion" ultimately express not conflict but cohesion. The validity of the institution in question (male dominance, kingship) is never disputed but is in fact reaffirmed, he maintains, for in the very act of ritually expressing hostility the participants declare acceptance of their everyday roles in the social system.[13]

As part of an elegant analysis of politics in the Kachin Hills region of northeast Burma, E. R. Leach (1954, paperback ed. 1965) presents a theory of religion and ritual which postulates interminable conflict as the very essence of social life. In Leach's view, religious behavior (and this includes telling myths as well as performing rituals) is a "symbolic statement which 'says' something" about how a society is organized (1965: 13, 286). Having already defined social structure as "a set of ideas about the distribution of power" (1965: 4), he argues that religious acts are symbolic statements about struggles for political power. In other words, instead of interpreting religion as support for the *status quo*, Leach asserts that in this basically egalitarian

---

[13] See also Turner (1957), in which Gluckman's approach is extended. Norbeck (1963) places Gluckman's observations in a wider perspective and refines some of his conclusions without calling into question the essential validity of his "functional" interpretation of ritual as a legitimizer of the social order. For a fundamentally different mode of interpretation see Rigby (1968).

society in which many people aspire to power, the principal function of ritual is to give symbolic expression to social relations predicated on conflict and the inevitability of shifts in political fortunes.

Another aspect of the relation between religion and social conflict comes to the fore in studies of sorcery and witchcraft.[14] Most social anthropologists look on witchcraft and sorcery not as *actions* carried out by witches and sorcerers but as *accusations* directed at persons who are said by others to be guilty of such actions (Middleton and Winter 1963: 3–4). Some accusations bring into the open smoldering resentment or distrust of people who are felt to be violating cultural norms or straining community relations; others express conflict between persons whose roles are in some sense imperfectly delimited or structurally at odds with one another (cf. Marwick 1952, 1965). The processes whereby a society works through accusations, defense, and perhaps counter-accusations are therefore understandable as exercises in conflict resolution.

To summarize, I have tried to make clear that whether the focus is on social cohesion, social conflict, or both, all this work takes as a point of departure the axiom that religion is understandable only when viewed in its social context and that its function or purpose is to help maintain the social system.

2. Religion is a foremost expression of a person's need to order his environment and experiences.

In this category are studies having to do with the world view (e.g., Horton 1962, Ortiz 1969), symbolism (e.g., Geertz 1966,

---

[14] The generally accepted distinction between these terms, deriving from Evans-Pritchard's study of the Azande (1937), is that a sorcerer utilizes toxic substances magically to poison his victim, while a witch bears intrinsic harmful powers within his or her person such that even a glance can sicken or kill a victim. In addition to Evans-Pritchard's pioneering work (cf. Gluckman 1944) and that mentioned in this paragraph, the following should also be consulted: Krige (1947), Wilson (1951), Nadel (1952), Mayer (1954); and for a general review, Mair (1969).

These are all African studies by social anthropologists. For comparison with the approach of cultural anthropologists to similar problems in American Indian religion, see Kluckhohn (1944) and Saler (1964). Kennedy (1967, 1968) compares Kluckhohn to Evans-Pritchard and comments on psychological explanations in anthropology.

Turner 1967), and various forms of structural analysis (e.g., Frake 1964, Lévi-Strauss 1962a, Needham 1960, Stanner 1964). In addition, I include the work of Evans-Pritchard (1956), Lienhardt (1961), and others (e.g., Kluckhohn 1949, Burridge 1965) in which religious thought is approached on its own terms and analyzed as a philosophical system (Evans-Pritchard 1956: 314–15). Despite obvious differences in emphasis, these authors have more in common than may be immediately apparent. For one thing, they are aware of one another's work, refer to it, and at times reinterpret it. For instance, Ortiz's study of the Tewa Indian world view focuses on the problem of dualism, which is central to the work of Lévi-Strauss, Needham, and others. Similarly, anthropologists interested in symbolism have commented extensively on Evans-Pritchard's discussions of how the Nuer equate birds with twins and substitute cucumbers for oxen in sacrifices (1956: chap. 5).[15] But more generally, all these studies exhibit a common concern with religion as an expression of basic human cognitive capacities for symbolic thought, for conceptualizing experience in terms of paired opposites (good-evil, and the like), and, most fundamentally, for endowing environment and experience with order and meaning.

A challenging introduction to the philosophical subtleties that may engage anthropologists who choose to work at this level is afforded by Evans-Pritchard's volume on the religion of the Nuer (1956) and a companion volume by his student and colleague, Godfrey Lienhardt, who studied the closely related religion of the neighboring Dinka (1961). By ordinary material standards these people, who live in the Nilotic Sudan, are indisputably "primitive," but the term hardly applies to their religions, both of which are revealed as possessing great depth and complexity. In addition, the authors themselves can be instructively compared, for although in fair agreement on theoretical matters they highlight somewhat different aspects of their subject. Evans-Pritchard's own religious disposition has, as he acknowledges (1956: vii; cf. 1962), influenced his mode of interpretation, especially in that he is more concerned than most of his contemporaries with the strictly philosophical and theological

---

[15] See various issues of *Man* (new series), vols. 1 and 2, 1966 and 1967.

dimensions of religion. This probably accounts for his tendency to explain Nuer thought with something of a Western theological bias: his translation of the Nuer term *kwoth* as "Spirit" or "God" (chap. 1), for instance, contrasts with Lienhardt's translation of the equivalent Dinka word as "Power" (1961: 28–32). Lienhardt is also representative of the greater number of contemporary social anthropologists in that he pays proportionately more attention to observed behavior, even though he clearly shares Evans-Pritchard's interest in religion as a system of thought.

But perhaps a more important point is that both authors are thoroughly aware of the importance of symbols and symbolism as vehicles of religious expression. Since symbolic analysis is now experiencing something of a whirl in anthropology, it is worth noting that these two representatives of the relatively conservative "Oxford school" of anthropology were well into the subject more than ten years ago. Nor were they alone; for the fact is that many other anthropologists, including Leach, Hallowell, Leslie White (1949a), and Gladys Reichard (1950) have expressed awareness of the importance of symbolism (cf. Spiro 1969). At the same time there can be little question that the subject has recently come to occupy center stage, partly perhaps as an anthropological expression of what Susanne Langer calls the "new key" in philosophy, partly also as the result of increasing exchanges of ideas and convergence of interests among European and American anthropologists.[16]

The anthropologist who has written most persuasively on the importance of pursuing symbolic analysis has been Clifford Geertz, especially in his programmatic essay on "religion as a cultural system" (1966). His framework is an elaborate definition for which the essay offers exegesis: "a religion is (1) a system of symbols which acts to (2) establish powerful, pervasive, and long-lasting moods and motivations in men by (3) formulating conceptions of a general order of existence and (4) clothing these conceptions with such an aura of factuality that

---

[16] For further discussion, especially on the relation of studies in symbolism to the work of Claude Lévi-Strauss, see Geertz (1968b). See also Middleton (1967), a reader which includes relevant papers by Leach, Wilson, Turner, Needham, and others.

(5) the moods and motivations seem uniquely realistic''
(1966 : 4). A companion essay on ''ideology as a cultural system''
(1964), read in conjunction with the other, makes for an instructive demonstration of the intimate connections between
religion and ''secular'' philosophy. The same holds true for his
study of Javanese religion and world view (1960), especially the
chapters of the Hinduistic *prijaji* variant. More recently Geertz
has written an illuminating comparison of the Islamic traditions
in Indonesia and Morocco (1968a), in the course of which he
raises questions about ''modernization'' to which we shall devote
attention later on.

But the man who has done most so far to place the study of
symbolism on a solid footing has been Victor Turner, a social
anthropologist who has concentrated on the ritual symbolism of a
single people, the Ndembu of northern Zambia (1961, etc.; see esp.
1967). Combining precisely recorded observations with bold and
sometimes far-reaching interpretations, Turner presents a picture of ritual as a set of symbolic actions and displays of symbolic objects which, taken together and considered in their
fullest ramifications, can be shown to embody a culture's fundamental precepts, core values, and axiomatic truths. Complete
analysis requires that each symbol be understood in triple perspective : one must know, first, what people say it means; second,
how it is used; and third, how it relates to other symbols. Turner
calls these the ''exegetical'' or ''interpretative,'' the ''operational,'' and the ''positional'' meanings of a symbol.

For example, in a paper on Ndembu circumcision ritual
(1962) he focuses attention on three key symbols, each of which,
he points out, is ''multivocal'' or ''polysemous'' (bearing many
meanings). The symbols in this case are three trees of different
species, each representing a stage in the initiates' symbolic
passage from immaturity to maturity. Boys are circumcised
under the first kind of tree, carried over the second, and seated
on a freshly cut log of the third while their wounds bleed.
Working first from native texts (''the exegetical level of meaning''), Turner shows how certain key characteristics of each tree
endow it and the ritual surrounding it with rich intricacies of
meaning: the first, because it secretes a white latex, signifies
motherhood, nourishment, matrilineal descent (hence Ndembu

social tradition), sexuality, procreation, bonds of kinship, and more; the second, because its wood beneath the outer bark is a brilliant white, signifies (along with a number of other white substances) through a complex network of further associations such fundamental values as strength, fertility, longevity, virtuousness, and so on; and the third, because it secretes a red gum suggestive of blood, adds a host of meanings deriving from that connection, the gist of which is that initiates die as children to be reborn as men.

Proceeding to the ways in which each symbol operates in the context of this particular ritual, then to how their meanings are modified by their positions in sets, Turner spins a complex web, the net effect of which is to suggest that very little of what matters in the lives of Ndembu initiates is omitted in the symbolism surrounding their ritual passage into adulthood:

> Each boy is sacramentally imbued with the whole Ndembu moral order, which is immanent in but also transcends the social order. . . . There are religious depths here that cannot be fathomed by the analysis of observational data. The symbols I have discussed have a fathomless lucidity of meaning which men of every grade of cultural complexity can grasp intuitively if they wish (1962: 172).

Anthropologists identifying themselves as "structuralists" are a rather diverse lot, ranging from "ethnoscientists" and social anthropologists to the all but unclassifiable Claude Lévi-Strauss. What they have in common is that they are not only structuralists but mentalists, for basically they are concerned with how ideas and concepts are organized in people's minds. Their work is grounded in the proposition that culture resolves into what Ward Goodenough identifies as two "orders of reality": a "phenomenal order," having to do with *observable* regularities in *behavior,* and an "ideational order," having to do with *discoverable* regularities in *thought* (1964: 11–12). The anthropologist sees and records the phenomenal order, then, but his goal is to discover the ideational order underlying and directing what he sees.

Interests of this kind have a long history in anthropology. The study of cognitive foundations of culturally patterned behavior dates back to the work of Durkheim and Mauss on "primitive classification" (1963, orig. 1903) and to that of Durkheim's student, Robert Hertz, on the significance of right and left hand in magical and religious thought (1960, orig. 1909). Recently a number of anthropologists have revived this particular form of inquiry with renewed attention to the theme of binary opposition and, more generally, to the subject of categories and categorization.[17] Their work suggests that the opposition between right and left is but one expression of a widespread, perhaps universal, characteristic of human thought, namely the propensity to operate in terms of paired opposites: good-evil, life-death, and so on, with one member of the pair positively, the other negatively, valued.

Unquestionably the most widely renowned spokeman for the structural approach in anthropology is Claude Lévi-Strauss. A prolific and controversial writer, Lévi-Strauss has attracted so much commentary and exegesis (e.g., Geertz 1967, Leach 1967) that I make no pretense of adding substantially to the discussion in this limited space. But it is possible to set his work in perspective. The essential point is this: whereas other anthropologists have for the most part contented themselves with the search for conscious or perhaps semiconscious cognitive designs, Lévi-Strauss has explicitly directed his attention to a search for *unconscious* foundations of human behavior (cf. Lévi-Strauss 1963: 18, 21, 281–82). His discoveries in that realm might be said to take binary opposition as a point of departure (and in that sense he is, as he of course recognizes, the heir of Durkheim, Mauss, and Hertz). But he carries the analysis several steps further: he discovers dialectical relationships in which contrasting pairs are symbolically united through cultural mediators— myth, ritual, social and cultural institutions—such that the paradox of their oppositeness (for example, life can only result in death) is resolved. The most fundamental opposition is that between nature and culture: a person is part of nature but experiences it through his culture, and cultural contrasts mirror those observed in nature (1962a, 1962b). But this is only the beginning. Moving in dialectical progression from synthesis to

---

[17] Some of the more important: Needham (1960, 1967), Beidelman (1961), Faron (1962), Yalman (1962), Leach (1964), Rigby (1966). Douglas (1966) is a highly original study of the significance of boundaries, categories, and categorical ambiguity.

synthesis, from one myth or institution to another, Lévi-Strauss argues that each synthesis is not only opposed to another but is ultimately united with it and with others at ever higher conceptual levels (1962a, 1964, 1967). Thus a myth emerges as far more than a just-so story, far more even than the basic charter for social action of Malinowski's analysis (1926); it becomes an artful expression of a person's most fundamental cognitive processes: his capacity to identify antithetical elements in his experience, to represent them symbolically, and thereby to resolve life's inherent paradoxes through the creation of cultural mediators (1964; cf. Yalman 1967).

The difficulty experienced by many British and American anthropologists in coming to grips with Lévi-Strauss's work is attributable, at least in part, to their affiliation with contrasting intellectual traditions, Anglo-American empiricism and French rationalism (Scholte 1966, Richards 1967). At the same time, many English-speaking anthropologists have been profoundly influenced by his writings, and evidences for convergence are apparent in much of the work under discussion here.

As a contrast to the Lévi-Straussian form of structural analysis, we might turn briefly to the work of Charles Frake, who is also concerned with cognitive structures but whose resemblance to Lévi-Strauss perhaps ends there. Frake has worked among the Subanun of the Philippines and published several papers on them, including a noteworthy study of their medical concepts (1961) and a "structural description" of their "religious behavior" (1964). His concern is not with large-scale excursions into the structure of the human mind but only with "an adequate ethnographic description of an aspect of culture" (1964: 11), specifically, Subanun culture and no other. His foremost problem, then, has to do with ethnographic method, and his purpose is to describe one segment of a culture as precisely and economically as possible. In characteristic "ethnoscientific" fashion (Sturtevant 1964) the cognitive structure which he discovers is categorical and hierarchical. For instance, Subanun religious offerings are interpreted as events involving exchanges between various kinds of "person" (the most inclusive categorical term for all participants), some of whom are "supernaturals," others "mortals." These two subcategories divide into their hierarchi-

cally ordered constituents. Under the subcategory "1. supernaturals," for example, one finds "1.4 gods," which includes
"1.4.2 raw-food-eating gods," which in turn includes "1.4.2.1
sunset gods," "1.4.2.2 sea gods," and so on. The goal is a complete, precise, and economical description of that segment of
Subanun culture definable as "religious behavior." What Frake
quite plainly rejects is anything resembling "intuitive impres-
sions of 'the meaning of religion in Subanun life' " (1964: 128),
to say nothing of statements on the meaning of religion in all
human life. His work, and that of other ethnoscientists, might be
summed up in the word "rigor," which appears often in their
writings and in which he modestly declares his paper to be de-
ficient (1964).

3. Religion supports man's efforts to survive in a world of
scarce resources, abundant perils, and endless suffering.

This statement is intended to cover a number of studies, again
quite diverse in emphasis but alike in that they take explicit
account of the fact that people must compete with one another
and with other occupants of their environments to satisfy life's
basic demands; that even the most successful competitors are subject to physical and mental suffering; and that immediate concerns for health, comfort, security, and survival outweigh all the
philosophy and theology people can ever devise. Some of this work
is predominantly biological and ecological in direction, being
concerned with a person's need to survive as an organism in a
competitive world. Some is psychologically oriented, concerned
with a person's need to explain and understand, and in a sense
thereby control, his fate.

The debt here to Malinowski seems plain, even though it is not
always expressed. Malinowski's cultural theories always focused
on peoples' *needs,* not only the biological needs common to all
animals but also the social psychological needs peculiar to our
species (Piddington 1957, Richards 1957). His eclecticism in this
regard gained him something of a reputation in professional
circles as a feeble theorist; it was said that he was imprecise,
tautological, and sociologically naïve (e.g., Fortes 1957, Parsons
1957). There is certainly some truth to this; but without ventur-

ing into a personal defense of Malinowski, I would add that his eclecticism and his concern with basic physical and psychological needs appear more respectable in the light of the widening horizons of modern anthropology. In this sense his cultural theories may prove, at least in part, to have been ahead of their time. There can be no question that we have come a long way since his time in deepening our understanding of some of the basic problems to which he directed attention; but it should be recognized that much of the work included in this section, though fully modern in tone and for the most part original in conception, is in harmony with Malinowski's dictum that to understand religion we must think not *only* about social and cultural systems but about the fundamental biological and psychological needs of the individual human beings in whose behavior those systems find expression.

To begin with, then, we may distinguish between two kinds of needs-oriented explanation. On the one hand are those which take as a point of departure the fact that people live in an environment, that they are themselves part of that environment, and that they must satisfy their basic biological needs within the limits of what it offers. On the other hand are those which move another step up the ladder, as it were, and begin with the fact that people have psychological needs that are peculiarly their own. We do not have to be overly rigid about this; the two approaches might be combined and some people have at least come close to doing so. But for our present purposes it may help to keep the distinction in mind.

Among social anthropologists only one man, Darryl Forde, has expressed abiding interest in the study of culture as peoples' adaptive mode. In his "Frazer lecture" on the religion of the Yakö of West Africa (1964: chap. 9), for example, we find that while he does not reject the sociological form of interpretation associated with Radcliffe-Brown, Forde is inclined to follow Malinowski's lead in arguing that social cohesion is but one element in a broader concern, namely, peoples' need to survive and to avert misfortune in a dangerous and demanding world. Thus he turns to the "underlying biological and ecological context" (1964: 262) for an ultimate explanation of Yakö religious belief and practice. In a paper on spirits, witches, and sorcerers he expresses much the same idea: supernatural beings are alternative "means for attaining material and social benefits and for averting threats to these"; and rituals "take on something of the character of an economic system" in which people make decisions and allocate resources in accordance with their perception of their needs and the risks attendant on seeking to satisfy them (1964: 213).

But it is in the United States, where anthropology and biology have not grown so far apart as has generally been the case in England, that anthropologists have gone furthest with ecological interpretations of religion. The outstanding accomplishment to date is almost certainly Roy Rappaport's *Pigs for the Ancestors* (1967a; summarized in 1967b), a carefully researched study of the ways in which rituals regulate ecological relationships in the New Guinea Highlands. Rappaport thinks of rituals as "part of the behavioral repertoire employed by an aggregate of organisms in adjusting to its environment" (1967b:18). He demonstrates that the killing and consumption of pigs, which is the central event in Highlands ritual, takes place at either precisely those times when people are exposed to stress calling for increased intake of protein or else when the pig population reaches proportions such that "the relationship of pigs to people changes from one of mutualism to one of parasitism or competition" (1967b: 25). But more than this he shows that in addition to the "local subsystem" of relations between humans and nonhuman inhabitants of their immediate environment, there is a more extensive "regional subsystem" in which neighboring human populations interact with one another as allies and enemies, as competitors for land, as intermarrying groups, and as partners in diverse forms of exchange. Ritual, a cultural invention intimately connected with most such interaction, thus emerges as a key regulator of critical bioecological relations among inhabitants of an environment.

No other work of this level of penetration has yet appeared. However, an anthropologist of similar persuasion, Marvin Harris, has recently published a substantial (and polemical) history of anthropological theory (1968) from the perspective of "cultural materialism," his thesis being that by and large anthropologists have ignored environmental and economic determinants of the behavior they proposed to explain. Earlier, in a controversial but trenchant examination of sacred cattle in India (1966), Harris argued that usages and taboos relating to these animals are wholly consistent with judicious economic behavior. It seems likely that further studies along these lines will appear in the next few years.

The most comprehensive statement in recent years on how religion serves psychological needs is to be found in the work of Melford Spiro. In his use of the terms "need" and "function," and in his basic thesis that religion enables the individual psyche to coordinate experience and to withstand trauma Spiro is clearly reminiscent of Malinowski, but his theoretical exposition is considerably more precise. Spiro defines religion as interaction with superhuman beings for the purpose of satisfying needs (1966: 96). And not just needs in the sociological sense, he argues; for although social solidarity may be an "unintended consequence" of religious behavior, such behavior must surely have intended consequences as well, namely, the satisfaction of felt psychological needs. He recognizes three categories of such needs (or "sets of desires"), each corresponding to a function of religion (1966: 106–17).

First are *cognitive* needs—for meaning, for clarification of that which is puzzling and obscure, for a sense of understanding and control over experience. In fulfilling this role, religion serves what he terms an "adjustive" function.[18] Next come *substantive* needs—for abundant food, health, fecundity, triumph over enemies, comfort, and security. Here religion serves an "adaptive" function. "Most, if not all, of these substantive desires," he observes, "can be classified as attempts to overcome or transcend suffering" (1966: 112). Third come *expressive* needs, by which he refers to the need to sublimate deep-seated drives and inclinations whose overt expression or even recognition might lead to intolerable anxiety and personality disintegration. In this case religion serves an "integrative" function.[19] In summary, Spiro, not unlike Malinowski, argues that to understand religion we

[18] See Spiro (1964) for exposition of this point. Geertz (1966) which appears in the same volume as the essay under discussion, touches on many of the same points and should be read with it.
[19] See Spiro (1952, 1965) for ethnographic illustrations of this function.

must think about those aspects of our psychobiological constitution that are specifically human in design. This is not to deny the validity of sociological explanations emphasizing the contribution of religion to the maintenance of society; but it is an error to mistake ''an explanation of society for an explanation of religion which, in effect, means confusing the sociological functions of religion with the bases for its performance'' (1966 : 122).

Recently Spiro published a study of Burmese ''supernaturalism'' (1967), that is, the non-Buddhist element in Burmese religion. The book is subtitled ''a study in the *explanation* and *reduction* of suffering'' (my italics), indicating that it is mainly concerned with the first two forms of psychological need (cognitive and substantive) identified in his theoretical paper. The essence of his argument is that whereas Buddhism offers no immediate release from suffering (it teaches that people suffer for demerits accumulated in their previous lives and that relief can be obtained only through ultimate release from all human feelings and desires), beliefs and practices relating to non-Buddhist spirits and demons furnish satisfying explanations for human misery and some hope of immediate relief through manipulation of these beings. Thus, although he concludes that Buddhism is overwhelmingly the more important of what he identifies as two coexisting religions, Spiro's concern here is with the one having most to do with sustenance and relief in this world.

A number of other students of Buddhism and Hinduism have also been drawn to comment on the contrast between the other-worldly or ''transcendental'' concerns of the so-called great religions and the mundane or ''practical'' concerns of folk religions existing side by side with them (Mandelbaum 1966, Ames 1964, Berreman 1964, Wax 1964). But there is another side to this picture. Some anthropologists (including Spiro) have discovered a practical aspect to these very same ''transcendental'' religions. For example, Manning Nash, who also worked in Burma, finds Buddhism and animism understandable only as complementary aspects of a single religious system serving people's needs for immediate and long-term security: ''Buddhism and the nats are not in conflict and nowhere in contradiction, but work mutually to give the villager a constant and rather clear view of the remoter ends of human existence while allowing him to deal with daily problems" (1963: 291). Spiro, too, although placing special emphasis on the relative immediacy of needs served by the two religions, notes that Buddhist ideology and religious behavior are not at all incompatible with rational economic behavior, that concerns with *karma,* merit, and rebirth do not mean the absence of ordinary human desires for comfort and security (1966b). For in the Burmese Buddhist's scheme of things—in his "behavioral environment" (1966b: 1163)—the future includes a very long period of time indeed, and religious investment in this life may be expected to bring substantial rewards in another.

In a lengthy paper on Buddhism in Thailand, in which sociological, psychological, and adaptive interpretations of religion are blended with notable skill, S. J. Tambiah (1968) takes an even firmer position on the practical orientations of Buddhist villagers. However much villagers may talk about rebirth and the next life, Tambiah says, he doubts "that an uncertain future result of this sort can gain precedence over consideration relating to this life of immediate experience" (1968: 42). He discovers these considerations in the complexities of interaction between lay people and monks, which he interprets as involving reciprocity between generations. For in this Thai village monkhood is an institution whereby younger and elder generations engage in a mutually beneficial transaction: "the older generation persuades its youth temporarily to renounce its vitality and sexual potency and undergo an ascetic regimen," thereby enabling the elders to gain sorely needed merit by supporting the young monks with gifts (1968: 105). In time these young men return to secular life and assume positions of prestige in the community deriving from their past role, and of course their turn comes to support similarly the generation that follows. Tambiah's exposition is more subtle and detailed than these few words may suggest; but it will perhaps be evident that in the course of a social anthropological analysis he has pointed out adaptive elements in Buddhism, in the sense of the immediate rewards it offers, and demonstrated that even in its "higher" manifestations Thai village religion is, in Leach's words

(1968 : 3), "a cult for the living, not a theology for the dead and dying."

To summarize now, it should be apparent that although a diversity of anthropological approaches to religion have emerged since Malinowski's time, certain basic principles and themes persist. Whatever their theoretical bias, nearly all anthropologists follow Malinowski's example by grounding their ideas in field experience and working outward from what they have personally observed. Nearly all accept some version of his argument that each religion is a unique configuration, a particular society's representation of the world and of what people must do to survive and prosper in it. And in line with this, many still follow his lead in contending that religion offers rational solutions to problems relating not to other worlds but to this one; hence, that the interpreter of other peoples' religions must keep sight of the solid benefits they derive from what may appear to be wholly spiritual or "transcendental" beliefs and practices.

V

The prologues are over. It is a question, now,
Of final belief. So, say that final belief
Must be in a fiction. It is time to choose.
                    Wallace Stevens, "Asides on the Oboe"*

With all this behind us, then, are we indeed any farther along than Malinowski was? Can we substantially improve on his statement, now nearly forty years old, that religion arises not "out of speculation or reflection, still less out of illusion or misapprehension, but rather out of the real tragedies of human life, out of the conflict between human plans and realities" (1931 : 641)? Not a great deal, it must be admitted. Anthropologists might now place more emphasis on the creative role of religion in bringing "plans" and "realities" into harmony, but the point is much the same.

---

* Reprinted from Wallace Stevens, "Asides on the Oboe," in *The Collected Poems of Wallace Stevens* (New York: Knopf, 1954) p. 250. Copyright © Alfred A. Knopf. Reprinted by permission of the publisher.

To the extent that we do now better understand the positive functions of religion in human affairs, we are in part indebted to advances made by physical anthropologists in the study of human evolution and to the implications that a few cultural anthropologists have begun to draw from them (Washburn and Howell 1960, Geertz 1962, Hallowell 1963). I refer to several closely related aspects of the development of our "human nature" during the later (hominid) phases of evolution. We have come to understand that in becoming hunters and tool makers our immediate ancestors initiated an evolutionary process whereby we became bearers of culture and users of symbols. Culture, we see now, is humanity's special adaptive mode; it is the human way of maintaining control over environment and experience.

We understand, moreover, that the basis of culture is symbolization. It must be emphasized that symbolic thought is not an ancillary talent to be turned on and off as the occasion requires. Symbolic thought is the human way of thinking, and symbolic behavior is the human way of behaving. This is not to insist that every last moment of our days is taken up with symbolic activity in the strictest sense, but it can be argued that even the simplest and most "physiological" of our actions are hedged round and shaped by a host of symbolic associations and culturally patterned usages.

Further, we have come to understand that two crucial components of the human personality have arisen in integral relation to our cultural-symbolic predispositions. These are foresight and self-objectification: the capacity to meditate on the future and to plan for it, and the capacity to conceptualize oneself as a person. Let me emphasize that we are not talking about possibilities for thinking and behaving; we are talking about definitive characteristics of human condition. It is "natural" and inevitable that a human being possess culture, use symbols, think about future events, and recognize his existence as a person. It follows, then, that whatever these capacities entail will be singularly, definitively, and indelibly human.

One thing they most certainly entail is religion. There is no dearth of anthropological definitions of religion (cf. Horton 1960, Goody 1961, Geertz 1966, Spiro 1966), but in order to develop this argument I shall venture one more: A people's religion is their beliefs and practices having to do with controlling extrahuman power and applying it to the service of human needs and purposes. Now let me explain how this relates to what we have been saying. It is an inescapable fact of life that human beings everywhere are forced to match their personal powers, such as they are, against an array of immensely powerful nonhuman organisms, beings (visible and nonvisible), and environmental happenings, nearly all of which are potentially destructive to human lives and purposes. It is inevitable that people should make every effort to control as much of that power as possible to insure that they are at times benefited by it and at very least not seriously harmed by it (cf. Aberle 1966, Glick 1967). In their efforts to comprehend and control forces much greater than they can personally muster, people are primarily dependent on symbolic behavior, on ritual recitations and actions designed to achieve what could never be achieved by more "straightforward" means. This is the behavior that I define as religious behavior.

The question might be raised at this point whether this adds anything to the insights expressed nearly a half-century ago in "Magic, Science and Religion." Only in this sense: In his more academic moments, when he was defining rather than describing magic and religion, Malinowski argued that magic is a "practical" art serving life's more immediate needs, while religion is "a body of self-contained acts being themselves the fulfillment of their purpose" (1954: 88). But when he turned to the question of what religions do for people, he made it quite clear that, in fact, their functions are not nearly comprehended in such abstract terms. For if religions everywhere are indeed concerned with problems of order, meaning, and ultimate purpose in human existence, they are no less concerned with the diverse ills, woes, frustrations, and fears that ordinary men and women face in the course of their everyday lives. Religions survive because they offer an indispensable boon: the anticipation of gaining some control over extrahuman sources of power, of turning that power away from harm and directing it to the fulfillment of human aspirations and designs. Near the close of his essay Malinowski observes that the function of *magic* "is to ritualize man's optimism, to enhance his faith in the victory of hope over fear. Magic expresses the greater value for man of confidence over doubt, of steadfastness over vacillation, of optimism over pessimism'' (1954: 90). But can we not say the very same thing about religion? Without carrying this further, I would argue that nearly everything Malinowski expresses in his essay applies not to magic *or* science *or* religion, but in part to magic *and* science *and* religion, and preeminently to religion.

Perhaps this will help place in perspective those very few persons (but including most social scientists studying religion) who profess to have no religion. What they are saying is that the extrahuman sources of power on which they depend are of a particular kind, namely those associated with Euro-American technology, and that where these are lacking, they accept relative powerlessness. If this is to be called the ''scientific world view'' or something of that sort, so be it; but it must be kept in mind that we are not talking about a Euro-American (or ''Western'') world view, only that of a minute and relatively new sect which originated during the Enlightenment. I am not being facetious, for the point bears on a central problem in the study of religion.

To assume that there is a ''Western'' world view which is ''rational'' or scientific in contrast to a ''non-Western'' world view which is ''magical'' or nonscientific (Wax and Wax 1963) overlooks the fact that the vast majority of Western people are just as concerned with traditional forms of nonhuman power as any other people. What distinguishes them is the particular idiom in which these concerns are phrased, but that is simply one manifestation of what we all know—that cultures are very diverse. What evidence is there to suggest that the Buddhism of a Thai villager and the indigenous religion of an East African herdsman resemble one another more or less than either resembles the religion of a devout Baptist in an Oklahoma town, a devout Jew in Tel-Aviv, or a devout Roman Catholic in Barcelona? All have to do with extrahuman sources of power. All speak of other worlds and other forms of being, but ultimately all refer back to human beings and to their very real problems in this world.

The major problem for students of religion in this new decade will be to gain better understanding of what happens when one religious view of the world encounters another. Often this will mean an encounter between Christianity and the religion of a less powerful people, although the apparent importance of this particular form of contact may be as much a reflection of our choices of research site as an accurate picture of what is happening in the world. In any event, it seems to be generally the case that the religions of people deeply embedded in conservative cultural traditions are sometimes shaken very hard indeed by contact with the world of secularism and technology. Geertz speaks of "the loss of power of classical religious symbols to sustain a properly religious faith" in Morocco and Indonesia, and he suggests that this is a widespread accompaniment to modernization (1968a: 102–4, cf. 1957). Undoubtedly this is so, but it is also true that in nations now committed to the "modern" way of life traditional religion lives on (Wyllie 1968). And is this not the case in America as well? God may be dead in some quarters of Berkeley and Cambridge, but there is nothing to suggest that he is not flourishing in Dallas, Omaha, and Salt Lake City. We might be reminded here that it is not scientists whom we send out to preach to the "natives" but missionaries— not representatives of a secular world view but representatives of the religious world view with which the great majority of Europeans and Americans still associate themselves and in which we have every reason to think they still repose faith. Undoubtedly we should begin to export the secular world view along with its technology, not to coax people to accept it (which in any event they are unlikely to do) but only so that they may understand it and not be left suspecting, as so many now do, that we have left out of their Bibles those critical passages giving insight into the origins of our technological powers.

Equally important, those of us who study people's responses to new religious ideas should not labor with the misconception that our world is one in which religion is disappearing. For, to the contrary, the evidence is that new religions are arising all the time, that people do not respond to new problems by abandoning religion but by developing a new religion on the ruins of the old. Thus the "revitalization movements" which have attracted much recent attention (Wallace 1956, Worsley 1968, Burridge 1969, LaBarre n.d.) appear to be nothing new in history but rather an integral dimension of social change, a natural phase in the social process. When accepted concepts of power, of its locus and control, prove to be insufficient for changing conditions, people revise their concepts to meet their new needs. The result, though we may label it a "cult" or a "movement," is in fact a new religion—a new way of looking at the world and of thinking about how people can best make their way through it. Because religion is part of humanity's natural state, when one religion dies there is always another to take its place.

The needs served by every religion include the requirement that the world make sense ethically and esthetically. But first and foremost we are talking not about theologies but about ways of coping with life. Many societies include mystics, but no entire group of people are so mystically inclined that they ignore the practical requirements of life in this world. No people sets cosmology before health, security, and whatever their culture has predisposed them to savor and enjoy in their everyday lives. We need more knowledge of what happens when religions are in competition for a people's allegiance; but most often I think we will find that the one which best meets the down-to-earth needs of people, which best satisfies their immediate desires, be it "great" or small, will be the one to triumph (Skinner 1958). For a competing religious idiom can hardly be expected in itself to persuade anyone to abandon his own traditional idiom; what one looks for are results. This is why when a native religion fails, it is usually not the religion of foreign missionaries that prevails but an altogether new religion compounded of old and new, designed to meet the needs of that particular people at that particular time.

In closing, let me repeat that in our own work we should be careful not to let nonbelief in *a* religion slip over into nonbelief in religion. In a world where new religions are being born nearly every day, it would be a colossal error to think that we are studying people who are somehow behind the times in continuing to believe and behave as they do. For the ultimate lesson of anthropology—one Malinowski had a large role in shaping—is that in the context of their own worlds people know quite well what is true, what is good, and what is right. As students of religion we have to believe them.

BIBLIOGRAPHY

Aberle, D.
  1966 Religio-Magical Phenomena and Power, Prediction, and Control. *Southwestern Journal of Anthropology* 22: 221–30.

Ames, M. M.
  1964 Magical-Animism and Buddhism: A Structural Analysis of the Sinhalese Religious System. In E. B. Harper, ed. *Religion in South Asia*. Seattle, Wash.: University of Washington Press.

Bateson, G.
  1958 *Naven*. Stanford, Calif.: Stanford University Press, 2d ed.

Beidelman, T. O.
  1961 Right and Left Hand among the Kaguru: A Note on Symbolic Classification. *Africa* 31: 250–57.

Benedict, R.
  1922 The Vision in Plains Culture. In Mead 1959.
  1923 The Concept of the Guardian Spirit in North America. American Anthropological Association, *Memoirs,* No. 29.
  1930 Psychological Types in the Cultures of the Southwest. In Mead 1959, pp. 248–61.
  1932 Configurations of Culture in North America. *American Anthropologist* 34: 1–27.
  1934 *Patterns of Culture*. Boston: Houghton Mifflin.

Berreman, G. D.
  1964 Brahmans and Shamans in Pahari Religion. In E. B. Harper, ed. *Religion in South Asia*. Seattle, Wash.: University of Washington Press.

Boas, F.
  1927 Religious Terminology of the Kwakiutl. In Boas, *Race, Language and Culture*. New York: Macmillan, 1940.
  1930 *The Religion of the Kwakiutl Indians*. Columbia University Contributions to Anthropology, No. 10, Parts 1 and 2. New York: Columbia University Press.

Burridge, K. O. L.
  1965 Tangu, Northern Madang Coast. In P. Lawrence and M. Meggitt, eds. *Gods, Ghosts and Men in Melanesia*. New York: Oxford University Press.
  1969 *New Heaven, New Earth*. New York: Schocken.

Dieterlen, G.
  1965   Systèmes de connaisance. In M. Fortes and G. Dieterlen,
         eds. *African Systems of Thought*. New York: Oxford Uni-
         versity Press.

Douglas, M.
  1966   *Purity and Danger*. London: Routledge and Kegan Paul.

Durkheim, E.
  1912   *Les formes élémentaires de la vie religieuse*. (Eng. trans.:
         The Elementary Forms of the Religious Life. London:
         George Allen and Unwin.)

————, and Mauss, M.
  1963   *Primitive Classification*. Trans. R. Needham. London: Cohen
         and West. French orig., 1903.

Evans-Pritchard, E. E.
  1937   *Witchcraft, Oracles and Magic Among the Azande*. Oxford:
         Clarendon Press.
  1956   *Nuer Religion*. Oxford: Clarendon Press.
  1962   Religion and the Anthropologists. In *Essays in Social An-
         thropology*. London: Faber and Faber.
  1965   *Theories of Primitive Religion*. Oxford: Clarendon Press.

Faron, L. C.
  1962   Symbolic Values and the Integration of Society among the
         Mapuche of Chile. *American Anthropologist* 64: 1151–64.

Firth, R.
  1936   *We, the Tikopia*. London: George Allen and Unwin.
  1955   *The Fate of the Soul*. New York: Cambridge University
         Press. Reprinted in Firth 1967b.
  1957   Ed. *Man and Culture: An Evaluation of the Work of Broni-
         slaw Malinowski*. London: Routledge and Kegan Paul. Re-
         printed by Harper Torchbooks.
  1961   Religion in Social Reality, chap. 7 of *Elements of Social
         Organization*. London: Watts & Co., 3d ed.
  1964   *Essays on Social Organization and Values*. L.S.E. Monog.
         on Soc. Anthrop. 28. London: Athlone Press.
  1965   A Brief History (1913–1963). *Dept. of Anthropology, Pro-
         gramme of Courses, 1965–66*. London: The London School
         of Economics and Political Science.
  1967a *The Work of the Gods in Tikopia*. L.S.E. Monog. on Soc.
         Anthrop. 1 and 2. London: Athlone Press.

    1967b   *Tikopia Ritual and Belief.* London: George Allen and
            Unwin.

Forde D.
    1954   Ed. *African Worlds.* New York: Oxford University Press.
    1964   *Yakö Studies.* New York: Oxford University Press.

Fortes, M.
    1945   *The Dynamics of Clanship among the Tallensi.* New York:
            Oxford University Press.
    1949   *The Web of Kinship among the Tallensi.* New York: Oxford
            University Press.
    1957   Malinowski and the Study of Kinship. In Firth 1957.
    1959   *Oedipus and Job in West African Religion.* New York:
            Cambridge University Press. Reprinted in C. Leslie, ed.
            Anthropology of Folk Religion. New York: Vintage Books,
            1960.
    1965   Some Reflections on Ancestor Worship in Africa. In
            M. Fortes and G. Dieterlen, eds. *African Systems of Thought.*
            New York: Oxford University Press.

————, and Dieterlen, G., eds.
    1965   *African Systems of Thought.* New York: Oxford University
            Press.

Fortune, R.
    1932   *Sorcerers of Dobu.* New York: E. P. Dutton.

Frake, C.
    1961   The Diagnosis of Disease among the Subanun of Mindanao.
            American Anthropologist 63: 113–32.
    1964   A Structural Description of Subanun "Religious Behavior."
            In W. H. Goodenough, ed. *Explorations in Cultural Anthro-
            pology.* New York: McGraw-Hill. Reprinted in Lessa and
            Vogt 1965.

Frazer, J. G.
    1922   *The Golden Bough.* London: Macmillan, abridged ed.

Gaster, T.
    1953   *The New Golden Bough.* New York: Criterion Books.

Geertz, C.
    1957   Ritual and Social Change: A Javanese Example. *American
            Anthropologist* 59: 23–54. Reprinted in Lessa and Vogt
            1965.

1960   *The Religion of Java*. New York: The Free Press.
1962   The Growth of Culture and the Evolution of Mind. In
       J. Scher, ed. *Theories of the Mind*. New York: The Free
       Press.
1964   Ideology As a Cultural System. In D. Apter, ed. *Ideology
       and Discontent*. New York: The Free Press.
1966   Religion As a Cultural System. In M. Banton, ed. *Anthropo-
       logical Approaches to the Study of Religion*. London: Tavis-
       tock.
1967   The Cerebral Savage. *Encounter* Vol. 28, no. 4, pp. 25–32.
1968a *Islam Observed*. New Haven, Conn.: Yale University Press.
1968b Religion: Anthropological Study. In D. Sills, ed. *Interna-
       tional Encyclopedia of the Social Sciences*. New York: The
       Free Press.

Glick, L.
1967   Medicine As an Ethnographic Category: The Gimi of the
       New Guinea Highlands. *Ethnology* 6: 31–56.

Gluckman, M.
1944   The Logic of African Science and Witchcraft. *Rhodes-
       Livingston Institute Journal* (June), pp. 67–71. Bobbs-
       Merrill reprint A–87.
1954   *Rituals of Rebellion in South-east Africa*. Manchester: Man-
       chester University Press. Reprinted in Gluckman 1963.
1955   *Custom and Conflict in Africa*. Oxford: Basil Blackwell.
1963   *Order and Rebellion in Tribal Africa*. New York: The Free
       Press.

Goodenough, W. H.
1964   Introduction. In W. H. Goodenough, ed. *Explorations in
       Cultural Anthropology*. New York: McGraw-Hill.

Goody, J.
1961   Religion and Ritual: The Definitional Problem. *British Jour-
       nal of Sociology* 12: 142–64.
1962   *Death, Property and the Ancestors*. Stanford, Calif.: Stan-
       ford University Press.

Hallowell, A. I.
1926   Bear Ceremonialism in the Northern Hemisphere. *American
       Anthropologist* 28: 1–175.
1934   Some Empirical Aspects of Northern Saulteaux Religion.
       American Anthropologist 36: 389–404.

1954　Psychology and Anthropology. In J. Gillin, ed. *For a Science of Social Man.* New York: Macmillan.

1955　*Culture and Experience.* Philadelphia: University of Pennsylvania Press.

1960　Ojibwa Ontology, Behavior, and World View. In S. Diamond, ed. *Culture in History.* New York: Columbia University Press.

1963　Personality, Culture, and Society in Behavioral Evolution. In S. Koch, ed. *Psychology: A Study of a Science,* Vol. 6. New York: McGraw-Hill.

1965　The History of Anthropology As an Anthropological Problem. *Journal of the History of the Behavioral Sciences* 1: 24–38.

Harris, M.

1966　The Cultural Ecology of India's Sacred Cattle. *Current Anthropology* 7: 51–66.

1968　*The Rise of Anthropological Theory.* New York: Thomas Y. Crowell.

Hertz, R.

1960　*Death and the Right Hand.* Trans. R. and C. Needham. London: Cohen & West. French orig. 1909.

Hodgen, M.

1964　*Early Anthropology in the Sixteenth and Seventeenth Centuries.* Philadelphia: University of Pennsylvania Press.

Homans, G.

1941　Anxiety and Ritual: The Theories of Malinowski and Radcliffe-Brown. *American Anthropologist* 43: 164–72. Reprinted in Lessa and Vogt 1965.

Horton, R.

1960　A Definition of Religion, and Its Uses. *Journal of the Royal Anthropological Institute* 90: 201–26.

1962　The Kalabari World View: An Outline and Interpretation. *Africa* 32: 197–220.

1967　African Traditional Thought and Western Science. *Africa* 37: 50–71 and 155–87.

Kennedy, J. G.

1967　Psychological and Social Explanations of Witchcraft. *Man* (n.s.) 2: 216–25.

1968　Psychology and Social Anthropology. *Man* (n.s.) 3: 301–4.

Kluckhohn, C. M.

1941   Patterning As Exemplified in Navaho Culture. In L. Spier,
        A. I. Hallowell, and S. Newman, eds. *Language, Culture, and
        Personality*. Menasha, Wisc.: Sapir Memorial Publication
        Fund.

1943   Covert Culture and Administrative Problems. *American An-
        thropologist* 45: 213–27.

1944   *Navaho Witchcraft*. Papers of the Peabody Museum of
        Archaeology and Ethnology, Vol. 22, no. 2, Cambridge, Mass.
        Reprinted 1962, Boston: Beacon Press.

1949   The Philosophy of the Navaho Indians. In F. S. C. Northrop,
        ed. *Ideological Differences and World Order*. New Haven,
        Conn.: Yale University Press.

1951   Values and Value-Orientations in the Theory of Action. In
        T. Parsons and E. Shils, eds. *Toward a General Theory of
        Action*. Cambridge, Mass.: Harvard University Press.

1956   Toward a Comparison of Value-Emphases in Different Cul-
        tures. In L. White, ed. *The State of the Social Sciences*.
        Chicago: University of Chicago Press.

Krige, J. D.

1947   The Social Function of Witchcraft. In W. Lessa and E.
        Vogt, eds. *Reader in Comparative Religion*. Evanston: Row,
        Peterson, 1958.

Kroeber, A. L.

1923   *Anthropology*. New York: Harcourt Brace Jovanovich, Inc.
1952   *The Nature of Culture*. Chicago: University of Chicago Press.

LaBarre, W.

forth- Materials for a History of Studies of Crisis Cults: A
coming Bibliographic Essay. *Current Anthropology*.

Leach, E. R.

1954   *Political Systems of Highland Burma*. Boston: Beacon
        Press, 1965, paperback ed.

1964   Anthropological Aspects of Language: Animal Categories
        and Verbal Abuse. In E. Lenneberg, ed. *New Directions in
        the Study of Language*. Cambridge, Mass.: Massachusetts
        Institute of Technology Press.

1965   Introduction. In B. Malinowski. *Coral Gardens and Their
        Magic*. Bloomington, Ind.: Indiana University Press.

1966   On the "Founding Fathers." *Current Anthropology* 7: 560–
        67.

1967   Ed. *The Structural Study of Myth and Totemism.* London:
        Tavistock.
1968   Ed. *Dialectic in Practical Religion.* (Cambridge Papers in
        Social Anthropology, No. 5.) Cambridge: Cambridge Uni-
        versity Press.

Lee, D.
1949   Being and Value in a Primitive Culture. *Journal of Philoso-
        phy* 46: 401–15. Reprinted in Lee. *Freedom and Culture.*
        Englewood Cliffs, N.J.: Prentice-Hall, 1959.

Lessa, W. A. and E. Z. Vogt, eds.
1965   *Reader in Comparative Religion: An Anthropological Ap-
        proach.* New York: Harper & Row, 2d ed.

Lévi-Strauss, C.
1962a   *La Pensée sauvage.* Paris: Librairie Plon. Eng. trans. *The
        Savage Mind.* London: Weidenfeld and Nicolson, 1966.
1962b   *Le totemisme aujourd'hui.* Paris: Presses Universitaire de
        France. Eng. trans. R. Needham. *Totemism.* Boston: Bea-
        con Press, 1963.
1963   *Structural Anthropology.* New York: Basic Books, Inc.
        (Orig. French ed., 1958.)
1964   *Mythologiques: Le Cru et le cuit.* Paris: Librairie Plon.
1967   The Story of Asdiwal. In E. R. Leach, ed. *The Structural
        Study of Myth and Totemism.* London: Tavistock.

Lévy-Bruhl, L.
1923   *Primitive Mentality.* London: George Allen and Unwin.
        Orig. French ed., 1922.
1926   *How Natives Think.* London: George Allen and Unwin. Orig.
        French ed., 1910.

Lienhardt, G.
1961   *Divinity and Experience: The Religion of the Dinka.* Oxford:
        Clarendon Press.

Lowie, R.
1924   *Primitive Religion.* New York: Boni and Liveright.

Mair, L.
1969   *Witchcraft.* New York: McGraw-Hill.

Malinowski, B.
1913   *The Family among the Australian Aborigines.* London: Uni-
        versity of London Press.

1916   Baloma: Spirits of the Dead in the Trobriand Islands. *Journal of the Royal Anthropological Institute* 46: 353–430. Reprinted in Malinowski 1954.

1922   *Argonauts of the Western Pacific.* London: Routledge & Kegan Paul. Reprinted New York: E. P. Dutton, 1961.

1925   Magic, Science and Religion. In J. Needham, ed. *Science, Religion and Reality.* London: Macmillan. Reprinted in Malinowski 1954.

1926   *Myth in Primitive Psychology.* London: Psyche Miniatures. Reprinted in Malinowski 1954.

1929   *The Sexual Life of Savages in North-Western Melanesia.* London: Routledge and Kegan Paul.

1931   Culture. *Encyclopaedia of the Social Sciences,* Vol. 4. New York: Macmillan.

1935   *Coral Gardens and Their Magic.* London: George Allen and Unwin.

1936   *The Foundations of Faith and Morals.* London: University of Durham. Reprinted in Malinowski 1962.

1944   *A Scientific Theory of Culture and Other Essays.* Chapel Hill, N.C.: University of North Carolina Press. Paperback Galaxy Book, New York: Oxford University Press, 1960.

1954   *Magic, Science and Religion and Other Essays.* Garden City, N.Y.: Doubleday Anchor Books. Orig. ed. New York: The Free Press, 1948.

1962   *Sex, Culture, and Myth.* New York: Harcourt Brace Jovanovich.

1967   *A Diary in the Strict Sense of the Term.* New York: Harcourt Brace Jovanovich.

Mandelbaum, D.
1966   Transcendental and Pragmatic Aspects of Religion. *American Anthropologist* 68: 1174–91.

Marett, R. R.
1914   *The Threshold of Religion.* London: Methuen, 2d ed.

Marwick, M. G.
1952   The Social Context of Cewa Witch Beliefs. *Africa* 22: 120–35 and 215–33.

1965   *Sorcery in Its Social Setting.* Manchester: Manchester University Press.

Mayer, P.
1954   Witches. Grahamstown. Rhodes University Inaugural Address.

Mead, M.
    1959   *An Anthropologist at Work: Writings of Ruth Benedict.*
            Boston: Houghton Mifflin.

Métraux, R.
    1968   Malinowski, Bronislaw. In D. Sills, ed. *International Ency-
            clopaedia of the Social Sciences.* New York: The Free Press.

Middleton, J.
    1960   *Lugbara Religion.* New York: Oxford University Press.
    1967   Ed. *Myth and Cosmos.* Garden City, N.Y.: Natural History
            Press.

Middleton, J., and Winter, E.
    1963   Eds. *Witchcraft and Sorcery in East Africa.* London: Rout-
            ledge and Kegan Paul.

Miller, R. J.
    1964   Cultures As Religious Structures. In J. Helm, ed. *Sympo-
            sium on New Approaches to the Study of Religion.* Seattle,
            Wash.: University of Washington Press.

Nadel, S. F.
    1952   Witchcraft in Four African Societies: An Essay in Com-
            parison. *American Anthropologist* 54: 18–29.
    1954   *Nupe Religion.* London: Routledge and Kegan Paul.
    1957   Malinowski on Magic and Religion. In R. Firth, ed. *Man
            and Culture.* London: Routledge and Kegan Paul.

Nash, M.
    1963   Burmese Buddhism in Everyday Life. *American Anthro-
            pologist* 65: 285–95.

Needham, R.
    1960   The Left Hand of the Mugwe: An Analytical Note on the
            Structure of Meru Symbolism. *Africa* 30: 20–33.
    1965   Review of L. Lévy-Bruhl, *Primitive Mentality. American
            Anthropologist* 67: 1291–93.
    1967   Right and Left in Nyoro Symbolic Classification. *Africa* 37:
            425–52.

Norbeck, E.
    1963   African Rituals of Conflict. *American Anthropologist* 65:
            1254–79.

Ortiz, A.
    1969   *The Tewa World.* Chicago: University of Chicago Press.

Parsons, T.
1957 Malinowski and the Theory of Social Systems. In Firth 1957.

Piddington, R.
1957 Malinowski's Theory of Needs. In Firth 1957.

Radcliffe-Brown, A. R.
1948 *The Andaman Islanders*. New York: The Free Press, 2d ed. Orig. ed., 1922.
1952 *Structure and Function in Primitive Society*. New York: The Free Press.

Radin, P.
1927 *Primitive Man as Philosopher*. New York: Dover.
1937 *Primitive Religion*. New York: Dover.

Rappaport, R.
1967a *Pigs for the Ancestors*. New Haven, Conn.: Yale University Press.
1967b Ritual Regulation of Environmental Relations among a New Guinea People. *Ethnology* 6: 17–30.

Redfield, R.
1962 The Primitive World View. In R. Redfield. *Human Nature and the Study of Society*. Chicago: University of Chicago Press.

Reichard, G.
1950 *Navaho Religion: A Study of Symbolism*. New York: Pantheon.

Richards, A.
1957 The Concept of Culture in Malinowski's Work. In Firth 1957.
1967 African Systems of Thought: An Anglo-French Dialogue. *Man* (n.s.) 2: 286–98.

Rigby, P.
1966 Dual Symbolic Classification among the Gogo of Central Tanzania. *Africa* 36: 1–17.
1968 Some Gogo Rituals of "Purification": An Essay on Social and Moral Categories. In E. R. Leach, ed. *Dialectic in Practical Religion*. New York: Cambridge University Press.

Robertson-Smith, W.
1889 *Lectures on the Religion of the Semites*. New York: Appleton-Century-Crofts.

Saler, B.
1964 Nagual, Witch, and Sorcerer in a Quiche Village. *Ethnology* 3: 305–28. Reprinted in J. Middleton, ed. *Magic, Witchcraft, and Curing*. Garden City, N.Y.: Natural History Press, 1967.

Sapir, E.
1949 *Selected Writings of Edward Sapir*, ed. D. Mandelbaum. Berkeley and Los Angeles, Calif.: University of California Press.

Scholte, B.
1966 Epistemic paradigms. *American Anthropologist* 68: 1192–1201.

Skinner, E. P.
1958 Christianity and Islam among the Mossi. *American Anthropologist* 60: 1102–19. Reprinted in J. Middleton, ed. *Gods and Rituals*. Garden City, N.Y.: Natural History Press, 1967.

Speck, F.
1935 *Naskapi*. Norman, Okla.: University of Oklahoma Press.

Spier, L.
1921 *The Sun Dance of the Plains Indians: Its Development and Diffusion*. American Museum of Natural History, Anthropological Papers, Vol. 16, part 7. New York: A.M.N.H.

Spiro, M. E.
1952 Ghosts, Ifaluk, and Teleological Functionalism. *American Anthropologist* 54: 497–503. Reprinted in Lessa and Vogt 1965.
1964 Religion and the Irrational. In J. Helm, ed. *Symposium on New Approaches to the Study of Religion*. Seattle, Wash.: University of Washington Press.
1965 Religious Systems As Culturally Constituted Defense Mechanisms. In M. Spiro, ed. *Context and Meaning in Cultural Anthropology*. New York: The Free Press.
1966a Religion: Problems of Definition and Explanation. In M. Banton, ed. *Anthropological Approaches to the Study of Religion*. London: Tavistock.
1966b Buddhism and Economic Action in Burma. *American Anthropologist* 68: 1163–73.
1967 *Burmese Supernaturalism*. Englewood Cliffs, N.J.: Prentice-Hall.

1969   Discussion. In R. F. Spencer, ed. *Forms of Symbolic Action.*
        Seattle, Wash.: University of Washington Press.

Stanner, W. E. H.
    1964   *On Aboriginal Religion.* Oceania Monograph No. 11. Syd-
            ney: University of Sydney. Originally six papers in *Oceania*
            30–33, 1959–1963.

Sturtevant, W.
    1964   Studies in Ethnoscience. *American Anthropologist* Vol. 66,
            no. 3, part 2, pp. 99–131.

Tambiah, S. J.
    1968   The Ideology of Merit and the Social Correlates of Buddhism
            in a Thai Village. In E. R. Leach, ed. *Dialectic in Practical
            Religion.* Cambridge Papers in Social Anthropology, No.
            5. New York: Cambridge University Press.

Turner, V. W.
    1957   The Politically Integrative Function of Ritual. Chap. 10 of
            Schism and Continuity in an African Society. Manchester:
            Manchester University Press.
    1961   *Ndembu Divination: Its Symbolism and Techniques.* Rhodes-
            Livingston Institute Papers, No. 31. Manchester: Manches-
            ter University Press.
    1962   Three Symbols of *Passage* in Ndembu Circumcision Ritual:
            An Interpretation. In M. Gluckman, ed. *Essays on the Ritual
            of Social Relations.* Manchester: Manchester University
            Press.
    1964a   Symbols in Ndembu Ritual. In M. Gluckman, ed. *Closed
            Systems and Open Minds.* Chicago: Aldine.
    1964b   Betwixt and Between: The Liminal Period. In *Rites de
            Passage.* In J. Helm, ed. *Symposium on New Approaches
            to the Study of Religion.* Seattle, Wash.: University of
            Washington Press.
    1966   Colour Classification in Ndembu Ritual. In M. Banton, ed.
            Anthropological Approaches to the Study of Religion. Lon-
            don: Tavistock.
    1967   *The Forest of Symbols.* Ithaca, N.Y.: Cornell University
            Press.
    1968   *The Drums of Affliction.* Oxford: Clarendon Press.

Tylor, E. B.
    1871   *Primitive Culture.* London: John Murray.

Wallace, A. F. C.
   1956   Revitalization Movements. *American Anthropologist* 58: 264–81.
   1966   *Religion: An Anthropological View.* New York: Random House.

Washburn, S., and Howell, C.
   1960   Human Evolution and Culture. In S. Tax, ed. *Evolution after Darwin,* Vol. 2. Chicago: University of Chicago Press.

Wax, M., and Wax, R.
   1963   The Notion of Magic. *Current Anthropology* 4: 495–518.
   1964   Magic and Monotheism. In J. Helm, ed. *Symposium on New Approaches to the Study of Religion.* Seattle, Wash.: University of Washington Press.

White, L.
   1949a   The Symbol: The Origin and Basis of Human Behavior. In *The Science of Culture.* New York: Farrar, Straus and Giroux.
   1949b   Culturological vs. Psychological Interpretations of Human Behavior. In *The Science of Culture.* New York: Farrar, Straus and Giroux.

Wilson, M.
   1951   Witch Beliefs and Social Structure. *American Journal of Sociology* 56: 307–13.
   1957   *Rituals of Kinship among the Nyakyusa.* New York: Oxford University Press.
   1959   *Communal Rituals of the Nyakyusa.* New York: Oxford University Press.

Worsley, P.
   1968   *The Trumpet Shall Sound.* New York: Schocken, 2d ed.

Wyllie, R. W.
   1968   Ritual and Social Change: A Ghanian Example. *American Anthropologist* 70: 21–33.

Yalman, N.
   1962   On Some Binary Categories in Sinhalese Religious Thought. *Transactions of the New York Academy of Sciences,* Series 2, 24.
   1967   The Raw: The Cooked: Nature: Culture. In E. R. Leach, ed. *The Structural Study of Myth and Totemism.* London: Tavistock.

6 SIGMUND FREUD AND HIS LEGACY: PSYCHOANALYTIC PSYCHOLOGY OF RELIGION[1]

Paul W. Pruyser

I INTRODUCTION

For a man who described himself in private correspondence as "a wicked pagan" and "a godless Jew," and whose daughter described his household as "totally non-religious" (Meng and Freud 1963: 17, 63, 11), Freud devoted a sizable portion of his voluminous writings to religion.[2] The explicit attention he gave it is an implicit recognition of the power that religion has over the minds of people, of the great logical and psychological puzzles it presents, and of the fascination it has not only for pious people but for "wicked pagans" as well. For Freud proceeded in regard to religion not only as a detached scholar, but also as an involved diagnostician making clinical judgments, as a concerned healer setting therapeutic goals, and at times as a polemicist contending

[1] The author is indebted to the following persons for a critical reading of the manuscript: Kenneth R. Mitchell, Ph.D., Ernst A. Ticho, Ph.D., and Philip Woollcott, M.D., all of The Menninger Foundation, and Seward Hiltner, Ph.D., of Princeton Theological Seminary.
[2] To give the reader ease in historical dating as well as opportunity for quick bibliographic checking, references to Freud's works (other than letters) are by date of publication as defined by the Standard Edition, followed in the case of quotation by the page number in the volume of the Standard Edition which comprises the quoted work.

about ideologies and *Weltanschauungen*. Teasingly, he wrote to his good friend Pfister in 1937 that he had just finished "a sizeable piece about some significant matters, . . . it is again about religion, so again it will not be pleasing to you" (Meng and Freud 1963: 144).

His first printed utterance about religion (1893), at the age of thirty-six, noted in a soberly psychiatric vein the cathartic effect of a religious practice, the Catholic confessional, "giving utterance to a tormenting secret" (1893a: 8), as well as certain forms of psychopathology in the religious, namely the "hysterical deliria of saints and nuns" (1893a: 11). At the time, any psychiatrist could have made such statements. His last public statement about religion (1939), written when he was in his eighties, raised near its ending the more encompassing and personally significant queries: ". . . how these . . . people have been able to acquire their belief in the Divine Being" and ". . . whence that belief obtained its immense power which overwhelms 'reason and science'?" (1939: 123) At the time, many psychiatrists could have asked such questions but refrained from doing so, probably because they took religious faith for granted instead of seeing it as a challenging problem. Freud's own striking answer was that the truth of religion is a "historical truth" (1927: 44, 1939: 129). But as the context of *Moses and Monotheism* (1939) and nearly all his previous statements about religion make clear, "historical truth" is not to be taken in the factual sense of dated and verified happenings, nor religiously as a divine self-disclosure, but in the psychological sense of archaic, primeval fantasy themes whose possible historicity is beyond verification but whose emotional legitimation is apparently enduring, inasmuch as the child remains the father of the man, and primitive people live on in modern ones.

II THE PERSONAL EQUATION IN FREUD'S SCIENTIFIC STUDY OF RELIGION

Since Freud himself would be the first to call attention to the role of the personal equation in all judgments about affect-laden issues, it is important to be aware of his "rationalistic, or perhaps analytic, turn of mind" (1914a: 212). These words are his own, when he described at the age of fifty-eight his marked enjoyment of works of art, especially literature and sculpture less often painting, as consisting largely in the attempt to explain to himself the source of their powerful effect on him. He acknowledged that he failed to do this with music and was almost incapable of obtaining any pleasure from it.

According to Jones (1953: 57), Freud loved nature and greatly enjoyed mountain walks; he was an excellent linguist and was well-read with an almost photographic memory. He was conversant with Jewish customs and festivals, had a fair amount of biblical knowledge, conversed and corresponded with several avowed Christians among whom was at least one professional theologian, and could not avoid being exposed to Austrian Catholicism, good and bad. He was also exposed to anti-Semitism, genteel and militant.

Much as he detested religious ceremony, he had to submit himself to a simple Jewish wedding because his country did not recognize a mere civil marriage. Though his biographer Jones reports that his Catholic nanny sometimes took him to church with her and that upon his return home after those church visits he was said to have "imitated preaching" these dubious events must have terminated when he was two and a half years old and were probably far more conflict-free than any Old World boy's seeing his first Punch and Judy show in the center of town. It seems that, though he rejected any imputation of religious interest, he fully accepted his keen intellectual interest in the phenomena and the roots of religion. To the end of his life he exposed his Jewish ancestry in the thematic selectivity of his investigations: like the Old Testament writers he focused his attention on the relations between fathers and sons. In addition, Jewish allegiance came through in occasional wry remarks about Christians in his correspondence with Jewish friends (Abraham and Freud 1965: 34, 46, 64).

Like many avowed unbelievers, Freud strove for intellectual honesty and tried to follow an impeccable ethic informed by historical awareness of the best in Western culture and admiration for the Greek and Latin classics. In his almost puritanical sobriety regarding questions of truth, for which he used exclusively a scientific yardstick, he was highly aware of an inevitable ambiguity in the impact of his propositions: on the one hand he was convinced from his psychotherapeutic work that the truth will eventually set a person free. On the other hand he knew from the same source that truth is at first a "bitter truth" which meets with fierce resistance. Any truth bearer is a challenger. Hence, as he put it in a letter to Singer in 1938: ". . . everything I write is bound to cause misunderstanding and—may I add—indignation." (Freud, E. L. 1960: 453–54). He did not succumb to the enticing praise of Pfister who, in boundless admiration for his "benefactor," wrote to him: "If you raised to your consciousness and fully felt your place in the great design . . . I should say of you: a better Christian there never was" (Meng and Freud, 1963: 63). On the contrary, he always knew, as an expert in the phenomena of transference, that people could be right for the wrong reasons, and that extraneous ideological premises could seriously distort the way in which his scientific propositions were registered by others. In his first historical sketch of the psychoanalytic movement he said: "The theological prehistory of so many of the Swiss throws no less light on their attitude to psychoanalysis than does Adler's socialist prehistory on the development of his psychology" (1914: 61). He believed that *purity of heart is purity of thought,* although he would have preferred to reverse the sequence of terms in Kierkegaard's dictum.

A slight impurity, however, is likely to beset even the best of challengers. It is the tendency to become provocative, as if these challengers brace themselves too much for an anticipated resistance whose force they overestimate. This may bespeak their own residual fear, their own residual ambivalence, their own ultimate uncertainty or, as might have been the case in Freud's speaking to the religionists, an underestimation of many avowed believers' own doubts. After all, lack of faith is a condition in which believers rightly claim to be the greatest experts. Moreover, belief in a divine Providence of the world had already started to decline not only in the disaffiliated but even in the faithful long before Freud noted how childish it is to cast the process of nature in the image of a quasiparent to whom one feels linked with libidinal bonds (1924). But provocation is close to watch-fulness, which is an asset in investigative work. Freud's vigilance quickly spotted the propensity of "pious souls," as he called them, to take the strong prohibition of murder in the Ten Commandments as proof of the loftiness of inborn ethical strivings in people, forgetting that strong prohibitions are only belatedly forged against equally strong (and demonstrable) impulses or wishes to commit the deed in the first place (1915 : 295–96). Such a statement is not provocative but *ad rem*.

And, thus, Freud's investigations of religion are not without traces of his militant dedication to an atheistic world view, a positivistic conception of truth, and the developmental orientation which prevailed during his lifetime (and under his own influence) in nearly all the sciences with which he dealt, from neuroanatomy to anthropology. These selective loyalties do not invalidate his observations and constructs about religion but only describe the steady perspective in which his data came to light and his concepts found their cogency. His turn of mind was indeed rationalistic and analytic, as he himself said. Disciplined scientific thought cannot do without these traits.

III FREUD'S CONTRIBUTIONS TO THE PSYCHOLOGY OF RELIGION

Although it is customary to present Freud's general concepts in chronological sequence, because he revised and amplified his theories in the light of fresh observations which exposed the shortcomings of earlier concepts, his statements about religion retained a remarkable stability during the long course of his literary productivity. Therefore, it makes sense to present his contributions to the psychology of religion topically, according to subdivisions which arise naturally from his writings. These are, in my view:

1. Origins and development of religion
   a. Phylogenetic
   b. Ontogenetic
2. Specific functions of religion
   a. What the ordinary person understands by his religion
   b. Religion as a system of beliefs, pledges, and doctrines

     c. Organization of thought in religion
     d. Religion as a means of social control
     e. The use of religious acts
     f. The role of feelings in religion
     g. Religion and reality testing
     h. Religion and sublimation

Since this chapter cannot be a primer on psychoanalytic psychology, which is, anyway, as yet more a loosely knit fabric of diverse and *ad hoc* theoretical fragments than the comprehensive and unified theoretical system it strives to be, it is important to keep in mind that the above topics are, as it were, specialized, if not spotty subperspectives within the larger global perspective of psychoanalytic reasoning. Inasmuch as there are empirical grounds for such "spottiness," a topical presentation would allow for a more faithful rendition of Freud's thoughts on religion than a streamlined whole could give.

Origins and Development of Religion—Phylogenetic

Both *Totem and Taboo* (1913) and *Moses and Monotheism* (1939) (the latter is in many respects an elaboration, written in several stages, of the former work) are discursive treatises with more than one thesis. Leaning on selected anthropological observations (controversial, according to many anthropologists), Freud held that wherever totemism is found, it is linked with exogamy. He concluded from this that the strength of the totemic incest barrier must be proportionate to the fear of incest in totemic peoples, which in turn is symptomatic of a substrata of strong incestuous wishes. He then analyzed the nature of taboo, to note its remarkable similarity to the "taboo sickness" (1913:26) in some modern people, namely, compulsion neurotics. In both cases there is ambivalence of feeling regarding acts that are at once highly desired and strictly prohibited, with the result that groups and individuals are suspended between awe and aversion. Taboo is a highly stylized prohibition which demands renunciation of a feverish wish. It plays on the fear that any violation will cause disaster; it leads to ceremonials of avoidance and often entails displacement from the original to other objects. If offense in thought or deed occurs (primitive omnipotence of thought equates thoughts and deeds), the restrictions are buttressed by more or less elaborate and ritualistic acts of expiation. Assuming that the oldest known taboos are imposed on killing the totem symbol and engaging in incest, Freud inferred that there must be strong inclinations toward these acts in the unconscious. Owing to this underlying temptation, taboo violation is contagious and is thus a social danger against which the social system must institute a rigorous defense.

Since primitive people were presumably closer (in time and mental organization) to the wish-fulfilling deeds against which the taboo was erected, their ambivalence was sharper than that of modern people. With the historical decline of ambivalence in evolving civilizations, the taboo also disappeared but not smoothly or totally. The long process of weaning from totemism goes through phases, which are determined by thought processes which move gradually from dominance by the pleasure principle to dominance by the reality principle. Just as thinking in human infants is at first characterized by omnipotence of thought, in which wishes create a fantasy world which prevails over external reality, so primitive peoples went first through an *animistic stage* in which they bluntly ascribed omnipotence of thought to themselves, enacted in magic rituals. It was an advance when, in the second *religious stage,* people assumed the intermediate position of ceding omnipotence to their gods but retaining some of it for themselves in order to influence these gods to favor the fulfillment of their wishes. Finally, in the *scientific stage,* people's omnipotence is overcome; they recognize their smallness in the universe and resign themselves to the superior forces of nature, including the appalling fact of death. But even in this latter stage, some remnant of the earlier omnipotence of thought lives on as belief in the power of the human mind to cope with the laws of reality. Religious thinking cherishes the object relation of child with parents in dependency; scientific thought adapts itself to reality and seeks its object in the wide, wide world. Modern people repeat ontogenetically the phylogenetic course: children have animal phobias, and the first sexual stirrings in childhood are markedly incestuous.

In *Thoughts for the Times on War and Death* Freud inferred from one form of the Christian atonement doctrine that the life-for-a-life theme indicates that the original crime or sin of humanity must have been a killing, indeed, a parricide: "the killing of the primal father of the primitive human horde, whose mnemic image was later transfigured into a deity" (1915: 293). This theme became more articulated in *Psychoanalysis and Religious Origins,* intended as a preface to Reik's *Ritual.* The parricide of the sons eventually resulted in social regulation through a set of moral restrictions: ". . . the oldest form of religion, totemism" (1919: 262). Freud added that later religions have the same basic content of (1) expiating the traces of that crime, and (2) proposing other solutions to the struggle between fathers and sons. In the same paper, the clinician in Freud notes that the ceremonials and prohibitions of obsessional neurotics show so much likeness to religious rituals that one might say these patients have "created a private religion of their own" (1919: 261).

The same themes recur in *Group Psychology and the Analysis of the Ego* (1921) but with greater emphasis on the father as a figure who gives love and protection and the duty of "good fathers" (for example, group leaders in the army and the church) to love their men equally, just as all group members are expected to love one another equally and justly. For Christians Christ is both a substitute of the (killed) father and an example of sibling love. But since religion is a group phenomenon, the ambivalent impulses tend to be split in such a way that "every religion is . . . a religion of love for all those whom it embraces," while the penchant toward cruelty and intolerance is directed to "those who do not belong" (1921: 98).

A passing remark in *The Ego and the Id* asserts that "religion, morality and a social sense—the chief elements in the higher side of man—were originally one and the same thing" (1923a: 37). It describes the ego-ideal as a substitute for the early longing for a loved father—"the germ from which all religions have evolved" (1923a: 37). In this statement, phylogenesis is clearly coupled with ontogenesis.

Finally, in *Moses and Monotheism* (1939) the religion of Aton, advocated by the Egyptian ruler Ikhnaton in an unsuccessful attempt to unite local cults into a pan-Egyptian religious system which would subordinate the priestly caste to the imperial pharaohs, was held up by Freud as the model and historical source of Jewish monotheism. Moses, who was reared in Egyptian royal circles, transmitted the Aton religion to the Jewish people while he was managing the exodus. In this work the emphasis is on showing the parallellism between the presumed or reconstructed historical sequence of the rise of Judaism from Jahwist henotheism to Mosaic monotheism on the one hand and the development of neurotic conflicts and symptoms in modern individuals on the other hand. It seems to me important to note that such neurotic conflicts may not have a shred of religiosity, except insofar as certain neurotic processes are like a "private religion." Similarly, the early Jewish religious systems do not require individual neuroticism in all the members of the Jewish people, except insofar as each member was affected by a corporate repressed memory of the original father-killing.

The thesis underlying Freud's comparison rests on the following conviction:

> . . . I have never doubted that religious phenomena are only to be understood on the pattern of the individual neurotic symptoms familiar to us—as the return of long since forgotten, important events in the primeval history of the human family—and that they have to thank precisely this origin for their compulsive character, and that, accordingly, they are effective on human beings by force of the historical truth of their content. (1939 : 58)

In essence Freud's comparison of the development of neuroses in individuals and the development of religious patterns of behavior in people is not instigated by an objective search for historical facticity but by his desire to answer the question: whence comes the sweeping power of religion (over reason) and whence the sweeping power of neurosis (over mental health)? Freud's curiosity about religion stemmed from his perplexity as a rational and ethical man whose sense of reality dictated that he acknowledge the relentless power of religion (which he saw around him as a citizen) and of neurosis (which he saw before him in his patients). As he himself put it: "If our work leads us to a conclusion which reduced religion to a neurosis of humanity and explains its enormous power in the same way as a neurotic compulsion in our individual patient" (1939 : 55).

The developmental model of the neuroses is: early trauma, defense, latency, outbreak of the neurosis, partial return of the repressed. This model, Freud held, is applicable to the phylogenetic development of religion. *Totem and Taboo* documents the aboriginal phases, *Moses and Monotheism* the later, more highly developed and refined phases of this ever-repeated sequence, from the rise of a Hebrew monotheistic father-religion to the modifications introduced by the Christian father-and-son religion. The book ends in a study of Jewish superiority feelings followed by the agonizing questions: ". . . how these . . . other people have been able to acquire their belief in the Divine Being . . ." and ". . . whence that belief obtained its immense power, which overwhelms 'reason and science'?" (1939: 123).

Origins and Development of Religion—Ontogenetic

It should be noted that most of the foregoing has dealt with the phylogenesis of religion. Yet the last two questions in the preceding paragraph have an exquisitely individual cogency and need to be answered in ontogenetic terms. It has always impressed me that Freud in his published work seems to have shirked the individual approach in seeking answers to his questions about religion. He never published a full-fledged case study that focused on the dynamics of religion in the life of a person. He said almost nothing about the details of religious education, either from the teacher's or the learner's point of view, except for his general aversion to it. Though he said much about the cognitive process in religion in *The Future of an Illusion* (1927), he did not make individual applications but spoke only globally of "believers" or "the faithful." Even if some of the clinical case studies he published contain remarks and observations about the patients' religious behavior, they are at best secondary to his purpose of presenting syndromes, symptoms, and dynamics.

In his comments on Schreber's autobiography (1911a), Freud noted many odd religious ideas and showed an interest in tracing their psychodynamic reasons and origins, but this is still far from coming to grips with the origins of belief in God and the dynamics of faith in Schreber's life. But his comments did show how Schreber's sexual conflicts necessitated certain kinds of theological innovation which brought his earlier acquired, conventional Christian belief system in line with his conviction that he was changed from a man into a woman. In other words,

Freud's treatment of the Schreber case shows the functioning of certain (odd, idiosyncratic, "sick") religious ideas in the whole of a paranoid system of thought through which Schreber attempted a new adaptation to his life's realities.

There is, however, much in Freud's observations about the general development of children (object relations, thought organization, Oedipus complex, superego and ego-ideal) that throws light on a presumably typical patterning of individual religious development. Most fundamental to all these observations is the recognition that the very young child is helpless and dependent on his parents in the same way that humankind feels helpless vis-à-vis nature and seeks protection from its overwhelming power. In *The Future of an Illusion* (1927) nature is both nurturant and threatening as is culture to its members, just as parents are both nurturing and threatening to their child. People both succumb to and rebel against the power of nature, just as children succumb to and rebel against the authority of parents. Intimate family dynamics as well as corporate pressures from society demand that the child learn to renounce certain wishes: those that would result in sexual license and those that would lead to aggressive assaults on others. Thus, from the beginning of an individual's journey into life, restrictions must be imposed and morals must be taught, in the hope that they will "stick" in such a way that society, the family, and the individual will benefit by having their anxieties lessened and their gratifications apportioned. The contract which society makes with individuals is: (1) to diminish the burden of instinctual sacrifices imposed upon people, (2) to reconcile them to those that must necessarily remain, and (3) to compensate them for these sacrifices.

The unconscious, however, knows no restrictions. As long as it is prevalent (as in early infancy, which is attuned to the pleasure principle), the frustrations of life, including temporary absences of the nurturant caretaker, are compensated for by the omnipotence of thought. This substitution has the power to create a wish-fulfilling perpetuation of mother or father through a fantasy image. In other words, a thought or protoconcept is born from a frustrated wish. Although such primitive thoughts will lose much of their vividness and realism when, with increasing operation of secondary thought processes, they are constantly

checked against the *prima facie* actuality of external reality
which produces the more tangible satisfactions, traces of the
compensatory fantasy images remain, probably for life. They
provide the nuclei of thought and feeling, of longings, of remi-
niscences of awe and bliss to which folklore, fairy tales, myths,
legends, and religion may add further charges and richer content provided, of course, that all these cultural goods are taught,
upheld as values, and socially reinforced. In most cases, religious
ideas are indeed taught, whether by a conscious and intentional
process of instruction or by inadvertent transmission through
unconscious acts or allusions of parents or even by the para-
praxias of swearing or involuntary prayer utterances. Though
Freud never seems to have stated these things explicitly, they are
axiomatic to his formulations.

What he did say was that the ego-ideal (between which and
the superego he made little systematic difference in *The Ego and
the Id*) is "the germ from which all religions have evolved"
(1923a : 37). It is a substitute for the early longing for a loved
father. Superego and ego-ideal are the results of processes of
identification with loving and rejecting, approving and disap-
proving, praising and blaming, opposing and protecting parents
whose external guidance patterns become, gradually, an internal
compass for behavior. They can bestow love upon the ego even
when outsiders would withhold love; they can bestow blame even
when outsiders might give praise. None of this is religious as
such; it is merely the beginning of moral self-regulation. But it
can quickly become religious because most religions entwine with
moral systems, because many religions consider conscience quasi-
divine, and because an "unseen father" under the corporate
pressure and in the established language of religion can easily be
transposed to a "heavenly father" of whose immanence in
human beings conscience is a sign, if not proof. Again, Freud
did not say this as I did, but he must have assumed these general
steps of individual religious origins and development. In *A
Religious Experience* Freud said in commenting on a letter he
had received from an American physician in a religious crisis
that "His ideas of 'father' and 'God' had not yet become widely
separated; so that his desire to destroy his father could become

conscious as doubt in the existence of God'' (1928b: 171). Apparently, then, he assumed that normally in the religious the real father and the idea of God do become separated and from that moment can be related to each other in various ways: for example, God will give what the real father has failed to give, God will (later) compensate for the miseries experienced on earth. Submission to the will of God in religious persons need not be matched by equal submission to one's father's will; in fact, it may be a sophisticated way of opposing one's father's will. But in the case at hand the fusion of father and God was still so prominent (as it presumably is in the very young) that the doctor's belated conversion experience was to be seen as ''complete submission to the will of God the Father'' (1928b: 171) and precisely in that sense a solution to the man's Oedipus complex.

Moses and Monotheism is forthright in stating that collective memories of the human group or ideational contents of former generations may leave traces in the subsequent individuals through genetic dispositions (1939: 98ff). This assumption is used to buttress the assertion that people have always known that they have had a primeval father whom they killed, and any repeat of such murders (Moses, Christ, and so on) may bring the old repressed memory back to consciousness. But *The Future of an Illusion* holds that many people do not have the ''rare experience'' (1927: 28) which in others seems to bear witness to the truth of proposed religious doctrines. Thus, these collective memory traces are not equally distributed through a population or are not equally potent. Reducing an individual's religiosity simply to the potency of some religious archetype would not do; something else must happen for religion to take hold of an individual.

Though there is no focal paper on the subject, there are scattered references in Freud's papers and books which indicate that he put much stock in a peculiar form of thought control he saw in religious people. In his commemorative paper on Charcot, Freud said that he had become familiar through this teacher with the literature on possession and witchcraft trials which taught him something about ''clerical phantasy'' (1893b: 22). Few people would deny today that ''thought control'' is an

appropriate description of some eras of Western history. Freud
elaborated this theme in different words when in later papers he
described the thought taboos presently found in people. He felt
that women are prone to be "scared away from *any* form of
thinking, and knowledge loses its value for them. The prohibition
of thought extends beyond the sexual field, partly through
unavoidable association, partly automatically, like the prohibiton
of thought about religion among men, or the prohibition of
thought about loyalty among faithful subjects" (1908: 199). The
case of *Little Hans* documents Hans's perplexity when he is left
wondering whether it is Mamma herself or God who is going to
determine whether his mother will have another child, and
Freud's footnote comment, *Ce que femme veut Dieu veut*
(1909a: 91), capsules the intellectual dishonesty which keeps
children in the dark. In *The Future Prospects of Psychoanalytic
Therapy* (1910) Freud noted that since the priesthood had
changed its attitude, hallucinations of the Virgin Mary in peasant girls had become rarer, thus indicating that what happens in
religious individuals depends in part on the control of corporate
prescriptions and proscriptions. In the case history of the Wolf
Man (1918) the patient's obsessional state became, before psychoanalytic treatment began, partially sublimated through religion but at a price: it impaired his intellectual activity, he lost
his zeal for learning, he dropped the acute questions regarding
God typical of his childhood, and he lost social interest.

Why does the ban on thought work in so many people? One
answer is that religious propositions give or promise wish-fulfillment (which is what makes them "illusions"). A second answer
is that people with successful superego development are transformed from foes of culture to its supporters. To be in tune with
one's conscience means having an internal lover independent of
external object relations. And to be in tune with public morality
and religion produces, apart from the satisfactions given by the
superego, the social expansion of the individual into a culture
bearer, a loyal citizen, a faithful believer, or a child of God, all of
which add their own narcissistic gratifications.

A third reason for the effectiveness of thought control through
religion is its defensive function: religion pretends to help the

individual against the forces of nature and sometimes of culture, provided one believes in its doctrines. Given Freud's definitions in *The Future of an Illusion* such belief means that one succumbs to the immediate persuasiveness of doctrine or cult and suspends critical intellectual questions. Since religion not only demands but promises so much, children as well as adults are always prone to follow the path of least resistance and compromise their intellect by giving in to the wish-fulfilling charms of the religious propositions.

I would like to add several more reasons to those that Freud advanced. Ages of sophistication have clad religion in rational forms on which considerable intelligence has been expended; thus, the child who is taught religion may sooner or later find great intellectual challenges not only about it but also within it. Ages of institutionalization have preserved religion not merely as a widely adopted "mode of thought" but have concretized it into a formidable set of social, political, economic, and even academic realities, to which any person from childhood on must make his adaptation. Even if one is opposed to it, one must be conversant with religion, or else one's naïveté will merit a bad mark. Neutrality to and diffidence about religion are almost impossible if one does not want to sever contact with a large chunk of reality and shrink one's enjoyments. Finally, ages of human endeavor have linked religion with an esthetic reality manifest in exquisite works of art, schools of art, and forms of art. Although Freud considered art a "mild narcosis" and esthetic enjoyment a "satisfaction through fantasy" (1930: 80–81), he also saw art as an erotic derivative, emphasizing, with his love for sculpture, the secondary sex characteristics of the human figure, while saying hardly anything about music (1930 : 83). To these enjoyments of art, erotic or narcotic, people feel rightly entitled, and the growing child can hardly avoid, while seeking the enjoyments of beauty, making contact with religion in one form or another, simply because religion is so patently present within the arts and vice versa. To this reality, too, the child brings not only wishes for satisfaction and needs for defense but also adaptive propensities. And if curiosity is another motive for seeking contact with religion (which includes a world view) or the world (which includes religion) a child or adult may aim for width of scope rather than precision in his reality contact.

Specific Functions of Religion

Though Freud wisely did not tie himself in his writings to an explicit conceptual definition of what religion is, he said something very important about its essence in a passage in *The Future of an Illusion* (1927 : 32–33) :

> Critics persist in describing as "deeply religious" anyone who admits to a sense of man's insignificance or impotence in the face of the universe, although what constitutes the essence of the religious attitude is not this feeling but only the next step after it, the reaction to it which seeks a remedy for it. The man who goes no further, but humbly acquiesces in the small part which human beings play in the great world—such a man is, on the contrary, irreligious in the truest sense of the word.

Whatever its social function, religion has for individuals above all a remedial, rescuing, or a kind of autotherapeutic function. This view of Freud is legitimate for a clinician. To look at things remedially is at least consistent with the professional identity of any healer, even when he ventures his interests beyond direct concern with patients. But he should remember that the truth of such a viewpoint is a clinical truth, which should neither have any ontological aspirations nor be equated with general scientific truth. Above all, clinical truth should not be elevated to an ideology or a quasireligion.

What the original person understands by his religion.   It follows from Freud's partial definition of religion that he would take special interest in those "remedies," or "rescue operations" as I would call them, which constitute a person's reactions to his feeling of impotence in the face of the universe. These run the gamut from special thoughts to special acts, or, as the religionist himself would say, from creed to cult. But while these thoughts may be consciously held and the acts consciously pursued, it is to be noted that the motives for engaging in these thoughts and acts may be largely unconscious. In fact, once the path into religion has been taken, religion itself tends to keep these motives from awareness. "In all believers . . . the motives which impel them to religious practices are unknown to them" (1907: 122–23). The original feeling of impotence and insignificance is presumed to be unbearable because of its unpleasantness; therefore one copes with it by taking recourse to those "rescue operations" which will either mitigate this feeling or replace it by a more acceptable affect—joy, hope, a sense of purpose, meaning, or mastery. The pious transform their feeling of impotence to another feeling: they know that "at heart they are miserable sinners" (1907: 123) and then deal with this feeling by certain observances. They do so not playfully, but seriously under the compelling force of the original misery, which they wish to eliminate from their minds.

In a modern phrase: religious behavior is coping behavior. Religious thinking is not at first a free use of the imagination, but an *anxious* search for substitutes to an *unpleasant* reality. Religious acts are at first not free movements, but driven motions (in postures, gestures, vocalizations, and so forth) with the magical qualities of rituals. The phenomenologist in Freud spotted right away the driven, obsessive, and compulsive quality of religious behavior in the ordinary person and held it fast as an essential quality of religion. For the ordinary person religion is not a playful option but a *must*, with its compellingness coming to him from all sides (inner and outer) with such force that its origins remain shrouded. Just as for the esthete *art comes from art* and not from the need to narcotize one's sensibilities in a dreary world, so for the religionist *religion comes from religion* and not from something else like a desperate need for fantasy formation.

And so the ordinary person has a certain repertoire that gives his religion content and validates it. He thinks, according to Freud, of a heavenly Father to whom he feels intimately related (1913, 1919, 1921, 1927, 1939); he thinks of this Father also as a Provider who governs the events of everything (1924, 1927); he accepts this Father's plan for curbing the instinctual promptings and postponing the satisfaction of the dearest wishes (1911b, 1927); and he even accepts the Father's Word (mediated, to be sure, by religious institutions) which halts curiosity from searching for nonreligious alternatives to coping with the sense of insignificance (1927). Because of this latter stricture religious thinking is to be seen as fettered thinking. It is unfree.

For the ordinary person, "You cannot exaggerate the intensity of . . . inner lack of resolution and craving for authority" (1910: 146). Religion gives to the ordinary person "solutions of the struggle between the father and sons," while at the same time "repeating once more the elimination of the father" (1919: 262). The ordinary person finds in his religion a stylized way of dealing with perennial themes born from perennial conflicts: guilt feelings and forgiveness, love and hate, freedom and authority, helplessness and power. Small wonder, then, that his religion is a *must* for him.

I find this phenomenology altogether correct, except that it seems to evolve from a rather narrow focus which keeps its sight on conflictual origins in the individual and in the human race. It excludes a priori the possibility of religion becoming conflict-free and shedding the motives of its origins for new motives. Like everything else, religion is subject to development (as Freud himself documented in his phylogenetic studies) in which it becomes thoroughly transformed. All religionists know this; the professionals among them aim at just those transformations. The question is how thorough these transformations can be. If one pursues the development of religion there may come a point that presents not only a semantic conundrum, but a profound problem with which many current theologians are struggling: can religious development proceed to the point that it eliminates itself? When does religion become so sophisticated, conflict-free, or "healthy" that one should no longer describe it as "religion" but as philosophy, value system, *Weltanschauung,* existential posture, or, as some theologians would say with a quasireligious word, "faith"? In pursuing this line of thought one returns full swing to the definition of religion and has to revise it. But Freud had explicit reasons for his dim views of religion's ever becoming conflict-free. These will be taken up in the later sections on reality testing and sublimation.

Religion as a system of beliefs, pledges, and doctrine.   "I believe that a large part of the mythological view of the world, which extends a long way into the most modern religions, is nothing but psychology projected into the external world'' (1901: 258). By implication, this statement from *The Psychopathology of Everyday Life* rests on a view of reality which takes the obvious world of the senses for granted and gives it the status of an uncontroversial reference point for all sane people. In Freud's espousal of this position, it was coupled with a suspicious attitude toward all metaphysics (1927: 28, 29, 32) in his time more fashionable than it is now. Freud did not attempt to define reality in any ultimate sense; he stuck to the position of positivism, if not naïve realism, when he spoke of reality principle, outer world, body, perception, internalization, and projection. I wish to emphasize that, unlike philosophers and theologians, clinicians must have their feet on the ground and abide by a rather pedestrian definition of reality if they are ever to correct the hallucinations, illusions, or delusions of their patients. They cannot allow themselves to be trapped in metaphysical debates about the ''really real.'' If a patient sees pink elephants on a white hospital wall or tries to press bugs out of his skin which he feels crawling there, he must be aided to better reality testing which shows nothing on the wall or in the skin. But Freud was more than a clinician, he was also a critical and a constructive thinker about cultural phenomena who built a large conceptual system with explanatory pretensions. It is intriguing that he recognized, only half in jest, the resemblance of some of his own theorems to mythology (1933), while he seriously endeavored at other times ''to transform metaphysics into metapsychology'' (1901: 259). Because of this ambiguity the word ''projection'' has many meanings in his works and ranges from a normal process of elaborating the sensory world with symbolic meanings to the pathological process, as happens in paranoia, of externalizing unto others certain obnoxious wishes of one's own unconscious.

From this platform (to which I shall return for different reasons on pp. 270–274), myth, fairy tale, legend, religious beliefs, and doctrines have much in common and are all different from positivistic reality thinking. They are charged with primary process elements; even when seemingly reasonable, they stand in the service of wish-fulfillment. They require poetic or convictional rather than factual language. Their truth, which Freud did not deny, is different from the truth of fact and logical reasoning. Their truth is historical in the special sense described earlier. Projection plays a large role in their formation.

In *The Future of an Illusion* Freud asked, "In what does the peculiar value of religious ideas lie?" His answer was, ". . . man's need to make his helplessness tolerable" (1927: 18). Religious ideas are part of a search for a source of power with which human beings could align themselves for personal comfort and social stability. This is clear in the demands placed on the gods: "they must exorcize the terrors of nature, they must reconcile men to the cruelty of Fate, particularly as it is shown in death, and they must compensate them for the sufferings and privations which a civilized life in common has imposed on them" (1927: 18). And, ". . . it is . . . natural to man to personify everything that he wants to understand, in order later to control it" (1927: 22). In this sense, religious ideas contain an innocuous form of projection which embroiders on the baffling world of the senses some interesting patterns—anthropomorphic patterns which synthesize some of humanity's efforts at solving problems of anxiety and guilt.

Inasmuch as love of God and love of fellow humans are not always spontaneous feelings but pledges which the religious individual makes, they represent efforts to renounce or suppress instinctual impulses—aggression, crass forms of egoism, or sexual licentiousness. From this basic pledge secondary pledges may follow such as expiation for misdeeds or evil thoughts, obedience to religious superiors, loyalty to doctrine and careful avoidance of doctrinal errors, watchfulness against backsliding, and so forth. Within the religious system, the basic pledge also involves the attitudinal set of faith which should be cultivated to such strength that doubt cannot seriously undermine it.

I think that Freud saw religious dogmas as the external reinforcers of the internal belief system and the wish-fulfilling function of personal beliefs as the validation of dogmatic truths. Dogmas are corporate phenomena whose tenaciousness (and excesses) depend on the degree to which they fulfill "the oldest, strongest and most urgent wishes of mankind. The secret of their strength lies in the strength of those wishes" (1927: 30). In a word, they are satisfiers. Perhaps the most sought-after satisfaction is the assurance of immortality. Because of this, dogmas can take certain liberties toward the reality of common sense, as illusions do; and they are therefore beyond proof or refutation by the ordinary or scientific means of validation. In religion one makes a contract with reality on terms that are entirely different from the contracts of science, the sense organs, or a secular ethic.

Thought organization in religion.   While "illusion" in the technical, nonpathological sense (1927: 30ff) is the status that Freud gave to religious ideas and dogmas, he was well aware of the enormous diversity of ideas *within* religion. Religious thought can depart from the merely illusory and become outright delusional. It can be spurious, crazy, obsessional, futile, primitive, archaic, magical. It can become tied to symptoms of mental illness or altered by idiosyncratic defense mechanisms.

The "hysterical deliria of saints and nuns" (1893a) have spawned crazy ideas, especially hallucinations. The "clerical phantasy" during witchcraft trials (1893b) has testified to delusions of sexual intercourse with devils not only in the accused, but also in the ecclesiastical accusers. Adoration of the Madonna's purity has often failed to give the Virgin her fair share insofar as it was driven mostly by the dynamics of sexual repression in women with a hysterical disposition (1905a). The seventeenth-century painter whose demoniacal possession Freud described could not adequately sort out Christ and the devil (1923b). Gross displacements can occur from religious ideals to the engagement in religious practices which elevate petty, time-consuming and wasteful ceremonials to divine status (1907). Useful and healthy as the repression mechanism is, if limited to specific ideas it can spread far beyond its intended purpose to become a blanket of amnesia, a feigned stupidity, or a general ban on the use of a creative and curious mind (1908).

In a word, religion, like other coping functions, may fail to solve the problems it sets out to solve or produce boomerang effects which pose new and unexpected problems. When a theological framework exists, it can be used for private oddities; it can be distorted; it can regress. Freud's remark that certain forms of mysticism may come to assume that "sin is indispensable for the enjoyment of all the blessings of divine grace"

(1927 : 37–38) properly hits religious dialectics having gone wild. Letter-magic in the prayers of the young Rat Man (1909b) turned words and letters into fetishes and was no more than a crass superstition. Schreber's private theodicy (1911a) was a flagrantly autistic piece of thinking, as was his belief that he had become God's wife.

So, while Freud focused in most of his formal works about religion on the irrational aspects of *all* religious thought and considered much of it "natural" given humanity's collective history and the experiences of each individual's childhood, as a clinician he differentiated between these "normal" features of religion and its pathological aberrations. He could not bring himself to speak of "healthy" and "sick" religion, for he found all religion, in a way, less than perfectly healthy. But he did distinguish between the general neuroticisms of everyday life and the full-fledged neuroses of patients who needed professional intervention in their painful suffering. Similarly he held that the pleasure principle is never obliterated by the reality principle but that everything depends on the proportion and the interaction between these two in the order of thought: all religion has a substantial primary process charge, but some religions or believers have far more of it than others.

The critique of religion that is inherent in Freud's statements about its ideas and thought organization warrants a quotation to place it in perspective: "I have said nothing which other and better men have not said before me in a much more complete, forcible and impressive manner. . . . All I have done . . . is to add some psychological foundation to the criticisms of my great predecessors" (1927 : 35).

Religion as a means of social control.   Every person craves an authority to aid him in his irresolution (1910). Society must impose renunciations of impulses upon its members and at the same time solicit from these members support for its authority (1927). Among the oldest forms of social regulation are totemism and taboos; both of them are directed to "the oldest and most powerful of human desires"—murder and incest (1913 : 22). Totemism and taboo also stand at the dawn of religion; therefore, religion and social control have long gone hand in hand. Religion deals with the very themes that lie at the roots of social thought: prohibiting murder, distributing power, regulating procreation, promoting workable balances between satisfaction and renunciation, replacing chaos with order.

But religion and society are not identical. Social ties and moral restrictions engender many societal forms, with or without religion. Conversely, religions do not uphold or benefit from all societal arrangements. In fact, since the early stages of humanity, the original ties between society and religion have gradually been loosened. Yet the thematic content of all religions retains the core of the original father-murder and the task of religions is "obliterating the traces of that crime or . . . expiating it by bringing forward other solutions of the struggle between the father and sons" (1919: 262).

Army and church are two examples of group process and social control (1921). Both have an exalted authority, hierarchically ordered in the leadership cadres, which represents each person's father. Both also foster lateral bonds among the members—*esprit de corps,* fellowship of love. When the upward bonds to the leadership are loosened (by poor leadership, for example) the members have a sense of panic that is the result of a defusion of libidinal and aggressive feelings formerly fused and channeled to the leaders. Both groups are examples of a special social process that replaces the individuals' ego-ideal by the external objects of the generals and officers, pope and priests, and Christ as the head of the church. Apart from these special object relations and special institutions, social control is mostly fostered internally through the ego-ideal: "a substitute for the longing for the father" (1923a: 37) and the character of the ego as "a precipitate of abandoned object-cathexes" (1923a: 29). Religion has much to contribute to all physic structures and through them exerts a noteworthy social control by means of self-regulation.

Under the influence of the Oedipus complex, its heir the superego tends to hold its moral contents in a parental mode (1924). Religion, because of its own imagery, tends to reinforce this propensity of the superego. By this token of thinking about morals in the parental mode, a powerful general transference occurs to all social institutions and persons in power positions. It carries Oedipal overtones and traces of sibling rivalry far beyond the family circle. The army and the church are only special illustrations in which transference relations are so patent that one cannot miss them; in more disguised and complicated ways they are found in school systems, industry, political parties, clubs, and, as Freud saw with his own eyes and with much chagrin, even in psychoanalytic institutes.

But religion provides far more than a cherished imagery for social control. It gives specific prescriptions and proscriptions. To give modern examples not listed by Freud: it may extol poverty and be against birth control; it may forbid its members to bear arms, or it may declare holy wars; it may enforce cumbersome rules for food preparation or put a ban on alcohol. Much political lobbying is done in the name of religion. Religious institutions may claim and get tax-exempt status and at the same time pour millions of dollars into relief work which, according to some, ought to be done by the state. It may declare itself against scientific findings, against intellectual curiosity, and for stifling anachronisms. Although Freud did not dwell on all these prescriptive and proscriptive items of religion, he said much about its ideological forcefulness and its "ban on thought," its failure to eradicate anti-Semitism (1939) and, above all, its failure to conquer the pleasure principle (1911b). The last point elicited strong feelings in Freud which come through in his paper on Dostoevsky: "A moral man is one who reacts to temptation as soon as he feels it in his heart, without yielding to it. A man who alternately sins and then in his remorse erects high moral standards lays himself open to the reproach that he has made things too easy for himself. He has not achieved the essence of morality, renunciation" (1928a: 177). Dostoevsky's morality, that is, his superego, was not very adequate; he ended up submitting himself to such incommensurables as the tsar, the God of Christianity, and an extremely conservative Russian nationalism (1928a: 177). The social control of religion, powerful as it is, also proceeds through compromises, not only with human nature but also with other social institutions.

Freud appreciated one of religion's luckier compromises in his comment that Christian asceticism (despite its many negative features) had in effect raised the psychical value of love since the waning days of the classical civilizations which no longer posed any barriers to sexual satisfaction so that "love became worthless and life empty" (1812 : 188).

The use of religious acts.   Dealing with patients who had predominantly neurotic symptoms (that is, they were disturbed but fairly well-organized) Freud saw many forms of behavior which bore a striking resemblance to traditional religious practices. From the moment he engaged in his psychoanalytic "talking cure" he was aware of the similarity between therapeutic abreaction and the cathartic effect of the religious confessional (1893a). In describing the secondary defenses of some of his patients, he spoke of "penitential measures," well aware of the religious ring of these words and, in fact, recognizing them as maneuvers to mitigate religious anxiety (1896). A comprehensive paper of 1907 documents the resemblances between neurotic ceremonials and religious rites: (1) their omission engenders pangs of conscience, (2) they are isolated from other activities, (3) details are carried out with great conscientiousness. He also noted differences: (1) neurotic ceremonials are more variable than the stereotyped religious rites, (2) neurotic ceremonials are private, while religious rites are public, and (3) the details of religious rites have conscious symbolic meanings, whereas neurotic ceremonials appear to be silly. This silliness is, however, only a surface impression. The neurotic ceremonials also have their symbolic meanings which can be brought to consciousness in the analytic process. This paper contains the famous aphorism that the obsessional neurosis is a private religious system and religion is a universal obsessional neurosis (1907 : 126–27). Freud added to the latter half of this statement that religion functions as "one of the foundations of the development of human civilization" (1907: 127). But, then, obsessional neurosis in the individual is seen as a wayward variant of the normal process whereby individuals are taught to become civilized, through the "do's" and "don'ts" (including those of religion) which are gradually internalized into the superego.

But then again it is noteworthy that within religion displacement of values may occur from the religious object to the rituals themselves! Hence the need for periodic reforms in religion, which aim at restoring the original value relations (1907: 126).

The fact that such displacements occur, however, is not to be shrugged off lightly as an unfortunate mishap: religious observances such as prayers and invocations are defensive and protective measures against a sense of guilt (the pious know they are miserable sinners) and means of securing aid in one's helplessness. They have an impelling character to ward off danger and to solicit friendly power.

Freud appreciated Reik's book on ritual; and by the time he wrote his foreword to it (1919), he had already had occasion to note some strange "private religious rituals" in the case studies he had meanwhile published. These convinced him all the more of the correctness of his thesis and at the end of his life, in *Moses and Monotheism,* he wrote with admiration of the religious reforms of Ikhnaton and Moses, whose new God demanded no sacrifice, spurned rituals, but asked for faith, truth, and justice (1939).

In placing as much emphasis as he did on the idea of God (as father) and the seeming universality of religious rituals, Freud implicitly defined religion as creed and cult. Both were, to him, the essence of religion, that "next step," "the reaction . . . which seeks a remedy" against the feeling of individul insignificance and impotence in the face of the universe (1927). But when he examined Jewish superiority feelings and described the progress in spirituality achieved by Mosaic religion (1939) he curiously omitted any mention of ritual in Judaism. He praised Judaism's intellectual bent—its accent on thoughts, words, records, schools, the Holy Book.

The role of feelings in religion.   Freud wrote far more about religious ideas than religious feelings. Unlike other students of religion he does not seem to have assumed that religion depends on experiencing specific emotions like awe or bliss or some other special sentiment. Consistent with his general thesis, which asserts that deities are held in love or hate by displacement from the original parental objects, the whole scale of affects which govern human relations is applicable to the relations between man and his gods. Even the root-feeling of helplessness vis-à-vis the universe and the sense of guilt over the primal father-murder which drive many people toward religion are not specific to religion; for many other people do not react to these by seeking the "remedy" that religion purports to be (1927).

He understood Schreber's emotional mixture of reverence and rebellion toward God to be like his dual feelings toward Flechsig and accepted Schreber's own description of his feeling of bliss as a sensation of very intense voluptuousness (1911a). "Reverence," "bliss," and "awe," are elicited by anything that has power—the gods, nature, social institutions, and human beings. They are part of the childhood perspective on things which leaves its traces in all adults. A byline in the paper on Schreber's *Memoirs* says, "One of my patients, who had lost his father at a very early age, was always seeking to rediscover him in what was grand and sublime in Nature" (1911a: 54).

Yet Freud must have had an intellectual appreciation of feelings germane to religion, or else he could not have written that taboo engenders awe and aversion and divides the world into the sacred and the unclean. What struck him profoundly was the bipolarity of feelings in taboo and elsewhere. In taboo-governed primitive religion the ambivalence is very marked; its modern parallel is demonstrated in compulsion neurosis (1913). It gives rise to irresistible urges to touch and painstaking ceremonials of avoidance, to accepting restrictions and breaking the restrictions, to acts of expiation and new indulgent acts. Taboos could disappear only when the ambivalence of people lessened, that is, when people became more civilized.

So in religion, as in all human relations, everything depends on the management of love and hate. Gods are loved and hated as people are loved and hated. But the idea of God also makes compensatory relations possible: the young Wolf Man solved one of his problems temporarily by fearing (hating) God and loving his father (1918). The same case shows what may happen when, as in Christianity, a son-god is added to the father-god: the Wolf Man, biblically instructed, could not love a god who had ordered Abraham to sacrifice his son Isaac, and he became indignant when the same omnipotent God did not prevent his own son from being sacrificed. For him, God represented the tormenting father whom he criticized by blasphemous thoughts. Similarly, in *A Religious Experience*, the American doctor lost his religious conviction momentarily when God allowed his patient, "a sweet-faced dear old woman'' (1928: 170–71), to suffer. His childish urge to destroy his own father became conscious at that time as doubt in the existence of God, until, through a later conversion, he ended up in complete submission to the will of God the Father.

Under the impact of the primal crime and every generation's wish to repeat it, guilt feelings are a central affect in religion. They give rise to many religious rites—the confessional, expiatory sacrifices, prayers for forgiveness, and commemorative acts which repeat symbolically certain aspects of the primal crime such as the Catholic Mass and Protestant communion services. The latter are a controlled and stylized ''return of the repressed'' (1939). But guilt feelings are also lessened for those who believe by the divine arrangements for atonement. In fact, inasmuch as Christianity is not only a father-religion but also a son-religion, the faithful can identify themselves with the Son in loving one another (1921: 94). There are, however, limits to such ''cruelty and intolerance'' appear in relation to out-groups (1921: 98). Freud felt that this imperfection should not be held too seriously against the faithful, for ''people who are unbelieving or indifferent are much better off psychologically in this matter'' (1921: 98).

Freud said little or nothing about anxiety as the basic motivating affect in the religious. There is no word about religion in his 1926 work, *Inhibitions, Symptoms and Anxiety*. He certainly did not speak of *Ur-angst* or existential anxiety in this regard. His persistent term is ''feeling of helplessness,'' a sense of powerlessness leading to a need for protection. Anxiety tends to be much more prominent as a secondary affect, as a consequence of espousing the idea of God and then having to face its implications: fear of God, fear of trespassing rules, fear of not fulfilling one's obligations, pangs of conscience, fear of being disloyal, fear of losing love of the deities or the religious community. Consideration of these fears brings up the question of reality testing, to which the next section is devoted.

Religion and reality testing.   In my understanding of Freud, the connecting term between feelings and reality testing in religion is *doubt*. Faith, whatever solace it gives, presents intellectual difficulties. Love and hate rarely appear in pure culture: ambivalence is rampant in relation with human and divine objects. This ambivalence gives rise to cognitive oscillations between faith and doubt. Religionists have always known the ambiguities of belief; hence their endeavors in apologetics and their need to write theodicies. Freud discussed several aspects of the faith-doubt tandem. He looked at the proposition *Credo quia absurdum* and found it unconvincing for himself and others. If religious truth is inwardly felt, how can it ever convince others who lack the subjective experience and can only take recourse to reason (1927: 28)? He also looked at the defense of various fictional systems epitomized in Vaihinger's "as if" philosophy and found it wanting: "A man whose thinking is not influenced by the artifices of philosophy will never be able to accept it" (1927: 29).

More importantly, Freud looked clinically at some concrete instances of the dynamics of doubting. I already mentioned twice the case of the American doctor who showed a sudden loss of faith and later solved his doubt by a new conversion experience (1928b). Then Freud saw in Dostoevsky up to the last moment of his life a wavering between faith and atheism. "His great intellect made it impossible for him to overlook any of the intellectual difficulties to which faith leads" (1928a: 187). In his comments on Schreber's *Memoirs* (1911a) he found that Schreber was a doubter who never had a firm belief in God, was convinced that God does not understand living people, and had profoundly negative feelings toward God which forced him to formulate a private theodicy in order to justify God's awful behavior toward him. In fact, Schreber went so far as to take over the divine role and develop megalomanic redeemer fantasies. Little Hans (1909a) was for a while swept by doubt when he was asked to believe that babies come from God rather than father and mother. The anal fantasies of the Wolf Man produced, with excessive ambivalence, the compulsive thought combinations "God-swine" and "God-shit" (1918: 17) and showed the sharpest criticism of the God he was taught to believe in. The Rat Man had to guard his elaborate prayers lest other phrases

with opposite intent forcefully insert themselves into his pious
utterings (1909b: 193).

The point becoming abundantly clear in these case fragments
is that the divine realities with which these patients struggle are
largely of their own subjective making; that they arise (in part)
from honest intellectual conundrums; that these homemade religious ideas are only feeble, nonsensical formulations of ambivalent feelings; and that religious doubts, no less than beliefs, take
their cues from the feelings that prevail in human relationships.
By Freud's clinical standard for reality testing these are all
autistic exercises: I dare say they would also be considered less
than acceptable by theologians and quite odd by the healthier
believers. But what are the standards for reality testing, and
how can there be any agreement on reality testing as long as
reality itself remains a controversial item?

Freud approached reality testing at three levels which he did
not always keep apart. First, as a practicing clinician he knew
the difference between firm reality contact in normal people and
poor reality testing in the mentally ill, including the finer grada-
tions in the latter which are captured in psychiatric nosology.
These differences hold, irrespective of whether anyone is religious or irreligious.

Second, he was sensitive to the basic differences in tempera-
ment, mood, or characterological "outlook" which give reality
an idiosyncratic color or tone for each person—the optimistic,
pessimistic, or neutral world views. There is a telling phrase in
one of his letters to Pfister: "You have the gift of throwing a
rosy sheen over the everyday life one takes part in so colourlessly
(Meng and Freud 1963: 91). And in another letter to Pfister:
"All the news that you give about yourself is not glad news, but
what right have we to expect that everything should be glad"
(Meng and Freud 1963: 132)? There is no evidence that Freud
saw Pfister's optimism as poor reality testing in need of correction, nor did he feel that Pfister's religiosity was a sign of failing
mental health or poor reality contact. It just intrigued Freud,
and his puzzlement is well put in one of his last letters to Pfister:
"That you should be such a convinced analyst and at the same
time a clerical gentleman is one of the contradictions that make
life so interesting" (Meng and Freud 1963: 142). At this second

level of appreciation Freud apparently felt that one could be at once religious and a clinically adequate reality tester, although that combination is an interesting problem for theoretical (non-clinical) psychoanalysis.

The third level is represented by another line from the 1930 letter to Pfister: "The question is not what belief is more pleasing or more comfortable or more advantageous to life, but of what may approximate more closely to the puzzling reality that lies outside us" (Meng and Freud 1963: 133). It is put more sharply in the polemical sections of *The Future of an Illusion* (1927) and the *New Introductory Lectures* (1933).

The 1927 work introduces a technical designation for religious ideas, namely, *illusion* and defines that designation positively and negatively. Illusions are "fulfillments of the oldest, strongest and most urgent wishes of mankind. The secret of their strength lies in the strength of those wishes" (1927: 30). And, "An illusion is not the same thing as an error; nor is it necessarily an error" (1927: 30). And "Illusions need not necessarily be false—that is to say, unrealizable or in contradiction to reality" (1927: 31). Later, "Of the reality value of most of them (religious doctrines) we cannot judge; just as they cannot be proved, so they cannot be refuted" (1927: 31). These definitional phrases suggest that prominence of wish fulfillment in any idea is not necessarily a falsification of reality. What they seem to mean, rather, is a warning: "Be on your guard" when your wishes are so strong you may have a colored or slanted view of reality and eventually falsify it. In the quoted phrases Freud was cautious enough to avoid ontological questions and assertions.

Other phrases in the same book have, however, a different ring: "scientific work is the only road which can lead us to a knowledge of reality outside ourselves" (1927: 31). This statement opts for positivism as the final criterion in defining reality testing, and because of its parsimoniousness it would have the practical result of declaring most human decisions to be based on illusory thinking, not only in religion and art, but also in commerce, mining explorations, agriculture, and all the rest. Freud obviously did not mean to go that far. Indeed, he was reflexive and complicated enough to consider his own alternative, the radical dedication to logic and necessity, somewhat illusory in its own way (1927 : 48). But then he backed up again by asking his imaginary religious interlocutor to "observe the difference between your attitude to illusions and mine" (1927 : 54), after having asserted earlier that "my illusions are not, like religious ones, incapable of correction. They have not the character of a delusion" (1927 : 53). These statements combine and confuse the three levels of reality testing.

Lecture 35 (1933) concludes with a lengthy section on the particulars of art, philosophy, and religion, in which the latter is described as a serious contender for truth with a wide following. Its tone is somewhat impassioned, and I think the key to its polemical quality lies in a sentence in the middle: "The struggle of the scientific spirit against the religious *Weltanschauung* is, as you know, not at an end: it is still going on to-day under our eyes" (1933:169). Thus, the argument arises from and centers on conflict and moves predictably to Freud's personal option for science as the only reliable approach to reality. In essence, however, it leaves reality undefined, except for what Rieff (1966) has described as Freud's preference for open-endedness, his "analytic attitude" or "anti-doctrine." If these intimations are correct, the question of reality testing is theoretically and practically relevant only at levels one and two. Level three has more to do with attempts to define *ultimate* reality, which is or should be alien to psychoanalytic intentions, than with the psychological function of reality *testing*.

Religion and sublimation.   Sublimation has always been a poorly defined concept in psychoanalysis. It originated in the context of the libido theory (1905b) and was meant to describe (without specifying the mechanisms involved) the deflection of infantile sexual aims to new aims which would meet with social approval, be commensurate with the person's age and capacities, and guarantee some satisfaction of the original wish which, in the meantime, had become unconscious. In sublimation an instinctual tendency or impulse is discharged through noninstinctual channels, on noninstinctual objects, with culturally defined aims, in culturally useful forms. Freud treated sublimation first as a defense mechanism and thought it might be connected with reaction formation (1905b). Later (1923a) sublimation was felt to involve displaceable energies, particularly those resulting from identifications. Still later, when the dual drive theory was formulated, *sublimation* was used specifically for libidinal aim deflection and *neutralization* for deflections of aggressive aims. Since ego-psychology and the adaptive viewpoints were articulated, however, there has been relatively little talk of sublimation. The term and the process have all but become absorbed by the synthetic, adaptive, and reality-testing functions of the ego.

Freud occasionally mentioned religion as sublimation and wrote (alluding with qualifications to the work of Jung and Pfister) that sexual dynamics can be represented, desexualized, in the highest ethical and religious interests of people (1914b). The Wolf Man case history (1918) includes the statements that the patient's Bible knowledge allowed him to sublimate his sadistic-masochistic attitudes and that the religious sublimation eventually impaired the patient's former intellectual activity. Elsewhere (1930: 97) sublimation is held to be "an especially conspicuous feature of cultural development"; it enables "higher psychical activities, scientific, artistic or ideological" to play their important role in civilization.

But if one turns to Freud's special works on religion, a different view arises. In *The Future of an Illusion* the word "sublimation" is mentioned only once, namely, by the imaginary and presumably religious interlocutor with whom the dialogue is artfully conducted. This man suggests that religion allows "of a refinement and sublimation of ideas" (1927: 52) by which the primitive, infantile traces of its origins can be left behind. Freud, without quite denying that religion may involve sublimation, stresses in his answer that religion is comparable to childhood neurosis (1927: 53), that the religionist is "more impatient, more exacting, . . . more self-seeking" (1927: 54) than the scientist; that religion asks that "the state of bliss begin directly after death" (1927: 54). Religion does not ask *enough* renunciation of infantile wishes, it is *too* gratifying, it consoles *too well*. Without openly saying so, Freud apparently felt that these features of religion militate against its being a true sublimation.

In *Civilization and its Discontents* (1930) the text reserves the applicability of sublimation to the work of the creative artist and the activities of scientists in solving problems and discovering truths. Religion is not explicitly given as an example; at best it is implied under the rubric of the "ideological" in the passage already quoted. In his elaboration of this passage Freud notes that one may at first be tempted to say that civilization seems to force sublimation upon the instincts but that on reflection the roles are reversed: "it is impossible to overlook the extent to which civilization is built upon a renunciation of instinct, how much it presupposes precisely the non-satisfaction of powerful instincts" (1930: 97). Thus, in sublimation renunciation comes first, and any system that satisfies the childish longing too readily in quasichildish ways, no matter how aim-deflected and with whatever object-displacements, is more akin to a childhood neurosis than to a sublimation.

There is another reason why Freud did not accept religion as a sublimation. Sublimation depends on talent and fortunate life circumstances that enhance it. Sublimation is a possibility only for the "happy few"—it is not for the masses (1930: 80, 97). Religion, however, is a mass phenomenon, or so Freud saw it. Its appeal, its power, its persistence, its wide following, its popularity—they all demonstrate how much it is directed to the ordinary person who pursues satisfaction whenever he can with the approval of his leaders and the gods that he invented. As *Totem and Taboo* put it, in the religious attitude, a person cedes some of his infantile omnipotence to his gods, but without seriously giving it up! Only the scientific attitude does away with this compromise; it submits "resignedly to death and to the other necessities of nature" (1913: 88) and, may I add, engages in active curiosity which is precisely what makes scientific work a true sublimation.

There may have been still another reason for Freud's critical caution about religion as sublimation. It stems from observations and inferences, by himself and others, about psychopathology in people with religious vocations. He alluded to hysterical deliria of saints and nuns (1893a), to witchcraft and demon possession (1893b), to the acceptance, by priests, of hallucinations of the Virgin in girls (1910), and to Pfister's study of von Zinzendorf's religious fanaticism (1914b). These are not just failing sublimations; in these constellations the path toward sublimation was never taken in the first place.

Freud felt that most religion not only falls short of sublimating the instinctual impulses, but is *ipso facto* an alternative to sublimation, an entirely different mode of problem solving. I think he would grudgingly acknowledge that some talented and curious religious minds could use religious ideation and activity in the manner of a true sublimation, but their number would always be small. Moreover, they would probably no longer be ''religious'' in the sense he gave to that word.

IV MAJOR PSYCHOANALYTIC STUDIES OF RELIGION SINCE FREUD

In the foregoing I have attempted to give a faithful presentation of Freud's ideas on religion. A few of my own thoughts were introduced only for didactic reasons: to put Freud's thoughts in sharp relief or to guard against possible misunderstanding. Since purity of theory and loyalty to basic concepts and assumptions have become important issues in psychoanalysis, my next endeavor to summarize major psychoanalytic contributions to the psychology of religion apart from Freud's own requires a few decisions. These are:

    1. To exclude from consideration the work of members of deviant schools and radical revisionist groups, not because I deem their work unimportant, but because they have proceeded from a different conceptual framework, which may merit separate exposition and elaboration.

    2. The focus must remain on the *psychology* of religion and therefore the views of sociologists, anthropologists, philosophers, and comparative religion scholars will remain outside the scope of this chapter, although I recognize that members of these disciplines have used, or been influenced by, Freudian views on religion. In addition, I lack expertise in these disciplines.

    3. The extensive and often polemical literature on "religion and psychiatry," which is such a hospitable collection of diverse bits and pieces from the helping professions but has so little focus on the psychology of religion, will be left out.

All three decisions imply the recognition that many students of religion have been influenced by psychoanalytic propositions but that there is an important difference between using snatches of psychoanalytic ideas eclectically and exploiting the full conceptual framework with all its explanatory potential.

Among Freud's immediate coworkers Reik, Rank, Pfister, and Jones played prominent roles in applying psychoanalytic principles to the study of religion. Freud referred to some of their works or built upon their observations. He also quoted Ferenczi (1916), who wrote very little about religion, but Freud used his concept of the infantile omnipotence of thought repeatedly to buttress his own views. Ferenczi (1926) in turn seemed to agree with most of Freud's statements on religion. In Reik's works (1923, 1946, 1951) data from comparative religion and observations about Judaeo-Christian dogmas and ceremonials were related to stages of libidinal development, particularly those capsuled in the libido theory. In essence they focussed on obsessive-compulsive traits. Rank's *Myth of the Birth of the Hero* (1914) centered on the psychodynamics of fantasy formation in myth and folklore which is part of the historical process of transfiguring human beings into deities or mythical entities.

Pfister's works (1917) drew on the professional knowledge of a Protestant theologian and practicing pastor, bringing together facets of historical theology, clinical data from parishioners, significant movements in Christianity, particularly the Reformation period, and case studies of religious leaders. Pfister's writings were capstoned by a large work on coping with fear through religion (1948) in which he tried to show that various theologies and religious traditions present different options in mitigating the inevitable anxieties that are the lot of humanity. Pfister wrote "from the inside of religion" as a participant-observer, and, when needed, as its apologist. (See his letter exchange with Freud.) He took keen interest in moral training and character building and felt that psychoanalytic principles formed a useful basis for mental hygiene. In tolerated opposition to Freud, Pfister felt that religion at its best has not only solace to offer mankind, but represents a respectable, indeed highly desirable, sublimation of libidinal and aggressive impulses.

Jones (1913, 1922, 1926, 1930) wrote several papers on the psychology of religion in which he traced psychodynamic implications of the shift from a single father-god to the Christian conception of the Trinity, the idea of the Holy Ghost, and Mariology. Except for trying to trace the origins of the Holy Ghost concept to feminine roots in the Great Mother religions, Jones did not add much to Freud's ideas on religion.

Pfister had already stated that religion contains far more than obsessive-compulsive features; in fact, he argued that thoughtful religionists had always fought against the dangers of these traits. Along with Pfister, many psychoanalysts have worked on this theme. Fromm's (1930) study of the development of the doctrine of Christ, which antedates his outspoken dissidence from classical psychoanalysis, was another attempt to correct Reik's and Freud's monotonous emphasis on compulsivity. He stressed the direct identifications which believers can make with Christ, the change from man-who-became-God to a God-who-became-man, and the gradual development of the female theme of the mother who nurtures the child.

Several members of the British school brought to religion a more positive regard. Flugel (1945), largely agreeing with Freud's analysis of religion, noted that in states of ecstasy a sense of unity with the divine is experienced which may reflect an intrapsychic fusion between ego and superego. He also saw Christianity as a son and brother religion rather than a father religion, felt that it aimed at wiping out the guilt of the remote past, and appreciated its nonviolence program, while acknowledging that its noble goals had not been realized, by and large. Flugel recommended that Christianity seek better canalization of emotions in active social programs, in a word, become more secular or humanistic. He admired Cattell's nonpsychoanalytic propositions.

Much more enthusiasm for the integrative power of religion, especially Christianity, is expressed in Marjorie Brierley's work (1951). Rather than arguing metapsychologically about the validity of the projection hypothesis, she was clinically concerned with the *kind* of attitudes projected onto God: a beloved ego-ideal, the sadistic superego components, or certain ego-attitudes such as the existential reality sense of a Cardinal Newman. She also highlighted the antiritualistic tenor of Christianity and saw the Eucharist as a complex symbol system which demonstrates that Christianity "caters not only for obsessional characters but also for a much greater variety of psychological types.'' Recognizing that some persons maintain a particularly affectionate relationship with their parents throughout life, she saw the possibility of a ''suckling experience to be so satisfactory that no later gratifications approach the same high level'' (Brierley 1951: 219). Mysticism could then be the answer to those needs. She differentiated between effectively and ineffectively religious people: in the former every aspect of the rich infantile life may become part of the religious experience, whereas in the latter unresolved infantile (or Oedipal) ambivalence patterns prevail. If basic human needs are satisfied in relation to God, personality may achieve a notable integration and sanctity of behavior may be enhanced.

Melanie Klein (1965) added clinical case material to show that the idea of God, if taught, may strengthen a child's omnipotence feelings and warp for life its reality sense in certain areas, so that utter nonsense and abject contradictions are accepted with credulity. The object-relations school represented by Guntrip (1961), Fairbairn (1954), and Winnicott (1965) has, of course, assessed the finer points of object choice, object displacement, and object splitting in the scale of interpersonal and person-God relations. The role of the transitional object in mystical experience was elucidated by Winnicott (1965: 185–86). Guntrip found human dependency a fact of life; and, insofar as it is a psychodynamic determinant of religion, the latter is not merely an infantile quest, but a perennial concern ''with the basic fact of personal relationships'' (Guntrip 1961: 383). Balint (1957) has schematized three characteristic positions: (1) the anaclitic relation which parallels longings for mystical union with the divine, (2) the idealization of the object, religiously exemplified in the cult of the Blessed Virgin, (3) the humiliation of the object, usually complemented by an idealization of the subject. A part of this position may foster demonology.

An excellent study by Eissler (1965) takes issue with the attempts made by some analysts, notably Zilboorg (1962) and Stern (1962), to turn Freud's critical assessment of religion into a sophisticated quasipsychoanalytic defense of religion, especially Catholicism. Eissler makes parenthetically the important observation that atheists (including Freud) do not necessarily have a special resistance to the idea of God. Their position may be conflict-free, whereas avowed believers are far more prone to experience some conflict in regard to their religion, if it were only because of its implications, ideals, and adhortations to honest self-assessment.

Hartmann's articulation of ego-psychology (1958) eventuated in detailed work by many psychoanalysts on cognitive processes, perceptual structures, ego-autonomy and ego-interests and the functions involved in adaptation with realistic compromises to drive derivatives, superego, autonomous ego needs, social demands, cultural opportunities, and the like paired with a full use of the earlier established conceptual framework of psychoanalysis. It made possible a new psychoanalytic psychology of religion whose descriptive acumen, explanatory power, and synthetic finesse are best demonstrated in Erikson's work.

Already in *Childhood and Society* Erikson (1950 [1963]) had called attention to the *mutuality* of attitudes and feelings that are basic to life. In picturing the trust ("basic trust") of infants he was not describing a solipsistic state but an aspect of reciprocal or mutual feeling tones within the smallest human group, each having an appeal value to the other. The emerging trust of the infant is supported by parental faith in the infant and in the viability of the parent-child relation. In the second edition of this book (1963) it is described more fully as a "trust borne of care." Erikson (1963: 250) also mentioned in the later edition that this trust is the "touchstone of the actuality of a given religion." In a much later article, *Ontogeny of Ritualization,* Erikson (1966: 604) suggests that ritualizations occur first in the nursery: "daily greetings affirming a strong emotional bond, . . . singular encounters of a sudden and mutual fusion in love or inspiration" and that these ritualizations are a "numinous element, the sense of a hallowed presence." They are continuous with religious observances, but what a difference between these sources (and qualities) of ritual and those obsessive-compulsive ones selected by Reik and Freud as essential to religion! For Erikson, rituals can be playful, they can combine familiar and surprise elements, they can symbolize at once belongingness and distinctiveness. In a word, they are not always linear products of ambivalence. Also, they clearly antecede any attempt at religious instruction.

Between these two works lies *Young Man Luther* (Erikson 1958), a milestone in the psychology of religion and a masterful demonstration of the potency of the psychoanalytic view. Given the space limitations of this chapter, only the most crucial dimensions of Erikson's approach can be summed up, and for didactic reasons I will do so enumeratively. In my opinion, they are:

1. The case study method is superb in showing how religion "fits" into the rest of life.

2. Any writer's personal equation on religion, being a unique perspective, is a powerful determinant in the discovery and selection of relevant data.

3. Psychoanalytic concepts are always to be attuned to the continuities of life, longitudinally and laterally, in all facets of mentation and behavior. I feel that most earlier psychoanalytic writers on religion did not carry this principle far enough and, therefore, were prone to end up showing religion as an infantile "foreign body," oddly separated from the rest of human pursuits and interests.

4. It is not enough to show the developmental source of motives; one must also show their developmental course and alterations, including the possibility that what is born from conflict may become conflict-free.

5. If life is a series of psychosocial tasks, the repeated initiatives people take in forming and changing their identities in life's course involve perpetual reassessments of past roles, past satisfactions and frustrations, past beliefs, past stupidities, past infantilisms, and so forth. Therefore, in regard to such patent cultural realities as religion, art, science, and moral values people seek everchanging adaptations in fluid proportions in which change rather than stability is the maturational goal. Fixity of beliefs is more likely to be a neurotic than a healthy phenomenon.

6. In analyzing the emotional and cognitive dynamics in Luther's theological innovations, as well as the emotional impact on Luther of theological propositions in the forms he had encountered, Erikson has shown the continuities between a man's life and his theology. In a word, the psychology of religion can and should deal with intricacies of theology just as it deals with prayer, worship, or mystical experience.

7. Erikson's use of psychoanalytic concepts has transcended, as it should, the awkward propensity to diagnostic labeling so characteristic of psychiatric writings. Much fine attention to detail is lost if one routinely calls rituals "compulsive" or "obsessional," repression "hysterical," sadness "depression," or suspiciousness "paranoid." Religious behavior is so diversified that the classical nosological

apparatus of descriptive psychiatry cannot capture its richness. Similarly, the question whether anything religious in any person or group is healthy or sick cannot be simply deduced from such labels.

8. Causality in psychoanalysis is not to be taken in the linear mode: important things are over-determined; everything has both a *because of* and an *in spite of* aspect; determinism is to be handled as cohesiveness of themes. Erikson's work seems to be attuned to these three aspects of causality in psychoanalysis, and because of this, Luther remained fully alive and as complex as ever in Erikson's study.

Several clinical papers by Lubin (1958, 1959) on partial identifications with numinous figures make good use of ego-psychological and Eriksonian concepts, as does the 1968 GAP report on the ''Psychic Function of Religion in Mental Illness and Health.'' These works, of which many more are needed, testify to the aptness of a statement by Ostow and Scharfstein (1954) : ''everything depends not on the bare issues of religion or irreligion, but on the quality of the religion or irreligion.'' Assessment of the quality of religion is of particular importance in studies dealing with drastic religious change, such as conversion experiences. Woollcott's paper on the conversion of St. Augustine (1966) exemplifies the viability of the ego-psychological approach.

Finally, the code of expository writing does not forbid me to describe my own recent book (Pruyser 1968) as an attempt to use psychoanalytic theory as broadly as possible and on as wide a front as manageable to the immensely varied phenomena of religion. My personal equation allowed an insider's view of religion-in-operation and gave opportunity to pair psychoanlytic constructs with phenomenological presentations of processes and issues. The phenomenological emphasis was introduced in the spirit of a much needed repair job, for it seems to me that the need for accurate and close-to-life description has often received short shrift in psychoanalytic studies of religion. My own study of religion was greatly enhanced by my identification as co-author with Menninger's general psychiatric work, *The Vital Balance* (1963). This work exploits the dynamic, economic, and adapative points of view in psychoanalysis in order to arrive at a continuum model of mental health and illness in which virtually all behavior can be seen as ways of coping with stress and unhappiness. If such a view is applied to the phenomena of religion, as I have tried to do, one can envisage a whole scale of religious coping devices ranging from healthy and efficient to unhealthy and inefficient, according to specifiable criteria.

V   TASKS TO BE DONE

What are the tasks ahead for those who find Freud's legacy viable and cherish the tools of psychoanalysis? In addition to the precepts I see demonstrated in Erikson's work, I offer the following immodest thoughts in all humility, well aware that many brains are needed to adapt them to researchable situations and modify them in the light of requirements of research design.

1. A large number of clinical case studies, clinical fragments, and illustrative vignettes have been devoted to documenting religious pathology or showing the encroachment of pathological states on religious beliefs and practices. Although such studies have not reached saturation level and should be continued, deliberate efforts should now be made to publish clinical portrayals of wholly or partly problem-free religious ideation and behavior in people who do seek professional help for intrapsychic and interpersonal conflict—if there are such cases! The caveat in the last clause is a bow in the direction of those who, with a variation on Juvenal, hold that *religio sana* is present only *in mente sana;* but the proposition as a whole is an invitation to all to replace controversial opinions by documented observations.

2. In gatherings of psychoanalytic psychotherapists one hears from time to time informal statements that religion, like money, is a topic which patients tend to guard by a self-imposed taboo. But one also hears quasiquantified statements to the effect that "one-third" or even "two-thirds" of the patients' discussion material is "religious"! It seems to me necessary to get such sayings out of the unverifiable opinion stage and into the open with adequate documentation, accurate counts, and definable criteria for the religious variable. But this will entail facing a series of hard questions. When is a statement, an association, a thought, a memory, or a feeling religious? Who does the assigning of items to the class "religious"? How does one draw the boundaries between this class and other classes, for example, beauty, morality, economics?

3. I have already alluded to another problem, closely linked with the foregoing suggestion, that is badly in need of research. Given the fact that some patients have held rather infantile religious beliefs and that they may have outgrown or relinquished these in treatment (which may be a paradigm of the normal course of growing up, without treatment), what modifications in the patient's thought or

activities provide the evidence that he is now "no longer religious" or "more mature in his religion"? As we saw earlier, Freud apparently used certain aspects of "primitive" thought in his definition of religion, particularly the idea of a Provider-God, and had therefore great difficulty recognizing the more intelligent forms of religion *as religion* for, at a certain stage of sophistication, they presumably turned into something else, like philosophy or ethics. How does one know that certain ideas or statements which replace earlier God-talk or church jargon are no longer religious? These questions, moreover, are not merely to be addressed to the psychoanalytic observers, but also to the patients themselves. Disenchantment with churches, opposition to childhood religion, criticism of doctrinal formulations, and departure from customary religious rituals—all these have been experienced by great religious leaders, prophets, and professional theologians. Such critical attitudes and signs of estrangement from earlier habits are not necessarily the end of religion in a person's life. They may be very religious gropings for new forms, experiments with new language games, or explorations in religion-in-the-making.

4. A final suggestion for research has to do with religious unbelief. Admittedly, this is a shaky notion, particularly when the word is used as a term of disapprobation by those who consider religious belief normative. The problem is illustrated (not defined) by the Freud-Pfister correspondence in which Pfister considered Freud "religious," while Freud insisted on his irreligiosity; by Zilboorg's insistence that Freud's posture of "unbelief" was due to specific resistances; and by a small book by Ruemke (1962) which suggests that religious unbelief is really a deplorable lack of something or an odd warping of the human entelechy. Precisely because there are such fierce opinions on this matter it seems to me important to produce case material that can throw some light on what so-called unbelief is, what its origins may be, what its course is in the flow of life, and—just as in the case of religious belief—how one defines it. Is religious unbelief merely a cognitive technicality and the avoidance of the religious language game, or does it say something about a person's loyalties, hopes, ethics, object relations, or affect constellations?

All four suggestions are addressed to clinicians or to scholars who use clinical research tools. For psychoanalysis is a clinical science. And clinical science is the appropriate path to that level of personality where the really interesting problems are, where experience is contradictory for good reasons, where affects have their disorderliness, and where human life shows its untidy features. Religion seems to me unthinkable without these features; hence, I put stock in the clinical approach.

BIBLIOGRAPHY

Abraham, Hilda C., and Freud, Ernst L.
  1965 *A Psycho-Analytic Dialogue. The Letters of Sigmund Freud and Karl Abraham, 1907–1926.* Trans. Bernard Marsh and Hilda C. Abraham. New York: Basic Books, Inc.

Balint, Michael
  1957 *Problems of Human Pleasure and Behavior.* New York: Liveright.

Brierley, Marjorie
  1951 *Trends in Psychoanalysis.* London: Hogarth Press.

Eissler, Kurt R.
  1965 Appendix 2, Further Notes on the Religious Controversy. In *Medical Orthodoxy and the Future of Psychoanalysis.* New York: International Universities Press.

Erikson, Erik H.
  1950 *Childhood and Society.* New York: Norton.
  (1963)
  1958 *Young Man Luther.* New York: Norton.
  1966 Ontogeny of Ritualization. In *Psychoanalysis—a General Psychology: Essays in Honor of Heinz Hartmann.* Rudolph M. Loewenstein, Lottie M. Newman, Max Schur, and Albert J. Solnit, eds. New York: International Universities Press.

Fairbairn, W. Ronald D.
  1952 Notes on the Religious Phantasies of a Female Patient. In *Psychoanalytic Studies of the Personality.* London: Routledge and Kegan Paul. And in *An Object Relations Theory of the Personality.* New York: Basic Books, Inc.
  (1954)

Ferenczi, Sandor
  1916 Stages in the Development of the Sense of Reality. In *Sex in Psychoanalysis,* trans. Ernest Jones. Boston: Richard G. Badger.
  1926 Obsessional Neurosis and Piety (1914). In *Further Contributions to Psychoanalysis.* London: Hogarth Press.

Flugel, John C.
  1945 *Man, Morals and Society.* New York: International Universities Press.

Freud, Ernst L., ed.
  1960 *Letters of Sigmund Freud.* Trans. Tania and James Stern. New York: Basic Books, Inc.

Freud, Sigmund

> *The Standard Edition of the Complete Psychological Works of Sigmund Freud.* James Strachey, ed. London: Hogarth Press. Dates according to volume.

1893a   On the Psychical Mechanism of Hysterical Phenomena: Preliminary Communication. Vol. II, 1955.

1893b   Charcot. Vol. III, 1962.

1896   Further Remarks on the Neuro-Psychoses of Defence. Vol. III, 1962.

1901   The Psychopathology of Everyday Life. Vol. VI, 1960.

1905a   Fragment of an Analysis of a Case of Hysteria. Vol. VII, 1953.

1905b   Three Essays on the Theory of Sexuality. Vol. VII, 1953.

1907   Obsessive Actions and Religious Practices. Vol. IX, 1959.

1908   "Civilized" Sexual Morality and Modern Nervous Illness. Vol. IX, 1959.

1909a   Analysis of a Phobia in a Five-Year-Old Boy. Vol. X, 1955.

1909b   Notes upon a Case of Obsessional Neurosis. Vol. X, 1955.

1910   The Future Prospects of Psychoanalytic Therapy. Vol. XI, 1957.

1911a   Psychoanalytic Notes on an Autobiographical Account of a Case of Paranoia (Dementia Paranoides). Vol. XII, 1958.

1911b   Formulations on the Two Principles of Mental Functioning. Vol. XII, 1958.

1912   On the Universal Tendency to Debasement in the Sphere of Love (Contributions to the Psychology of Love II). Vol. XI, 1957.

1913   Totem and Taboo. Vol. XIII, 1955.

1914a   The Moses of Michelangelo. Vol. XIII, 1955.

1914b   On the History of the Psychoanalytic Movement. Vol. XIV, 1957.

1915   Thoughts for the Times on War and Death. Vol. XIV, 1957.

1918   From the History of an Infantile Neurosis. Vol. XVII, 1955.

1919   Psychoanalysis and Religious Origins. Preface to Reik's *Ritual:* Psychoanalytic Studies. Vol. XVII, 1955.

1921   Group Psychology and the Analysis of the Ego. Vol. XVIII, 1955.

1923a   The Ego and the Id. Vol. XIX, 1961.

1923b   A Seventeenth-Century Demonological Neurosis. Vol. XIX, 1961.

1924   The Economic Problem in Masochism. Vol. XIX, 1961.

1926   Inhibitions, Symptoms and Anxiety. Vol. XX, 1959.

1927   The Future of an Illusion. Vol. XXI, 1961.

1928a   Doestoevsky and Parricide. Vol. XII, 1961.
1928b   A Religious Experience. Vol. XXI, 1961.
1930   Civilization and Its Discontents. Vol. XXI, 1961.
1933   New Introductory Lectures on Psychoanalysis. Vol. XXII, 1964.
1939   Moses and Monotheism. Vol. XXIII, 1964.

Fromm, Erich
1930   Die Entwicklung des Christusdogmas. *Imago* 16 : 305–73.

Group for the Advancement of Psychiatry
1968   *The Psychic Function of Religion in Mental Illness and Health.* (GAP Report 67) New York: Group for the Advancement of Psychiatry.

Guntrip, Henry J. S.
1961   *Personality Structure and Human Interaction.* New York: International Universities Press.

Hartmann, Heinz
1958   *Ego Psychology and the Problem of Adaptation.* Trans. David Rapaport. New York: International Universities Press.

Jones, Ernest
1951   All from Essays in Applied Psychoanalysis 2. London: Hogarth Press.
1913   The God Complex.
1922   A Psychoanalytic Study of the Holy Ghost Concept.
1926   The Psychology of Religion.
1930   Psychoanalysis and the Christian Religion.
1953–   The Life and Work of Sigmund Freud. 3 vols. New York:
1957   Basic Books, Inc., vol. 1.

Klein, Melanie
1965   *Contributions to Psychoanalysis, 1921–1945.* London: Hogarth Press.

Lubin, Albert J.
1958   A Feminine Moses: A Bridge between Childhood Identifications and Adult Identity. *International Journal of Psychoanalysis* 39 : 535–46.
1959   A Boy's View of Jesus. In *Psychoanalytic Study of the Child,* Vol. 14. New York: International Universities Press.

Meng, Heinrich, and Freud, Ernst L.
  1963   *Psychoanalysis and Faith: The Letters of Sigmund Freud and Oskar Pfister.* Trans. Eric Mosbacher. New York: Basic Books, Inc.

Menninger, Karl, Mayman, Martin, and Pruyser, Paul W.
  1963   *The Vital Balance.* New York: Viking Press.

Ostow, Mortimer, and Scharfstein, Ben-Ami
  1954   *The Need to Believe.* New York: International Universities Press.

Pfister, Oskar
  1917   *The Psychoanalytic Method.* Trans. Charles Rockwell Payne. London: Kegan Paul, Trench, Trubner and Company.
  1948   *Christianity and Fear.* Trans. W. H. Johnston. London: George Allen and Unwin.

Pruyser, Paul W.
  1968   *A Dynamic Psychology of Religion.* New York: Harper & Row.

Rank, Otto
  1914   *The Myth of the Birth of the Hero.* Trans. F. Robbins and Smith Ely Jelliffe. New York: Journal of Nervous and Mental Disease Publishing Company.

Reik, Theodor
  1923   *Der eigene und der fremde Gott.* Leipzig/Vienna/Zurich: Internationaler Psychoanalytischer Verlag.
  1931   *Ritual: Psychoanalytic Studies.* Translated by Douglas
  (1946) Bryan. New York: Norton. Translation (1946), New York: Farrar, Straus and Giroux.
  1951   *Dogma and Compulsion: Psychoanalytic Studies of Religion and Myths.* New York: International Universities Press.

Rieff, Philip
  1966   *The Triumph of the Therapeutic.* New York: Harper & Row. See especially chapter 4.

Rümke, Henricus C.
  1962   *The Psychology of Unbelief.* Trans. M. H. C. Willems. New York: Sheed and Ward.

Stern, Karl
    1962   Anything Can Be Reduced to the Irrational—but Does It
            Help? A Review of Gregory Zilboorg, *Psychoanalysis and
            Religion. New York Times Book Review* 6 (May 6) : 18.

Winnicott, Donald W.
    1965   *The Maturational Processes and the Facilitating Environ-
            ment.* New York : International Universities Press.

Woollcott, Philip
    1966   Creativity and Religious Experience in St. Augustine. *Jour-
            nal for Scientific Study of Religion* 5 : 273–83.

Zilboorg, Gregory
    1962   *Psychoanalysis and Religion.* Ed. Introduction Margaret S.
            Zilboorg. New York : Farrar, Straus and Giroux.

7 BEYOND WILLIAM JAMES

James E. Dittes

I INTRODUCTION

The coordinators of this volume ask me to discuss the "central propositions" of *The Varieties of Religious Experience* (James 1902, hereafter VRE). How William James would hoot at the assignment, in characteristically good-humored irritation. Thought, least of all James's, has no center; thought, least of all James's, cannot be captured by propositions. Thought, most of all James's, is a living flow.

"Central propositions" is the language of structure. But, for James, structure entombs the mind. Experience is so much richer than any success of the mind in comprehending it that efforts to locate and organize thought are as likely to hinder as to aid the mind in its proper quest, which is always to seek that which is "beyond" its present confinements.

To focus on "central propositions" may suggest that disciplined thinking is an end in itself or that it yields products to be arrayed and admired in a museum (including those museums called scholarly journals or books or classrooms or even, perhaps, Gifford Lectures). But, for James, critical, disciplined thinking has a *purpose*—to enable us to live more effectively in our world—and in such *use* is its importance and its validity.

"Central propositions" implies dicta that claim attention as insights of permanence and wide generalizability, a kind of building block added to humanity's gradually accumulating tower of knowledge. But, for James, the discoveries and formulations of the mind have a type of validity that is "here and now," "for me," as well as "maybe." To build with them is to build a futile tower of Babel; solid towers can be built only of inert, inorganic, squared and smoothed blocks; and thought, for James, is living, organic, magnificently uneven in contours, and wonderfully rough in texture.

To label a seventy-year-old book a "classic" and to search out its "central propositions" whether to adapt or to test or to restate, as instructions for this volume would have us do, seems to presuppose that the author of the "classic" has or claims a distinctively direct pipeline to reality. It suggests that William James's "propositions" may be especially isomorphic with the structures of reality or that it is worthwhile or possible to test them to see whether they are. It suggests that William James may have discovered especially accurately how things really are and that we need to share or, at least, to test this discovery as formulated in his "propositions." But William James would say that he has reported how things are *for him* and that there is not any "really are" beyond how they are for him, any more than the way things are for him need to be for us.

Thus, the assignment leads to a confrontation: In his own view, William James is not taken most seriously and most authentically when he is looked to for his propositions. Confrontation is not unwelcome in the Jamesian view nor an unlikely place to make fruitful discovery. But it makes us realize at the outset that to write about the relation beween William James and the social science of our time may be to identify estrangement more than continuity.

The conception of this book asks: How have James's ideas been advanced, tested, elaborated, and extended by social scientists since his book? The simple fact is that James's ideas have *not* been advanced, tested, and so on. His ideas are summarized in historical surveys but do not feed into contemporary empirical research or substantive discussion in the psychology of religion. Typically, James is revered in the first chapter of a textbook then ignored in the substance of the book. His ideas are not tested, debated, or applied, as are those of other "classical writers" discussed in this book. If James's writing *is* invoked in contemporary discussion, it is to add James's language—and thus his blessing and prestige—to the writer's own ideas.

This "neglect" represents the important, though usually implicit, recognition by most researchers and theorists that James's

ideas cannot be so used without ripping them out of their
context. James's ideas were not offered, the lectures were not
intended, the book was not written for the purpose of contributing to a common enterprise of accumulating scientific generalization. They were offered to express a personal outlook, an attitude,
a philosophy, a spirit. In James's own view nothing is more
crucial than the context and the function of an idea. Ideas for
him do not have, as they do for the contemporary scientific
outlook, reference to a constant, objective reality, equally per-
ceptible to all observers in the same way, observers whose perception is gradually clarified, gradually made more like the reality
itself, as they share their individual perceptions and ideas about
this reality. For James, an idea about reality and, for that
matter, reality itself, exists for particular persons in particular
circumstances. The ideas are *for* the thinker, here and now. Since
their purpose is not to make a rendering as isomorphic as
possible with some objective reality "out there," there is no point
in talking about James's ideas as though they were to be
validated or corrected by rigorous test to see how accurately they
do render the objective reality.

James does not take the stand, in his Gifford Lectures, of the
pioneer looking for others to follow, to build upon foundations he
is laying down. For example, he does not, as is the custom of
those of us steeped in the spirit of an accumulative scientific
corpus that informs the idea of this book, acknowledge lacunae
and imprecisions with pious reference to "future research." He
is, instead, offering his matured reflections. Others may follow,
he would be the first to welcome them, but they will follow with
their matured reflections. The emphasis is equally on "their"
(reflecting especially the pluralism of his outlook—the "varieties" of the title) and on "matured" (reflecting especially the
element that may be labeled "pragmatism" in his outlook—the
"experience" of the title). He would expect others to advance
their views vigorously, with no more timidity or apology for
being "only" their views than James has advanced his own;
what one finds validly tested in his own experience has the best
claim; to search for the transcending absolute is to chase illusion.

Since James's ideas are the report of how one man, a man who happened to delight in the expectation that others would find things to be different, finds things to be, there is not much point in asking about the degree to which the scientific community has shared or not shared his ideas as to how things are.

Thus we have the anomalous situation that the man most often and justifiably cited as the father of American psychology of religion has left no school or following or system or impact of the kind ordinarily regarded as a founder's heritage. There is no distinctive Jamesian psychology of religion any more than there is a distinctive Jamesian psychology.[1] James can be appropriately regarded as the founder of American psychology of religion not for the psychological theories or psychological data or psychological method he offered, but for his philosophical position or perhaps more accurately, philosophical temper or outlook. He championed an attitude toward religion and toward the universe and toward investigation which justified, even encouraged, psychological study.

James was a philosopher. Or, perhaps more accurately, he was philosophical, not the possessor or announcer of a philosophy. What he had to offer and has to offer is a distinctive philosophical temper, an outlook, a *spirit,* to use the highly appropriate word chosen by his literary executor and biographer Ralph Barton Perry for his own exposition of William James's mind, *In the Spirit of William James* (1938).

As John Smith (1967) writes:

> James was philosophical in a way that is, unfortunately, not as widespread today as it was at some time in the past. For him, to be

---

[1] The most frequently cited contribution by James to psychological theory, as such, is the exception that proves the rule. The theory of emotions to which James's name is often attached, along with that of the Dane, C. Lange, may be and has been taken as a straightforward psychological theory of the kind I have argued here James did not produce, at least in the psychology of religion—a theory to be tested against data to see how accurately it can account for them. It patently does not fit the data. The "theory" can be read much more plausibly and much more straightforwardly as an expression of James's radically empirical or pragmatic or functional epistemology. The theory, in James's own epigrammatic formulation, "we feel sorry because we cry, angry because we strike, afraid because we tremble" (1890: 450), clearly does not arise from analysis of data nearly so much as from James's philosophical and dispositional preference to give priority to the more behavioral elements and to make the more cognitive elements derivative, having validity only as they are rooted in overt function, in the empirical.

philosophical meant viewing every subject against the background of man and his place in the universe; it meant being aware that there is always more to your subject than you are able to capture at one time and from one perspective. Being philosophical on his terms was as much an attitude and a temper of mind as a standpoint or a position to be articulated in a particular system . . . the philosophical influence was evident less as a matter of doctrine and more as the persistent attempt to think critically and comprehensively.

James not only thought *with* the concepts and principles he found necessary for expressing the results of his investigations, but thought *about* them as well.

Perhaps we could even venture to say that he thought *through* them. He made his concepts transparent—and his English style cannot be separated from his thought—enough that his mind spirit shows through as much in spite of them as with them.

If, with any integrity, we are to consider William James with reference to contemporary social scientific study of religion, it must be this philosophy, this spirit that we consider, this attitude toward religion, toward the realities religion points to, and toward the processes of knowing and of investigating. If we consider particular psychological statements, it must be as these express this spirit, not to see how closely these psychological statements correspond with any particular facts or other theories at our disposal. The next section will demonstrate in some detail how even James's most striking psychological statements are better understood as expressions of this outlook or philosophy or spirit than they are as scientific propositions.

This exercise may or may not seem fruitful to contemporary scientists. James's spirit seems remarkably contemporary. Secularism, pluralism, existentialism, confrontation, involvement, search for authenticity, the struggle of the individual against the establishment—these are the characteristics of James's spirit. However, though these may be the characteristics of some parts of our culture, they are not the characteristics of the scientific parts of our culture. Some of the battles James was fighting would be viewed by contemporary scientists as on their behalf; he can be quoted and proof-texted for his opposition to a monolithic, supernatural, reductionistic understanding of religious phenomena, a view that precludes psychological investigation. Because his philosophy insisted on taking religious phe-

nomena seriously as *phenomena,* he fought battles that paved the
way for scientific study. But because James was opposed to
established, exclusivistic, monolithic reductionism of any kind,
not just *religiously* established monopolies, his philosophy can be
turned against much of contemporary science just as well. Because he insists on taking religious phenomena seriously, as
phenomena with an authority and importance in themselves, he
raises constant objection against attempts to capture these phenomena in the name of science.

Psychology, and indeed all science, is beset with a persistent
and ongoing battle between those who place the highest values on
regularity, generalizability, reproducibility, and those who
would place still higher values on individuality, depth, richness,
and "meaning." James stands with the latter, endorsing, even
insisting upon individual distinctiveness and depth. Since the
debate is still so lively and James has so many allies, it might
seem of no more than historic interest to retrace his early arguments. Yet his own formulation—a blend of pluralism in ontology and radical empiricism and pragmatism in epistemology—
may still represent a distinctive, important, and instructive
position, a somewhat different and more sophisticated formulation of the issues than, for example, many of his disciples and
spokesmen may achieve today.

This chapter will now proceed in three further sections. First,
it will try to make good on the assertion that the pronouncements
in *The Varieties of Religious Experience* are better seen as
expressions of a philosophy or spirit than they are as entries into
an accumulating scientific corpus. Those of James's observations
that seem the most likely candidates for "central propositions"
will be reviewed, and it will be seen how these, rather than
formulating propositons, express a spirit. This kind of inductive,
empirical, case study approach to discerning James's spirit is the
most characteristically Jamesian method we could use. So, after
having examined several materials in the book, we should have
an understanding of the spirit which animates it. Second, however un-Jamesian as may be such a concession to would-be
synthesizers and makers of "central propositions," the next
section will attempt a more systematic statement of the philosophy or spirit. The final section will attempt to apply this spirit

critically to some issues, mostly methodological, in contemporary social scientific study of religion.

II BEYOND THE PSYCHOLOGY
TO THE SPIRIT

If the study of religion has yielded any insight in our time, it is an understanding of the paradox of institutionalization: the religious spirit demands a body, but this body preempts the spirit. The transcendent, or the response to the transcendent, finds cultural forms and expressions which are supposed to reflect and point to the transcendent but which turn out to veil the transcendent; and forms receive the response due the transcendent. Something like that has happened to the spirit of William James. He delivered the Gifford Lectures, *The Varieties of Religious Experience,* as a series of rich and varied expressions of his outlook, his spirit. *"The Varieties* can scarcely be called a systematic treatise on the psychology of the religious life. Professor James had a thesis to prove. The philosophy that appealed at once to his heart and mind was pluralistic idealism. James therefore sought support in the religious life for his hypothesis that the universe is a protean world of spiritual beings"[2] (Uren 1928: 61). James's skepticism for questionnaires and his use of case studies, his arguments on the validity of mysticism and the constructive potential of mental illness, his affirmation of a "beyond" and "over belief," his construction of types—rightly read, all these and other parts of the book point us not just to themselves but to the spirit that has called them into being. But, as idolatry and fundamentalism are easier than faith in a transcendent beyond form, so it is easier to select certain "fruits" of James's spirit and to hold these up as the "central propositions" which most of us prefer to find. We tend

---

[2] Uren shares the understanding I am proposing as to James's strategy and as to what the book is and is not. But I think it clear that James had not only a thesis of a pluralistic universe to demonstrate but also his pragmatic theory of knowledge. By the same token the way James goes about presenting the lectures is as much a clue to these dimensions of his spirit as is the material he describes in them.

to absolutize, as *the* key to James, expressions and arguments
that James was content, even insistent, to leave tentative and
open and even to leave behind, as he moved "beyond." (James
was the first to go "beyond William James.") Even Uren
(1928), whose insight into the unsystematic nature of this book
was quoted with approval above, subsequently insisted on the
most systematic codification I have ever seen of these lectures.
He endeavors "to isolate and classify the numerous types which
are treated by James with irritating desultoryness" (Uren
1928: 80), and he offers an elaborate scheme of well-labeled and
well-defined types and subtypes, and the insights that James
wanted such excursions to yield for the reader are utterly
obscured.

If it is tempting and easy to rend selected elements of James's
thinking out of context and to nominate these to a centrality
they do not deserve (a pseudocentrality that obscures the communication of his spirit), part of the problem is that James also
writes "out of context." He threw himself into each chapter in
his *Psychology* as though it *were* the key to all psychology, and
then he abandoned it and moved beyond to the next chapter and
threw himself into *that* in the same way. So he conducts himself
in the Gifford Lectures. He ventures to write about each "variety" as though it provided the central proposition our coordinators and, perhaps, our readers would like. One can, like Uren,
be irritated at such carelessness, discount such lapses, and proceed to arrange all in a super organization. Or one can suppose
that James means to do exactly what he is doing and that this
style is only one more clue to the message he wants to get across.
He does after all make the message obligingly explicit from time
to time.

> But why in the name of common sense [sic] need we assume that
> only one such system of ideas can be true? The obvious outcome of
> our total experience is that the world can be handled according to
> many systems of ideas, and is so handled by different men, and will
> each time give some characteristic kind of profit, for which he cares,
> to the handler, while at the same time some other kind of profit has
> to be omitted or postponed. (VRE: 120)

James does not propose to get hung up on any one encounter and
lose the "beyond."

This section proposes to consider, one after another, several of the ideas that could be, and have been, offered as "central propositions." It will show that James did discuss each one as though it were the key. It will also show that James clearly invited his hearers and readers to move "beyond" each one. I propose to "demythologize" each of these central propositons to discover the spirit of William James which is "beyond" any of these statements of William James.

Two Types

If William James is to be cited for actual, constructive theorizing in the psychology of religion, it is for his famous types: "The contrast between the two ways of looking at life which are characteristic respectively of what we called the healthy-minded, who need to be born only once, and of the sick souls, who must be twice-born in order to be happy. The result is two different conceptions of the universe of our experience" (VRE: 163). It is with these types that he is most often represented in textbooks whose writers and readers have typically tried to see how they could make still other instances fit into these types.

But rather than trying to make these types *the* distinctive Jamesian key to comprehending religious experience, they might be advised to linger over these types no longer than did James. "It is true that he introduced distinctions such as 'once-born' and 'twice-born,' for purposes of classification. But he attached little importance to them" (Perry 1948: 333). The distinction that James seems to offer so absolutely on page 163 looks different on pages 477f.

> From this point of view, the contrasts between the healthy and the morbid mind, and between the once-born and the twice-born types, of which I spoke in earlier lectures, cease to be the radical antagonisms which many think them. . . . But the final consciousness which each type reaches of union with the divine has the same practical significance for the individual; and individuals may well be allowed to get to it by the channels which lie most open to their several temperaments . . . so that in many instances it is quite arbitrary whether we class the individual as a once-born or a twice-born subject. (VRE: 477f)

These types are important, but they are important for the representations they give in *their* chapters of the philosophy-spirit-method approach of James to the study of religion. And it contradicts that spirit with ironic severity to wrest these types out of context and try to discover how religious persons or experiences can be sorted into one type or the other. In presenting these types, James wanted us to understand something about religious experience and human nature (that *is* the subtitle of the volume, "A Study in Human Nature"), but what he wanted his hearers to understand was not simply that these two types can be distinguished.

James's distinction between the healthy-minded and the sick soul bears an obvious, though perhaps superficial, correlation with the still more famous types to be suggested by Max Weber within three years of the Gifford Lectures and to be elaborated and solidly established within a decade by Ernst Troeltsch: the distinction between the church and the sect.[3] Church-sect has been subjected ever since to seemingly endless (in both meanings of the word) debate: Which are the crucial defining characteristics? What instances fit which category? (Undoubtedly such discussion will be both continued and rebuked in this volume.) Although I have read and heard much debate as to the proper use and definition of James's types, I am not aware of empirical research that has rendered them the degradation, from James's point of view, of trying to demonstrate the types empirically through factor analysis or even scaling.

There is, undoubtedly, a variety of reasons that James's types have escaped the degree of obsession and preoccupation that have harassed church-sect. There have been fewer psychologists of religion than sociologists of religion to argue with each other, for one thing. And these psychologists of religion have generally been attracted to the more dynamic formulations of the same distinction (between the suppression and acknowledgement of conflict and "evil") announced by Sigmund Freud in his manifesto *The Interpretation of Dreams* while James was preparing the Gifford Lectures (without, so far as is apparent, being informed by or about Freud's thinking at the time). But perhaps psychologists have avoided preoccupation with how well the

[3] Weber first pairs the terms "church" and "sect" after a sentence that could be mistaken for James's account of his distinction. Weber describes the one "as a sort of trust foundation for supernatural ends," and the "other as a community . . . of the reborn" (Weber 1958: 144f.).

types fit the facts because they implicitly recognize a different intention for James's types.

Perhaps the difference in intention between James's types and the sociologists' is as simple as hearing James want to say "there *are* two types" and hearing Troeltsch want to say "there are *two* types." Theoretical types, like their more recent statistical counterparts, factors, do two things. They collect like characteristics, and they separate unlike. But James, like the most sophisticated users of factor analysis, was totally unwilling to generalize beyond his own accumulation of data; the groupings that emerged made sense of the instances at hand, but different data, or even a different way of viewing the same data, could easily yield different groupings. James was particularly unwilling to suppose that his "factors" exhausted the "space." Nothing could have been more repellent to him than the aspiration "to account for all of the variance." It was enough for James to poke gentle fun at the established view of religion held by his hearers by calling it, ironically, "healthy-minded," and by demonstrating one alternative style, an underdog that turned out to have at least as strong claims for validity. (He could never assume Freud's more radical contention that the self-repressive style that the Establishment preferred could actually be dysfunctional, yielding pathology. In James's father's house there were many rooms, enough even for Victorian Henry as well as Yankee William.)

The description of the two types comes early in the book, the first thing after three essentially introductory lectures. This is not, in my judgment, to announce these as the banner psychological concepts to be announced in the lectures, but to establish, in their own way, that there *is* variety. It just takes two. Having established this decisively, the types have served their purpose, and there is not the slightest hesitation about going on to looking at similar and different data in different ways. The very next chapter introduces the "divided self," a category that has troubled no end of more "logical minded" (James's epithet) readers (for example Uren 1928), who have agitated themselves over whether this is a third type or a subtype or whether it fits in to the overall scheme begun by "healthy-minded" and "morbid-minded" in some different way. The difficulty makes James's point for him, even though it goes too often unheeded: there is no "overall scheme," experience is too rich for one.

He concludes the chapter on healthy-mindedness with as eloquent and explicit appeal for pluralism as is found in the book, including such resounding sentences as

> But why in the name of common sense need we assume that only one such system of ideas can be true? . . . and why, after all, may not the world be so complex as to consist of many interpenetrating spheres of reality, which we can best approach in alternation by using different conceptions and assuming different attitudes, just as mathematicians handle the same numerical and spacial facts by geometry, by analytical geometry, by algebra, by the calculus, or by quarternions, and each time come out right? (VRE: 120)

He is characteristically tactful enough not to address this attack directly against the Establishment's view of religion, which I do think he means to be chiding. But its climactic position at the end of this chapter can hardly intend otherwise.

All this contrasts with the treatment commonly given church-sect. Sociologists have generally succeeded in discussing their types as though they were intended to give a mapping of the universe, rather than an account of the inner coherence of certain segments of it. However, this turns out to be a misunderstanding of Troeltsch's intentions, too. Paul Gustafson (1967) has argued impressively that Troeltsch intended to be developing the coherent implications of two theologically derived dimensions, rather than account for all possible empirical observations. And others (for example, Johnson 1957, 1971; Eister 1967) have suggested that Troeltsch, too, was chiefly concerned to peg his types "simply as two among other alternate or variant forms" (Eister 1967:88).

The style with which James works is also important to notice in connection with these types as elsewhere. One looks in vain for the definition of these types, for the itemization of those characteristics which definitively put an instance in one or the other. He enumerates rather than defines. He adds instance to instance, loosely linked. Careful conceptual summary would subtract from, not add to, the description of actual events, which is where the "essentials" lie.

If the chapter on healthy-mindedness has, as its end, the appeal for pluralism quoted above, and the chapter on the sick soul continues this appeal by demonstrating the greater adequacy of this underdog of religious styles, these two chapters carry another message as well. The criterion of adequacy is made clear. "The world *can be handled* according to many systems of ideas, and is so handled by different men, and will each time *give* some characteristic kind of *profit,* for which he cares, to the handler, while at the same time some other kind of profit has to be omitted or postponed" (VRE: 120, my italics). "The method of averting one's attention from evil, and living simply in the light of good is splendid *as long as it will* work. It will work with many persons; it will work far more generally than most of us are ready to suppose. . . . But it breaks down *impotently* as soon as melancholy comes" (VRE: 160, italics added). In the middle, then, of his essentially descriptive, static account, James introduces functionalism—pragmatism, as he will later call it—not as a style of psychological analysis, but as a criterion of philosophical evaluation. "Here is the real core of the religious problem: help!" (VRE: 159). Validity is more likely to be found where responses to such need are found. Such judgment is closer to the judgment of the religious traditions themselves ("In as much as ye did it unto the least of these. . .") than it is to those contemporary judgments which presuppose that functional analysis invalidates rather than validates. If a social scientist ventures to demonstrate the functions of religion, to show how religion answers the cry for help, perhaps even in ways not consciously recognized by the religionist, he may be ennobling religion, in James's view, but debasing it ("reducing" it, we say) in others' eyes. Not just religionists (for example, Havens 1968), but social scientists, too, are suspicious of the functional and seem to assume that *either* religion serves discernible functions *or* it is true. The serving of functions, which James exalts as a criterion of value, is still apologized for (for example, Bellah 1970) or scolded (for example, Berger 1967; Nash and Berger 1962) as degrading.

But another criterion intrudes, partly between the lines, a familiar criterion by now. Healthy-mindedness, the spirit of the once-born, is dubious in part just because it suggests a oneness. James must have in mind here, in part, the buoyant absolutism of Emerson and, perhaps, even of his own father, which he found wanting. It too simply denies the conflicting components of experience.[4]

The two types, in summary then, point more to the philosophical principles of pluralism and pragmatism than to any empirical ordering of phenomena.

Mysticism

If the healthy-minded–morbid-minded distinction occupies the prime place after the introductory lectures, mysticism occupies the climactic place. James contributes to this notion of the climactic status of mysticism by saying at the outset of the chapter that he has been building up to it throughout the lectures. And here he offers the oft-quoted statement, "One may say truly, I think, that personal religious experience has its root and center in mystical states of consciousness. . . . Such states of consciousness ought to form the vital chapter from which the other chapters get their light"[5] (VRE: 370).

Is mysticism, then, the key, the epitome, the model, the essence, the foundation of religious experience? Well, James is capable of treating any current topic as though it were the whole or the key to the whole, for the very simple reason that while he is discussing it, it is. But we need to read to the end of his chapter on mysticism and also, of course, consider the other topics which alternatively serve the same function. At the end of the chapter we discover that, far from an absolute, mysticism is

---

[4] I say that healthy-mindedness implies a monism, despite James's apparent word to the contrary, "Now the gospel of healthy-mindedness, as we have described it, casts its vote distinctly for the pluralistic view" (VRE: 130). If James was not above a gentle irony in his designation of "healthy-mindedness," it may be recurring here. In any case, James is speaking here of what might be called—though he had more regard for the niceties of language than to do so—"vertical pluralism." Healthy-mindedness is pluralistic to the extent that it discards (James's younger Viennese contemporary would have said "represses") evil and conflicts into a distant and distinct world, beyond its own conscious experience. The remaining world of experience remains safely monistic.

[5] Mysticism, interestingly enough, was a type that Troeltsch added to church and sect, apparently to move in two directions which correspond to the two dimensions we are finding fundamentally in James's thought. Troeltsch apparently wanted to demonstrate more of the diversity of religious types. He also apparently wanted to find more opportunity for discussing their function.

characteristically relative. It may claim an authority over those who experience it, but none over the rest of us. James writes with an absolute firmness only when he is combating absolutism.

> Once more, then, I repeat that non-mystics are under no obligation to acknowledge in mystical states a superior authority. . . . They offer us *hypotheses*. . . . What comes [in mystical experience] must be sifted and tested, and run the gauntlet of confrontation with the total context of experience, just like what comes from the outer world of sense. (VRE: 417-19, italics in original)

James does not dispute it as a fair reading of his purposes to suppose that "I have undermined the authority of mysticism" (VRE: 421).

James, indeed, wants us to have respect for mysticism, not because it represents the essence of religious experience so much as because it represents the essence of some values very important to his spirit. James used his lectures on mysticism to carry on two running battles, each occupying about half of the chapter. The first half of the chapter wages battle against the absolutistic pretensions of rationalism (and in favor of a pluralism of consciousness). The second half battles against the stultified pretensions of "established" mystical traditions (and in favor of more functional understanding and of attention to pragmatic effects). Actually, in a sense, it is a single running battle, the same that occupied most of his career. He challenges the pretensions of the established system wherever he finds it oppressive and idolatrous, which seems to be about wherever he finds it, in this case both among mystics and among antimystics.

> I am against bigness and greatness in all their forms, and with the invisible molecular moral forces that work from individual to individual, stealing in through the crannies of the world like so many soft rootlets, or like the capillary oozing of water, and yet rending the hardest monuments of man's pride, if you give them time. The bigger the unit you deal with, the hollower, the more brutal, the more mendacious is the life displayed. So I am against all big organizations as such, national ones first and foremost; against all big successes and big results, and in favor of the eternal forces of truth which always work in the individual and immediately unsuccessful way, underdogs always, till history comes, after they are long dead, and puts them on the top. (Henry James 1920, II: 90)

Mysticism is defined as an experience of knowledge that "defies expression" (VRE: 371). The principal mark of mysti-

cism is, on purpose, a negative one. Mysticism provides a repudiation, if its validity can be acknowledged, of the primacy of
rationalism. This was a repudiation devoutly to be wished, "our
normal waking consciousness, rational consciousness as we call it,
is but one special type of consciousness, whilst all about it,
parted from it by the filmiest of screens, there lie potential forms
of consciousness entirely different" (VRE: 378). James set out
in this chapter not so much to describe the essence of religion as
finally and climactically to help his hearers rend that filmy
screen and to discover that they, too, are capable of experiencing
forms of consciousness quite different from the feeble rationalism on which they were wont to rely. He starts out with innocent
guile assuring his hearers in the first paragraph that he is on
their side of the filmy screen. He is separated from mystical
experience "almost entirely." Then step by step, with gradual
escalation, he reminds them—us—that after all we do have
glimpses of such things, glimpses which we can find nonthreaten-
ing and even authentic. First, "aha" experiences of recognition
and perception, then *déjà vu,* then dreams, then, briefly, trances.
Then alcohol, which he wryly suggests has been "long since
branded as pathological," apparently wanting to remind us how
far behind the filmy screen we have already gone. Then nitrous
oxide which James had experimented with.

At this point his presentation reaches a climax. He has led his
hearers and readers gradually into an appreciation of mysticism,
not just so they could appreciate and understand mysticism—
one is hard pressed to find any "psychology of mysticism"
anywhere in the chapter—but so that they would come to appreciate that understanding of reality that mysticism points to.
"No account of the universe in its totality can be final which
leaves these other forms of consciousness quite disregarded. . . .
They forbid a premature closing of our accounts with reality."
This is the message: do not cheat yourself by closing your
account with reality. This is the message to which much of the
book is directed; mysticism is in its climactic place in the book
because it makes the point insistently. And James has been especially careful in constructing this lecture to make sure his
hearers are led gently enough to this point so that they can
accept the message as deriving from their own experience and

not as alien and exotic. James can end his brief homiletic pressing of the point, as he does (''those who have ears to hear, let
them hear'') with some confidence that he has opened ears to the
hearing of his message of an open, pluralistic universe. Having
opened ears and having announced the message they are to hear,
James bombards his hearers with ten pages of personal accounts
of mystical experiences—some drug-induced and some ''religious
mysticism pure and simple''—with virtually no comment.

The end of this series of cases almost certainly must have been
the end of Lecture 16. For at this point James makes the transition from the discussion of mysticism ''as it comes sporadically''
to a discussion of ''its methodical cultivation'' within the established religious traditions (VRE: 391), which have sometimes
even generated ''a codified system of mystical theology'' (VRE:
397). This transition is the signal to make the transition in mood
from the trust and openness accorded the disestablished to the
guardedness and suspicion accorded the established. Testimony
is still taken even from these ''methodical'' mystics when this is
useful to attack the pretensions of rationalism. ''Saint Ignatius
confessed one day to Father Laynez that a single hour of meditation at Manresa had taught him more truth about heavenly
things than all the teachings of the doctors put together could
have taught him'' (VRE: 401). But a new note of challenge
creeps in, lest these established mystics lay claim to too much
authority over the rest of us. The challenge gradually escalates
from this mid-point to the end of the chapter where the claims of
mysticism to be a decisive religious authority are soundly repudiated with such remarks as I have quoted above.

The challenge is, in part, on familiar ground, that of pluralism
of consciousness and, hence, pluralism of reality and, hence,
pluralism of authority. We are reminded that religious mysticism itself comprises richly varying moods and experiences, so
that any one can hardly be norm or authority. We are reminded
that ''religious mysticism is only one half of mysticism'' (VRE:
417); although the ''other half'' is presently largely relegated to
''textbooks on insanity,'' it too still needs to be heard from. And
we are finally reminded that mysticism is only one of the varieties of religious experience. If the call, ''those that have ears to
hear, let them hear,'' is an appeal to unblock ears too long tuned

to only a narrow band of hearing, it must also, in the last analysis, remind us that there are those who do not have ears to hear.

But the challenge comes too from the other principal force within James's spirit, his pragmatism. Mystics may report many wonderful and amazing experiences and even develop means for codifying and cultivating these. But such an experience has value and deserves to be taken seriously—even for the mystics themselves, much less by the rest of us—only if it meets one clear test. "Its fruits must be good for life" (VRE: 392). "To pass a spiritual judgment upon these states, we must . . . inquire into their fruits for life" (VRE: 404). James's seemingly unqualified enthusiasm for mysticism in the first half of the chapter now gives way to the guardedness with which he puts mystics to this test; notice the conjunction he chooses now that he is well into this part of his discussion: "Saint Ignatius was a mystic, *but* his mysticism made him assuredly one of the most powerfully practical human engines that ever lived" (VRE: 404, my italics added).

One could try to tease out of James's discussion some fragments of actual psychological study of mysticism. The most notable such fragment would be his summary description (VRE: 407–13) of the qualities of mystic consciousness. He summarizes this by saying that mystic consciousness is optimistic "or at least the opposite of pessimistic," and that it "harmonises best with twice-bornness." But several things need to be noted to put this description into context. First and most amusingly almost, is the polite disregard he shows here for the distinctiveness of the types of healthy-mindedness and morbid-mindedness to which he earlier devoted so much attention, a disregard which was interpreted in our last section. It doesn't offend James, as it does the systematizers of his thought, to find mysticism both optimistic and twice-born. Second, this descriptive summary is exceedingly brief and tucked in near the end of the chapter. Third and crucial, this description has a context and an explicit purpose, a "function." He says at the outset that he is going into this description to see what evidence he can find for the authority of mysticism.

He follows this descriptive material and concludes the chapter with a systematic three-point statement. These summarize the three principal messages he has wanted to get across in the course of his discussion of mysticism. He summarizes them in the reverse order from that in which we have found them in the chapter. First, whatever authority mysticism possesses, it comes from its pragmatic outcome, the "truth that comes to a man [that] proves to be a force that he can live by" (VRE: 414), and this becomes a very strong authority indeed, rendering the mystic even *"invulnerable"* (VRE: 415) to whatever demands social propriety and rationalism may want to inflict upon him. Second, however, even the claims of mysticism are severely limited by the consideration of pluralism within and without mystical consciousness. And third, the appeal of the first half of the chapter is now recapitulated: mysticism holds out a hope to all of us to move beyond the confining rationalistic cells in which our own consciousness may be fettered. William James's discussion of mysticism is far less important for what he wants us to know about mysticism than it is for what he wants us to know through mysticism about the spirit with which he approached this subject and all matters.

Saintliness

With this new affirmation of the pragmatic (or, as James was then still calling it, the "empirical") test, perhaps we should look to what he says about the "fruits" of religion for a "central proposition." What counts is the pay-off of religious experience in helping a person move through actual life experiences. This must be a clear deduction from James's presuppositions, and he obliges us in making it and in providing a total of five lectures—a fourth of the total and by far the most pages given to any topic—to "saintliness." He opens this section by calling this discussion of "the practical fruits for life" the "really important part of our task" (VRE: 254). "The collective name for the ripe fruits of religion in a character is Saintliness. The saintly character is the character for which spiritual emotions are the habitual centre of the personal energy" (VRE: 266). And at the outset of such a crucial discussion, James even ventures to write as though he had hold of a universal: "and there is a certain composite photograph of universal saintliness, the same in all religions, of which the features can easily be traced" (VRE: 266). He proceeds with an elaborate and definitive-sounding catalogue. Having itemized these validating fruits for 100 pages, he is still ready to answer "yes" to the question "as to whether religion stands approved by its fruits. . . . The whole group [of saintly attributes] forms a combination which, as such, is religious, for it seems to flow from the sense of the divine as from its psychological center" (VRE: 361). But then, two paragraphs before the end, the real William James stands up, after this long but temporary investment in the promotion of saintliness.

> Let us be saints, then, if we can. . . . But in our Father's house are many mansions, and each of us must discover for himself the kind of religion and the amount of saintship which best comports with what he believes to be his powers and feels to be his truest mission and vocation. There are no successes to be guaranteed and no set orders to be given to individuals, so long as we follow the methods of empirical philosophy. (VRE: 368)

His discussion of saintliness, as thorough and commanding as it is, is not to describe or endorse any of these particular fruits of religion so much as it is to insist that it is to the fruits, the pragmatic outcome, that we must look for validation, not to premises or to logic or to absolute givens. James would hardly be surprised or chagrined that the catalogue of virtues and other outcomes, to which he devoted one-fourth of his lectures, would appear today to be the most dated and the most neglected. What counts as a good outcome depends in large measure on the culture and the expectations and values within which the outcome occurs. Pragmatism is hardly a criterion of value, but only a direction, showing one where to look for criteria. "How is success to be absolutely measured when there are so many environments and so many ways of looking at the adaptation?" James asks at the end of his discussion of saintliness (p. 367). "It cannot be measured absolutely; the verdict will vary according to the point of view adopted." The pragmatism does not so much yield to the pluralism as blend with it. And new "environments" and new "ways of looking at the adaptation" will generate new catalogues of desirable outcomes.

Religion As "Sui Generis"

There is one other strong candidate for the position of "central proposition." Though it has no chapter by itself, proof-texts can be found distributed throughout the lectures. William James is frequently taken as a champion of those who would regard religion as *sui generis* and oppose the "reduction" of religion by analyzing it with categories rooted "outside" religion. He was indeed such a champion—in a sense and in a context. It is important, though, to understand just what he did say. For he patently did not mean and would not approve of some of the views he is sometimes taken as endorsing.

The *sui generis* argument, in varying form and on varying grounds, claims that religion or religious phenomena are inadequately understood if they are understood with categories or variables or theories that could be or have been used to analyze other, nonreligious phenomena.[6] There are grounds for invoking James as a supporter of this argument: the undoubted respect which he accorded religious experiences and those who reported them, the scorn he heaped upon "medical materialism" and other such simple-minded reduction of religious experience to organic and pathological causes, and the fact that he does not invoke in his discussion of religious experiences any of the psychological concepts he had labored through a decade earlier in his general psychology text.

But the principal purpose of *The Varieties of Religious Experience* was to wrest religion from a distinctive preserve under the sovereignty of a religious Establishment and to claim the

[6] The *sui generis* argument is often accompanied by or confused with, but is logically quite distinguishable from the more extreme phenomenological argument: Religious phenomena are inadequately understood if they are understood with categories different from those used by the subjects experiencing the phenomena. The *sui generis* argument is often accompanied by or confused with, but is logically quite distinguishable from the more general, antiscientism argument: The validity of the religious experience may not be challenged by any psychological analysis, of whatever variety.

same rights for psychology in this former preserve as in all other
domains of human experience. As Paul Pruyser puts it clearly in
listing the propositions advanced by James, the first is "that
religious phenomena are continuous with other psychic phenomena" (Pruyser 1969 : 3).

As part of his strategy to make this point, James's first
chapter—in this connection, we should probably remember that
it was his first *lecture*—is of considerable importance. Except as
such a tactic, it seems otherwise unaccountable why he would
begin the entire lecture series with a discussion of "Religion and
Neurology." This lecture accomplished two things. (1) He identified the most extreme of the reductionists—those referring
religious experience to the bodily functions—and thereby acknowledged the chief apprehension and resistance his audience
would have to his lectures; by being able in good conscience to
share the offense they felt by this extreme (physical) reductionism, he was able to win a hearing for his own more moderate reductionism. (2) He was also able, continuing the task which
belonged to his times and to his own personal vocational development, to emphasize the distinction between physiology and psychology and to make his vigorous claim for the propriety of purely
psychological investigation of religious experiences. To attack
the sovereignty of the medical Establishment over his topic was
good warm-up, perhaps even throwing his listeners off guard, for
his attack on the religious Establishment's claim to sovereignty
over religious experience.

Having thus claimed his right to treat religious experience as
he would any other object of psychological investigation, James
proceeded to do just that. It happens that his way of treating
anything was to take it very seriously in its own right and to
take it fresh. It is on principles far more fundamental than the
sui generis character of religious experience that he treats his
material with respect and does not try to employ psychological
categories developed elsewhere. His affirmation is of the *sui
generis* character of each experience, not just religious experience. He does not bring categories from his psychology textbook
into his study of religion anymore than he carries categories
from one chapter to another of his psychology text or anymore
than he carries the same analytic categories from one chapter to

another in *The Varieties of Religious Experience*. He treats religious experience as no less *sui generis* than any experience, but also no more so. In analyzing any particular instance of religious experience, he does not hesitate to move freely through the total psychological experience, so far as he has it accessible. He sets up no boundaries marking religious off from other experience.

I can find no counterpart in James's thinking and certainly no warrant in his spirit for such notions as a distinctive religious sentiment or the idea that "peak experiences" are removed from other psychological functions and somehow of a different order, to mention characteristic suggestions of two later Bostonian psychologists (Allport and Maslow) with whose names and ideas James is often linked in this matter. Indeed, James is quite explicit about the notion of a " 'religious sentiment' which we see referred to in so many books, as if it were a sort of mental entity" (VRE: 28). "As there just seems to be no one elementary religious emotion, but only a common storehouse of emotions upon which religious objects may draw, so there might conceivably also prove to be no one specific and mutual kind of religious object, and no one specific and essential kind of religious act" (VRE: 29).[7]

There is another issue closely related to that of the *sui generis* question. The genetic fallacy is frequently attacked, scientism put in its proper place, and the validity of religious experience protected by insisting on the sharp distinction between psychological analysis and judgments of validity. To know, even with certainty, the psychological history and function of a belief or a practice says nothing for or against the truth of the belief, the

[7] It is another definitional question, not particularly relevant here, as to whether religion is psychologically single or multiple. Theorists' positions on *this* question, however, are closely correlated with their positions on the *sui generis* question. This is perhaps predictable both logically and psychologically. Those who draw a tight boundary between religious and other experience tend to make it a single boundary. Religion is more clearly distinct from other phenomena when it is a single phenomenon. To admit of differentiation within the domain of religion, as to speak of "The Varieties of Religious Experience," seems to be associated with a willingness to permit the lowering of the (protective?) barrier between religion and other human realms; just as the society that most acknowledges pluralism and differentiation within is most likely to admit contacts outside of its borders.

appropriateness of the practice, or any objective reference for either; adjudicating such questions as these presumably is the business of philosophy or some other discipline, not psychology. That kind of division of questions may be appropriate, indeed, it is one I would advance (1969: 605), but it is far from James's position. This kind of separation of scientific questions from questions of value and validity—the "we build the bomb, you decide how to use it" mentality—is absolutely antithetical to James's own spirit, especially in its pragmatic emphasis. There is no world apart from the working, functioning world. So there is no world of value and no references or criteria for validity apart from the world of psychological functions. Value and validity are established precisely by and only by function.

How then must we understand the passages which can be and are proof-texted as indicating James's support of such a distinction? He indeed casts livid and unambiguous scorn on attempts to disparage and discredit religious experience by relating it to pathological or glandular or other mean origins and functions. But if William James scorned the evaluation of religious experience according to its origins and roots we need to be clear what he advocated instead. It was not the separation of the evaluative question from functional analysis. Rather, it was the distinction between what amounts to two different kinds of functional analyses. He did not oppose *evaluation* based on *origins* because he wanted to separate evaluation from fact, but because he insisted on evaluation based on *outcome*. It was not that William James as philosopher refused to evaluate religious experiences on the basis of what William James as psychologist could discern. It was rather a question of what the psychologist would look at and, hence, what the philosopher would judge by. It was the fruits, not the roots, of religious experience—as of any experience—which were to provide the criteria. James disposed of the mean origins quickly in his first chapter but devoted five chapters, one-fourth of the book, to "Saintliness." The origins of the experience, that is past, and like all pages once turned, is of little interest to the here and now. What effects does the religious experience have on his behavior now? That is the crucial question. What if authoritarians and the prejudiced are attracted to established religions these days, as we now know from unequivocal research findings that they are. That would hardly even be interesting information to James. The question is whether the religion does anything to affect them.

James had one more important comment to make on the problem of reductionism. This derives more from his pluralism than his pragmatism. It consists of taking the meanness out of mean origins. If his move just discussed above consists of bringing the "big questions" down to the level of experience, perhaps the move mentioned here consists of bringing the "lower origins" up to the level of experience. Even if one were to grant pathological roots, for example, what is so discrediting or disparaging or devaluating or invalidating about that, anyhow? As James would not put it, pathology is part of the creation with equal rights and equal likelihood of yielding truth and value. To suppose otherwise is a prejudice and stereotype not unlike any other special prejudice. To discredit any idea by pointing out that the speaker is insane is not so different from trying to discredit it by pointing out that the speaker is, for example, Oriental or female. In fact, of course, there is more than a hint in James's celebration of the other and of the different, in his suspicion of the established, in his sympathy with the underdog, that, if anything, he expects a little more validity and insight and goodness to come from the outcast.

Summary of "Central Propositions"

This search through the beginning, the climax, and the heart of VRE for "central propositions" leaves us with one disconcerting impression. James was capable of writing as though he were offering firm absolutes—highly generalizable, tightly defined analytic categories; a descriptive catalogue of universal phenomena; definitions and criteria of authentic religion—then of renouncing these. The reader may well feel abandoned and exposed if he thought the structure James was inviting him to enter was a solid abode; for James it turns out to be only a transient tent, serving James fully and well and serving him temporarily. This nomadic style of mind, delighting in movement and thriving in the anticipation of what is yet to come, baffles and offends some, who can live only in clearly located stable structures; James's

younger colleague at Harvard, Josiah Royce, found him verging
on irresponsibility. This is why there is on purpose no Jamesian
school of psychology. In writing his *Principles of Psychology,*
as in writing *The Varieties of Religious Experience* he becomes
totally immersed in the substance and tools of each chapter, as
though *it* were the key to the whole; then moves on feeling no
more desire to "integrate" the chapters one with another or to
fashion a comprehensive system than he would want all his
dinner guests or all the members of his family cast in the same
mold.

Boring (1950) epitomized James's mind as "positive yet
tolerant" and Allport (1961) celebrated his "magnificent tentativeness." But to call William James "tolerant" or "tentative"
is like saying that his writing style was "not cumbersome."
There is a fierce, positive affirmation in this nomadic style of
mind which is the whole point of James's message and is his
legacy. This message is on purpose in the way he worked, fully as
much as in what he said.[8] The shiftiness which may frustrate
the systematizing reader looking for the essence of James's
thought should be heeded by that reader as the best clue he may
get to that "essence." To understand William James best on his
own terms we must not listen and appraise what he says (propositions, central or otherwise) so much as we discover what his
statements are doing for him; what function do they serve in the
largest context of his life that we can apprehend? What *process*
do they reflect? So, to know William James best, we find ourselves assessing not the content of his mind but its quality, his
style, his temper, his basic attitudes, his spirit.

"On the whole" is a frequent and telling phrase in VRE, one
about which James became self-conscious toward the end of the
lectures (see, for example, pp. 321, 368), perhaps challenged by
the more systematically minded and therefore impatient Scotch
listeners. The phrase, of course, expresses his essential "tentativeness," to stick with Allport's word. " 'On the whole'—I fear we
shall never escape complicity with that qualification, so dear to
your practical man, so repugnant to your systematizer"

---

[8] And, in poor imitation, it is a message I have tried to communicate as
much in the way I have presented the preceding paragraphs fully as much
as in their content.

(VRE: 321). But the phrase also points to the grounds for that "tentativeness"; it expresses the affirmation that is expressed by the tentativeness.

The authority William James acknowledged was that of experience itself, the "blooming, buzzing confusion" from which one fashions his *Weltanschauung* and to which he then submits his cognitive abstractions for correction and renewal. This ore of experience, though crude, remains richer and grander than any attempts to refine it. There is always a "more" to experience, both a qualitative "more" and a quantitative "more," into which one may, nay must dip again and again.

To identify this root conviction, from which so much else derived, one might speak of James's "reverence for life." But this phrase has now been preempted to cover a decidedly un-Jamesian pallid, constricted, imperious legalism. For Schweitzer, the phrase expresses and generates restriction; it emphasizes the distinction between self and others and yields mostly a narrowing of choices. It mostly adds to the "thou shalt nots" of life. To reclaim the phrase to suit James, we should have to refuel it with relish and gusto and openness, with a lust to relate to life, to be subject to its discoveries.

Here is the personal zest, the "chivalry of soul"—Royce's phrase—reaching out to embrace others, all others, in conversation and correspondence that made immediate intimates of all and antagonized none. As James Ward wrote to William James ten days before he died, "Yours, my dear friend, has been a successful life and surely it has been a happy one, for I know of no-one more universally beloved. I, at least, never heard an ill word of you from anyone" (Perry 1948: 355f). Dwight Eisenhower (1967) described his method of handling someone who "has acted despicably, especially toward me. I try to forget him. I used to follow a custom—somewhat contrived, I admit—of writing the man's name on a piece of scrap paper, dropping it into the lowest drawer of my desk, and saying to myself, That finishes the incident, and so far as I am concerned, that fellow." Somehow people did not seem to act despicably toward William James, and such disposal would have meant to William James an avoidable loss, a loss not to the "fellow" but to himself. James welcomed, even celebrated the different *other*—other person, other idea, other culture—not in spite of the difference, but, with an insight only now being forced on American society's attitude toward social minorities, *because* of the difference. The different is beautiful.

To go "beyond" is always urged by James because in the "beyond" is still more of the rich rewarding life which James finds in the here and now.

III THE "BEYOND" IN JAMES: ALWAYS A "MORE" AND AN "OUTCOME"

"Beyond" As "More": A Throbbing Pluralistic Universe

William James grew up in a family of strong, distinctive personalities, of diverse talents, of interests pulling in all directions, of vigorous convictions constantly contending across the dinner table and across the Atlantic, perpetually on the move, seldom living in the same house for as long as a year, its own diversity regularly augmented by a stream of stimulating household visitors; yet he grew up in a family remarkable also for its mutual support and affectionate cohesiveness. The final book James published was a celebration of *A Pluralistic Universe,* and some of his most memorable contributions to psychology are caught in such phrases as "a stream of consciousness" and "blooming, buzzing confusion." There is a straight line from the experience to the philosophical position and psychological insights. James had every reason to conclude that people not only did, but perhaps more importantly, *could* live in the context of a reality that was "redundant and superabundant," to quote Bergson's summary of James's metaphysical position.[9] Where some people can find support for a sense of rightness and direction, an identity, a satisfaction of fundamental personal religious and metaphysical yearnings only in closely structured social and ideological systems, James had every reason to suppose that a

---

[9] In his introduction to the French translation of *Pragmatism* cited by Perry (1948: 351).

person most readily found himself not in spite of, but verily in the middle of contention and multiplicity and change, the tug and pull of sensations and ideas and wills. And, given his pragmatic, radically empirical epistemology (to be discussed later), if this is how and where people found themselves, this is how the universe is. Educated throughout boyhood by a succession of tutors who came and went or, more accurately, were found here and there as the James family came and went; forbidden by his father's suspicion of organized education to accompany a friend to college, even when James was finally permitted to subject himself to the formal structures of scientific study at Harvard; these scientific studies remained only a fragment of his ever-fragmented education.

> He was perpetually grazing and ruminating, wandering wherever the pasturage was good. Fortunately two notebooks of the year 1862–63 have been preserved, in which appear—along with items extracted from the lectures of Agassiz on "Geology and the Structure and Classification of the Animal Kingdom," and Joseph Lovering on "Electrostatics, Electrodynamics and Acoustics"—pencil drawings, historical and literary chronologies, sayings of Charles Pierce, an outline of the French Revolution, and abstracts of Buchner's *Kraft und Stoff*, Max Muller's *History of Ancient Sanskrit Literature*, Farrar's *Origins of Language*, and Jonathan Edward's *Original Sin*. The entries in these books, and in an Index Rerum begun in 1864, range over the whole field of literature, history, science, and philosophy. They indicate a mind as energetic and acquisitive as it was voracious and incorrigibly vagrant. (Perry 1948: 71)

Fully satisfied by such knowledge that came in illuminating bursts, feeling no need to struggle for synthesis, James could readily suppose that the reality itself was similarly burstlike with an infinite plurality of bursts always to come. The "beyond" which constantly lured his restless mind from one idea to another, from one solution to another, was always the beyond of others, never the beyond of the One which lay behind or above or around the immediate.

> The power of his mind lay largely in its extreme mobility, its darting, exploratory impulsiveness. It was not a mind which remained stationary, drawing all things to itself as a centre; but a mind which traveled widely—now here and now there—seeing all things for itself, and making up in the variety of its adventures for what it lacked in poise. (Perry 1948: 66)

And if the diversity of ideas one person found was to be welcomed, so also was the diversity of ideas brought by the confrontation of one person with another. His most faithful and staunchest philosophical adversary was his younger colleague and friend Josiah Royce. Near the end of James's life, Royce testified to the nature of the relationship and to the nature of James's attitude toward those who held contradictory ideas:

> James found me at once—made out what my essential interests were at our first interview, accepted me, with all my imperfections, as one of those many souls who ought to be able to find themselves in their own way, gave a patient and willing ear to just my variety of philosophical experience, and used his influence from that time on, not to win me as a follower, but to give me my chance. . . . Whatever I am is in that sense due to him. . . .
>
> Sometimes critical people have expressed this by saying that James has always been too fond of cranks, and that the cranks have loved him. Well, I am one of James' cranks. He was good to me, and I love him. The result of my own early contact with James was to make me for years very much his disciple. I am still in large part under his spell. If I contend with him sometimes, I suppose that it is he also who through his own free spirit has in great measure taught me this liberty. (Perry 1948: 162)

In his social judgments James was a liberal but most definitely not of the brand who proposed the management of other people's lives for their own welfare. He might today even be called a radical for his unequivocal endorsement for letting each one do his own thing or, as he put it with characteristic greater elegance, letting the "bird fly with no strings tied to its leg" (Perry 1948: 140).

James's celebration of this diversity in each person's experience and between persons, was suggested and was justified by his conviction that the nature of things is just so diverse. James does *not* see us in the position of the blind men feeling different parts of the elephant—exactly the opposite. For that image implies several things which are not true for James: (1) that there is a synthesis, a oneness which could be built from our multiple perceptions; (2) that our individual distinctive perceptions are somehow the product of an inadequacy or defect in our own perceiving; and (3) that the particularity we happen to comprehend is somehow an accidental product of where we happen to be standing, rather than, as James would have it, the particular validating and validated product of our own directed energy and searching. (If one observer perceives a leg and another a tusk, in James's view it is because one in some sense, is "looking for" a leg the other "looking for" a tusk.)

When one has perceived a truth or insight to the satisfaction of his criteria for the validity of evidence (in James's case the pragmatic radically empirical functional criteria), then that is truth. That is as absolute a truth as he can expect or needs to find and, by James's extension, as there is. Though aware and delighted that there are other truths, one does not disparage his own personal finding by thinking of it only as a shadow of a truth which is potentially clearer, or a part of a truth which is potentially more complete or to be integrated with other truths. This would be illusion and futility.

The affirmations of pluralism *can* be grudging, merely tolerant and not really affirmations at all. One can concede, as a kind of practical inconvenience or an embarrassment to be overlooked, that there are realities other than those one has perceived, discoveries other than those one has made, but without being affected by this acknowledgement. One continues with his own commitments to his own views of reality, his own discoveries, his own methods, *as though* they are absolute. He has a pious paragraph at the end of his article saying, "Of course, there may be other approaches and other interpretations," but he does not show any interest in seeking them. He agrees to take part in a symposium called "Various Approaches to . . ." or "Various Views of . . ."; but he does not listen to the other speakers. But James actively pursued the "beyond." He genuinely celebrated the "other." One solution was no sooner formulated than the question had to be reopened in search for new solutions. He eagerly moved from chapter to chapter in the *Psychology* and *The Varieties of Religious Experience,* moving from one conceptual framework to another, exploring and exploiting each fully and decisively but no more feeling the need to stick with the framework adopted in one chapter while he was in the next than he did the need to integrate all the frameworks into a single systematic whole.

The affirmations of pluralism *can* be inhibiting and stifling. If there is such an infinite variety of reality and of approaches to reality, why take any one seriously? "Sure, I'll be on the symposium; what do you want me to talk about?" "Find out which research grants are easiest to get this year; we'll submit a proposal for that." Against such stifling carelessness, James's epistemology is a vigorous corrective. One does not pick truth off a cafeteria serving table, passively accepting something that has been served up by someone else. Truth is harder earned than this and, therefore, well earned. Truth yields only to more active, directed search. One approaches the food table with a specific appetite and *this* must be satisfied, or there is no meal. Perhaps it can be satisfied from the cafeteria line but, more characteristically, the appetite must move on to the kitchen and there direct preparations afresh. The truth has to work for you, or there is no truth. To be a philosopher—and, presumably, a scientist—one must be an active participant, even a partisan, never a mere spectator. If one does not have a specific *will* to believe, there is nothing to believe. Reality must be wooed and courted before it will yield its secrets, and then only to the particular suitor. Nothing could be more different from pallid relativism—anything goes—than James's demand for energetic self-direction and self-investment in the approach to reality. James's empiricism could not be further removed from the shotgun empiricism of heedless, mindless searching to which questionnaire respondents, computer programmers, and journal readers are too much subject today. One approaches reality with a clear question, formulated out of the heat and heart of one's own searching—we might say scientific theories—or one does not get an answer.

The affirmation of pluralism, the affirmation of the beyond, of the discovery yet to come, is always an extension of the affirmation of the validity and vitality of the discovery already made; it is not a compensation for the defects of the present discovery. James is affirming a doctrine of creation and, perhaps, of redemption far more readily than he can countenance a doctrine of the fall or of sin. One *can* be humble about his own views, tolerant of others', and hopeful for new insights all on the basis of his awareness of the defects of his own views. One can believe, on the principle of human fallibility, that he must expect to move beyond any conclusion, however hard won and however valid it may seem. Yet not so with James. He moved joyfully from idea to idea, from solution to solution, even as he moved from friend to friend, from career to career, from place to place, expecting the most from the next because the last had had so much to offer him. James abandoned painting as a career only after he was good at it and was sure he enjoyed it through a period of total immersion in painting. He almost left Agassiz's botanical collection expedition in the Amazon out of despair—"If there is one thing I hate it is collecting" (Perry 1948: 21)—but he stuck it out and came to write nostalgically about the trip. And he came home to make a career and a philosophy of being a collector. James rejected the absolutism that he found in his father and in Emerson, for example, and later in Royce, not because he found this absolute so overwhelming and terrifying that its yoke had to be thrown off—a view that makes relativists of some as they experience the absolute's judgment—but, rather, James discarded the absolute as too puny. He found life too rich, the universe too fast-moving and full to be gauged by a single absolute. "James relished this . . . chaotic plenitude which experience exhibits when it is restored to its primitive unselectedness" (Perry 1938: 127). "He was scarcely out of his infancy before he began to be a nostalgic cosmopolitan, flying from perch to perch, now yearning for home, now equally eager to escape—liking it where he was *and* longing for the better far away" (Perry 1948: 48). It is that final "and" (which I have italicized), the affirmation of the beyond out of the affirmation of the here and now, that is James's spirit. Is this "healthy-mindedness?" Hardly. Is this "tough-mindedness?" Perhaps. But those are categories developed for other purposes, and why suppose that they have to be found appropriate for this occasion?

"Beyond" As "Outcome": Knowledge Is in the "Happening"

Before finding himself in the academic career of philosopher and psychologist, William James experimented with two other careers, one which he enjoyed and one which he disliked. At the age of eighteen he became a painter, but having tested his talents and found them substantial, he left the career, satisfied, to move on. In his early twenties, he began studying science and medicine, found much of this not to his liking, and, accordingly, was able to wrench himself from it only after prolonged torment.

When James's philosophy is called "empiricism," we would do better to think of the empiricism of the painter rather than the empiricism of the scientist. To know something, for James, is to take a very active role in the discovery, to make perceptions that are shaped by the vigorous interaction and expectation and actual experience. To know "empirically" is no more to be the passive recorder or collector of events and objects, as James too often found science to be, than the painter is engaged in making a photographic reproduction. The knowledge one thus gains from expectation consumated by experience is *his* knowledge. Presumably, it does not contradict others' knowledge, just as the painter's product can be viewed by others intelligibly and with appreciation. But one hardly expects, as the scientist typically does, that the validity of his knowledge will be tested precisely by the degree that it is identical with the knowledge of others. The reason for this, the force of the *"his,"* is not just the metaphysics of pluralism—reality does not just present itself differently to different persons—but is also in the necessity for personal investment in the act of knowing.

"To know" carries two rather distinct kinds of meaning in English. To know is to have information about, usually of impersonal facts. To know is also to be acquainted with, to be familiar with; in this sense, perhaps the word's basic usage is with reference to persons. "I know John Smith's telephone number" suggests a very different type of knowledge from "I know John Smith." Perhaps the archaic usage of "to know," referring to sexual familiarity, is an intense form of the second usage. Other languages have two different words for these two different meanings. But the single word in English permits the more ready extension of knowledge as personal acquaintance and familiarity to apply to impersonal objects and events and experiences. Perhaps this is why English-speaking philosophers have seen the richest possibilities in empiricism. In any case, this is what James does.

"Pragmatism" is the particular radical form of empiricism which is generally applied to James's theory of knowledge. (Actually, the pragmatism is offered by James as a kind of supplement or a substitute for the more immediate, intuitive familiarity which is the preferred, but seldom accessible, form of knowledge. But if one has to have mediated "knowledge about," then let it follow from the principles of pragmatism.) Knowledge is validated by its practical consequences. Something is true to the degree that it works, rather than something works to the degree that it is true, to follow the aphorismic formulation of which James's theory of emotion is a direct echo (we are sad because we cry and angry because we strike).

At first glance, such a theory of knowledge would seem to give primacy to external events and practical pay-off; and in the political sphere today, the notion of pragmatism does conjure up the image of a mindless politician without inner conviction or principle led to decisions by the calculation of maximum votes in the next election. But this is exactly the wrong way to understand James. Pragmatism actually calls our attention much more to inner direction and personal initiative in the process of knowing than it does to "objective" events. Though it is the pay-off that is decisive; something has to be paid off. Though the results are essential to establish knowledge, the results are defined by *expectations* which are even more fundamental and equally indispensable. An event *is* a result only as it is a response to directed probing. There is no answer without a question. Much as some conditioning theorists would like to overlook the fact, it still seems to be a fact that "reinforcement" or "reward" is effective only insofar as it meets an inner need or drive. Even Pavlov's dogs had to be hungry to salivate even to food, much less to bells, which is just as important to understand as the fact that they would stop salivating to bells if they never got food. James would enjoy, for his illustration of such self-direction and especially for its illustration of the dominance of the underdog's self-direction, the cartoon in which the rat brags that he has the psychologist trained: "Everytime I press this bar he gives me something to eat." He might also understand that advertisers are as hooked on the particular motive they are trying to appeal to as their audience is hooked by their manipulation of those motives.

It is no wonder that a commentator finds himself almost anthropomorphizing pragmatism.

> It stresses the act of initiative. Such knowledge is not a pure re-
> ceptivity, but an attack—inspired by a desire for truth or a state
> of discontent, and guided by a plan of campaign. It is a project
> framed or expectation entertained in advance, and then executed, so
> far as experience permits. . . . It does not attack at random, but
> selects an objective which promises to remove its present quandary.
> (Perry 1938: 72)

One takes aim at a target, then almost hurls himself at the
target to see if his sighting was true. In such an account of how
truth is wrested from experience, we are undoubtedly justified in
hearing more than a slight autobiographical overtone. This was
James's style of life. Perhaps it is epitomized in an incident
recounted by H. G. Wells in his *Autobiography* (Knight
1950: 61). James was visiting his brother Henry in the latter's
proper English home in Rye. He heard that G. K. Chesterton was
staying at the inn next door. He wanted to see Chesterton. So
what else but to take the gardener's ladder, climb up, and peep
over the wall—a move of "scandalous directness" that "terribly
unnerved" the thoroughly Europeanized Henry who, of course,
would have all experience as muted and indirect—and sometimes, it even seems, as pointless—as possible. The correct way to
meet Chesterton was through proper mediators and according to
proper forms.

> This vivacity, this eagerness and gusto, marked James from an early
> age—as a "son and brother." His sister Alice once said of him that
> he seemed "to be born afresh every morning." "He came down from
> his bedroom *dancing* to greet me," said his father. . . . He was an
> overflowing and inexhaustible fountain—a fountain, be it remarked,
> and not a channeled stream. (Perry 1948: 373)

James apparently took more congenially to lectures and to
letter writing than to more formal book writing, probably because the former has a clearer target to which the author can
direct himself; and self-direction is the name of the game.

If William James's pluralism is, to some degree, a reaction
against his father's search for and claim for absolutes, his insistence on personal investment—with pay-off of the investment—
as the necessary condition for discovery, stands in counterpoint
to his brother's placid, passive, interminable, and indirect descriptions. William once posed the contrast in a letter to his
brother: "but why won't you, just to please Brother, sit down

and write a new book, with no twilight or mustiness in the plot, with great vigor and decisiveness in the action, no fencing in the dialogue, no psychological commentaries, and absolute straightness in the style?'' (Perry 1935, Vol. 1: 424) (Notice that by 1905 ''psychological commentaries''—at least Henry's, and perhaps others'—belonged among those verbal exercises that miss the point of experience.)

His brother's prose meanderings annoyed James for the same reason that he had no patience with what he regarded as the trivial preoccupations of the religious and scientific Establishment. Such indirectness, such infatuation with peripheral and unsorted details denied and prevented authenticity. To be genuine is to be carried to the heart of a matter and to a clear pay-off by the ''acute fever'' of one's own inner experience by the active anticipation of the encounter. An important part of the agenda for *The Varieties of Religious Experience* is the search for the criteria of authentic religion. This is important testimony to the impossibility in James's view of separating ''fact'' from ''value,'' but it is even more important to notice the criteria he chooses. Early on (VRE: 8) he links the ''acute fever'' with ''effective fruits'' and before the first chapter is over has referred to ''inner happiness'' and ''serviceability for our needs'' and to ''immediate luminousness'' and to ''moral helpfulness.'' These criteria, like the five lectures James gives to ''Saintliness,'' refer, as those of a pragmatist should, to fruits, to good effects. But these fruits, these effects, all refer, as those of a Jamesian pragmatist should, to the personal search that forms the target for the outcome.

It is ironic that Gordon Allport, who in many ways should be regarded as a disciple of James, lost this tension of pragmatism when he came to establish criteria for authenticity. ''Extrinsic'' religion was to be disparaged, in contrast with the more committed and personal ''intrinsic'' religion, in large part for its ''utilitarianism'' (Hunt and King 1971). The extrinsically religious person ''uses'' his religion, and this makes it degraded religion in Allport's view. But to James usefulness belongs more clearly on the side of authentic religion than its opposite. James would, of course, want to share with Allport some concern for better and poorer uses. Perhaps, paradoxically, the pragmatist is more readily alerted by his very concern for function, to different quality of functions being served, as contrasted with the one who, offended by utilitarianism, dismisses all outcome as a criterion in favor of the more static and remote concept of sentiment.

James was hardly disposed to separate religion and the psychological investigation of it as somehow entirely different types of human enterprise. The criteria for value and authenticity in the one are criteria for value and authenticity in the other. Whether in religious inquiry or scientific inquiry or any other enterprise, pragmatism refers to the investment of the self in a particular set of circumstances and to the pay-off by those circumstances of that investment. With only casual or slight investment there can be only slight pay-off and, hence, slight "knowledge." This must be the fate of the atheoretical, purely "empirical" foray, even also of the study guided by relatively trivial hypotheses. Only the risky plunge of the big expectation, mobilizing one's most significant expectations, is likely to have a big pay-off and, hence, important knowledge. But what if the risk proves too risky and the circumstances do not pay off the expectation? Much as William James admires and trusts moral and psychological struggle, he is almost too "healthy-minded" to consider the possibilities of epistemological failure, that the circumstances will say "no" to one's expectations. And he is definitely too healthy-minded and non-Freudian to consider the possibility that expectations and investment will make one continue to perceive "yes" even after circumstances have said "no." But there is, after all, the completely open-ended, pluralistic universe, rich with possibilities and awaiting one's next investment.

IV   WILLIAM JAMES BYPASSED

If psychology of religion has gone "beyond" William James, it has been by bypassing him. His psychology is not employed by the field, and, far more importantly, his spirit does not inspire it. If William James is honored as the "father" of the psychology of religion, it is in a very special sense, which can be interpreted in terms of ambivalence appropriate to the psychology of religion. He is revered as a great and distant hero but hardly heeded. He is the liberating Moses, who called down a plague on the houses of both the religious and the medical Establishment and who led the psychology of religion into independent existence. But his recommendations as to how that independent existence should be conducted are ignored as thoroughly as the builders of the golden calf ignored those of the law-giving Moses. This estrangement must be insisted on here, even though this disrupts the format of this book.

However, if James's relation with current research *is* one of estrangement, then *this* relationship is what can be reported here. If we have gone "beyond" James by neglecting him, this is the kind of "beyondness" that needs to be discussed here. We can still venture to appraise the field in the light of James. But this means being bold enough to try to do just that, to speak the judgment his spirit speaks about our current state of affairs. Some of the most admired and most celebrated characteristics of our contemporary "scientific study of religion" contradict essential affirmations of William James's spirit. We may be right, or he may be right. But it is the role of this chapter to take James as the norm, and from that perspective our unreflective adulation of and obedience to what we mean by empiricism and objectivity and generalizability has made golden calves of these and other characteristics of our own research. We readily assume, without thinking about it, that the more "empirical" and "objective" and the more generalizable is our research, the better it is. To read William James carefully is to make ourselves reexamine—or, perhaps, examine—our received faith in such virtues.

"Empiricism" As a Golden Calf

The suggestion is frequently and seriously made these days by researchers in religion (for example, Barton 1971: 853) that what we most need is a data bank, the accumulation in one computer memory of the data collected on all the diverse samples with all the diverse instruments that are investigated. The idea seems to be that if one set of data has defects, the remedy is in the accumulation of more such sets of data. In fact, so many data banks have already sprung up in the last decade that they are now being coordinated by an Association for the Development of Religious Information Systems, with a newsletter and a directory (Moberg 1971). The data bank idea easily can be understood as proposing, "What we need are more data, any data."[10] As such, it is a natural extension of many prevailing trends in our current research. More research is generated and guided by the availability of data than by the informed curiosity of the researcher. The availability of the data is permitted to generate the research questions asked of the data, more than are research questions, formulated because something seems worth asking, permitted to generate the collection of decisive data.

Such promiscuous empiricism is evident in the frequency of secondary analysis of data, a practice which the data bank proposes to encourage and to institutionalize. One defect of such secondary analysis is that the data, collected for one purpose, have to be strained in order to fit new questions; secondary analysis can seldom answer questions as decisively as newly-designed research. The other defect is the one James's thinking alerts us to, that *questions* have to be strained and foreshortened in order to fit the available data; secondary analysis can seldom *ask* questions as decisively as newly-designed research.

Such promiscuous empiricism is evident when items are written and administered freely, only to see what relationships turn up in the analysis. I was once telephoned by a person designing what turned out to be a prominent piece of survey research. He invited me to include ten questions in his instrument. "We have that many columns left on our last IBM card," he explained. I declined the invitation. If the appendix to the report reveals that the questionnaire has contained more items that were unused than used in the analysis, we have a right to wonder what direction the researcher initially gave his research beyond the kind of

[10] The rather indiscriminate recommendation for more empirical data is precisely the urgent appeal made by the author of one popular text in psychology of religion, his recommendation as to what is most needed to advance the field (Clark 1958). The irony that makes this one example worth picking out from the many almost ritualistic recitals of this appeal by many authors is that this author professes to be a close disciple of William James.

blind faith that data, any data, would be illuminating. The computer encourages such faith by its easy generation of huge correlation matrices and factor analyses. The traditional warning to would-be factor analysts that "you only get out what you put in" is hardly a warning when the researcher does not really suppose that there can be any more compelling or sovereign input than raw data, any data.

Promiscuous empiricism is evident in research which is based on and shaped to readily available popular instruments. Thus, a few published and publicized measures of religiosity are used repeatedly, most notoriously the Allport, Vernon, Lindsey Study of Values, even still Thurstone's scales, more recently Allport's and Ross's intrinsic-extrinsic scales or Faulkner's and DeJong's (1966) "5-D" scales. This popular use persists despite well-established serious psychometric shortcomings and, more seriously from James's perspective, despite the fact that there is frequently little relationship between the concepts of religion implied by the instruments and those that the researcher has proposed to study, sometimes even dubious relationship between the concepts actually measured by the instruments and those claimed by the inventors of the instruments (Cf. Clayton 1971; Dittes 1969; Hunt 1968; Hunt and King 1971). Equally contrary to James's spirit is the use of a few standardized personality tests, correlated over and over again with these few measures of religiosity. Still more odious to James and still more common is the use of the easily available measures of church attendance and church affiliation as a measure of religiosity.

Promiscuous empiricism is evident, too, in some practices in the reporting of research, as well as in the conduct of research. It is present in the research report that gives great, if not exclusive, attention to the procedures without suggesting how or even that these procedures issued out of particular theoretical questions and were designed to answer them. It is present, too, in the research report that opens with a long list of previous studies on the topic or even abstracts of their results without telling us how these accumulate to generate or to leave questions to be answered by the new research. The author gives the impression that it is his contribution to add, almost randomly, one more set of empirical results to the previous catalogue and that such a contribution is not only satisfactory, but commendable. Such research reports usually end with the author's ritualistic recommendation that "more research is needed on this question," without telling us how future research should be guided by his own findings. This is further evidence of the kind of raw empiricism that relies on data for data's sake.

Promiscuous empiricism is also present in review and encyclopedia articles that abstract a long series of empirical findings, a sentence or a paragraph to each, without organizing the results or without telling us what we know and do not know as a consequence of these studies or how the studies could have been better done so we could find out more. It is also present in methodological surveys and critiques that hold each piece of research up to some essentially arbitrary and rote-learned methodological criteria (size of sample, randomness of sample, interjudge reliability of observations, length of scale, size of factor loadings, orthogonality of rotation, two-tailed p-value, and the like) without telling us how particular criteria and criticisms issue out of the need certain kinds of questions have for certain kinds of data and controls. (As will be demonstrated shortly, for example, some kinds of questions require selected, even biased samples, a point not readily accepted by those more concerned with the purity, rather than the relevance, of data.) It is also present in research reports that announce the new findings in abstract, quite out of the context of preceding research and theorizing, as though any new data are so commanding, so sovereign, that the presentation and interpretation of them is all that is required.

It is necessary now to be clear about the grounds by which William James would find defective such golden-calf-like glorification of data for data's sake, the tendency that seems epitomized by the proposal for a data bank. First, we must be clear about the seeming irony that "empiricism" is a label appropriately attached to James's philosophy, yet that philosophy is invoked here to rebuke the "empiricism" that has just been described. The difference, however, is no less than the difference between "active" and "passive." The investigator (even that name is a misnomer) who is content to record whatever data readily come his way is leaving out the most essential component of the empirical process, his own aggressively active search and expectation. The infinite richness of reality which James celebrated does not mean that truths are available at every hand for the plucking. It means, instead, that truth is available only to the one who approaches this "blooming, buzzing confusion" with a purpose and expectation. Discovery and insight are yielded to one who looks *for*, not to one who merely looks around. Reality is such that it offers and requires a kind of partnership with the investigator, a partnership that is consummated in the *experience*. Data can be noted by a computer, but reality, including its abstraction into data, can be *experienced* only by a person who has approached with questions that he feels to be personally real and urgent for answer. There is just below the surface in James's conviction—but only just below the surface—the criterion of risk, which his successors a generation or two later would invoke under labels such as "existentialism." Until one risks a genuinely disconcerting disconfirmation, until one risks the negative answer to a personally crucial expectation, he is not probing reality sufficiently to discover anything. Until one makes an investment that he might lose, he does not earn the pay-off. James wrote as a motto inside the front cover of his copy of Locke's *Essay* this sentence from that book.

> He that will not eat till he has demonstrated that it will nourish him, he that will not stir till he infallibly knows the business he goes about will succeed, will have little else to do but sit still and perish. (Perry 1948: 298)

James was to show how, as an alternative to such passive perishing, one who takes the risk finds the nourishment in the eating and in the stirring, the success.[11]

The accumulation of data governed by little more than randomness or convenience is generally rationalized in terms of the collective enterprise that is science. This is expressed most crudely and most ritualistically in the sentence at the end of the research report that says, "It is hoped that others will continue this line of research." Quite apart from the question as to whether a "line" has been established, as claimed, and apart

---

[11] The criterion of risk was less than fully explicit in James's mind because his experience of the richness of the universe and the plurality of its affirmations made him not take more seriously than in principle the prospect of disconfirmation.

from the degree of pretension in supposing that others should follow one's own lead, James's philosophy has to raise serious question about whether others *can* continue one's own research. This appeal to collectivity—an abdication of individual initiative and responsibility more common in all segments of late twentieth-century American culture than in James's time—tends to contradict the requirement for direction and initiative in inquiry, insofar as such direction is more readily, if not exclusively, the fruit of individual search. There is, further, a degree of irresponsibility in so easily assuming that an incompleted inquiry can be completed by others. If valid discoveries derive from energetic, self-initiated inquiry with the full mobilization and investment of self, then others cannot pick up where one leaves off; and one should not leave off undone. Until one achieves the discovery that yields an authentic pay-off, it may not be too much to say that he has done nothing. If the criterion of discovery is in the pragmatic pay-off, there is no criterion for stopping short of the pay-off and no reason to proceed beyond it, at least not along the same line; after the pay-off, it is time to ask new questions and to start a new line.

However, it is not just James's pragmatism, but also his pluralism that has to be invoked against the crude empiricism. To prize the accumulation of facts is to presuppose clearly, if not explicitly or deliberately, a *uni*verse in contrast to James's *pluri*verse. If we as scientists act and talk as though we were slowly putting together the pieces of a jigsaw puzzle, this assumes that the pieces provide one coherent picture that already exists, though diffused, among the pieces and that one day will be fully seen. The promiscuous empiricism assumes, whether it says so or not, that one piece of the jigsaw puzzle is as good as any other; since all are going to fit together eventually, one might as well contribute the piece he has easily at hand, rather than search for one which more obviously fits something.

For James, reality is discerned more fully by the more penetrating investment into experience, not by the accumulation of more experience. Each "piece" of reality is not like the jigsaw fragment that displays only a tiny portion of the design but manifests it obviously to all eyes, needing only to be accumulated with other fragments for the design to be disclosed. Rather, each "piece" of reality is more like the cell that carries in its chemistry and genes the design of the whole body, but only in potential; it needs cultivation and nourishment for the design to become manifest.

The promiscuous empiricist maintains an attitude of passive deference before the data, the same attitude of passive deference one yields to an absolute, for he indeed treats each piece of data as a representative of an absolute; and it is this attitude that James finds preventing scientific discovery. For James the world is not a thing out there to be discovered by pieces, small or big. The world is dynamically responsive to whatever serious inquiry one makes. But unless one initiates serious, directed inquiry, there will be *no* response.

"Objectivism" As Golden Calf

In the same post-Freudian, postwar period that has rediscovered sin in many forms and by many labels—distortion wherever human will is permitted sway—science, especially social science and especially social science exploring material as elusive as religion, has striven mightily to purge human will out of its procedures. This would appall William James, who thought it not only proper but indispensable that inquiry be shaped by human concerns and who scoffed at the pretension that purified rationality could capture an objective "truth," a perception of reality that would be "true" regardless of the perceiver. In our pantheon of golden calves, "objectivism" is the principal figure and "empiricism" only one of its faces. Sometimes the blessing of "objectivism" is invoked to sanction behavior that is largely the result of laziness and cowardice as in the instances of promiscuous empiricism cited previously in which we passively record whatever data are most conveniently at hand, then rationalize our sloth as "objectivity." More often, however, objectivism is more energetically, even fiercely served by us, with a single-minded fidelism as devoted and as constricting as any in the "religious" populations we study. (In James's lexicon, "single-minded" would be a term hardly distinguishable from "mindless.") We are determined, with as fervent a moralism as any we study, to exercise *control,* as we and other moralists both clearly say, lest our own personal concerns surface and affect the outcome to distort, as moralists always see it.

The Protestant ethic is linked with the rise of science no less than with the rise of capitalism. If humanity's capture of the moon is the proud triumph of science and capitalism and, hence, the proud triumph of WASP Middle America (Mailer 1970), then psychology and sociology of religion have been, to a remarkable degree, the enterprise of American Protestants[12] and thus an enterprise putting high value on self-control. *Its* proud triumphs, less spectacular but hardly less profaning than the scientific domestication of the moon, include intricately stratified random samples, scale reliabilities of .90 and more, books full of contingency tables, 100 x 100 correlation matrices, and the extraction of a dozen orthogonal factors, down to eigen values of less than 1.00.

In obeisance to objectivism, reliability is one of our prime offerings. Preoccupation with reliability gives expression to our concern to prove that something is "out there"; if we were more concerned with "what" that "something" was, we would be more concerned with conceptualization and with validity and with careful prediction. The dissertation writer and every other writer of a research report typically goes to far greater pains to demonstrate the reliability of his measures than to any other part of his analysis. This is not without reason, for this is what critics most easily pounce on. During five years as a journal editor I have watched and even contributed to the shaping of manuscripts by the norms of the field. "Greater reliability" or "more information about reliability" is the demand that editorial consultants have most often made, regardless of what other flaws the submitted manuscripts may also have had.

To find that responses are correlated among different items or

---

12 The Protestantism of these fields can be established by any tally of institutions where such courses are taught or by a tally of authors in journals or in textbook bibliographies. It is "remarkable" in light of the fact that psychology, sociology, and the study of religion more generally are decidedly *not* Protestant preserves. The recent transformation of the American Catholic psychological and sociological societies into organizations focused on the psychology and sociology of religion provides the principal exception that proves the rule; these changes are probably best understood as part of the Protestantization, in the present sense, of American Catholicism.

between one time and another gives reassuring evidence that there is something "really" "there." Reliability evidence gives the researcher the right to talk about it which he would not earn by having the conceptualization of "it" clear in his own mind; and indeed the reliability gives him the right to talk about it, whether or not that "it" is clear in his own mind. It is profoundly comforting to our present scientific spirit to find that the "it" is *not* dependent on the particular circumstances of asking the questions or the particular wording of one question or the particular perceptions and expectations of one investigator. For, in our judgment, these particularities harbor vicissitudes and accidents and individual subjective interpretations, and, hence, "error," as we resoundingly dismiss whatever appears only in the individual instance. Reality, for us, is evidenced by regularity and communality and reproducibility and homogeneity, precisely for the reason that these characteristics reassure us that we have kept out of our inquiry the subjective and the individual, which we regard as contaminating instrusion. But it is precisely for this same reason, the exclusion of the individual's subjective involvement, that James regarded these characteristics of regularity and homogeneity as barriers to reality.

It is in our determination to establish interjudge reliability that we most explicitly take the investigator out of the investigation. As we also say in the verbal (but seldom behavioral) honor we accord the norm of reproducibility, only what can be shared and agreed upon is real. Whatever is idiosyncratic and, hence, what is most likely to issue from the interaction between the observed material and observer's own history and expectations, whatever is most functional for him, whatever, James would say, is most likely a clue to truth, that is what we discard as error.

We treat the "response sets" of our subjects as we do our own; we rigorously control their contamination. Might responses be influenced by social desirability or yea-saying or ethnic background or intelligence or by unconscious desires to please or to frustrate the experimenter? Then, by all means, eliminate these influences from the results. Treat them more like excrement than increment, and exercise necessary—or more than necessary— "control." In fact, of course, these "response sets," this evidence of interaction between the research situation and the subjects' history and motives, may be indicators or vehicles of characteristics and behavior actually of crucial importance to the investigation. The "personality" that is measured after discarding such "sets" is a mutilated and unreal personality. Are other variables correlated with social desirability or social class? This may well disclose rather than disguise important insights. This is a point that has been alluded to by one of those who has felt himself in William James's tradition (Allport 1965). The therapist makes a similar point when, tempted to resent the disrupting intrusion of his patient's illness into the very structure of the therapy as resistance and transference, he seizes on this disrupting intrusion as the most illuminating, as well as most accessible, instance of that illness (for example, Dittes 1967).

James would, and did, make the same point more strongly in the case of the investigator's "response sets." To excise the interaction of *his* history and motives with the research materials is to mutilate the investigation and to lose crucial insights.[13] Perhaps the anthropologist has learned the best of the social scientists how to exploit responsibly his personal involvement with the materials, rather than to try to excise it.[14] As a "participant observer" the anthropologist, not unlike the clinical psychologist, may make himself a subject, a special, trained sample of one, available for thorough "interview." Or he may recognize, in contrast to the current popular search for "non-

[13] However, there are limits, even for pragmatist James, as to how much significance and insight can be attributed to the functional relationship between the investigator and his materials. "The 'function' of Titchener's 'scientific' psychology—is to keep the laboratory instruments going and to provide platforms for certain professors. Apart from that it seems to me more unreal than any scholasticism," he noted once. (Letter to Mary W. Calkins, September 19, 1909. Perry 1935, Vol. II:123.)

[14] Correspondingly, during my five-year tenure as editor of the Journal for the Scientific Study of Religion (1967–71), it is my judgment, a judgment I would submit to any jury of the journal's readers, that a roster of the most significant and incisive manuscripts would include a heavy over-representation of those by anthropologists followed closely by historians and clinical psychologists. And, perhaps not irrelevant to the methodological point at issues, the roster of anthropologists includes an over-representation of women, whose reputed talents at internalized, embracing judgments may provide an enviable relief from the superrigorous scientism that, by contrast, resembles desperate efforts to prove virility, even to the point, as suggested above, of promiscuity.

obtrusive'' measures and, again, like the therapist, that he *is* an added variable and that he can use subjects' reactions to him as a special index. Or he may use his own emotional response to another person as a point of entry into understanding the life of that person. For example, if as interviewer he finds himself feeling and behaving extremely protectively toward the interviewee (helping through pauses, rephrasing questions, being reassuring about the quality of the answers, and the like) *this*—his own reactions—may be the best evidence forthcoming as to dependency characteristics of the interviewee, characteristics that may be most relevant to understanding his religiosity. In summary, then, the investigator can use himself in at least three ways: (1) as a fellow-subject, responding to a situation in parallel and presumably representatively, along with other subjects; (2) as a controlled stimulus from which he can gauge and interpret subjects' responses; (3) as a kind of living meter, responding to subjects' responses. All of these ways recognize, rather than deny, that the interaction of researcher and subject is a complex sociopsychological situation and that the complexities can be used to enhance the investigation. Such an intent seems to me to be an expression of William James's spirit.

Erik Erikson, in a study that, perhaps, belongs in the domain of the social scientific study of religion, provides one illustration of the use of himself as an investigative tool. The first quarter of his *Gandhi's Truth* (1969) could be read as a methodological postscript to his book on Luther (1958). In telling how he went about studying Gandhi, it is as though he is making rejoinder to those who criticized the Luther book for lacking historical objectivity. It is as though he is saying, ''All right, I will study a more contemporary figure, so I can interview witnesses firsthand; but their story turns out to be just that, *their* story. I will study archives faithfully; but they turn out to tell mostly about the whims of archivists.'' ''Facts'' are elusive and chimerical. But, by contrast, there is yet an avenue to truth, and it seems to be William James's avenue, as well as Norman Mailer's. So Erikson emphasizes the first person. He narrates the events, trivial and grand, by which Gandhi gradually came to have a hold over his interest. He carefully reports his own reactions as he interviews Gandhi's adversaries and allies as clues to Gandhi's experience with these same people. And he unleashes, in the middle of the book, a blistering "Dear Mahatma" letter, in which his own anger and disappointment with Gandhi unlock and channel the most insightful analysis the book has to offer of Gandhi's personality.

There are some more modest "uses of the person" that still seem consistent with James's spirit and yet may be more acceptable to the contemporary social scientist than the risky Erikson-Mailer model that may seem to threaten loss of control or at least loss of rigor. Two of these invite the investigator to make fuller use of himself in the way he does factor analysis and content analysis; a third invites him to make fuller use of his "subjects."

Factor analysis. There is a conventional schizophrenic charade that is played out in the way that we usually perform and report factor analysis. The situation needs someone like William James to say out loud what we all know: "The emperor has no clothes." Typically, a great amount of highly "subjective" personal intuition, personal wisdom, and personal "looking *for*" goes into the conduct of the factor analysis. What items to include, and even before that, how to write them? What program to use, especially whether to aim for orthogonal or oblique rotation, and whether to go in for second-order factors? Which factors to interpret and which to dismiss as "uninterpretable?" What size loading to use as the cut-off criterion for including items on the factor? And, most notoriously of all: How to label and to interpret the factors? All of these crucial decisions and others[15] require exercise of skill, art, and intuition by the investigator and are, as they should be, governed by what *he* is looking *for*. This is science in the spirit of William James, probably the closest most social scientists get to conducting their craft in this spirit.

But when it comes to displaying our work to colleagues, the

[15] The decision as to the number of factors to extract and the very crucial decision about locating the rotated factors are now more often left to the arbitrary criteria of the computer although in the best factor analytic studies the investigator still exercises his art and wisdom on these decisions as well.

heavy norms of objectivism take over. We disguise our own art, rationalize the decisions, and represent them as subject to totally objective criteria. Whereas our examination of the items and our "looking *for*" certain outcomes has almost always influenced the choice of the floor criterion as to what size factor loadings will be included on a factor, we almost always represent the decision as the reverse; it is part of the conventional charade to write as though a decision about criterion value has been arrived at independently and then has determined the inclusion and exclusion of items on a factor. As strongly as we dare, we write as though the labeling and interpretation of factors were objectively "given" by the distribution of items and their loading, rather than depending at least as much on the particular "bent" of the mind that is doing the interpreting. One important exception to this reporting convention appears in a very influential paper by Morton King (1967), a sociologist who, though—or perhaps because—he is scrupulously rigorous where it counts, apparently does not feel the need to pay false obeisance to objectivism :

> Factor and cluster analyses do not test hypotheses. They merely put data into a form which can be compared to a theoretical model. Since there is no accepted mathematical procedure for making such a comparison, it must be made by the researcher—using his best judgment, maximum objectivity, and familiarity with the data. (King 1967 : 175)

This double standard between the performance and the reporting is by no means dishonest. It is perfectly legitimate to rationalize one's judgments, to see and to show how well they can fit objectively stated criteria. What is to be deplored, from James's point of view, is not so much the objective packaging as the obscuring of what is so packaged. Let this talent and art of the investigator be proudly displayed, partly to give credit where credit is due, partly to enhance the skill with which this art is performed by making it more public and hence more subject to mutual learning and criticism but mostly so that we can better comprehend each one's particular discovery by seeing where he was coming from and where he was aiming. Despite the impression we apparently like to create with those long tables of numbers, there is not, James insists, a fixed, given reality out there, imposing fixed rules of access. But rather the reality is disclosed in the interaction of the searcher's search and the material that responds to his search.

Content analysis.   When an interview or a document or other extended sample of behavior is to be analyzed, this can be done with molecular or with global judgments. The task is to make inferences from discrete and diffuse material to an efficiently few and theoretically relevant set of categories. Most typically, the researcher defines small units (for example, the sentence or the minute) and concrete categories for the judges to sort or rate or score the units by. This makes the judges' task easy, guarantees the maximum reliability (which is what those dissertation readers and manuscript reviewers will be especially looking for), and reserves for the chief investigator (or perhaps for the reader) and usually for the most hurriedly prepared part of the manuscript, the task of extending the inferences from the more concrete categories of judgment to the more abstract categories of interpretation. For example, investigators (Long, Elkind, and Spilka 1967) find it a routine and simple judgment to classify the content of children's prayer ("family" or "pets" are the two examples they give us); reliability is obviously high. But the interpretations they make from arranging these categories by age are rather sweeping (and characteristically occupy less manuscript space than the description of the categories and the process of judgment): "with increasing age the content of prayer became more personal and individualistic, but at the same time less egoistic and self-centered" (1967: 107). We are not really permitted to trace the line of inference from the highly reliable concrete judgments to these profound and subtle interpretations.

On the other hand, the global interpretations can be entrusted in the first place to the judges. Their ability to recognize in the children's words such distinctions as "more personal" or "less egoistic," based on their intuition, experience, training by the investigator and by each other (and specifically not excluding their own personal history with children, with prayer, and with "personal" and "egoistic" attitudes) is probably as reliable and as valid as the authors' inferences of these characteristics from a count of content categories. This is precisely what these same authors did in another part of this study. A global judgment was made on a three-point scale as to the degree of "differentiation and abstraction" with which a child discusses "prayer." The definitions for the three points on the scale help the reader to retrace and to have confidence in the judgment of these categories from the protocols. Reliability among three judges was high, varying between .92 and 1.00 for the statistic that was used. It is also clear that the authors felt able to make more thorough, more careful, and more illuminating analysis of these data, a fact not unrelated, I would surmise, to the fact that these data included the richness of the more global, more personally demanding judgments.

Scales.   The same principle applies in the construction of questionnaires for subjects as in the construction of rating scales for judges. Will the respondent be asked to report—highly reliably, of course—concrete details (church attendance, belief in afterlife) from which the researcher will infer "religiousness" or "orthodoxy?" Or is it possible that the respondents' definition of "religious" and their ability to estimate it can be relied on at least as well as the investigator's inferences from his contrived measures? As good a way as any estimating a person's religiousness may be to ask him. (As in Allen and Spilka 1967, in which a single self-report item—suitably masked by calling it a religious identity scale—yielded results equivalent to those of several more elaborate measures.)

There is a kind of tyranny, which offends James's spirit, in one person (the survey researcher and psychometrist) providing the language (the scale items and response categories) with which another person (the respondent) must express himself. James's objection, we should be clear, is not a tender-minded, humanistic complaint about the intrusion of science into depths beyond the reach of science, nor is it a worry about invasion of privacy. His is tough-minded scientific concern for validity. The imposition of one mind on another is a barrier to truth, in whatever guise that imposition takes place. Validity is enhanced—James's pluralism—by finding ways to encourage the expression of others' distinctive views and is enfeebled by relying on a single view. Validity is enhanced—James's pragmatism—by relying on the formulations of those most invested and most earnestly searching, those in an "acute fever" (VRE: 8), and is enfeebled by relying on the formulations of those whose knowledge and experience of religion is "secondhand" (VRE: 8). Since the social scientist's experience of religion is most typically of this "secondhand" type or perhaps the lingering memories of childhood experience or adolescent aspirations and antagonisms, his formulation of the parameters of religion is hardly to be most trusted by James.[16]

The reply (for example, Pahnke and Richards 1963, or Glock and Stark 1966: 4) that respondents *do* answer the questions quite misses the point here being raised. The check marks, or their verbal equivalents, are the respondents', which means that people are willing and able to accommodate themselves to any stimulus material. But the words are the investigators' and reflect *their* view of what "mysticism" or "orthodoxy," for example, ought to mean to the respondents. We simply do not know how the respondents would express their own "mysticism" or "orthodoxy" nor whether the degree of "mysticism" or "orthodoxy," as the respondents might express it, is even correlated with their responses to the investigator's items.

Between the extreme of simply asking the respondent to report on his "religiousness," or "orthodoxy," or "mysticism," and the extreme of providing the social scientist's own Procrustean terms with which to report, there is another procedure, which seems to be more in the spirit of William James than not. If

---

[16] Social scientists *do* develop "acute fever," of course, and engage in earnest search, but not often in pursuit of orthodoxy and salvation. Fevered search develops in pursuit of scientific hypotheses and categories. This is as it should be, according to James, who presumably would encourage the scientist's hot pursuit, even to the point of generating items and scales. But this is different from providing language with which to measure more phenomenologically derived descriptive categories. So, the researcher who has conceptualized a variable, such as dogmatism, and who wants to detect and understand it, ought to be encouraged, it would seem to follow from James, to devise scales or other methods for giving expression to *his* conception. But this is different from writing items to measure what is lodged in the conceptions and the searching of the respondent, such as his "orthodoxy." That can be known best by finding ways for him to give expression to his own searching.

there are to be items and scales measuring belief or religiousness, at least they can be generated by those who hold the belief and practice the religion. This is the procedure followed, for example, by Monaghan (1967), Spilka, Armatas, and Nussbaum (1964), Vergote (1969), and Yinger (1969). They have, in effect, invited the subjects to be collaborators in developing the measurements. They have shared with the subjects the concept(s) to be assessed and have invited them to suggest and to criticize items. A variant of this procedure, one used, for example, by Gray (1970) and by Sommerfeld (1968) is to go to the official documents of a religious tradition; these may still be the repository of some "acute fever," probably more than the social scientist can muster at any rate. The outcome of such procedure has to be one of greater validity, whether by Jamesian criteria, or any other.

Generalizability As Golden Calf

In a great many research reports, perhaps a majority, the first table of data does not tell us any of the results of the study but instead tells us about the characteristics of the sample. The size of the sample and its representativeness are paraded and carefully documented. So are the procedures—randomization, stratification, solicitation, follow-up (sometimes complete with an appendix of the enticing letters that have been used to recruit cooperation)—by which the large and representative sample has been achieved. There is an important audience for this information, for the adequacy of the sample becomes the most visible and most vulnerable criterion for the adequacy of the research. Rules are clear and generally well-accepted for what makes a good sample, more so than for what makes good research in other respects. So critics—whether dissertation readers, manuscript reviewers, journal editors, authors of reviews and surveys, fellow researchers—fasten on these rules; and research is more often accepted or dismissed for adequacy of sample (judging chiefly by my experience as a journal editor reading consultants' critiques) than on any other grounds.

The importance we have come to attach to large and representative samples and to the techniques for getting them partly reflects the appeal of objectivism. The advanced technology of sampling gives us a reassuring sense of control against "bias," as we say in connection with samples, a sense that we are detecting something that is "really" "there."

The drawing of good samples also reflects something of what was described earlier as "promiscuous empiricism," the collection of data that are most easily available, rather than data that are sought out to be most suited to particular purposes of the investigator. This may seem an unfair assertion, since adequate samples are intended precisely to overcome such promiscuity as the distribution of the instrument to whatever sophomore psychology class or church organization is most conveniently at hand. But from the point of view of James, whose typical samples were individuals selected precisely for their important peculiarities, careful random sampling techniques can still be a serious cop-out; the researcher is still accepting a sample that is most easily available to him—accepting the going standards of size and representativeness and the technology for achieving these—when he does not have any more theoretically incisive basis for constructing a sample that will yield the most decisive and interpretable results.

The principal appeal of good samples, however, is precisely that we are after highly general conclusions. We want results, in our research or others', that can be generalized to the widest possible population across differences of age, sex, social class, intelligence, personality, denomination, region; even, so far as possible, across differences of nationality and culture; across any other peculiar differences that might be associated with sample selection or response rate. Social science and, perhaps especially, a still struggling social science such as is the study of religion unambiguously accords highest status to concepts and to empirical results of the highest possible generality.

James, if he were willing to marshal some Freudian perspectives (and there is no reason to think that he wouldn't, if he could *use* them) might find something profoundly self-defeating, even self-abusive, in the urge for generalization. For in giving expression to this urge, social science repudiates what it knows best; it renounces all those sources of variance that it is best equipped, even mandated, to study. There is a curious kind of identity-burying, even suicidal streak in social science in the tendency, as soon as a source of variance is established, to relegate it to the category of variables to be *controlled* for, rather than to hold it up for further study and reflection. One is reminded of the puritan, of whatever denomination or era or discipline saying: ''Whatever is lively and exciting and has an influence, overcome it, neutralize it, deny it.'' As with the ''response sets'' discussed earlier, these established sources of variability are very easily dismissed as contaminators rather than conveyors, as disguisers rather than disclosers of important effects. Their defect seems to be their particularity, the limits they set on generalization.

This appeal to consider differences between groups (James would press even more for considering differences between individuals) as an important effect to be welcomed and studied, not obscured and controlled, is one way of giving expression to James's pluralism, his conviction that reality is more truly seen in its diversity than in the search for oneness. But James's point needs to be made still more radically. To study variance among denominations, for example, is still a task of high generality, covering many denominations, usually with the implication that results are generalizable to all denominational differences. Would the social scientist ever do better to study only one denomination, one age group, one social class; would he be better off accepting a low response rate because he wants to study only those most motivated to respond? Does the search for generalization, even for comparison across groups, obscure important effects that can be discerned only within a particular group? James would insist so, invoking not only his conviction about the pluralism of reality and the apprehension of reality only in particularity and diversity, but also the views we have summarized here as pragmatism. If something is so only to the degree that it is serving functions, responding to active search, then we ought to look for that something, if not only among those with the ''acute fever'' James admired, then at least among those with a little warm interest. And the researcher also might be encouraged to have at least enough ''warm interest,'' if not more energetically directed search, to select the sample appropriate for his study. The sample, like all other elements of the research, must work *for* him. One can hardly study the dimensions of religiosity among nonreligious persons or the structure and functions of beliefs among nonbelievers. Yet researchers try, dutifully including everyone who turns up in a random sample of the population and dutifully trying to build up the response rate; whereas a purposive selection from the sample, including the self-selection of immediate responders, may give a much more appropriate sample for the study at hand. There is not only James's philosophic argument that to study what is common is to lose out on what is significant. There is also clear empirical evidence that the more comprehensive, heterogeneous sample in some cases washes out significant effects (Bahr, Bartel, and Chadwick 1971, Barton 1971: 839, Dittes 1967, 1969, Maranell 1971) and that some research is more likely to yield results when samples are restricted to the greater homogeneity of a single denomination or even a relatively low response rate (for example, Feagin 1963, King 1967, Campbell and Fukuyama 1970).

The trouble is that we have been made so fiercely aware of the real bias that *is* introduced when our sample is limited in a way *irrelevant* to our hypothesis (for example, a college student population to test hypotheses appropriate for much less sophisticated and less wary population) that we have overreacted with an addiction to generalizability and find a great deal of difficulty bringing ourselves to select or acknowledge limited samples which are distinctively *relevant*. Thus, a researcher whose purpose is essentially to replicate previous studies (for example, Finner 1970) still finds himself apologizing that his sample shares the same limitations as those he is replicating, although for his purposes this is a distinct virtue. Thus, many studies of "projection" of paternal characteristics onto God have overlooked the necessary condition that theories of projection imply persons clearly possessed of motives provoking projection, and they have proceeded with their broad, unselected samples.

Not to know what characteristics of a population are appropriate to select is not to know clearly or urgently enough the questions one is addressing to his research. To concentrate on mechanical processes of selecting a sample, processes that claim for a virtue only greater generalizability of "answers," is to avoid being clear about the questions. And this posture—being an "answer person" without being an earnest inquirer—is as good a way as any to identify the characteristics of the contemporary social scientist that separate him from the spirit of William James.

BIBLIOGRAPHY

Allen, Russell O., and Spilka, Bernard
    1967   Committed and Consensual Religion: A Specification of Religion-Prejudice Relationships. *Journal for the Scientific Study of Religion* 6: 191–206.

Allport, Gordon W.
    1961   Introduction. *Psychology: The Briefer Course by William James.* New York: Harper & Row.
    1966   The Religious Context of Prejudice. *Journal for the Scientific Study of Religion* 5: 447–57.
————, and Ross, Michael J.
    1967   Personal Religious Orientation and Prejudice. *Journal of Personality and Social Psychology* 5: 432–43.

Bahr, Howard M., Bartel, Lois Franz, and Chadwick, Bruce A.
    1971   Orthodoxy, Activism, and the Salience of Religion. *Journal for the Scientific Study of Religion* 10: 69–75.

Barton, Allen H.
    1971   Selected Problems in the Study of Religious Development. In Merton P. Strommen, ed. *Research on Religious Development: A Comprehensive Handbook.* New York: Hawthorn Books, Inc.

Bellah, Robert N.
    1970   Confessions of a Former Establishment Fundamentalist. *Bulletin of the Council on the Study of Religion* Vol. 1, no. 3, pp. 3–6.

Berger, Peter L.
    1967   A Sociological View of the Secularization of Theology. *Journal for the Scientific Study of Religion* 6: 3–16.

Boring, Edwin G.
    1950   *A History of Experimental Psychology.* 2d ed. New York: Appleton-Century-Crofts.

Campbell, Thomas C., and Fukuyama, Yoshio
    1970   *The Fragmented Layman: An Empirical Study of Lay Attitudes.* Philadelphia: Pilgrim Press.

Clark, Walter Houston
    1958   *The Psychology of Religion.* New York: Macmillan.

Clayton, Richard R.
    1971   5-D or 1? *Journal for the Scientific Study of Religion* 10:
            37–40.

Dittes, James E.
    1967   *The Church in the Way.* New York: Scribner.
    1969   Psychology of Religion. In *Handbook of Social Psychology.*
            Vol. 5. Gardner Lindzey and Eliot Aronson, ed. Reading, Pa.:
            Addison-Wesley.

Eisenhower, Dwight D.
    1967   *At Ease: Stories I Tell My Friends.* Garden City, N.Y.:
            Doubleday.

Eister, Allan W.
    1967   Toward a Radical Critique of Church-Sect Typologizing.
            Journal for the Scientific Study of Religion 6: 85–90.

Erikson, Erik H.
    1958   *Young Man Luther: A Study in Psychoanalysis and History.*
            New York: Norton.
    1969   *Gandhi's Truth: On the Origins of Militant Nonviolence.*
            New York: Norton.

Faulkner, Joseph, and DeJong, Gordon
    1966   Religiosity in 5-D: An Empirical Analysis. *Social Forces* 45:
            246–54.

Feagin, Joe R.
    1964   Prejudice and Religious Types: A Focused Study of South-
            ern Fundamentalists. *Journal for the Scientific Study of
            Religion* 4: 3–13.

Finner, Stephen L.
    1970   Religious Membership and Religious Preference: Equal In-
            dicators of Religiosity? *Journal for the Scientific Study of
            Religion* 9: 273–79.

Glock, Charles Y., and Stark, Rodney
    1966   *Christian Beliefs and Anti-Semitism.* New York: Harper &
            Row.

Gray, David B.
    1970   Measuring Attitudes toward the Church. *Journal for the
            Scientific Study of Religion* 9: 293–97.

Gustafscn, Paul M.
    1967   UO-US-PS-PO: A Restatement of Troeltsch's Church-Sect
            Typology. *Journal for the Scientific Study of Religion* 6:
            64–68.

Havens, Joseph, ed.
    1968   *Psychology and Religion: A Contemporary Dialogue.* Prince-
            ton, N.J.: D. Van Nostrand.

Hunt, Richard A.
    1968   The Interpretation of the Religious Scale of the Allport-
            Vernon-Lindzey Study of Values. *Journal for the Scientific
            Study of Religion* 7: 65–77.
    ———, and King, Morton
    1971   The Intrinsic-Extrinsic Concept: A Review and Evaluation.
            Journal for the Scientific Study of Religion 10:339–56.

James, Henry, ed.
    1920   *Letters of William James.* 2 vols. Boston: Atlantic Monthly
            Press.

James, William
    1890   *The Principles of Psychology.* 2 vols. New York: Henry
            Holt.
    1902   *The Varieties of Religious Experience: A Study in Human
            Nature.* New York and London: Longmans, Green. New
            York: Random House Modern Library.

Johnson, Benton
    1957   A Critical Appraisal of the Church-Sect Typology. *Ameri-
            can Sociological Review* 22: 88–92.
    1971   Church and Sect Revisited. *Journal for the Scientific Study
            of Religion* 10: 124–37.

King, Morton
    1967   Measuring the Religious Variable: Nine Proposed Dimen-
            sions. *Journal for the Scientific Study of Religion* 6: 173–85.

Knight, Margaret
    1950   *William James.* Hammondsworth: Penguin Books.

Long, Diane, Elkind, David, and Spilka, Bernard
    1967   The Child's Conception of Prayer. *Journal for the Scientific
            Study of Religion* 6: 101–9.

Mailer, Norman
    1970   *Of a Fire on the Moon.* Boston: Little, Brown and Company.

Maranell, Gary M., and Razak, W. Nevell
  1970   A Comparative Study of the Factor Structure among Professors and Clergymen. *Journal for the Scientific Study of Religion* 9: 137–41.

Moberg, David O., ed.
  1971   *International Directory of Religious Information Systems.* Milwaukee, Wis.: Department of Sociology and Anthropology, Marquette University.

Monaghan, Robert R.
  1967   Three Faces of the True Believer: Motivations for Attending a Fundamentalist Church. *Journal for the Scientific Study of Religion* 6: 236–45.

Nash, Dennison, and Berger, Peter
  1962   The Child, the Family, and the "Religious Revival" in Suburbia. *Journal for the Scientific Study of Religion* 2: 85–93.

Pahnke, Walter N., and Richards, William A.
  1966   Implications of LSD and Experimental Mysticism. *Journal of Religion and Health* 5: 175–208.

Perry, Ralph Barton
  1935   *The Thought and Character of William James.* 2 vols. Boston: Little, Brown.
  1938   *In the Spirit of William James.* New Haven, Conn.: Yale University Press.
  1948   *The Thought and Character of William James.* Briefer Ver-
  1964   sion. Cambridge, Mass.: Harvard University Press. New York: Harper & Row.

Pruyser, Paul W.
  1969   *A Dynamic Psychology of Religion.* New York: Harper & Row.

Smith, John
  1967   William James as Philosophical Psychologist. 75th Anniversary Address for the Division of Philosophical Psychology. American Psychological Association, Washington, September 3, 1967.

Spilka, Bernard, Armatas, J., and Nussbaum, June
  1964   The Concept of God: A Factor-Analytic Approach. *Review of Religious Research* 6: 28–36.

Sommerfeld, Richard
   1968   Conceptions of the Ultimate and the Social Organization of
           Religious Bodies. *Journal for the Scientific Study of Religion*
           7: 178–96.

Uren, A. Rudolph
   1928   *Recent Religious Psychology: A Study in the Psychology of
           Religion.* New York: Scribner.

Vergote, Antoine
   1969   Concept of God and Parental Images. *Journal for the Scien-
           tific Study of Religion* 8: 72–78.

Yinger, Milton
   1969   A Structural Examination of Religion. *Journal for the Sci-
           entific Study of Religion* 8: 88–99.

8 H. RICHARD NIEBUHR AND THE PARADOX OF RELIGIOUS ORGANIZATION: A RADICAL CRITIQUE*

Allan W. Eister

A "classic work" in any field, generally speaking, seems to be one that is referred to frequently in subsequent work or that sets a direction of investigation, establishes a vocabulary, or proposes a style or framework of interpretation which other scholars accept and follow. By any or all of these criteria, H. Richard Niebuhr's *Social Sources of Denominationalism* (1929) qualifies as a classic work in Christian ethics and in the theological study of the Christian church in its social contexts. By the same token it would seem also to qualify as a classic in what continues to be called, rather loosely, the sociology of religion.

Niebuhr, however, was not a sociologist, either by training or by intent. His appointment at Yale was to a chair of Christian ethics in a leading Protestant theological seminary; and *The Social Sources of Denominationalism* was not, as he himself was the first to acknowledge in the preface (1929: vi) a social science monograph.

For these and other reasons which should become apparent as we proceed, any attempt to assess the value of Niebuhr's work for the social scientific study of religion inevitably raises sets of

* I wish to express my thanks to the several scholars who have read an earlier version of this paper and given me the benefit of their criticism and comment: Bryan R. Wilson, James Gustafson, Reed Whitley, Benton Johnson, Samuel Mueller, Dunbar Moodie, and Robert Towler.

problems concerning the applicability of his concepts, the transferability of interpretations from one discipline to another, unrecognized biases, and related questions which must be given attention before one can hope to arrive at any judgment about the worth of his contribution to the scientific study of religion or, indeed, about what exactly the nature of that contribution was.

However "sociological" Niebuhr hoped or intended to be in his analyses, it is reasonably clear from the context of his writing that religious organizations—particularly the Christian church—must be, for him, more or other than merely subjects for detached observation and study. Primarily, he was a churchman and a theologican.

But even if his theologically slanted insights and purposes are called into question (as they have been in some measure, for example, by Charles Y. Glock and Rodney Stark [1965:152n] or by N. J. Demerath III [1965: 152n, 186n]) his work might still not be faulted on that score alone since, as it seems clear, many views attributed to Niebuhr by other scholars were not, in fact, taken as he intended them to be taken or understood within the same framework of assumptions in which he himself worked. The latter problem seems to inhere in any attempt to interpret the work of any scholar from the perspective of another discipline. And it may well be magnified in any attempt to evaluate that work.

Despite the hazards of possible misinterpretation, however, the central problem to which I would like to direct attention in this paper is whether or not Richard Niebuhr's analysis of the relationship between religious organization and societal structure (or selected aspects of it) and the concepts which he used are appropriate or reliable guides for sociological or for more general social scientific investigation of religion in society today. Indirectly and by extension, since Niebuhr drew heavily on the work of Ernst Troeltsch, concepts and interpretations of the latter will also need to be considered here.

Without doubt, Niebuhr's work, and especially *The Social Sources,* which was published in 1929, has had a marked and important influence on the thinking of Americans who have written on the sociology of religion whether as recognized sociol-

ogists or as students of what has often been more aptly called
"religious sociology."

Among sociologists Howard Becker (1932: 624–28) and several of his students, notably in this connection J. Milton Yinger
(1946: 27ff) acknowledged debts to H. Richard Niebuhr; and
virtually every textbook or general treatise in American sociology of religion gives attention to Niebuhr's sect-to-church hypothesis or to other of his ideas about how economic, political,
and other social structures and interests shape the institutional
expression of Christianity. (Although *The Social Sources* seems
to be widely known among European scholars, it is much less
frequently cited there, judging from a rapid survey of recent
publications, for example, Matthes 1965, 1969: 54, Schneider
1962, Laeyendecker 1967: 106ff, W. Stark 1967, Wilson 1959:
3–15, 1967, Isichei 1964, Martin 1962.)

Similarly, in more empirically-oriented sociological research,
one discerns in the work of Russell R. Dynes (1954, 1955) or
Benton Johnson (1953, 1957), for example, conceptions of religious organization deriving from Niebuhr or from Troeltsch.

More directly, Liston Pope's *Millhands and Preachers* (1942,
see also 1948) (originally presented as a Ph.D. dissertation in
religion at Yale) and numerous other studies produced by
seminarians and other scholars in the fields of Christian ethics
and theology bear the imprint of Niebuhr's thought (Muelder
1945, Douglas 1945: 89ff, Mead 1954: 300ff, Whitley 1955, 1959,
Shippey 1958, Lee 1960a, 1960b, Marty 1959, 1960).

Both the way relationships between church and society in the
United States have been perceived and the problems for investigation which grew out of this perspective reflect wide awareness
of *The Social Sources of Denominationalism*.[1] Even where a
scholar so thoroughly grounded in empirical details about given

---

[1] References to Niebuhr's ideas range widely from direct, explicit citations
to specific statements he made about sect or church "characteristics" (or
about the "sect-to-church process") to what can only be inferred as responses to interpretations of religious organization shaped by Troeltsch and
by Niebuhr. Thus, for example,

Reed (1943), Goldschmidt (1933), Clark (1945, 1946, 1948), Eister
(1950), O'Dea (1954), Berger (1954, 1958), Hoult (1958: 83), Stanley
(1958), Moberg (1960, 1961, 1962), Vernon (1960), Demerath (1961),
Vallier (1963), Scanzoni (1965), Glock and Stark (1965), Steinberg
(1965), Glock, Ringer, Babbie (1967).

sects as is Bryan R. Wilson (1961, 1966) takes issue with one or
more of Niebuhr's specific characterizations of "the sect," a
standard base of reference is apt to be *The Social Sources*.[2]

Clearly, to try to assess Niebuhr's work in relation to the still
emerging theoretical and methodological framework for the scientific study of religion or even to clarify, or report accurately,
the aims which he set for himself and his fellow theologians is a
somewhat delicate task for one who has not formally studied
Christian ethics nor been in close or direct contact with Christian theology, particularly as it bears on problems of locating
and preserving the "Christian character" or purposes of nomi-
nally Christian religious organizations. The same or approximately the same problems, one might add, appear with respect to
the work of Ernst Troeltsch. However, since Niebuhr, like
Troeltsch, has had and continues to have such impact on the
sociology of religion that his work cannot be ignored, the task is
one that has to be undertaken with whatever training a social
scientist has.

To approach Richard Niebuhr's work in this spirit—to ask, in
effect, whether or not sociologists *can* follow his lead (or indeed
that of any other committed Christian student of the church and
society) without running the risk of abridging certain canons of
scientific investigation—may appear to be a very negative way of
going about the matter. It may have the advantage, however, of
bringing issues more sharply and more directly into focus.

The thesis, among others, that will be argued here is that
neither Niebuhr nor Troeltsch has supplied social scientists with
the kinds of conceptualizations of religious organization that
social science requires and that Max Weber's conceptions of the
nature and basis of religious organization (and of the dynamics
of religious organization) are both more suitable and more
appropriate for social scientific use than those advanced by
Niebuhr and by Troeltsch.

Before pressing the argument further by trying to identify
what the canons of scientific inquiry are as they apply to the
study of religion, we should perhaps first try to establish what it

---

[2] A significant exception to the general statement in this sentence is found
in Paul M. Harrison (1959), where the prime reference is not to *The Social
Sources* but to Niebuhr (1956).

was that Niebuhr sought to accomplish, what he himself had to say about his own hopes and purposes. Probably the best expressions of these latter are found not in *The Social Sources of Denominationalism*, which was his first book, but rather in his later writing. Particularly clear and forthright statements are found, for example, in his essays in *The Church Against the World* (1935) and in *The Kingdom of God in America* (1937).[3] In the preface to the latter he commented specifically on what he had tried to do in his first book:

> In . . . *The Social Sources of Denominationalism,* I sought to discover the nature of the relation of religion to culture and to throw light on the complexity of American Christianity by examining the influence of social forces on faith and by tracing the sociological pattern of race, class and sectional interests as it manifested itself in the denominations. The account left me dissatisfied at a number of points. Though the sociological approach helped to explain why the religious stream flowed in these particular channels it did not account for the force of the stream itself; while it seemed relevant enough to the institutionalized churches it did not explain the Christian movement which produced these churches; while it accounted for the diversity in American religion it did not explain the unity which our faith possessed despite its variety; while it could deal with the religion which was dependent on culture it left unexplained the faith which is independent, which is aggressive rather than passive, and which molds culture instead of being molded by it. (Niebuhr 1937)

This is a frank expression of what was primarily a believer's concern for the place which religion, and particularly a faith which he himself avowed, occupied in a society and culture of which he was also a part. The "sociological analysis" to which he referred was being used, and Niebuhr undoubtedly thought properly so, in the service of other purposes than the deliberately detached, neutral description of "religion in society" to which social scientists like Max Weber and most sociologists in the

---

[3] I am reminded by Professor James Gustafson who worked closely with Richard Niebuhr as a colleague at Yale Divinity School that Niebuhr's views underwent considerable change in the period between the writing of *The Social Sources* and these later books. These changes were affected both by what Niebuhr observed of the turmoil through which the German church was passing, particularly in the early 1930s and by his own and his responses to others' developing insights. Such changes might, of course, alter considerably his ability to recall in retrospect what all of his original objectives may have been.

tradition of Durkheim and the major American training centers in sociology felt professionally obliged to confine themselves. A knowledgeable social scientist will detect in Niebuhr's statement connotations in the words "culture," "social forces," "explanation" which reflect an orientation quite distinct from those ordinarily intended or implied in scientific usage.

In *The Church against the World* (1935: 1) Niebuhr had been even more explicit in identifying his primary loyalties and the purposes to which his sociological analyses were to be put: "The point of view is from within the church . . . [of one who] having been convinced of the truth of the gospel, knows no life apart from it."[4] Further, he saw his church as menaced by a flood of circumstances which were threatening to engulf it and which he hoped in some measure to combat: "We live . . . in a time . . . when the church is imperiled not only by external worldliness but by one that has established itself within the Christian camp" (Niebuhr 1935: 1).

It was already apparent from the opening chapter in *The Social Sources*, which Niebuhr had entitled *The Ethical Failure of the Divided Church*, that he was intending something more or other than a merely descriptive-historical account of the reasons for structural separation within the Christian church in the United States or a disinterested sociological analysis of the process. Passages in this and subsequent chapters almost resound with the ringing and severe judgments of an Old Testament prophet. For Niebuhr, a divided church was utterly *wrong;* and "denominationalism," that is, separate organizations, whether in the form of churches or of sects or other, was iniquitous and plainly contrary to the spirit or will of God as expressed in the gospels. Worse still, the fault or sin of a divided church was seldom admitted to—indeed, scarcely even *recognized*—by many Christian Americans. Thus:

> Denominationalism in the Christian church is . . . an unacknowledged hypocrisy. It is a compromise, made far too lightly, between Christianity and the world. Yet it often regards itself as a Christian achievement and glorifies its martyrs. . . . It represents the accom-

[4] Later (Niebuhr 1935: 154) wrote, "The dependence of man upon God and the orientation of man's work to God's work require that *theology must take the place of the psychology and sociology* [of religion] which were the proper sciences of a Christianity which was dependent on the spirit of man."

modation of Christianity to the caste-system of human society. It carries over into the organization of the Christian principle of brotherhood the prides and prejudices, the privilege and prestige, as well as the humiliations and abasements, the injustices and inequalities of that specious order of high and low wherein men find the satisfaction of their craving for vainglory. The division of the churches closely follows the division of men into the castes of national, racial and economic groups. It draws the color line in the church of God; it fosters . . . misunderstandings . . . self-exaltations, the hatreds of jingoistic nationalism . . . the spurious differences of provincial loyalties [and] seats the rich and poor apart at the table of the Lord. (Niebuhr 1929 : 6)

To begin with, then, denominations and denominationalism were to be viewed pejoratively as expressions of failure in Christian religious organization. Beyond this Niebuhr seems not to have been particularly concerned about the *defining characteristics* of denominations as such or about the way they were to be distinguished from churches on one hand and sects on the other. Throughout *The Social Sources,* denomination and church (except when Niebuhr was referring to the Church of Christ) were used interchangeably. It was enough that they were fragments of what, in his opinion, should have been, at least in spirit, an undivided whole, and what he was attempting to do was to locate the social sources of *division.* More than this, he was writing to alert fellow Christians to the anti-Christian character of their disunity and to pursuade them that such a situation was intolerable if they intended to take their faith seriously.

It is not clear from what he wrote, however, whether in speaking of denominationalism he was using the word to refer to the separate and more or less autonomous *structures* into which the Christian church was organized or whether he was referring primarily to *attitudes* of pride—in class, race, ethnic group, nation, or region—which he saw as supporting division. Much of both, he felt, stemmed as much from unawareness or blindness on the part of nominal Christians to their failures as it did from deliberate intent; much of it was the unconscious product of structural forces or conditions in society at large. His task, as he saw it, was to expose these conditions and challenge his fellow churchmen—clergy and laity together—to corrective action.

But there were basic difficulties which needed to be understood, and it was to his theological understanding that he turned for the kind of interpretation and explanation that was, to him, most important.

Without some knowledge and appreciation of this the social scientist who tries to "borrow" from Niebuhr is not only apt to misunderstand much of what he wrote but to distort his interpretations in the process. On the same grounds, however, Niebuhr's concepts, if not his enterprise as a whole, require of social scientists implicit value judgments which it is not proper or possible for them to make *as social scientists,* and it may commit them to goals or purposes which could conflict with their purposes as social scientists.

Theologically, the root problem seemed to Niebuhr to lie in the fact that the Christian gospel, Christian faith, and Christian ethics exist as radically alien in a world of which they are not a "natural" part. Paradoxically, they can exist *only* in this state. Necessarily, if Christianity is to become "real" in the world or have any relevance to it, it *must* be embodied in some kind of "sociological" or "organized" form. But in the process of becoming organized, it takes on characteristics of "the world" which reflect the nature of that world, which is invariably "corrupting" in its influence. The result, inevitably, without divine intervention is a sinful, "compromised" expression of the faith.

Described somewhat differently, the situation is one in which pure, perfect, ineluctable spiritual phenomena are given institutional or organizational embodiment or structuring which violate or deny in some measure what is "true," "good," or essential about faith. Ultimately, if I understand Niebuhr's position, this is the basis of "compromise" although there are many more expressions of human compromise, deliberate or otherwise, besides this irreducible and "necessary" form of it. It is not clear from Niebuhr's usage of the word how much he meant to regard as the unchosen product of unrelenting necessity, that is, of "requirements of the situation" over which the actors could not be said to have control (and for which they could not be held responsible theologically) and how much chosen by human beings acting consciously in pursuit of various private or "worldly" divisive interests. But the concept of *compromise* is central to the framework of his interpretation of religious organization.[5]

At this point we might deviate briefly to take note of Ernst Troeltsch's quite different conception of compromise in Christian religious organizations. Very briefly, he had identified three patterns or "principles" of organization or association within the Christian tradition—the churchly, the sectarian, and the mystic. Each of these "sociological types" was governed by its own conception of Christian imperatives; all were "legitimately Christian," and the three patterns were *alternatives,* not necessarily developmentally related in the sense in which Niebuhr saw "the church" as an "outgrowth" of the sect.

For Troeltsch (1931: 335) the "church type" was that kind of Christian organization which seeks to bring as many souls as possible to salvation—to "conquer the world for Christ"—by gaining maximum organizational strength and power and then moving to fasten Christian values upon "the world" in order to "cover the whole life of humanity." By contrast, the sect and the mystics are not interested in the salvation of society or in gaining power or influence in it. To "the world" and its fate most sectarians, presumably, would be indifferent. Theirs was rather a more single-minded kind of determination to try to live up to the ethics of Jesus as their various sect leaders understood and interpreted these. Mystics, finally, stood one step further

---

[5] Several readers have suggested that I am reading too much into the word "compromise" in suggesting that Niebuhr and those who used the concept as he did were, in fact, caught up in a peculiarly *Christian* conception of it and that using it from the standpoint of a Christian's understanding of Christian ethics is not different from using it without such "inside" insight; or, to put it otherwise, that an "outsider" can as readily identify and describe compromise of Christian ethics as an "insider." I do not agree that this was the case, at least with respect to Niebuhr or to Troeltsch. I do feel obliged to record their views that compromise, even as Niebuhr used it, was a neutral term, denoting only a degree or measure of deviance from a norm which is "publicly accessible"—readily understandable and capable of being described by anyone. Compromise in this sense would be a matter of "obvious" discrepancy or of logical inconsistency or of "goal displacement" and nothing more. I do not believe that this *was* all that Niebuhr had in mind or that his conception was so devoid of implicit "loading" as those who have insisted that it is have been willing to recognize. Further evidence, incidentally, of the peculiarly theological and Christian character of compromise as *Troeltsch* used it can be found in the latter's concluding statement to *The Social Teaching of the Christian Churches* (1931: 999–1000).

along in the degree of their detachment from the world, their primary goal being to achieve or try to maintain a sense of union with God. Ideal-typically they did not or could not care whether their lives were models of ethical perfection, much less whether the world could be saved. In each case Troeltsch assumed that, within broad limits, a choice of "organizational principle" was open. Both church and sect types as well as the mystical principle, Troeltsch emphasized, had existed in the primitive church, one in the tradition of Paul the other in the tradition of Jesus, and *both* were, to him, legitimate "organizational expressions" of Christianity. Historical circumstances, combined with a broad and ambitious sense of mission on one hand and a wide range of sociological and psychological processes and motivations on the other, produced the medieval "universal church," but the "sect principle" even then was never lost.

In any event the "compromise" of which Troeltsch spoke was always a "church type" response, not, as for Niebuhr, a response of which sects *might* be equally capable. Compromise for Troeltsch was primarily a matter of weighing gains against costs which *churches* engaged in, in principle at least, in the ultimate service of Christian and spiritual ends. With Niebuhr, as we have seen, compromise was something more devastating; it was a condition inescapably imposed upon *all* Christian religious organizations to the extent that they were organized, and it was always deleterious and detrimental.

At first Niebuhr seems to have accepted Troeltsch's view that the compromises which Christians were making were largely a matter of choice, though he wrote with less tolerance of the church. Thus, for example,

> Christendom has often achieved apparent success by ignoring the precepts of its founder. The church, as an organization interested in self-preservation and in the gain of power, has sometimes found the counsel of the Cross quite inexpedient as have national and economic groups. In dealing with such major social evils as war, slavery and social inequality, it has discovered convenient ambiguities in the letter of the Gospels which enable it to violate their spirit and to ally itself with the prestige and power those evils had gained in their corporate organizations. (Niebuhr 1929: 33)[6]

[6] The "analogous insight" to which I refer is Herbert J. Muller's (1952) thesis that civilizations have invariably failed because of the impossibility of realizing in their social structures the central values to which they are presumably committed. See esp. pp. vii–ix.

These are the opening sentences of *The Social Sources,* and they seem to set the tone for subsequent analysis and interpretation. On the following page, however, there is an arresting statement which seems to reject, if not deny the imputation that "ethical failure" is the result of deliberately chosen compromise and to look for the explanation elsewhere. Indeed, it has very much more the quality of the "tragic flaw" concept in Greek drama, suggesting that Niebuhr was aware of other and perhaps more profound difficulties standing in the way of the realization of Christian ethics or of the Christian spirit in "the world":

> No idea can be incorporated without the loss of some of its ideal character. When liberty gains a constitution, liberty is compromised; when fraternity elects officers, fraternity yields some of the ideal qualities of brotherhood to the necessities of government. And the gospel of Christ is especially subject to this sacrifice of character in the interest of organic embodiment, for the essence of Christianity lies in the tension which it presupposes or creates between the worlds of nature and of spirit, and its resolution of that conflict by means of justifying faith. (Niebuhr 1929: 4)

In this statement Niebuhr seems to be asserting, without exploring its fuller implications, the idea that *organization per se*—any organization and every kind of human organization—contains the seeds of its own failure; or, to put it another way, *all* organizations are foredoomed to severe frustration in any efforts they make to realize ideal purposes or objectives, particularly those having to do with spiritual or ethical values. Instead, however, of treating the "ethical failure" of the Christian church as a particular instance of a more general paradoxical condition common to many kinds of groups, Niebuhr chose to confine his analysis narrowly and exclusively to religious organization within Christianity. Christianity, he goes on to say, by way of explanation:

> demands the impossible in conduct and belief; it runs counter to the instinctive life of man and exalts the rationality of the irrational; in a world of relativity it calls for unyielding loyalty to unchangeable absolutes. . . . Organize its ethics—as organize them you must . . . and the free spirit of forgiving love becomes a new law, requiring interpretation, commentary, and all the machinery of justice—just the sort of impersonal relationship which the gospel denies and combats. Place this society in the world, demanding that it be not of the world, and strenuous as may be its efforts to transcend or sublimate the mundane life, it will be unable to escape all taint of conspiracy

and connivance with the worldly interests it despises. (Niebuhr
1929: 4–5)

From this sort of "situational compromise" presumably there is
no escape since "Christian ethics will not permit a world-fleeing
asceticism which seeks purity at the cost of service. At the end, if
not at the beginning, of every effort to incorporate Christianity
there is, therefore, a compromise" (Niebuhr 1929: 5).

At this point Niebuhr seems to abandon the possibility of
maintaining any distinction between compromise that is *chosen*
by sinful humans and compromise which is *imposed* upon human
beings by necessity, as a condition of their existence at least as
Christians. What I understand him to be saying here is that
ultimately the Christian church will be preserved from destructive compromise, if it is to be preserved at all, *only* by the grace
and power of God, although he does express the hope at the very
end of *The Social Sources* that unity, at least, might still be
gained for the church through self-denying, sacrificial behavior
on the part of repentant Christians acting as chastened human
beings.

Very clearly this conception of *compromise* as applied to the
definition of the church, if not the whole *idea* of "compromise"
(whether applied to *churches* or to *denominations* and, in the
case of Niebuhr, to some kinds of *sects* as well), is so saturated
with theological connotations both by Niebuhr and by Troeltsch
that it could be argued that it ceases to be usable by social
scientists who are not privy to the "true" or "authentic" interpretation of Christianity and its demands upon its adherents.
Since it seems to be in the nature of things religious that rival or
alternative interpretations of even the most apparently *un*equivocal precepts arise, this in itself seems to pose operational problems for social scientists, although these are perhaps not unique
to *Christian* religious organization. Still, only those who understand the "true character" of the Christian ethic or the Christian message can hope to identify or distinguish what is
"compromise" and what is not. Such judgments as these are *not*
judgments which social scientists *as social scientists* seem to be
competent to make; and emphasis on the point seems justifiable
since *compromise* as Troeltsch and Niebuhr use the concept in
describing their "types" of religious organizations connotes

something *more* than mere consistency or inconsistency between word and deed: Something uniquely and peculiarly Christian is implied as being involved in the judgment and in the defining "operation."

If social scientists use concepts in which such judgments are *implicit,* that is, built into the definitions themselves (as in the case of *church* or *denomination*) on the basis of procedures that do not readily lend themselves to explicit specifications and thus cannot be made accessible to *all* scholars equally, they, the social scientists, that is, could be guilty of making value judgments unwittingly and, hence, necessarily also uncritically. Even where this is not the case, that is, where the social scientist believes he *can* specify the operations by which he determines the presence or absence of "compromise," there are still questions which a thorough-going methodological skeptic must raise about the validity, if not the reliability, of such determinations. The issues seem sufficiently significant or complex, perhaps, to justify the further discussion to which we now turn.

It is not unusual in the social sciences, though probably examples are rapidly becoming rarer, to find words in which implicit value judgments are encased. But the task of exposing the "soft spots" in such words is much more difficult in the case of some concepts than in others. On the surface such words as "church" or "sect"—or even "denomination"—might not seem to pose particularly formidable difficulties. Yet these have been so widely and variously defined and with such varied degrees of ideological and theological weighting beyond what has already been suggested that there seem to be good reasons for questioning whether or not they should continue to be used in social scientific discourse at all, let alone in research on religous organization where precision, reliability, and value neutrality (that is, freedom from either favorable or pejorative connotation and valuation of the phenomena being described) are essential.

Unfortunately, too many students of religious organization have tried to communicate their hypotheses and their findings using several of these concepts *without clarifying the referents in each case, without giving each the critical scrutiny that concepts in social scientific usage should be given, and without holding to any fixed or standard definitions.* This seems to have been particularly characteristic of the concepts "church" and "sect" and of the range of extensions, modifications, or refinements which various students have devised to fit the variations in organization, structure, or some other aspect of specific empirical cases. Sometimes they have been revised apparently in order to permit the student to emphasize some particular facet of religious organizations which happens to interest him. The result, as is increasingly being argued elsewhere, has been a veritable jungle of alleged and untested combinations of traits said to be characteristic of "church," "sect," "denomination," "cult," and so on. Whether indeed, as has been pointed out rather frequently by now,[7] the alleged traits in each instance do, in fact, "belong together" in some system of interrelated items, much less whether what is most basic or crucial to the whole can be identified and what the order of magnitude of importance of each item for every other is, is information that until rather recently was not often demanded. Or if it was sought, it was not so rigorously pursued as some of the more dramatic or impressive forms of quantitative analysis in the social sciences have made possible. Definitions grew spongey or additional traits were arbitrarily added in such profusion (or subtracted equally arbitrarily in some cases) so that it ceased to be possible to identify clearly what the concept in question included and what it excluded. All of these, to repeat, were problems of definition of concepts of religious organization which fell outside the peculiar problem of implicit bias in concepts like "church," "sect," and "denomination" to which attention has already been drawn.

There are other sources of conceptual weakness to which it seems necessary to point in both Niebuhr's and Troeltsch's uses of these words. But before considering these it might be helpful to try to determine, if we can, what there is about religious organizations which has seemed to discourage social scientists from treating them as genuine *systems of functionally interrelated traits* or as sets of quantitatively interrelated items which can be described in terms of latent structure analysis or some other

---

[7] See several articles on "Church-Sect Reappraised" in the *Journal for the Scientific Study of Religion* 6 (1967): 64–90; Glock and Stark (1965: 245–46); Peter L. Berger (1954, 1957, 1963); Benton Johnson (1957, 1963) and A. W. Eister (1949, 1950).

variation of factoral ordering. For I am inclined to believe that it is not merely a matter of methodological training or prejudice that accounts for the paucity of attempts at quantitative defini-tion of religious organizations as clusters of variables identifiable as types of sociological groups or of group structures. All of this, one suspects, has something to do specifically with the nature of ideal-types and of the kinds of phenomena for which they are intended to be used.

A helpful cue for locating the basic generic difference that separates those kinds of *models* that are capable of being de-scribed or stated in quantitative terms (with functional interre-lationships expressed in the form of multivariable equations) from *ideal-types* is found in Pitirim A. Sorokin's (1947: 145ff) distinction between "causal-functional" and "logico-meaning-ful" relationships. Religious phenomena, presumably, are *par excellence* examples of actions (and structures) saturated with "meanings," few of which, at least in minds of Christian theologians and ethicists and of many social scientists as well, can be satisfactorily translated into quantitative factors, that is, variables or attributes, or should be so treated.

But the crux of the matter, perhaps, lies deeper, namely, in the totally different "principle of explanation" on which the ideal-type as distinguished from the functional model (and indeed all systems of quantitatively describable relationships) rests. While this is not the place to attempt full discussion of this particular problem, perhaps it can be suggested that whereas "explana-tion" in the case of functionally related phenomena consists in locating constant or reliable (and thus predictable) orders and magnitudes of relationship, it takes an entirely different form in the case of the "logico-meaningful" relationships, as in the case of the ideal-type, where it is enough to "understand why" actors are acting as they do in terms of their "subjectively intended meanings." As I have argued elsewhere (1967a, 1967b), *explana-tion, in the case of the ideal-type,* consists in constructing (or verbally *re*constructing) on the basis of an empathic "inside look" into the "typical reasoning processes" of "typical actors" in "typical situations," plausible or convincing hook-ups or linkages between ends or "intended goals" of these typical actors and the various kinds of means (and organizations or "programs of means") by which they are seeking to gain their ends. Once these are "understood" the action is "explained."[8] For some, no further investigation is needed or wanted.

Being able to identify the intended goals or objectives of actions in social situations and to describe what the actors, with or without the concurrence of the observer, regard as the means that are necessary or "appropriate" to achieve them, while not regarded by some social scientists as constituting satisfactory scientific "explanation" (presumably because of unreliability), nevertheless comes close to what many others are attempting to accomplish through their research and analyses. Included in what is being discussed here is so-called *Verstehende Soziologie,* although there are other examples of it which could also be cited in the social sciences. The point, however, is that *both* "committed Christian" scholars and "totally"—or nearly totally—"disinterested" social scientists have tried to carry on their studies within this mode and idiom of inquiry.

And it may, as we have argued, account for a greater latitude—or tolerance of imprecision—in conception and definition of religious organizations (churches, sects, denominations, cults, and so on) than might be acceptable to social scientists with more exacting methodological norms and procedures. The phenomena, in any case, in the opinion of an apparently large number of scholars, are too complex, too diverse, or too "qualitative" in character to be defined in fixed, standard form. Some appear to be assuming that to try to establish a standard definition, operationally or by other means, is not only impossible but might rob them of the opportunity for creative insight, dull their sensitivity to nuances, or otherwise hamper their interpretations in some way. Yet, even if in some fashion verifiable propositions could be produced without consensus on rigorously defined concepts or precise specification of the traits universally contained within each type (whether it be an ideal-type or simply an ordinary "taxonomic" type), a minimal need for clear and consistent conceptualization exists, at least within the framework of the scholar's own analysis and hopefully within

---

[8] And the more difficult to understand of Max Weber's criteria for ideal-types, namely, "adequate causality," appears to be satisfied.

that of a given field or discipline if not within the realm of scientific language in a more inclusive sense.

All of this is by way of suggesting that an additional major criticism of Niebuhr's work as a possible contribution to the scientific study of religion might properly be leveled against his varied and inconsistent allusions to—one can scarcely call them definitions of—church, sect, *or* denomination as specific socio-logical types. We have already noted the problem with reference to *denomination*. Niebuhr's conception of the *church* lacked also a fixed sociological specification. There are passages in his writing where the *church* is regarded as embracing the whole of Christendom—the totality of all Christians living and dead. Elsewhere the church is *any* religious organization. Or, citing Weber and Troeltsch jointly as his source, Niebuhr (1929: 19) identifies as a church an inclusive type of religious organization into which one is born willy-nilly, baptized, and ordinarily subsequently confirmed. Still elsewhere (1935: 3) he speaks of the church as "the company of those who know they have found a savior,"[9] implying later that the church ought to think of itself and be regarded by others as a kind of ongoing social movement, ever on guard against the organizational "compromises" and "institutionalization" as he had identified and defined them in *The Social Sources.*

But if *protean definitions,* shifting and imprecise as they are, pose difficulties for social scientists because of their lack of standardization and, hence, their unreliability, these defects, as we have argued earlier, still fall short of those that are inherent in any attempt to define concepts, such as "church" or "denomination," *on the basis of such a value-loaded notion as "compromise"* applied, as Troeltsch and Niebuhr and their followers have variously sought to apply it, to Christian organizations. To repeat, so long as what constitutes "compromise" of the "right" or the "true" or authentic Christian principle—or ethic or "spirit" or sacrament or whatever—cannot be strictly and objectively defined (and thus rendered as a reliable social scientific concept, equally accessible to all social scientists regardless of

---

[9] This statement *is* taken out of context and may not, as one reader charges, be either fair or appropriate. "The statement," he writes, was a normative statement, "obviously not intended to be sociologically descriptive."

their personal religious training, background, or faith), definitions incorporating the idea of "compromise" or demanding
reference to it would seem to have no place in social science
usage. More than mere variation in definition is involved here.
As we have pointed out earlier, the social scientist who concurs
in the conception of "sect" as "uncompromising" and the
"church" as "compromising"—or the sect as *relatively* less and
the church as relatively more "compromising"—without demanding unambiguous, possibly even operational, specification of
what is being denoted by these words runs a serious risk of
committing himself unwittingly to a Christian value judgment
which he ought not or cannot, as a neutral or objective scholar,
make. At the very least it lies outside of the range of his technical competence to determine if it requires, as Troeltsch and
Niebuhr brought to it, a *Christian* understanding of Christianity's social organization.

There are at least two additional assertions about new religious movements, particularly about sects, which Niebuhr, and
in one case Troeltsch also, makes which must be regarded as
highly questionable and, possibly, so poorly substantiated that
they become misleading if not carefully specified in their use.
These have to do with the notions (1) that "vital" religious
commitments and interest exist primarily if not exclusively
among the "lower classes," specifically, among the poor, and (2)
that sects, as one form in which such commitments are expressed,
are by their "very nature," as Niebuhr (1929: 19) asserted at
one point, "valid only for one generation." The latter has
been vigorously and, if one relies upon empirical cases for evidence, effectively challenged by Bryan Wilson (as we shall note
later) and by Harold Pfautz and by J. M. Yinger, both of whom
pointed to instances where "sectarian" values and attitudes
seem to be successfully transmitted over more than the generation of original converts.

There is a point which must be made in connection with this
latter issue, however, and it is related to the totally alien or
discrete vocabularies, purposes, and goals of Niebuhr as a theologian, churchman, and Christian ethicist on one hand and of
Wilson, Pfautz, Yinger, and others as sociologists on the other.
When Niebuhr spoke of the "validity" of the sect for only one

generation we must assume that he was speaking of a condition of the movement as a *Christian* phenomenon and that he was again using criteria to which sociologists were not referring, did not wish to refer and, as social scientists, were not able to refer. Social scientists are interested not in evaluating the *quality* of the sect as a Christian agency in the world but look rather to its characteristic attitudes, social control mechanisms, and capacity to endure as a type of social group having certain ascribed "ideal-type" traits.

The question of whether or not *only the poor* are capable of founding or sustaining sectarian values, attitudes, and patterns (which both Niebuhr and Troeltsch seemed to be asserting) is a complex one. Niebuhr (1929: 29), for example, quoted approvingly and at length from Troeltsch's *Social Teaching of the Christian Churches:*

> The really creative, church-forming religious movements are the work of the lower strata. Here only can one find that union of unimpaired imagination, simplicity in emotional life, unreflective character of thought, spontaneity of energy and vehement force of need, out of which an unconditioned faith in divine revelation, the naivete of complete surrender and the intransigence of certitude can arise.

A few pages earlier (1929: 21) Niebuhr had written, "the rise of new sects to champion the uncompromising ethics of Jesus and 'to preach the gospel to the poor,' has again and again been the effective means of recalling Christendom to its mission."

In a similar vein, but with a certain measure of qualification, Troeltsch (1931: 334) had written:

> Very often in the so-called "sects" it is precisely the essential elements of the Gospel which are fully expressed. . . . There can be no doubt about the fact . . . the sects, with their greater independence of the world, and their continual emphasis upon the original ideals of Christianity, often represent in a very direct and characteristic way the essential fundamental ideas of Christianity.

Troeltsch was even more direct (1931: 44) regarding the class status of those with supposedly strongest or most intense religious feeling.

> On such a foundation alone is it possible to build up an unconditional authoritative faith in a Divine Revelation with simplicity of surrender and unshakeable certainty. Only within a fellowship of

this kind is there room for those who have a sense of spiritual need, and who have not acquired the habit of intellectual reasoning which regards everything from a relative point of view.[10]

Perhaps such assertions were intended to apply only to sects in the Christian tradition with its emphasis upon the positive value of poverty—although Troeltsch did *not* qualify his remarks in this respect—and perhaps they were intended to apply only to sects and not to other "fragmented" divisions in the Christian church, such as Niebuhr's "churches of the middle class" (for which *religious* fervor was never claimed).

For Niebuhr "the poor"—or "the disinherited," as they are referred to more generally in the second and third chapters of *The Social Sources*—had a certain apparently "natural" nobility (even though it may be only an "exaltation of the typical virtues of the class"):

> Hence one finds here, more than elsewhere, appreciation of the religious worth of solidarity and equality, of sympathy and mutual aid, of rigorous honesty in matters of debt, and the religious evaluation of simplicity in dress and manner, of the wisdom hidden to the wise and prudent but revealed to babes, of poverty of spirit, of humility and meekness. Simple and direct in its apprehension of the faith, the religion of the poor shuns the relativization of ethical and intellectual sophistication and by its fruits in conduct often demonstrates its moral and religious superiority. (Niebuhr 1929: 31)[11]

Such statements, unsupported by documentation and especially by *testing* against negative evidence, cannot—or ought not—be taken seriously by social scientists. Yet, as we shall see, there is some evidence that there has been *some* inclination to accept without further question or without rigorous scrutiny the idea that only the "disinherited" are capable of initiating or of sus-

[10] Samuel Mueller has reminded me that, within Roman Catholicism at least, a high positive value being placed on poverty, especially voluntary poverty, it is to be expected that many "new" Christian movements would emphasize a status of poverty whether or not this accorded with the adherents' original or actual socioeconomic position.

[11] It must be noted, however, that Niebuhr was emphatic in his denial of the "proletarian character" of *all* faith. Sects but not religious faith were to be viewed as characteristically "of the poor." See Niebuhr (1929: 77).

Bryan Wilson, commenting upon this quotation, suggests that the virtues Niebuhr was listing here had less to do with any propensity on the part of the poor to specific types of "sectarian" response than they did with the social experience of poor people in a more general sense.

taining a sect type of religious organization. (One effort to which we shall give attention later on has been made to expand the categories of "the disinherited," originally confined, presumably, to the poor and perhaps the politically weak as well, to "the deprived," which would include, in addition, those who are ethically alienated from the central structures of the society and some others besides.[12] Whether or not this extension proves to be viable or acceptable in the light of empirical evidence drawn from actual cases of new religious movements and, particularly, *sects* remains to be seen.)

Although Niebuhr's view of the origins of sects among the disinherited seemed to repeat Troeltsch's, there *is*, on closer examination, a considerable difference. As we have already noted briefly, this difference exists *both* in the *dynamic* of sect development *and* in the *relation between* church and sect. In Troeltsch's view, sects or, more exactly, the *sect principle* (by which he had meant to designate that strain or element within the Christian tradition which "cared more for the radical law of the Scriptures and the way of life of genuine Christians" than for the ecclesiastical ideals of unity and universality under the sacramental grace of an all-powerful God) had existed within the primitive church, but had been so overshadowed by the power and attractiveness of the medieval "ecclesiastical ethic" (if not by the sheer grandeur of the Roman church's organizational achievement) that it did not "reappear" until toward the end of the eleventh century. The sects which arose at this time appeared to Troeltsch to be more an expression of concern for personal religious feeling (as distinguished from sacramental piety) than of "protest" on the part of the poor. Furthermore, as we have

---

[12] See Glock and Stark (1965: 242–59) on "deprivation" as an alternative concept to "disinherited." Whatever the merits of the proposed substitution (or extension) of the one concept for another, it seems clear that at least "psychic deprivation" if not "organismic" and possibly other forms of deprivation as Glock and Stark define these would *not* be congruent with Niebuhr's hypothesis about the peculiar tie between poverty and the rise of Christian sects. "Psychic deprivation" simply wouldn't be an adequate equivalent, I feel sure.

By the same token, it seems highly questionable whether Werner Stark's thesis in *Sectarian Religion*, which accounts for sects largely on the basis of rejection of authority (political or other) by emotionally disturbed leaders, would be acceptable to Niebuhr.

also noted, where Troeltsch saw both the church principle and
the sect principle as authentic expressions of Christianity, both
implicit in the early Christian movement and both necessary for
the satisfactory expression of Christianity, Niebuhr saw the
church type, as Troeltsch described it, as *especially unsatisfac-
tory* as an organizational expression of the faith. Troeltsch's
(1931: 340–41) comment on the subject had been the assertion
that

> both types are a logical result of the Gospel, and only conjointly do
> they exhaust the whole range of its sociological influence, and thus
> also indirectly of its social results, which are always connected with
> the religious organization.
>
> In reality, the Church does not represent a mere deterioration of
> the Gospel, however much that may appear to be the case when we
> contrast its hierarchical organization and its sacramental system
> with the teaching of Jesus.

While Troeltsch *did* regard the church principle as standing
closer to the Pauline Christ and the sect principle as closer to the
man Jesus, he did *not* regard the sect as the sociological predecessor to the church:

> the sects are essentially different from the Church and the churches.
> The word "sect," however, does not mean that these movements are
> undeveloped expressions of the Church-type; it stands for an inde-
> pendent sociological type of Christian thought. (Troeltsch 1931:
> 338)

Nor did he regard Christianity or the Christian movement as
having begun as a Jewish sect. On the contrary he retains the
word "sect" for more specific application to one form of organizational expression of the new religious faith. "It is . . . clear,"
he wrote toward the beginning of *The Social Teachings of the
Christian Churches* (1931: 42–43), "that the rise of Christianity
is a religious and not a social phenomenon." It was, as it developed, *not* merely a movement to recall a wayward Judaism to
its "true" nature or purposes; that is, a "Jewish sect"; it was a
movement, a new religious tradition, intended to displace an
older covenant or "dispensation" with a new and more valid
one. It was, in short, much more than simply an effort to challenge a "compromised" ecclesiastic structure in a religious
tradition, weakened or distorted as a result of such "compromise." It *was,* however, as both Niebuhr and Troeltsch agree, a

faith which took strongest root among the poor and the disinherited (Niebuhr 1929 : 32).

For Niebuhr (1929 : 32–33) this latter fact alone seems to have cast the earliest Christians into some form of the sect type, though not *merely* as a socioeconomic ''protest'' movement.

> The development of the religion of the disinherited is illustrated not only by the history of various sects in Christianity but by the rise of that faith itself. It began as a religion of the poor, of those who had been denied a stake in contemporary civilization. It was not a socialist movement, as some have sought to show, but a religious revolution.

But, following his thesis, when

> the new faith became the religion of the cultured, of the rulers, of the sophisticated, it lost its spontaneous energy amid the quibblings of abstract theologies; it sacrificed its ethical rigorousness in compromise with the policies of governments and nobilities; it abandoned its apocalyptic hopes as irrelevant to the well-being of a successful church.

and,

> Now began the successive waves of religious revolution, the constant recrudescences of religions of the poor who sought an emotionally and ethically more satisfying faith than . . . the metaphysical and formal cult of Christianity had come to be.

Quite apart from the important differences we find between Niebuhr and Troeltsch in their respective theoretical conceptions of church and of sect and of the possible *developmental* connection between them which the former but *not* the latter scholar stressed, there are similarities in their overall conceptions of these two forms of religious organization which bear directly on the questions we have raised concerning their appropriateness for social scientific use. For both Niebuhr and Troeltsch, church and sect were intimately, indeed almost inextricably, bound up with their own personal perceptions and understandings as Christians of the Christian faith. This poses an almost insoluble problem for the social scientist who wishes to use the sect concept comparatively, that is, as an analytical tool for studying sects in other than the Christian tradition.

Perhaps the simplest, most direct way of making the point here is to try to restate what it is that Niebuhr and Troeltsch identified as characteristics of sects. Clearly these may *or may not* be characteristic of sects in non-Christian traditions or, indeed, even in Christian but non-Western settings, as, for example, Africa.

At least three of these characteristics have been cited. *All* sects according to the "model" proposed by Niebuhr based in part on Troeltsch, (1) can arise only among "the poor" since only they have the qualities requisite for maintaining "sectarian" patterns, (2) will be marked by a primary concern for *ethical* purity or lack of "compromise," and (3) will inevitably tend to develop toward a denominational structure, which can be loosely called a church, if not toward an institution which is "officially established" in some way.

Now it requires only a modicum of knowledge about sects in Islam or even in Judaism to recognize the provinciality of conceptions based solely upon organizational patterns found within Christendom. Even here, however, as R. L. Wishlade (1965: 2–4) has astutely pointed out, there may be a variation too great to be covered by some further extension or refinement of the sect concept (which has often been the way of responding to instances where empirical cases have not fallen neatly into the pattern). It was more characteristic for representatives of the white "churches" to challenge and oppose government policies than for representatives of "white sects" to do so.

In the case of the Muslim sects, if the Shi'ites and the successive subdivisions which grew out of this tradition may be taken as examples, it was *neither poverty nor ethical concern* nor "protest" so much as concern for maintaining a "true" or valid line of authority within Islam which provided the basis for sectarian movements.

Similarly, within the Sunni tradition, neither the moral strictness of the Kharidjites nor the severe "unitarianism" (especially the hostility to the "cult of saints" which had developed within Islam) of the Muwahhidun (or Wahhabis as they were called by their opponents) seemed to be an expression of religious concern associated with poverty or low socioeconomic status within the Muslim community. In Ibn Khaldun's (1958: I, 333, II, 76ff) analyses of Islam, other factors than socioeconomic status clearly emerge as important in determining how rigorously or how faithfully Muslims would practice or adhere to the principles of their faith. In any case, poverty was not erected into a central value or an ideal standard.

Nor, in Islam, is "the world" in the sense of secular political-communal organization viewed as threatening or as much a potential source of "compromise" or "corruption" of the faith itself (or of the ethical principles most closely related to it) as appears to be the case with Christianity. To be sure "worldliness" was a source of concern to some Muslims, but it was more a matter of *laxness* and "falling away" from strict adherence to religious duties rather than of cooperating with secular political authority (for the sake of gaining or maintaining power and influence) which was viewed as the chief threat to "the faith." Formal political organization and *control* of the community were, in fact, *enjoined* upon "good Muslims" as duties. They were *not* something from which they should shy away or which they should avoid as "worldly" and, therefore, contaminating.

Possibly for a similar reason, namely, the close association of religious authority and communal organization, sects in Judaism seldom fall into the kind of pattern described either by Niebuhr or by Troeltsch. The Sadducees, for example, who are usually identified as a Jewish sect, were an elite group. Although the Pharisees are described in some sources as "plebeian"—a group to which "the masses looked for religious leadership"—the social composition of this sect "did not always follow rigid class-lines; not a few of them were men of wealth and influence (Ausubel 1964)."[13] Not enough appears to be known about such groups as the Hasideans, the Therapeutae, the Yudghanites, the Karaites to provide clear evidence of the socioeconomic status of their members.

Whether these considerations constitute sufficient evidence for supporting the contention that "church" and "sect" as these concepts have been absorbed into the sociology of religion more or less directly from Niebuhr and from Troeltsch are too closely tied to the Christian faith and its value structure to be usable for social scientific purposes generally, that is, as we have argued, that they lack the neutrality necessary for concepts which sociologists can use in comparative and cross-cultural study of reli-

[13] See also articles on Pharisees, Sadduccees, Karaites, and others in Werblowsky and Wigoder (1966: 299).

gious organizations, is a question to which we can now return. Even in the analysis of religious organization and the dynamic of organizational change within the Christian tradition itself there is, as we have pointed out, a question as to whether the social scientist, in using the concept of "sect" or the concept of "church" as they are presently defined and widely used, may not be passing judgment on whether or not Christian principles and Christian ethics are being abridged, or, as the theologians would have it, "compromised." If there is legitimate question at this point about the concepts, there is more serious difficulty in utilizing these concepts when one moves outside of the Christian tradition. What are needed, it would seem, are organizational structural concepts which are more specifically and narrowly *sociological*. "Sect," of course, *could*, perhaps, be one, and, for at least some of the non-Christian religious traditions, "church" (or its organizational equivalent) *could* be another. Freed from the implicit biases which we have identified as existing where "the church" is identified as "compromised" and "the sect" as at least relatively "uncompromising" (in relation to what Christian theologians and probably they alone may lay claim to defining as the authentic Christian values), such concepts presumably would be not only neutral but capable of general applicability.

Here precisely is where the conceptions of "church" and "sect" as they were formulated by Max Weber can be shown to be superior for social scientific purposes to those formulated by the theologians and Christian ethicists, Troeltsch and Niebuhr; for Weber makes no reference whatsoever to whether or not *either church* or *sect* is "compromised." A *church*, for Weber, is, strictly speaking, simply a religious organization which claims monopolistic authority and into which one is born, whereas a sect is a *voluntary* religious association to which one must apply for membership and be judged worthy or not to be permitted to join (or remain) in the group.

Weber distrusted the validity of any analysis where the observer favored one over another of the objects of his investigation. I think it would be fair to say that he was not only not at all interested in whether or not a Christian sect as a sociological type was "less compromised" or "closer to the ethic of the

Sermon on the Mount'' than the church as a type, but it seems likely that he would have ruled such a judgment as inappropriate if made as a substantive judgment by a social scientist or used as the basis for any would-be social scientific definition of the sect as a sociological concept or type. Not even the operation of *verstehen* or interpretive understanding would seem to permit such a judgment to be made since something more is involved here than merely entering empathically into the minds of the actors, difficult as that operation would be. To locate what the aims or goals of an actor are and how he perceives the various means that he recognizes or accepts as available to him for reaching his ends in Weber's sense is not the same kind of mental or intellectual operation as Troeltsch and Niebuhr called for. Where social scientists might, under some circumstances—and assuming they accept the validity of the methods of *Verstehende Soziologie*—be able to identify *inconsistency* between professed goals and chosen means, to identify *compromise* calls, we repeat, for knowledge which they *as social scientists* simply do not have.

It is clear from what Weber (1947: 156–57) wrote about *church*, moreover, that he shared little with Troeltsch, and less with Niebuhr, in his conception of this type of religious organization:

> What is most characteristic of the church, even in the common usage of the term, is the fact that it is a rational, compulsory organization with continuous organization and that it claims a monopolistic authority. It is normal for a church to strive for complete imperative control on a territorial basis and to attempt to set up the corresponding territorial or parochial organization. So far as this takes place, the means by which this claim to monopoly is upheld, will vary from case to case. But historically its control over territorial areas has not been nearly so essential to the church as to political corporation. . . . It is its character as a compulsory association, particularly the fact that one becomes a member of the church by birth, which distinguishes a church from a "sect." It is characteristic of the latter that it is a voluntary association and admits only persons with specific religious qualifications.

Elsewhere (1946: 306) he wrote:

> Affiliation with the church is, in principle, obligatory and hence proves nothing with regard to the member's qualities. A sect, however, is a voluntary association of only those who, according to the principle, are religiously and morally qualified. If one finds voluntary reception of his membership, by virtue of religious probation, he joins the sect voluntarily.

Even wider fissures can be said to open up between Weber's ideas about the essential characteristics of churches and of sects (and the relationships of the latter to low socioeconomic status) and those of Niebuhr and of Troeltsch but especially, the former. In Niebuhr's brief reference to Weber in *The Social Sources* he picked up the latter's emphasis on the structural differences between church and sect to which we have just been giving attention, and he cited (1929: 17) both Weber and Troeltsch as having "demonstrated how important are the differences in the sociological structure of religious groups in the determination of their doctrine." His own work, as we have seen, was an attempt to demonstrate a quite different relationship or process, namely, the effect of the environing social structure on the character of the religious groups. Furthermore, he went very much further in asserting an association between the structural and other characteristics of sects and the lower-class status attributed, *ex hypothesis,* to their members than did Weber. In fact one searches almost in vain in Weber's writing for anything approaching either Niebuhr's or Troeltsch's axiomatic assertions about these matters.

Although Weber (1963: 101) did concede that "the lowest and most economically unstable strata [which for him included not only "the poor" but also what he regarded as certain categories of the lower middle class] are . . . susceptible to being influenced by religious missionary enterprise," he quite plainly did not look especially to the poor, as Troeltsch and Niebuhr in a somewhat more limited sense did, either for religious fervor or for lofty ethical sensitivity or concern. To the contrary, "Only in a limited sense," he wrote (1963: 101) "is there a distinctive class religion of disprivileged social groups." Although the latter's "particular need," especially in comparison with the " 'sated' and privileged strata," "is for release from suffering . . . their need for religious salvation, where it exists may assume diverse forms" (1963: 101, 108).

Earlier he had noted that a religion of salvation may very well have its origin with socially *privileged* groups, since the requisite leadership qualities cannot be said to be confined to membership in a particular class. Furthermore, neither can the protests of the "disprivileged" (including here the politically as well as the economically "deprived" and their need for salvation) be expected, as a matter of course, to take the form of religious sectarianism. "Insofar as the modern proletariat has a distinctive religious position, it is characterized by indifference to, or rejection of, religion common to large groups of the modern bourgeoisie" (1963: 100). But it is not necessarily likely in his view to express itself in the form of religious fervor or piety: "the classes of the greatest economic disability, such as slaves and free day laborers, have hitherto never been the bearers of a distinctive type of religion" (1963: 99). Nor, presumably, do they hold a monopoly on the sectarian type of religious organization. In Islam it was as frequently either nomads or warriors as it was representatives of the poor who voiced deep concern about what they regarded as effete and sybaritic departures from the "original" Muslim values of stern and simple piety. In Weber's chapter, "Judaism, Christianity and the Socio-Economic Order" (1963: 246–61), again there is no attempt to connect the emergence or creation of sectarian patterns to low socioeconomic status, at least in the first instance.

On the whole, in his discussions of religion and the "disprivileged" Weber seems to have been more concerned with powerlessness than with poverty as such; but even then there is little or no basis for inferring that he saw a close or necessary relation between *sect* and low socioeconomic status. Although such association may exist, it was not, for Weber, the critical or defining basis on which the concept of "sect" (as distinguished from "church") rested. He scarcely mentioned sects at all in his discussion of the religious interests (and their expression) among the nonprivileged. (The latter, in Weber's view, included others than the "lower classes" or "the poor" only, but *not* so broad a spectrum of categories as that suggested by C. Y. Glock and Rodney Stark (1965: 242–59) as constituting "the deprived.")

The sect, one might say, was to be defined not in terms of what it rejects (as "compromise") or protests but rather in terms of what it asserts or affirms in positive terms—its "sect ideal" or, as Weber suggested, its identifying *"sect principle."* Further, it was to be defined in terms of the kind and intensity of internal social control and organization mobilized in support of that principle, whatever it may be (whether a given ritual practice or set of practices, a principle for ''insuring'' legitimate succession of religious authority, an ethical norm or set of standards, or whatever else within a given religious tradition the sectarians might select as *the* right, the correct, or the superior path, interpretation, standard, or dogma).

One of the clearest and most readily identifiable structural consequences for the *sect* as a type of religious organization or group is the one upon which Weber in fact fastened, namely, the practice of accepting or excluding members on the basis of the extent of their adherence to the specified norm or standard or ideal.[14] It would seem to be *this* rather than the question of whether or not the *standard* of the sect was ''*un*compromised'' (as distinguished from the ''compromised'' standard—and compromising tendencies on the part of its members—of the church as a type) which becomes central to the definition of ''the sect.'' By defining the sect in terms of strong or intense concern on the part of its members for their ''ideal''—their identifying principle—rather than primarily as a protest group or as a group intent upon promoting conflict, it becomes possible to include within the general type not only those groups which are in direct, open, or aggressive opposition to ''the Establishment,'' ''the world,'' or other religious organizations but also those who are, as they claim, truly *indifferent* to these and often literally withdrawn from the power structure and sometimes from the economic system of their environing society. Of course, insofar as any strong positive assertion of a given dogma, ritual practice,

---

14 However, as both Joachim Wach (1951: 203) and Bryan Wilson (1967: 9) have pointed out, there are definite limits to what kind of ''standard'' or ''sect principle'' could qualify. Wach wrote:

> It seems necessary . . . to address a warning to those sociologists who have taken a special interest in sectarianism. They should not overlook the fact that religious bodies are not, certainly not primarily, associations for the fostering of any material or even ideal purpose, though such notions do, of course, play a part; but that they desire to be worshipping groups and should be understood and interpreted with this intention so long as it is not disproved.

Wilson has also reminded his fellow sociologists, ''The sect is not an interest association. . . . It regards itself as engaged in the maintenance of faith and in the distribution of blessings, towards the salvation of men. . . . Its aim is the implementation of the will of God, so far as this is given to men.''

ethical standard, principle of religious authority, or other puta-
tive "sect principle" as the *only* correct or proper one for a
given religious tradition—and superior to the beliefs and practices of other groups in the same religious tradition—constitutes
an instance of implicit, if not explicit, "aggression" upon the
latter and can, in this sense, be a kind of invitation or provocation to hostility from without, it might be argued that all sects
are conflict groups. But this seems to depend upon how the sect
and its "defining principle" are viewed *from without* at least as
much as it does upon how aggressive the particular sect in question wishes to be. Such questions can be left open for empirical investigation, in any case, rather than being "foreclosed by
definition," provided one is willing to define the sect in the more
narrowly structural terms of a group sharing what is to them a
vitally important standard of membership, jealously guarded and
reenforced by vigorous exercise of social control within the
group.[15]

In the end this may be the strongest argument for keeping the
sociological definition of "sect" (as of "church" or any other
type of religious organization) to a minimal statement of its
structural character, leaving empirical research to determine
what additional characteristics are, in fact, associated with
specific manifestations or instances of the type, how closely, and
under what conditions. (This argument in favor of parsimony
and for greater emphasis on inductive discovery as distinguished

[15] It was with considerations of this sort in mind that I (1950: 67–77) tried
some years ago to devise an ideal-type definition of *sect* against which to
examine a particular religious movement—Moral Rearmament or The Oxford
Group:

> the sect is a rigorously organized group of people who by their conduct
> indicate that they have chosen to "live apart" from society in general
> according to what they conceive to be important and imperative standards.
> Partly as a result of conflict, which is usually generated between the sect
> and the larger society in which it is embedded, and partly out of concern
> generated within the group itself for the protection and inviolate preserva-
> tion of its own ideals, the sect is, characteristically, a closed group with
> rigid qualifying tests, or disciplines, for elected members.

The operative distinction between *sects* (as religious movements) and
cults, as Glock and Stark (1965: 245) have identified this, is that the latter
"are religious movements which draw their inspiration from other than the
primary religion of the culture, and which are not schismatic movements in
the same sense as sects, whose concern is with preserving a purer form of the
traditional faith."

from the more deductive theoretical elaboration of a heuristic concept may run counter to the practice of the "ideal-type" method as it is commonly understood in American sociology of religion; but it may have the merit of discouraging mere speculation over which combinations of characteristics or traits "belong" together in "the sect" or which comprise "the church.")

Besides Weber's conception of "sect" there are a number of other alternative sociological definitions which differ from Niebuhr's and which it might be useful to cite very briefly for the additional light they shed on what was distinctive about the latter's approach. Ellsworth Faris and Robert C. Angell, for example, proposed a theory of sects which identified them as essentially a kind of creative response to conditions of social disruption or unrest. Thus Angell wrote (1941: 150, 169) in language strongly reminiscent of W. I. Thomas, R. E. Park, and E. W. Burgess:

> Since ours is a time of rapid change and considerable disorganization, we should expect the rise of . . . sects, for they are one way in which new definitions of the situation appear. . . . In the days of their youthful enthusiasm for the ideal, sects form moral communities almost completely dissociated from the world about them.

However, his *basic* conception of the sect he himself regarded as Weberian: "A sect is closed to the outside world, a group of believers who wish to follow a sacred pattern of life. New converts are accepted only after rigid scrutiny of their qualifications. . . . In short, in Max Weber's phrase, a sect is 'a whole of qualified people.' "

Ellsworth Faris (1955: 77) had written in a vein somewhat similar to Angell's at about the time Niebuhr's *The Social Sources* was first published: "Arising at a time when the fixed order is breaking up, or tending to break up, the sect is the effort of the whole community to integrate itself anew. It is the order arising from social chaos." From this point he proceeded to devise a theory of his own to account for the origin and for the cohesiveness of sects that was quite different from Niebuhr's and, by contrast to Weber's austere definition of the sect, rather elaborately embroidered. "The sect," Faris declared (1955: 79), "is originally constituted . . . by those who have split off from existing organizations" under conditions of "unrest and confusion [which have loosened] . . . the bonds of union" within those organizations and presumably, within the community or society generally. When this state of affairs prompts "a few kindred spirits" to seek each other out and to form the nucleus of a new group—indeed, of a new social order—a sect is born. "It is very rare," Faris continues, "that the original motive is separation, but when the divergent nucleus excites opposition and achieves group cohesiveness, the stage is set for a new sect."

While there are some parallels in Faris's and in Niebuhr's ideas about the ways sects may develop, there is no reference at all in Faris's (1955: 79) concept of the sect (as there is none in Weber's) to this type of religious organization as being the characteristic form of religious organization among the poor or the disinherited and less "compromising" in respect to Christian ethics:

> The first stage [of a sect] is typically a stage of conflict, though the methods of warfare vary according to the standards of the times. Many of the organizations are short-lived. . . . When group consciousness and morale characterize the original company or cadre of the sect there is often more or less rapid growth by accretion or by the attraction of others.

While adults may want to join sects for a wide variety of reasons, according to Faris (who seems here only to be ruminating speculatively, that is, without data), and do, in fact, succeed in getting themselves admitted without necessarily meeting the "religious tests" for membership, it is *conflict* not value consensus which welds the group into a cohesive group with rigorous patterns of social control:

> Just why they [members of sects] are attracted is a very interesting problem. It is often assumed that the chief appeal is to men of like temperament. . . .
> Conflict unites the sect, creates *esprit de corps* and heightens morale. . . . In this conflict period of the life of the sect, the tendency is toward exclusiveness wherever feasible. Certain economic relations with "the world" are necessary, but the cultural life is protected. There is always a tendency to be an endogenous tribe. (Faris 1955: 79, 81)

However, to Faris (1955: 78):

> The set forms of the constitution of the sect vary so much that the details must be regarded as chance or accidental. The problem here

is very similar to the problem of an invention, differing chiefly in that the sect is a collective affair while an invention is individual.

Examples of other attempts on the part especially of American sociologists to define "sect" and the ways in which these definitions differed from Niebuhr's conception could be discussed, but to do this would probably carry this critique unnecessarily far afield. Another and possibly more fruitful line of inquiry would be to attempt to trace in some detail the references sociologists writing since Niebuhr have made to his work and the contexts in which his ideas have been placed. On that assumption, in any case, we shall turn to this final task of this paper presently.

The fact that both H. Richard Niebuhr and Ernst Troeltsch were, as we have emphasized, Christian theologians whose central concern was not for the detached or for the comparative study of religious organizations but for ways in which religious organizations served to express the Christian faith or to facilitate, modify, limit, or distort it has been demonstrated, I believe, to have a marked effect on their conceptions of religious organizations. These "effects," we have argued, have limited the value of their concepts for social scientific use, calling into question their appropriateness (or their reliability) for use in objective analysis.

It seems important to note, however, in this connection that not *all* scholars with essentially Christian or ethical-theological concerns as their primary interest incorporated into their concepts the same kinds or degree of implicit value judgment which, I believe, we can identify in the cases of Niebuhr and of Troeltsch. Joachim Wach (1944), for example, seems to have succeeded rather well in his formal definitions of *ecclesia, sect,* and other types of religious organizations in keeping his concepts somewhat more narrowly structural.[16] Valuable as it might be to

---

[16] As Wach recognized elsewhere (1959: 188, 207), however, "considerable differences exist between the approach of the sociologist and that of the theologian" and he concluded:

As it is the task of the historian and the sociologist to study the genesis, development and structure of all these groups [churches, denominations, and sects], so it is the function of the theologian who is religiously committed constantly to examine and revise the theological presuppositions upon which the basic concept of the ecclesias of his own community rests, in the light of an ever-continuing study of and meditation upon the teaching of Christ.

explore Wach's concepts further in this light, we cannot do this here.

Up to this point in our critique we have relied upon what Niebuhr and, on occasion, Troeltsch, has himself written. This is not, however, a completely satisfactory basis on which to try to assess the worth of Niebuhr's or of Troeltsch's contributions to the social scientific study of religious organization, since, as we noted toward the beginning, what it is that a scholar says or means to say may not be grasped or accurately conveyed by those who subsequently cite his work. The latter can too easily lift concepts or ideas out of context and unwittingly put them into others. In short, we need to reckon with the possibility of "conceptual drift," if not outright distortion, even when this is not intended.

Ordinarily, where the problem is recognized, the ideal solution is to "go back to the original sources." In the case of church-sect theory, however, social scientists have not shown a strong or determined inclination to do this so that we now confront a lush undergrowth of conceptualization in which the basic issues tend to be obscured. To cut into this is difficult but necessary even though it will have to be done here in only limited and "programmatic" fashion.

Merely to list books and articles in which reference is made to *The Social Sources* by social scientists would in itself constitute a fairly arduous task, yet in the space which remains we shall try to review briefly some of the uses to which Niebuhr's conceptions and interpretations have been put.

It may help the organization of the discussion here to point out that there are two major themes or clusters of ideas, both broadly "sociological" in character, which are commonly identified with H. Richard Niebuhr. One of these is explicit in the title of his book, *The Social Sources of Denominationalism*. The other is the so-called sect-to-church (or, as some would have it, the sect-to-denomination) hypothesis.

Failure to keep these two sets of ideas clearly in mind *as separate* has caused confusion, contributing to the present situation as far as church-sect theory and research are concerned. The former of the two themes is a broader theory of the social sources of *divisions* within the Christian church. Niebuhr was concerned here not with sects as such but with divisions of *all* kinds, whether into churches or sects or "denominations," the latter of which, in Niebuhr's broad usage, *could* include both churches and sects insofar as either was caught up in the toils of worldly necessity and worldly pressures. The other was a theory of the dynamic of sects. Clearly he was not concerned in either case with precise descriptions of *structural* characteristics of organization which, for sociologists, are critically important.

Of these two major themes found in Niebuhr's work it is difficult to say which has had more attention. Often, unfortunately, they have been loosely scrambled together with consequences which may well have been dysfunctional for the development of a solid sociology of religious organizations.

Almost from the beginning the social sources (loosely, the sociological "causes") of divisions in religious bodies theme was linked with the sect-to-church (or denomination) theme. Niebuhr himself seems to have thought that Troeltsch was implying that there was such a connection.

Troeltsch, as we noted, did see a close connection between vital and creative religious faith, lower-class status, and "essential" Christian ideas. It is not surprising that, if one were to view Christianity as originating as a *sect*, connections of the sort Niebuhr made would be thus drawn. The fact is, however, that Troeltsch apparently did *not* see sect and church as *sequential* organizations, but rather as equally valid, alternative, and authentic forms of expression of the Christian religious tradition. Both were almost equally ancient forms of organizational expression, latently, if not always actually, present *side by side* from the beginning. He did not, as we have noted, think in sect-*to*-church terms, much less in sect-to-denomination terms attributed to him by sociologists who did not read him carefully. (Moreover there was, as we have noted, serious question about whether he did, in fact, view early Christianity as "sectarian," since at one point he spoke of it as an entirely *new* faith.)

Nevertheless, Niebuhr came to be viewed as the successor to Troeltsch who had developed the latter's "typology" from a sociologically sterile to an analytically fruitful formulation, giving it a dynamic character which made it relevant for adaptation and application to the American Protestant religious organizational experience. As one leading sociologist (Johnson 1957: 89) wrote of church-sect:

> Richard Niebuhr deserves the credit for adapting the typology [of Troeltsch] to research in American Protestantism. Recognizing it as unwieldy and perceiving its "static" nature, he attempted a reformulation based upon what he considered the essential differentiating criteria between Church and Sect. . . . Troeltsch had observed that Sects must make some reconciliation with the "world" or suffer extinction. Niebuhr proposed that the typology be used to study the processes by which Sects effect this reconciliation. This is the origin of the well-known hypothesis that Sects develop ultimately into Churches—that is, that the attitude toward the secular culture in time undergoes a change from harsh rejection to a degree of toleration or even acceptance.

One of Niebuhr's graduate students, Liston Pope, who was not a sociologist, produced what has since been hailed as a sociological classic expounding this thesis. And at a time when American social scientists were keenly aware of upward social mobility on one hand and of a kind of rough "class determination" of social behavior (including the organization of religious movements and structures) on the other, no one asked any very searching questions about all this.

Although they frequently took issue with Niebuhr on particular points and either modified or extended some of his ideas, many sociologists seemed ready to accept the general formulation which combined a theory for the emergence of sects with a theory to account for their survival and subsequent development in what became an almost routine orthodoxy in the "sociology of religion."

Many sociologists, in any case, found in Niebuhr's sect-to-church (denomination) hypothesis something which they wished to use, even if only as a foil in some cases. Becker (1932), Yinger (1946, 1957), Pfautz (1955, 1956, 1964), O'Dea (1954), Berger (1954, 1958), Stanley (1958), Wilson (1958, 1959, 1961, 1966), Moberg (1960, 1961, 1962), Vallier (1963), Glock and others (1965, 1967), Demerath (1965), John Scanzoni (1965), Demerath and Hammond (1969), and many others in these and other writings have cited Niebuhr's thesis with varying degrees of readiness to accept or reject.

Howard Becker (1932: 626–27) proposed to identify all the "compromised" divisions of the Christian church in America (which Niebuhr had been willing to refer to interchangeably as "sects" or as "churches of the disinherited," or as "churches of the middle class," and so on) as *denominations* or, rather, as examples of a new "ideal-type"—the denomination.

Pfautz (1955)[17] and later Moberg (1960, 1961)[18] insisted upon regarding still another ideal-type, which they identified as "the cult," as existing *prior in time* to "the sect" (and as succeeded not necessarily or always directly by "the denomination" but sometimes by what Yinger (1946: 22, 1957: 150–52) and they, and others who joined them (Wilson 1958), proposed to call "the established sect").

Although scholars who quoted Niebuhr or referred to his work were generally careful to acknowledge the qualifying statements and the exceptions which he himself had written into his hypothesis, the variations and some of the more subtle points tended to be lost in the face of the beguiling notion that new religious movements rising among the poor, the uneducated, and the powerless were what brought vitality and fervor (and a minimum of compromise) to religion but that, within a while and for a variety of reasons including a general rise in economic status often resulting from abstemious lives and so forth, these movements would "sacrifice" or lose one kind of power in order to gain another as their members climbed the socioeconomic ladder.[19] Whether by loss of members to the less fervent organizations "higher" on the scale or by internal processes of development, which transformed the sects themselves into "churches" or denominations (Moberg 1962:272), the result was approximately the same, and the whole seemed to be adequately accounted for in terms of Niebuhr's thesis, as it was understood.

There were, however, significant variations and refinements,

---

[17] "The modal sequence," Pfautz (1955: 123–24) wrote, "involves a transition from cult through sect to denomination."

[18] "Much evidence," Moberg wrote (1960: 100ff.), without, however, citing specific cases, "supports the hypothesis that a new religious body typically emerges as an amorphous cult which develops into a sect and then, if it survives, gradually changes its characteristics to become a denomination which, in turn, becomes the source of new sects."

[19] The prominence of this view owes much to the popularity given it by Niebuhr's student at the Yale Divinity School, Liston Pope, whose Ph.D. thesis was published under the title *Millhands and Preachers* (1942).

and we should mention at least one of these. Niebuhr himself had pointed out (as Werner Stark 1967b, Benton Johnson 1957, and J. M. Yinger 1957 have noted) that Calvinism and Calvinist sects followed a somewhat different course and pattern of development than did certain other sorts of new religious movements and organizations in Protestantism. However, where Stark (1967b: 62) viewed Calvinism as a socioreligious structure which was, from the outset, a "narrow . . . bourgeois church" Johnson (1957: 91) saw it as the branch or strand among Protestant traditions within which the sect-to-church processes was best exemplified and the hypothesis best substantiated:

> There is a very good reason, to suspect that the Sect-to-Church hypothesis was a generalization of rather limited application anyway. Most research within this framework has been done on Calvinist-type denominations, indeed denominations of a revivalistic, moralistic sort. . . . In other words a particular kind of ethico-ritual system has been focussed on. . . . Those radically "anti-worldly" groups which Troeltsch would unhesitatingly have called Sects cannot be understood so clearly in terms of the Sect-to-Church hypothesis. The major historical trend of the Amish, the Shakers, or to a lesser extent the Quakers can scarcely be understood as a simple process of "accommodation" to the values of the outer society. It seems safe to say that, despite some astute and valid observations that Niebuhr makes in presenting his Sect-to-Church hypothesis, the actual developmental sequence he poses is pretty much confined to Calvinist Sects in a mobile society. Certainly the proposition cannot continue to be entertained in its present form because most of Protestantism cannot be placed in the Church category.

Whether or not Niebuhr would agree with Johnson's conclusion as to the particular strain of Protestantism within which his thesis would likely prove to be most accurate or applicable, it seems possible that he might accept Johnson's judgment regarding his sect-to-church hypothesis: that its "usefulness is now more or less limited to the conceptualizing of a developmental sequence that seems to take in some areas of American Protestantism." However, Niebuhr (1929: 28, see also 18–20) had written in *The Social Sources,* though at some pages removed from his original and most vivid statement of the thesis:

> One phase of the history of denominationalism reveals itself as the story of the religiously neglected poor, who fashion a new type of Christianity which corresponds to their distinctive needs, who rise

BEYOND THE CLASSICS?

in the economic scale under the influence of religious discipline, and who, in the midst of freshly acquired cultural respectability, neglect the new poor succeeding them on a lower plane.

One phase—not the entire process of division and subdivision within the church.[20]

Scanzoni (1965: 327), following what he (and Demerath and Hammond [1969: 160] as well) regards as the much more carefully and thoroughly worked out propositions about sect development formulated by Bryan Wilson, also demands more clear-cut and explicit limitation in the application of the general thesis.

Wilson (1959) very early in his work on sects had raised doubts about a number of specific points in the sect-to-church (denomination) hypothesis as it had been formulated by Niebuhr in *The Social Sources*. He called into question Niebuhr's assertion (1929: 19), "By its very nature the sectarian type of organization is valid only for one generation," and at various points in his *Sects and Society* (1960) Wilson seemed at least somewhat dissatisfied, as I long have been, with the stark assertion frequently made (or implied) by Niebuhr and perhaps to a lesser degree by Troeltsch as well that the *sect* as an ideal-type is necessarily and exclusively a religious organization of "the poor," the politically powerless, or the uneducated.[21] On the basis of evidence drawn from his intensive studies of sects, Wilson (1961: 3, 9, 1966: 200ff), like Pfautz (1956, 1964) rejected both the one-generation life span thesis for the ideal-type sect and the sect-to-denomination (or church) sequence as an inevitable or invariant pattern.

On the issue of the relation of social status to sect interest Wilson's position is not *quite* so clear: "New religious movements," he writes (1966: 201), "are frequently vehicles for sections of society which are otherwise unaccommodated socially and religiously. When the productive relations of society are

---

20 Other sources, it will be recalled, included sectionalism, racism, nationalism, ethnicity. Niebuhr (1934) is probably his clearest and most satisfactory statement of the *sect* concept from the point of view of the sociologist.
21 Wilson's later work (1970) further argues that Niebuhr was mistaking the part (that is, *some* sects) for the whole (*all* sects), and from this point he went on to delineate several "subtypes" of sects which he identifies as conversionist, revolutionist, introversionist, manipulationist, thaumaturgical, reformist, and utopian.

changing, new groups of men find some need for a reinterpretation of their position. New classes seek then their own transcendental justification.'' The general statement appears to be
equally applicable to any class in the social order. In the face of
major social change *all* classes are subject to dislocation and may
need to "seek then their own transcendental justification," but
in the context of his further comments it seems apparent that
Wilson has in mind primarily the same "lower classes" to whom
Troeltsch and Niebuhr had referred; for the "new classes" of
whom Wilson speaks are described as "being excluded from the
existing distribution of social honour and religious sanctity."
Under these conditions,

> Their demand for status, for gratification, is likely to respond to
> the transcendental promise of status *in the next world* if the imme-
> diate prospect of status in this one is withheld. And yet what the
> history of Protestant denominationalism makes evident is that there
> is no agency so effective in providing men with improved status and
> respectability *in this world* as that which promises them these things
> in the next. Becoming religious, accepting the promise for deferred
> reward, is itself an agency not only of discipline but also of en-
> hancing status in this world. The sect which persuades men that they
> are the poor, "the least the lost the lowest and the last," promises
> them ultimate salvation in the after-life, also offers a foretaste of
> heaven in the assembly, establishes its own inner status structure,
> induces members to behave in respectable ways to each other, and
> to conduct themselves as saints *manqués* in the wider society. It is
> part of the return to fundamentals manifested by groups that
> emerge in this way. (Wilson 1966: 201–2)

A similar restatement of the theory, blending Niebuhr's two
major theses and adding some modifications, appears in Glock,
Ringer, and Babbie (1967), where Niebuhr is cited as having
noted that "the economically deprived were more likely to form
or join fundamentalist rather than liberal religious groups."
Those authors comment (1967: 78–79):

> This tendency was attributed to a greater need for experiencing
> religion emotionally than simply observing it ritually. Niebuhr
> further suggested that the ethics of hard work and asceticism com-
> monly found among the fundamentalist sects had the effect of ul-
> timately resolving the economic hardships of their followers. As
> members of the sect followed the injunctions to work and save, they
> became more prosperous and the sects came to take on a more
> church-like ritualistic character.

Similar, but not identical; for here "the dynamic" presumably or ostensibly moving the sect toward denomination or church is not precisely or specifically the loss of fervor in the second generation, the desire for power or respectability or status as such, but simply improvement in economic position. Interwoven as all of these may prove, in fact, to be, their association in the theory as it stands has more the look of a speculated "ideal-type" formulation (constructed on the basis primarily of the theorists' experience or general historical understanding of what might plausibly be expected to go with what), rather than one drawn out on the basis of testing for intercorrelations among multiple factors in actual, historical-empirical cases.

It should be repeated here that the general statements of the theory actually blend together at least two *separate* themes, each of which should be examined separately before it is accepted in the more complex, "scrambled" form in which it is usually reasserted.

For the sake of clarification we have identified one of these theses as Niebuhr's "developmental thesis" and include in it all of his ideas relating to the "sect-to-church" (or denomination) process. The other has been identified as his "structural division thesis" taken to include all of his ideas, including those derived from Troeltsch, relative to the correlations which he saw between social class (and other structural divisions of society) and the structural divisions within "the church."

What we have observed up to this point in our review of citations to Niebuhr's work (especially *The Social Sources*) are references either to his "developmental thesis" or to ideas that combine this with certain other theories about the class character of new religious movements (that is, the socioeconomic statuses of their members) and a variety of alleged psychological and other "reasons" for their origin.

Several sociologists, however, were evidently not so much interested in the developmental processes of sects or in Niebuhr's theories about them as they were in his ideas about the social bases of structural diversity synchronically or cross-sectionally considered and in the correlations of class, status, party, race, region, ethnic group, and national identification with style and type of religious organization and behavior.

Thus, for example, Walter R. Goldschmidt (1933) writes: "Richard Niebuhr furnished us with a text so universally apropos that I cannot but introduce my discussion . . . with his words: . . . 'The division of the churches closely follows the division of men into the castes of national, racial, and economic groups.' " Hoult, Dynes, Shippey, O'Dea, and Berger all refer to this aspect of Niebuhr's thought, not necessarily to the exclusion of interest or awareness in the developmental processes, but as distinct from the latter.

Hoult (1958), for example, refers to Niebuhr's "influential work" in the analysis of "group factors which have led to Christian religious differentiation," and Dynes (1955) took the proposition that "churchness is associated with high socio-economic status and sectness . . . with low socio-economic status" as the basic proposition to be tested in his research.

Glock and Stark (1965: 165) cite Niebuhr as one of the classic sources for what they describe as the typically social scientific view that "theological disputes among the denominations [may be regarded] as rhetorical 'superstructures' produced by and obscuring the 'real' reasons—such as class—behind the conflicts."[22]

O'Dea's (1954), Berger's (1954), and Demerath's (1965) references to Niebuhr appear to regard his ideas about the relationship of religious affiliation and socioeconomic status as of at least as much importance for research purposes as the sect-to-denomination hypothesis.

So nearly universal is the acceptance of the association between low socioeconomic status and "the sect" that it is difficult to find social scientists who have given this proposition the searching critical examination which all scientific propositions normally receive and without which most stand in danger of being erected

---

[22] Niebuhr himself had not gone so far. Writing about himself in the preface to the *Social Sciences* (p. vii) he said simply:

The effort to distinguish churches primarily by reference to their doctrine and to approach the problem of church unity from a purely theological point of view appeared . . . to be a procedure so artificial and fruitless that he [the author] found himself compelled to turn from theology to history, sociology and others for a more satisfactory account of denominational differences and a more significant approach to the question of union.

into self-perpetuating stereotypes, wherein the student sees only what he is conceptually prepared to "see."

Niebuhr himself (1929: 65, 70, 72, 77) had concluded, we recall, that not *all* "new" religious structures began as lower-class movements; some, like the Calvinist churches, might well be thought of as beginning not as lower-class sects but as middle-class denominations. Even Methodism, although he identified it as "the last great religious revolution of the disinherited in Christendom," was "far removed in its moral temper from the churches of the disinherited in the 16th and 17th centuries" and exhibited elements of an "original middle-class point of view."

Two important alternatives to Niebuhr's "structural division theory" should be noted: Glock's and Stark's "deprivation theory" for the origin of new religious movements (to which reference has already been made) and Rodney Stark's (1964) theory of radical secular political movements and organizations as *alternative* channels for the expression of lower-class frustration and discontent in contemporary societies.

Dissatisfied with a thesis which seemed to confine the dynamics of new religious movements—the drive or the thrust of "sectarianism"—exclusively to the economically disinherited (the poor) or the politically weak, Glock and Stark propose an extension of the sources of strain to include not merely "absolute" disabilities or handicaps—economic deprivation (poverty) social deprivation (absence of power and prestige), organismic deprivation (absence of physical and mental health) ethical deprivation (frustrated values), and psychic deprivation (absence of meaning to existence)—but also relative ones and those *not* confined to the lower socioeconomic strata. Thus, "religious needs" and "religious faith" and fervor could, theoretically, surface anywhere in the social structure. "Sectarianism" however, is *not* clearly identified as a possible mode of religious response and organization equally throughout the social order.

Stark (1964) represents a point of view in the sociology of religion which, while generally accepting Niebuhr's "structural division thesis," strips it of its interpretative content (in the sense in which Niebuhr "intended" it to be taken) and proceeds to a wholly "external" examination of the relationship between economic (and political) deprivation on one hand, affiliation with (and involvement in) organized religion on another, and participation in (or affinity for) radical political parties on a third. The result is an open-ended kind of inquiry into the whole problem of the relationship between poverty and sectarianism which is quite different from the a prioristic type of approach represented by social scientists who uncritically followed the methods and usage of Troeltsch and of Niebuhr.

It is probably not possible at the end of a long essay on Niebuhr's work to summarize briefly the arguments or to draw together in the form of a simple conclusion all that would be relevant to the assessment of his contribution to the social scientific study of religion, much less to try to weigh the influence which he has had on the sociology of religion in America or elsewhere. Nor can we predict what sociologists or other social scientists may or will yet find provocative in his work. Evidence that Niebuhr's work *is* widely known can be found readily enough, as we have earlier noted, in the numbers of citations to that work one encounters both in American and in European and other publications.[23] Such references, it might be observed on the basis of a not very systematic inspection, seem to be directed almost solely to *The Social Sources of Denominationalism* and only rarely, if at all, to his later books from which, as we have suggested, one gets a clearer understanding of Niebuhr's interest

[23] At the same time it should be noted, perhaps, that there are no references at all to *The Social Sources* (or to H. Richard Niebuhr) in some bibliographies and elsewhere where they might have been expected—''Trend Report and Bibliography for Sociology of Religions,'' Current Sociology 5 (1965), published by UNESCO; or David Riesman (1955). Liston Pope, but not Richard Niebuhr, is mentioned in a report on *Sect, Cult and Church in Alberta* by W. E. Mann, the executive secretary of the Toronto Diocesan Council for Social Services of the Church of England in Canada.

Possibly because his conceptions of sect are considered to apply too specifically to U.S. groups to be useful in European contexts, or for other reasons, Niebuhr is not mentioned, for example, in any of several essays on Protestant sects appearing in the *Archives de Sociologie des Religions* written by Jean Seguy and by others—for example, ''Les sectes d'origine protestante et le monde ouvrier francais au XIX siecle,'' ''Sectes chretiennes et developpement,'' or ''L'ascese dans les sectes d'origine protestante.'' Nor does there seem to be any reference to H. Richard Niebuhr in an early essay by Carl Mayer (which Professor James Luther Adams has kindly put at my disposal) titled ''Sekte u. Kirche,'' *Heidelberger Studien*, Vol. III, 6 (Heidelberg: Verlag der Weiss'schen Universitätsbuchhandlung, 1933).

in denominations, whether churches *or* sects, and in the Christian church.

The position which we have taken in this paper is that several of Niebuhr's concepts, as well as propositions he developed in using them, have not been sufficiently carefully or critically examined by social scientists who have used them or, at the least, that many who have used them have done so without adequate awareness of the full implications of their content as he fashioned them for his own use as a Christian churchman, theologian, and ethicist. What seems likely to endure, whatever may be the judgment of the reader, concerning specific concepts like "church," "sect," "denomination" (or such propositions as Niebuhr's sect-to-church hypothesis or the relationship between low socioeconomic status and "sectarianism") is the emphasis which he gave to the principle that all forms of religious organization are profoundly and inescapably affected by the social and cultural contexts in which they exist.

This basically sociological insight, however, now needs to be carried a step further in the service of the objectives we have set for ourselves in this paper. Any serious attempt to assess the impact of Richard Niebuhr's work on the scientific study of religion cannot, on sociological grounds, stop with any merely logical analysis of the "adequacy" or inadequacy of his concepts for scientific purposes. Nor would it be enough to rest the case upon a historical review of studies which have used his concepts or drawn upon his theories, even if the review were more detailed and searching than what we have attempted to do here. Stated as succinctly as possible, the question we must ask now is this: Can we, on the basis of what we know (or think we know) about contemporary attitudes toward religion, predict an increase or a decline in the attention likely to be paid to Niebuhr's views in the near future? This is a question, as I see it, which can be raised quite apart from the question of whether his concepts are or are not capable of being used in rigorous social scientific analysis; it is a sociological rather than a logical or methodological question.

Prognostication being the risky enterprise that it is and sociological information on which such prognostication rests being scanty and unreliable as it is, at least on this point, any projections one attempts to make probably should remain in the realm of modest conjecture. Yet perhaps some trajectory might be drawn.

If it is, in fact, true (as Peter Berger 1970 and many others have argued) that "most recent sociology of religion has been a sociology *of the churches*" both in Europe and in the United States, then it seems reasonable to expect that, with the unmistakable surge of interest in "religion outside of the churches"— in "new religions," cults, and "underground churches" as well as "privatized" spiritual questing—all theories about religious organizations as such, Niebuhr's included, might lose "relevance." And this might well happen even before the question of the validity (or invalidity) of those theories and concepts has been settled or even throughly aired.

Of course, the idea of "religion outside of the churches" has been around for some time. Thomas Jefferson spoke of himself as "myself, a sect alone"; and theologians from Soren Kierkegaard to Dietrich Bonhoeffer and Rudolph Bultmann, not to mention dozens of other figures, Protestant and Catholic, have made the critical distinction between faith and structure. (For Jews, given the communal and "familistic" nature of their religious practice, at least until comparatively recently, it was scarcely an issue.) But such ideas were, apparently, largely confined to the few rather than shared by the many and were much less effectively acted upon. For the most part, presumably, those who were "religious" went to church or at least identified themselves in some way with "organized religion." As a result "religion outside of the churches" may well have had very little sociological expression, although it may be necessary here to remind ourselves that even under the most "favorable" conditions for churchly religion, there seem to have been times and places in American history where "seekers" found themselves "unchurched," a circumstance which may have contributed in part to the proliferation of sects in some localities or among some classes of the population.

Today all this seems to have been changed. Apparently, there is felt to be, if anything, a surfeit of "organized religion" or at least of local congregations whether in rural or in urban or even in suburban places coupled with an apparent disinclination on the part of many to identify "being religious" with "being a member of a church." With some exceptions there seems to be something less than an insistent, overpowering drive to organize and staff new congregations. New congregations *are* being organized, of course, but apparently not in proportion to the increases in numbers of the population. For many young people religious *movements*—cults especially—appear to hold greater interest or have stronger appeal. Parallelling this shift from churches ("religious organizations") to the more amorphous "religious movements" seems to have been a shift from what some students of the history of religion have called a "theology of transcendence" to a "theology of immanence" with a concomitant decline in interest in "external" forms and structures of all sorts. If this is indeed the trend, then we may expect perhaps to find students of religion turning less often to H. Richard Niebuhr and more often to students of the "new religions" or, rather, to the more varied and fluid forms in which "religion" may be expected to manifest itself. While undoubtedly much attention will continue to be given to religious organizations and their problems—those of internal structuring of clergy and other roles, of enhancing the values of rituals, of engaging or not engaging in "social action," and the like—relatively speaking, it does seem rather unlikely that such interest will dominate the sociology of religion.

BIBLIOGRAPHY

Ausubel, Nathan, ed.
    1964   *Book of Jewish Knowledge*. New York: Crown.

Angell, R. C.
    1941   *The Integration of American Society*. New York: McGraw-Hill.

Becker, Howard
    1932   *Systematic Sociology on the Basis of the Beziehungslehre and the Gebildelehre of Leopold von Wiese*. New York: Wiley.

Berger, Peter L.
    1954   The Sociological Study of Sectarianism. *Social Research* 21: 467–85.
    1958   Sectarianism and Religious Sociation. *American Journal of Sociology* 64: 41–44.
    1970   *A Rumor of Angels*. Garden City, N.Y.: Doubleday.

Clark, S. D.
    1945   The Religious Sect in Canadian Politics. *American Journal of Sociology* 51: 207–16.
    1946   The Religious Sect in Canadian Economic Development. *Canadian Journal of Economic Political Science* 12 : 439–53.
    1948   *Church and Sect in Canada*. Toronto: University of Toronto.

Demerath, Nicholas J., III
    1961   Social Stratification and Church Involvement: The Church-Sect Distinction Applied to Individual Participation. *Review of Religious Research* 2: 146–54.
    1965   *Social Class in American Protestantism*. Chicago: Rand McNally.
————, and Hammond, Phillip E.
    1969   *Religion in Social Context*. New York: Random House.

Douglas, H. P.
    1945   Cultural Differences and Recent Religious Divisions. *Christendom* 10 : 89ff.

Dynes, Russell R.
    1954   Church-Sect Typology: An Empirical Study. Unpublished Ph.D. dissertation. Ohio State University.
    1955   Church-Sect Typology and Socioeconomic Status. *American Sociological Review* 20 : 555–60.

Eister, Allan
    1949   The Oxford Group Movement: A Typological Analysis. *Sociology and Social Research* 34: 116–24.
    1950   *Drawing-Room Conversion: A Sociological Account of the Oxford Group Movement.* Durham, N.C.: Duke University Press.
    1967a Toward a Radical Critique of Church-Sect Typologizing. *Journal for the Scientific Study of Religion* 6 : 87.
    1967b In a review of John C. McKinney, *Constructive Typology and Social Theory.* In *American Sociological Review* 32: 515–16.

Faris, Ellsworth
    1955   The Sect and the Sectarian. *American Journal of Sociology* 60 : 75–89.

Glock, Charles Y., Ringer, Benjamin B., and Babbie, Earl R.
    1967   *To Comfort and to Challenge: A Dilemma of the Contemporary Church.* Berkeley and Los Angeles, Calif.: University of California Press.

Glock, Charles Y., and Stark, Rodney
    1965   *Religion and Society in Tension.* Chicago: Rand McNally.

Goldschmidt, Walter
    1933   Class Denominationalism in Rural California Churches. *American Journal of Sociology* 49 : 348–55.

Harrison, Paul M.
    1959   *Authority and Power in the Free Church Tradition.* Princeton, N.J.: Princeton University Press.

Hoult, Thomas F.
    1958   *The Sociology of Religion.* New York: Dryden Press.

Isichei, Elizabeth A.
    1964   From Sect to Denomination among English Quakers. *British Journal of Sociology* 15 : 207–22.

Johnson, Benton
    1953   A Framework for the Analysis of Religious Action with Special Reference to Holiness and Non-Holiness Groups. Unpublished doctoral dissertation, Harvard University.
    1957   A Critical Appraisal of the Church-Sect Typology. *American Sociological Review* 22: 88–92.
    1963   On Church and Sect. *American Sociological Review* 28: 539–49.

Khaldun, Ibn
    1958   *The Muqaddimah: An Introduction to History,* Vol. III.
            Trans. Franz Rosenthal. New York: Pantheon Books for
            the Bollingen Foundation. See also his comments on the
            Kharijites in Volume I.

Laeyendecker, Leonardus
    1967   *Religie en Conflict: De zogenaamde sekten in sociologisch
            perspectief.* Meppel: J. A. Boom.

Lee, Robert E.
    1960a   The Organizational Dilemma in American Protestantism.
            Union Seminary Quarterly Review 16: 9–19.
    1960b   *The Social Sources of Church Unity.* Nashville, Tenn.:
            Abingdon.

Martin, David
    1962   The Denomination. *British Journal of Sociology* 13: 1–14.

Marty, Martin E.
    1959   *The New Shape of American Religion.* New York: Harper &
            Row.
    1960   Sects and Cults. *Annals* 332: 125–34.

Matthes, Joachim
    1965   *International Yearbook for the Sociology of Religion,* ed.
            Koln u. Opladen No. 1.
    1969   *Kirche U. Gesellschaft: Einfuhrung in die Religionssoziolo-
            gie II.* Reinbek b. Hamburg: Rowolt.

Mead, Sidney
    1954   Denominationalism: The Shape of Protestantism in America.
            Church History 23: 300ff.

Moberg, David O.
    1960   Does Class Shape the Church? *Review of Religious Research*
            1: 110–15.
    1961   Potential Uses of the Church-Sect Typology in Comparative
            Religious Research. *International Journal of Comparative
            Sociology* 2: 47–58.
    1962   *The Church as a Social Institution.* Englewood Cliffs, N.J.:
            Prentice-Hall.

Muelder, Walter G.
    1945   From Sect to Church. *Christendom* 10: 450–62.

Muller, Herbert J.
    1952   *Thesis in the Uses of the Past.* New York: Oxford University Press.

Niebuhr, H. Richard
    1929   *The Social Sources of Denominationalism.* New York: Holt, Rinehart and Winston.
    1934   Sects. *Encyclopedia of the Social Sciences* 13: 624–31.
    1937   *The Kingdom of God in America.* Chicago: Willett, Clark.
    1946–47   The Norm of the Church. *Journal of Religious Thought* 4: 9y.
    1956   *The Purpose of the Church and Its Ministry.* New York: Harper & Row.
————, Pauck, Wilhelm, and Miller, Francis P.
    1935   *The Church against the World.* Chicago: Willett, Clark.

O'Dea, Thomas F.
    1954   Mormonism and the Avoidance of Sectarian Stagnation: A Study of Church, Sect and Incipient Nationality. *American Journal of Sociology* 60: 285–93.

Pfautz, Harold W.
    1955   The Sociology of Secularization: Religious Groups. *American Journal of Sociology* 61: 121–128.
    1956   Christian Science: A Case Study of the Social Psychological Aspect of Secularization. *Social Forces* 34: 246–51.
    1964   A Case Study of an Urban Religious Movement: Christian Science. In E. W. Burgess and D. J. Bogue, ed. *Contributions to Urban Sociology.* Chicago: University of Chicago Press.

Pope, Liston
    1942   *Millhands and Preachers.* New Haven, Conn.: Yale University Press.
    1948   Religion and the Class Structure. *Annals of the American Academy of Political Social Science* 256: 84–91.

Reed, H. W.
    1943   The Growth of a Contemporary Sect-Type As Reflected in the Development of the Church of the Nazarene. Unpublished Ph.D. dissertation, University of Southern California.

Riesman, David
    1955   Some Informal Notes on American Churches and Sects. *Confluence* 4: 127–59.

Scanzoni, John
  1965   Innovation and Constancy in the Church-Sect Typology. *American Journal of Sociology* 71: 320–27.

Schneider, Siegfried, ed.
  1962   Ausgewälte Internationale Bibliographie zur Neueren Religionssoziologie. In *Kolner Zeitschrift f. Soziologie u. Sozialpsychologie* 6.

Shippey, Frederick A.
  1953   Sociological Forms of Religious Expression in Western Christianity. *Religion in Life* (Spring), pp. 3–15.

Sorokin, Pitirim A.
  1947   *Society, Culture and Personality.* New York: Harper & Row, 145 ff.

Stanley, Manfred
  1958   Sect-Church: A Reformulation. Paper presented to annual meeting of American Sociological Society. Seattle, Washington.

Stark, Rodney
  1964   Class, Radicalism, and Religious Involvement in Great Britain. *American Sociological Review* Vol. 21, no. 5, pp. 698–706.

Stark, Werner
  1967a   *The Sociology of Religion,* Vols. II and III. London: Routledge and Kegan Paul.
  1967b   Sectarian Religion. *The Sociology of Religion,* Volume II. New York: Fordham University Press.

Troeltsch, Ernst
  1931   *The Social Teaching of the Christian Churches,* Vol. II. Trans. Olive Wyon. London: George Allen and Unwin.

Vallier, Ivan
  1963   Roman Catholicism and Social Change in Latin America: From Church to "Sect." Paper presented at annual meeting of the American Sociological Society, Los Angeles.

Vernon, Glenn M.
  1960   Religious Groups and Social Class: Some Inconsistencies. *Papers of the Michigan Academy of Sciences, Arts and Letters* 45: 295–301.

Wach, Joachim
    1944   *Sociology of Religion.* Chicago: University of Chicago Press.
    1951   *Types of Religious Experience, Christian and Non-Christian.*
            Chicago: University of Chicago Press.

Weber, Max
    1946   *From Max Weber: Essays in Sociology.* Trans. and ed. H. H.
            Gerth and C. W. Mills. New York: Oxford University Press.
    1947   *The Theory of Social and Economic Organization.* Trans.
            A. M. Henderson and Talcott Parsons. New York: Oxford
            University Press.
    1963   *The Sociology of Religion.* Trans. Ephraim Fischoff. Boston:
            Beacon Press.

Werblowsky, R. J., Wigoder, Zwi and Geoffrey
    1966   *The Encyclopedia of the Jewish Religion.* New York: Holt,
            Rinehart and Winston.

Whitley, Oliver
    1955   The Sect to Denomination Process in an American Religious
            Movement. *S. W. Soc. Sci. Quarterly* 36: 275–82.
    1959   *The Trumpet Call of Reformation.* St. Louis, Mo.: Bethany
            Press.

Wilson, Bryan R.
    1958   Apparition et Persistance des Sectes dans un Milieu Social
            en Evolution. *Arch. de Sociol. des Rel.* 5: 140–50.
    1959   An Analysis of Sect Development. *American Sociological Re-
            view* 24: 3–15.
    1961   *Sects and Society.* Berkeley and Los Angeles, Calif.: Uni-
            viersity of California Press.
    1966   *Religion in Secular Society.* London: Watts.
    1967   *Patterns of Sectarianism,* ed. London: Heinemann.
    1970   *Religious Sects.* New York: McGraw-Hill.

Wishlade, R. L.
    1965   *Sectarianism in Southern Nyassaland.* London: Oxford Uni-
            versity Press for the International African Institute.

Yinger, J. Milton
    1946   *Religion in the Struggle for Power.* Durham, N.C.: Duke
            University Press.
    1957   *Religion, Society and the Individual.* New York: Macmillan.

EPILOGUE

I

If the title *Beyond the Classics?* is a little enigmatic, the original title, which was not to have displayed the question mark, would, it turns out, have been more than a little misleading. The Society for the Scientific Study of Religion's Twentieth Anniversary Convention theme, which the foregoing essays were designed to reflect, was one of "taking stock." We recruited authors and made assignments with the assumption that their reviews of studies of religion since the classics would reveal considerable accumulation, that scholarship of the past few decades has gone "beyond" the understanding of religion contained in those works.

Alas, these essays call into question how much accumulation there has been. They contain significant numbers of citations, of course. Some, even, are brilliant bibliographic records, constituting chapters in intellectual history. But though authors of this volume *find* subsequent literature, they have found less *consolidation* in it than might at first be expected. Contemplating Whitehead's aphorism, "A science which hesitates to forget its founders is lost," might lead us to the conclusion that the social scientific study of religion is lost. Marxian scholars, it seems, still quarrel over Marx; Freud's successors debate yet the question of what is authentic Freudianism; the view of primitive religion so startlingly portrayed by Durkheim has yet to be unambiguously applied to contemporary society; Malinowski at least presaged the questions about tribal religions still being asked today. And so on with the other great social scientific scholars whose attention to religion has rightly earned them titles as authors of classics.

Are we lost? Is the scientific study of religion without essential progress or direction after a century or more of work inspired by a handful of classics? No doubt members of our discipline differ in their beliefs regarding how far we have strayed, but there can be little doubt, based on these essays, that the *accumulative* record is meager indeed. Little can be cited in the way of orderly growth based on classical foundations. Several interpretations of this situation might be advanced; together, they constitute reasons for our not having gone very far beyond the classics:

1. Perhaps even more than in social science generally, the classical writers in the scientific study of religion have been raised to sainthood. Not only has Whitehead's warning been ignored and we have hesitated to forget our founders, but also have their writings been regarded as "sacred." The effect has been, therefore, a large amount of scholarly attention to the founders' ideas and their "true interpretation" rather than their empirical testing. This is probably the case with Marx and Freud more than with the other classicists discussed in this volume, although the interpreters of Weber and Durkheim also have been known to debate which is the truer of competing true exegeses. In the Marx and Freud instances, moreover, such exegetical "schools" have led even to mutually hostile political factions or therapeutic camps. To be sure, their writings on religion have had no such large-scale pragmatic consequences, but the explicators have been no less involved in plumbing the mysteries of their masters. The essays by Birnbaum and Pruyser contain vivid illustrations; as the set of contributors makes clear, however, debate about all these masters continues on.

2. Along with the saintly stature accorded the classics has come a tendency to forget the questions which they addressed. Subsequent work has frequently followed the means but forgotten the ends by emulating a great work without being concerned for the issues that made it great. Those who have pursued Catholic-Protestant differences in "capitalistic spirit," even in the face of Weber's warning that doing so would be tangential to his original concern, may serve as a prime example. "Fundamentalists" can as well be found reading the gospels of Marx, James, Freud, Durkheim, and so on, however. (This charge, it should be noted, is not that subsequent work has necessarily been of poor quality. It is not quality we are discussing here but the absence of significant accumulations of work.) Instead of surpassing their founders, then, social scientists of religion often focus and refocus on the classics. The fault lies not wholly with the followers, it is true; the classics differ themselves in how clearly they laid out a program for future research. Thus, the accumulated record following Niebuhr's *The Social Sources* is considerable, and, even though Eister questions the validity of it all, it was the existence of this record which allows him to do so. Glick documents a sizeable literature which has been generated by Malinowski, in part, it could be argued, because Malinowski stated clearly his own questions. The opposite might almost be said of Durkheim; his originat-

ing question may be clear enough, but its application in any but "primitive" contexts is certainly not.

3. The Introduction to this volume pointed out how little the classical writers were aware of one another and how little, therefore, their books reflect one another. A similar charge might now be made of those who have followed the masters; relatively little attention has been given to bridging the classics. Instead, scholars have tended to locate themselves in one camp and stray only seldom from it. The early work of Talcott Parsons (1937) and, later, some essays of Robert N. Bellah (1958; 1964) are notable exceptions to the rule, but even these are largely integration of sociological concepts. The inclusion of psychological and anthropological concepts is limited. Thus, those working within a Freudian frame of reference, say, have little help in moving toward a Marxian, a Durkheimian, or Niebuhrian frame as well. The practice of ignoring one another continues, in other words.

4. There is a marked separation of theory and quantitative data in the social scientific study of religion. More even than in other fields of inquiry, perhaps, the careful, convincing, hard data-oriented studies of religion are generally only tangential to the theoretical concerns which are identified in the classics and which make them classics. Quantitative empirical studies are rare enough in the scientific study of religion, but many of those that do exist are mere catalogues of facts, while many others, excellent in methodological terms, are informed less by the classical literature than by client questions. Frequently arising in a context of the real organizational concerns of religious bodies, many studies have devoted time and attention to authentic questions, no doubt, but they conclude with little to do with the classical issues. This, of course, is the other side of our second point. There, researchers were seen to have ignored the ends in pursuit of means; here, the means of social research are seen to be directed frequently toward other ends. Either way, the chances of going beyond the classics by accumulative effort are slim indeed if the profound questions they posed are left unattended. The exceptions help document the rule. The excellence of Bryan Wilson's work on sects (1961, 1967), of Bellah's (1957), Nelson's (1969), and Little's (1969) pursuits of the Weber question, or of Erickson's biographies in the Freudian mode (1958, 1969) are beyond dispute. But, while empirical, they are not quantitative and thus constitute more "examples" than "evidence" of theoretical refinement. This last sentence, let it be noted, is not a call for crude empiricism; it is, however, an acknowledgement that quantification may allow for readier accumulation of evidence.

In summary, therefore, if the scientific study is not lost, neither can it claim any orderly progress. And this after a relatively long period of time, considering the short history of all of social science. We may not be floundering, but the record of the essays in this volume documents clearly that the mass of studies—some major, some minor—do not go far beyond the classics.

A fifth factor, considerably subtler, would seem to be identified in these essays as another stumbling block on the path to an accumulated social scientific study of religion. It has to do with the fact that *religion* is the subject matter, which therefore makes the setting of any agenda or program for orderly research more difficult. Perhaps the notion that religion is somehow ineluctable, unique, nonpareil, is the issue. The classicists, these contributors seem to be saying, did not treat religion as they would have treated other phenomena. They postulated instead the profound, almost elusive, nature of the sacred side of life; and programs for research do not flow automatically from such penetrating analyses, it is suggested. Profound and elusive themes generate profound but elusive agendas, they seem to conclude; and those who have followed have frequently lost sight of the agenda.

The essays convey the message in a variety of ways. Dittes, writing on William James, is clear enough in his judgment that James, generally seen as offering a scientific classification of religious appetites, was *originally* attempting something quite different. And that something, says Dittes, has not even been properly identified, let alone built upon. Consider the similarity in tone, however, as Pruyser comments on what he regards as incorrect development in Freudian theory:

> Much fine attention to detail is lost if one routinely calls rituals *compulsive* or *obsessional,* repression *hysterical,* sadness *depression,* or suspiciousness *paranoid.* Religious behavior is so diversified that the classical nosological apparatus of descriptive psychiatry cannot capture its richness. (p. 282, italics in the original)

Or Benjamin Nelson's:

> In my view, Weber seems to have been largely correct in his interpretations of the historical developments. What his original critics missed—what many continue to miss today—is the critical fact that "capitalism" in a narrow sense was not the central interest of Weber's essays on the Protestant ethic. . . .

The burden of Eister's essay is different, of course, in insisting that Niebuhr's church-sect distinction, because at base theological and not empirical, is therefore not usable by social science. But even here the challenge Eister presents is to *rescue* classical insights by properly seeing Niebuhr's profound intent, not to abandon the obvious empirical puzzle of religious organizations. Finally, along this line might be mentioned Glick's assertion that those anthropologists who see culture as "religious structure" or religion as "cultural system," that is, "the proposition that religion is another term for, or at very least an essential dimension of human designs for living," are closest to Malinowski's ultimate goal in ethnography.

This failure by subsequent scholars of religion to pursue the profound, if implicit, agenda of the classics would appear to be a failure shared generally in the social sciences, however. As has been noted (Hanson 1958: 71), scientific breakthroughs come through "abduction" or leading away, not through deduction or induction. Perhaps, we might say, the classics of the scientific study of religion enjoy their stature because they have abducted us, led us away to new insights, relationships, or root ideas. However, science, being more than breakthroughs, requires also the accumulation or consolidation following the breakthroughs. The insight must be converted into a paradigm if a science is to develop. The new idea must yield to systematic restatement, which in turn calls for an obvious and agreed-upon methodology. The work of one period must not only inspire the work of the next period but in addition must *compel* it. While the classics of the present volume have obviously inspired considerable work, they have compelled very little. Restatements are hardly systematic, and alternate methodologies abound.

If social science generally does not yet measure up fully as a science in the sense that its compelled, accumulated record is meager (Kuhn 1962), then it is not surprising that the social scientific study of religion would also lag behind. Indeed, religion, having in some degree regarded science and the scientific perspective with suspicion, may have been especially resistant to scientific scrutiny. Therefore, even though the classical writers in the social scientific study of religion appear also as founders in the social sciences generally, their contributions in religion may have generated even less accumulative work than their other contributions.

II

Needless to say, the observation that the social scientific study of religion's needed paradigm has not yet arrived is not a call for self-imposed orthodoxy. Accumulative progress may tend to produce a momentum which sloughs off competing ideas, problems, or methods; these the proper study of humanity must always allow for, even if a dominance necessarily goes with those following the paradigmatic mold. The call, then, is not to drive out infidels, but to discover a program. It is not to freeze the agenda, but to get busy on the items already there.

The fear of a rigid orthodoxy in our work may be naïve, anyway, because the hope for a paradigm in the future may be unrealistic. Little significant change in the scientific study of religion appears likely. The issues identified by, at least attributed to, the classics continue to arrest us; the controversies they engendered linger on; and suggestions for change (such as this one) keep getting offered. Moreover, the scholar's academic home base—whether anthropology, psychology, sociology, or what—contributes to the confusion by imposing disciplinary divisions into the "discipline" of religion studied scientifically. (Actually one significant countersign is the scholarly group for which this book was prepared, The Society for the Scientific Study of Religion. Its steady gain in members and intellectual stature may, at the least, lead to the blurring of external lines by those who would share a focus of study.)

Even more serious is the challenge held out by those who doubt if religion *can* be studied scientifically. Those who question whether it can be so studied join forces on occasion with those who question whether religion *should* be so studied. The results frequently are monumentally trivial, but so, too, is the hoped-for goal further delayed. Perhaps this is as it should be. Perhaps the charges of reductionism are warranted. Perhaps those who would admit new evidence into the sciences of humanity are correct. It is not our place here to argue that question, nor is it our intent. But the emergence even of the question signals a failure of nerve in the scientific study of religion. The paradigm, clearly, is not just around the corner.

All hope is not lost however. Our gloomy forecast could indeed be proven wrong by the events of the coming decade. We said in the Introduction that periods of rapid social change are sometimes made to appear rapid by scholars who, by offering new interpretations of the world help us see the difference between the old and the new. The classical writers, we suggested, are accorded their honor in part because they identified the religious dimensions of such change. Several indications suggest the possibility of "rapid" social change in our time if there are persons who will identify it. If they do and if the present age is judged to be one of meaningful turmoil, it, too, will have its religious dimensions and thus the possibilities for their scientific study. No program can be laid out, of course; our incapacity for that is precisely the result of having no paradigm. However, three *levels* of investigation seem appropriate in the scientific study of religion in our age, and we conclude this volume with brief mention of them.

1. There is, first, the analysis of religion at the macroscopic level of the total society. Durkheim's assertions about the Arunta, which he himself, no doubt, intended to update for modern France, have all manner of possible application today, the "civil religion" investigations being cases in point. So, too, have we seen that Weber's notion of rationalization has present-day relevance, especially in developing nations. Malinowski's understanding of religion made for a wholistic view of social life, as did Freud's continual return to ideas of a mass psyche, a cultural memory, and so on. All of these classical writers, in fact—William James being a likely exception —addressed issues at the society-wide level.

In our day, then, from the deliberate creation of new nations to the ascension by science to the position as supplier of dominating cultural images we are surrounded by opportunities to pursue the classical interests at a macroscopic level. As one example, what is the mix of tribal beliefs, missionary imports, and newfound destinies as elaborated by leaders of new nations? As another, what is happening to notions of guilt and responsibility in the legal and correctional fields as a result of new understanding of the forces which produce delinquent or deviant behavior?

At the risk of stretching a comparison, we might suggest that the present situation affords many opportunities for restudying religion globally. Where the classicists were concerned with the shift of societies into the industrial age, however, today's scholars must attend as well to the shift into a postindustrial age. Thus, there seems little question but what the world of work-leisure is heading toward massive change. Marxist and Weberian notions regarding the role of ideas and economic position are, therefore, subject to renewed testing in new settings. What are the religious ramifications for societies built on abundance rather than shortage? For societies coming to realize the expendable nature of the physical environment? For societies that have the technology for controlling population in both size and gender? For societies where the gap between professed ideal and actuality is, if not greater than ever before in human history, at least observed by greater numbers?

2. Second is the scientific study of religion at the organizational level. Standing out at this level, no doubt, is the upheaval in the Roman Catholic church, which, though receiving considerable attention already from social scientists as well as theologians, is deserving even more because of its centrality in the contemporary religious scene. In less dramatic form are the correlative confrontations in Protestantism and Judaism as they reduce their hostility and defensiveness toward "science" and accommodate to "modernity" instead. Though demythologizing has a history now decades old among theologians and clergy, it is perhaps correct to say that similar movements among the laity are only now gaining favor. What happens to the uniqueness of religious organizations if, in maintaining relevance, they relinquish most of what distinguishes them from non-church voluntary associations?

The classical writers discussed in this volume dealt more, it is true, with churches as they *became* voluntary associations. In the ensuing five to ten decades, churches' *voluntary* status has become standard but now their *churchliness* is seriously debated. The occupational locations of ex-pastors, ex-nuns, and one-time seminarians attest to this debate, but whether the clergy role has secularized or whether comparable roles—for example, teaching, social work, community organizing, and the like—have sacralized is a question of some moment.

Niebuhr, of course, of the writers discussed in this volume was the chief student of religious organizations *qua* organizations. Marx and Weber also advanced a number of ideas about ecclesiastical behavior, however, which can well be tested and refined in present-day arenas. Urban sects represent one such arena, as they both proliferate and disappear, as do the Oriental or other mystical bodies which seem to be gaining new footholds outside of the East. And not to be forgotten is the ecumenical movement, be it actual merger, cooperative association, or simply reducing mutual hostility. What can probably be asserted in all these instances is the change—incipient, if not already present—in the *organization* of religious sentiments. A mode of religiousness that emerged in the middle centuries of the West is very likely undergoing significant metamorphosis. It may occur in our lifetime and a number of the classics provide insights into how this might be studied.

3. A third level of analysis is possible in the scientific study of religion: the level of individual religious consciousness. If, for example, laypeople now also routinely "demythologize," what does this mean for their religious lives as individuals? The classical writ-

ers talked at this level only rarely, and we followers also remain
hesitant to pursue the seeming elusive nature of individual religious
expression.

Classification of individuals is not the issue here; contemporary
social science can provide as many classifications, including religious
classifications, as one might want. But these, in religion, have tended
to be *with respect to a given orthodoxy*. When it is orthodoxy itself
which is made problematic, then new classification schemes are
clearly called for. When for example, do people *feel* religious? If,
as anecdotal evidence suggests, answers can appear quite unrelated
to the existence of churches, what is one then to make of contemporary religion?

The "psychologists," James and Freud, would seem most relevant
to questions asked at this level, though the anthropologist, Malinowski, had a remarkable sensitivity to individual nuance which appears
over and over again in his writings on religion. More importantly
from a research strategy standpoint, many of the ideas to be tested
at global and organizational levels require or at least are served
by, information gathered at the individual level, where social science
has made greatest methodological strides. Therefore, it might be
said that almost any of the questions from any part of the classical
literature in the scientific study of religion are appropriately addressed at the microscopic level. After all, scholars of religion need
reminding as much as other social scientists: if anything happens in
society, it is persons who do it. Global trends and ecclesiastical
changes always turn out to have their individual counterparts.

We would not minimize either the importance or the difficulty
posed by questions such as these at each of the three levels. Moreover, the scientific study of religion is not without a number of
excellent contemporary studies which reflect the agenda as implicitly established by the masters.

Our thesis here is only that, beginning with a spectacular set
of classics by Marx, and by those that followed him, the scientific
study of religion has still not consolidated the traditions of problem finding and methodology which would indicate how these
contemporary phenomena should be approached. As we said
before, present-day researchers may be inspired but hardly compelled by the classics as they take up these questions. It is our
hope, as well as one of the purposes of this book, that in the
future this situation will no longer exist. After all, if the social
scientific study of religion is worth doing at all, it both deserves
sustained effort and promises accumulated knowledge. As of now,
it is probably accurate to say that we are not very far beyond
the classics.

BIBLIOGRAPHY

Bellah, Robert N.
    1957   *Tokugawa Religion*. New York: The Free Press.
    1958   The Place of Religion in Human Action. *The Review of Religion* 22: 137–54.
    1964   Religious Evolution. *American Sociological Review* 29 (June): 358–74.

Erickson, Erik H.
    1958   *Young Man Luther*. New York: Norton.
    1969   *Gandhi's Truth: On the Origins of Militant Nonviolence*. New York: Norton.

Hanson, Norwood R.
    1958   *Patterns of Discovery*. New York: Cambridge University Press.

Kuhn, Thomas S.
    1962   *The Structure of Scientific Revolutions*. Chicago: University of Chicago Press.

Little, David
    1969   *Religion, Order, and Law*. New York: Harper & Row.

Nelson, Benjamin
    1969   *The Idea of Usury,* rev. ed. Chicago: University of Chicago, Press.

Parsons, Talcott
    1937   *The Structure of Social Action*. New York: McGraw-Hill.

Wilson, Bryan R.
    1961   *Sects and Society*. London: Heinemann.
    1967   *Patterns of Sectarianism*. London: Heinemann.

ABOUT THE
CONTRIBUTORS

Norman Birnbaum is professor of sociology at Amherst College. He has taught at Harvard University, the London School of Economics and Political Science, Oxford University, and the University of Strasbourg. He is currently chairman of the Committee on the Sociology of Religion of the International Sociological Association. He has held a Guggenheim Fellowship, and is a contributing editor of *Partisan Review*. His recent publications include: *Sociology and Religion* with Gertrud Lenzer (Prentice-Hall 1968); *The Crisis of Industrial Society* (Oxford University Press 1969); *Toward a Critical Sociology* (Oxford University Press 1971).

James E. Dittes is professor of psychology of religion at Yale University, where he is a member of the psychology department, the Divinity school faculty and director of graduate studies in the department of religious studies. He is currently president of the Society for the Scientific Study of Religion and has been editor of the *Journal for the Scientific Study of Religion*. He is the author of *The Church in the Way* (Scribner's 1967) and *Minister on the Spot* (Pilgrim Press 1970) and of summaries of psychology of religion in the *Handbook of Social Psychology* and the *International Encyclopedia of the Social Sciences*. He is currently on sabbatical on a senior fellowship from the National Endowment for the Humanities.

Shmuel N. Eisenstadt is professor of sociology at the Hebrew University, Jerusalem, Israel. He has also been visiting professor at the London School of Economics, Universities of Harvard, Michigan, and Chicago, as well as Carnegie visiting professor at the Massachusetts Institute of Technology. He has received the 1964 McIver Award of the American Sociological Association. Professor Eisenstadt's major areas of interest include sociological theory, comparative sociology, political sociology. Among his recent publications are *The Protestant Ethic and Modernization* (Basic Books, Inc. 1968); *Political Sociology* (Basic Books, Inc. 1970) which he edited; *From Generation to Generation* (The Free Press 1971); *Social Differentiation and Stratification* (Scott Foresman 1971).

Allan W. Eister is professor of sociology and chairman of the department of sociology and anthropology at Wellesley College. A former officer and member of the Council of the Society for the Scientific Study of Religion and for some years book review editor of its journal, he planned the 1971 meetings of the Society and is presently engaged in editing selected papers from that conference. His primary research interest is in new religious movements and the theory of cults and of sects.

Leonard Glick is professor of anthropology and Dean of the School of Social Science, Hampshire College. He has carried out ethnographic studies in New Guinea and the West Indies. In addition to the anthropology of religion, his interests include psychological anthropology, history of ethnology, and problems relating to ethnic diversity.

Charles Y. Glock is professor of sociology, University of California, Berkeley, and director of the research program in religion and society at the University's Survey Research Center. He was formerly director of the Survey Research Center and also has served a term as chairman of the department of sociology. Past-president of the Society for the Scientific Study of Religion, he has written extensively in the sociology of religion. His works include *Christian Beliefs and Anti-Semitism* (Harper & Row 1966), and a new book, *Religion in Sociological Perspective* (Wadsworth 1973).

Phillip E. Hammond is professor of sociology at the University of Arizona. He is secretary of the Society for the Scientific Study of Religion and currently engaged in studies in law and retirement as they relate to religion. Among his recent publications are *School Prayer Decisions: From Court Policy to Local Practice* with K. M. Dolbeare (University of Chicago Press 1971), and *American Mosaic: Social Patterns of Religion in the U.S.* with Benton Johnson (Random House 1970).

Benjamin Nelson is professor of sociology and history in the graduate faculty of the New School for Social Research. His *Idea of Usury: From Tribal Brotherhood to Universal Otherhood* has recently appeared in a second enlarged edition at the University of Chicago Press and Phoenix Books. Since its inception in 1956 Professor Nelson has been a principal advisory editor for humanities and social sciences for Harper Torchbooks, and he continues to be general editor of three series of paperback books issued by that company. He has served as vice-president and member of the Council of the Society for the Scientific Study of Religion, is a charter member of the American Society for the Study of Religion, and has recently been named president of the American Council to the International Society for the Comparative Study of Civilizations.

Talcott Parsons is professor of sociology at Harvard University, where he has been since 1927. He has been president of the American Academy of Arts and Sciences, the American Sociological Association, and the Eastern Sociological Society. Professor Parsons's major areas of interest include higher education, comparative institutions, and sociological theory. Among his recent publications are *The System of Modern Societies* (Prentice-Hall 1971), a companion volume to *Societies: Evolutionary and Comparative Perspectives* (Prentice-Hall 1966), and he has a forthcoming book on American universities written in collaboration with Gerald M. Platt and Neil J. Smelser which will be published by the Harvard University Press.

Paul W. Pruyser, Ph.D., is a clinical psychologist at the Menninger Foundation in Topeka, Kansas. After having been director of the Foundation's professional training programs, he is now Henry March Pfeiffer Professor in that institution. His main professional interests are personality theory, the teaching of clinical mental health knowledge and skills, and the psychology of religion. He is also visiting professor of psychology at McCormick Theological Seminary in Chicago. He has twice been vice-president of the Society for the Scientific Study of Religion and is on the editorial board of the Society's *Journal,* the Bulletin of the *Menninger Clinic,* and *Pastoral Psychology.* He is coauthor with Karl Menninger and Martin Mayman of *The Vital Balance* (1963) and author of *A Dynamic Psychology of Religion* (1968).

73 74 75   12 11 10 9 8 7 6 5 4 3 2 1